The Cambridge Companion to the Drum Kit

The drum kit is ubiquitous in global popular music and culture, and modern kit drumming profoundly defined the sound of twentieth-century popular music. *The Cambridge Companion to the Drum Kit* highlights emerging scholarship on the drum kit, drummers, and key debates related to the instrument and its players. Interdisciplinary in scope, this volume showcases research from across the humanities, sciences, and social sciences, all of which interrogates the drum kit, a relatively recent historical phenomenon, as a site worthy of analysis, critique, and reflection. Providing readers with an array of perspectives on the social, material, and performative dimensions of the instrument, this book will be a valuable resource for students, drum kit studies scholars, and all those who want a deeper understanding of the drum kit, drummers, and drumming.

MATT BRENNAN is Reader in Popular Music at the University of Glasgow and the author of *Kick It: A Social History of the Drum Kit* (Oxford University Press). His previous book, *When Genres Collide* (Bloomsbury), was named as one of Pitchfork's 'Favourite Music Books of 2017'.

JOSEPH MICHAEL PIGNATO, Professor at the State University of New York, Oneonta, is a 'musician, educator, and music business visionary' (Tape Op Magazine). He is co-author of *The Music Learning Profiles Project* (Routledge) and leader of the acclaimed avant jazz collective Bright Dog Red, which records for Ropeadope Records.

DANIEL AKIRA STADNICKI is a SSHRC Postdoctoral Fellow at McGill University. He has worked as a session drummer for over two decades in the Canadian folk, world, and pop music scenes, garnering Juno nominations, Gold Records, Canadian Folk Music Awards, among other accolades.

Cambridge Companions to Music

Topics

The Cambridge Companion to Ballet
Edited by Marion Kant

The Cambridge Companion to Blues and Gospel Music
Edited by Allan Moore

The Cambridge Companion to Choral Music
Edited by André de Quadros

The Cambridge Companion to the Concerto
Edited by Simon P. Keefe

The Cambridge Companion to Conducting
Edited by José Antonio Bowen

The Cambridge Companion to the Drum Kit
Edited by Matt Brennan, Joseph Michael Pignato and Daniel Akira Stadnicki

The Cambridge Companion to Eighteenth-Century Opera
Edited by Anthony R. DelDonna and Pierpaolo Polzonetti

The Cambridge Companion to Electronic Music
Edited by Nick Collins and Julio D'Escriván

The Cambridge Companion to the 'Eroica' Symphony
Edited by Nancy November

The Cambridge Companion to Film Music
Edited by Mervyn Cooke and Fiona Ford

The Cambridge Companion to French Music
Edited by Simon Trezise

The Cambridge Companion to Grand Opera
Edited by David Charlton

The Cambridge Companion to Hip-Hop
Edited by Justin A. Williams

The Cambridge Companion to Jazz
Edited by Mervyn Cooke and David Horn

The Cambridge Companion to Jewish Music
Edited by Joshua S. Walden

The Cambridge Companion to the Lied
Edited by James Parsons

The Cambridge Companion to Medieval Music
Edited by Mark Everist

The Cambridge Companion to Music in Digital Culture
Edited by Nicholas Cook, Monique Ingalls and David Trippett

The Cambridge Companion to the Musical, third edition
Edited by William Everett and Paul Laird

The Cambridge Companion to Opera Studies
Edited by Nicholas Till

The Cambridge Companion to Operetta
Edited by Anastasia Belina and Derek B. Scott

The Cambridge Companion to the Orchestra
Edited by Colin Lawson

The Cambridge Companion to Percussion
Edited by Russell Hartenberger

The Cambridge Companion to Pop and Rock
Edited by Simon Frith, Will Straw and John Street

The Cambridge Companion to Recorded Music
Edited by Eric Clarke, Nicholas Cook, Daniel Leech-Wilkinson and John Rink

The Cambridge Companion to Rhythm
Edited by Russell Hartenberger and Ryan McClelland

The Cambridge Companion to Seventeenth-Century Opera
Edited by Jacqueline Waeber

The Cambridge Companion to Schubert's 'Winterreise'
Edited by Marjorie W. Hirsch and Lisa Feurzeig

The Cambridge Companion to the Singer-Songwriter
Edited by Katherine Williams and Justin A. Williams

The Cambridge Companion to the String Quartet
Edited by Robin Stowell

The Cambridge Companion to Twentieth-Century Opera
Edited by Mervyn Cooke

The Cambridge Companion to Wagner's Der Ring des Nibelungen
Edited by Mark Berry and Nicholas Vazsonyi

Composers

The Cambridge Companion to Bach
Edited by John Butt

The Cambridge Companion to Bartók
Edited by Amanda Bayley

The Cambridge Companion to the Beatles
Edited by Kenneth Womack

The Cambridge Companion to Beethoven
Edited by Glenn Stanley

The Cambridge Companion to Berg
Edited by Anthony Pople

The Cambridge Companion to Berlioz
Edited by Peter Bloom

The Cambridge Companion to Brahms
Edited by Michael Musgrave

The Cambridge Companion to Benjamin Britten
Edited by Mervyn Cooke

The Cambridge Companion to Bruckner
Edited by John Williamson

The Cambridge Companion to John Cage
Edited by David Nicholls

The Cambridge Companion to Chopin
Edited by Jim Samson

The Cambridge Companion to Debussy
Edited by Simon Trezise

The Cambridge Companion to Elgar
Edited by Daniel M. Grimley and Julian Rushton

The Cambridge Companion to Duke Ellington
Edited by Edward Green

The Cambridge Companion to Gershwin
Edited by Anna Celenza

The Cambridge Companion to Gilbert and Sullivan
Edited by David Eden and Meinhard Saremba

The Cambridge Companion to Handel
Edited by Donald Burrows

The Cambridge Companion to Haydn
Edited by Caryl Clark

The Cambridge Companion to Liszt
Edited by Kenneth Hamilton

The Cambridge Companion to Mahler
Edited by Jeremy Barham

The Cambridge Companion to Mendelssohn
Edited by Peter Mercer-Taylor

The Cambridge Companion to Monteverdi
Edited by John Whenham and Richard Wistreich

The Cambridge Companion to Mozart
Edited by Simon P. Keefe

The Cambridge Companion to Arvo Pärt
Edited by Andrew Shenton

The Cambridge Companion to Ravel
Edited by Deborah Mawer

The Cambridge Companion to the Rolling Stones
Edited by Victor Coelho and John Covach

The Cambridge Companion to Rossini
Edited by Emanuele Senici

The Cambridge Companion to Schoenberg
Edited by Jennifer Shaw and Joseph Auner

The Cambridge Companion to Schubert
Edited by Christopher Gibbs

The Cambridge Companion to Schumann
Edited by Beate Perrey

The Cambridge Companion to Shostakovich
Edited by Pauline Fairclough and David Fanning

The Cambridge Companion to Sibelius
Edited by Daniel M. Grimley

The Cambridge Companion to Richard Strauss
Edited by Charles Youmans

The Cambridge Companion to Michael Tippett
Edited by Kenneth Gloag and Nicholas Jones

The Cambridge Companion to Vaughan Williams
Edited by Alain Frogley and Aiden J. Thomson

The Cambridge Companion to Verdi
Edited by Scott L. Balthazar

Instruments

The Cambridge Companion to Brass Instruments
Edited by Trevor Herbert and John Wallace

The Cambridge Companion to the Cello
Edited by Robin Stowell

The Cambridge Companion to the Clarinet
Edited by Colin Lawson

The Cambridge Companion to the Guitar
Edited by Victor Coelho

The Cambridge Companion to the Harpsichord
Edited by Mark Kroll

The Cambridge Companion to the Organ
Edited by Nicholas Thistlethwaite and Geoffrey Webber

The Cambridge Companion to the Piano
Edited by David Rowland

The Cambridge Companion to the Recorder
Edited by John Mansfield Thomson

The Cambridge Companion to the Saxophone
Edited by Richard Ingham

The Cambridge Companion to Singing
Edited by John Potter

The Cambridge Companion to the Violin
Edited by Robin Stowell

The Cambridge Companion to the

DRUM KIT

....

EDITED BY

Matt Brennan
University of Glasgow

Joseph Michael Pignato
State University of New York, Oneonta

Daniel Akira Stadnicki
McGill University

CAMBRIDGE
UNIVERSITY PRESS

University Printing House, Cambridge CB2 8BS, United Kingdom

One Liberty Plaza, 20th Floor, New York, NY 10006, USA

477 Williamstown Road, Port Melbourne, VIC 3207, Australia

314–321, 3rd Floor, Plot 3, Splendor Forum, Jasola District Centre, New Delhi – 110025, India

79 Anson Road, #06–04/06, Singapore 079906

Cambridge University Press is part of the University of Cambridge.

It furthers the University's mission by disseminating knowledge in the pursuit of education, learning, and research at the highest international levels of excellence.

www.cambridge.org
Information on this title: www.cambridge.org/9781108489836
DOI: 10.1017/9781108779517

First published 2021

A catalogue record for this publication is available from the British Library.

ISBN 978-1-108-48983-6 Hardback
ISBN 978-1-108-74765-3 Paperback

Contents

Figures

Tables

Music Examples

Notes on Contributors

Vincent Andrisani, PhD, is an instructor in the School of Journalism and Communication at Carleton University. He writes and lectures on the topics of sound, media, and communication, and his work has appeared in outlets such as Sounding Out! Blog, TEDxSFU, and *Tapuya: Latin American Science, Technology, and Society*. Before his career as an academic, Andrisani spent several years as a performing musician in the city of Toronto. Although he plays live much less these days, he maintains a healthy regimen of Stone-Killers to keep his hands in shape.

Paul Archibald is a Bristol-based drummer and lecturer in music. Current projects include Rob Heron & the Tea Pad Orchestra and Free Nelson Mandoomjazz, currently signed to RareNoise Records. International touring (e.g. Jazzfest Berlin, OctLoft China), local festival exposure (e.g. Glastonbury, Wilderness, Bestival), as well as regular radio play (BBC 2, 3, 4) feed into his teachings on the live music industry. Having previously lectured in the sociology of popular music at the University of Bristol, Archibald lectures on research methods and the popular music industry at the British and Irish Modern Music (BIMM) Institute, Bristol.

Steven Baur is Associate Professor of Music at Dalhousie University in Halifax, Nova Scotia. He has published widely on topics in nineteenth- and twentieth-century music from both 'popular' and 'classical' traditions, from Ringo to Ravel and from Musorgsky to the mambo. His work appears in the *Journal of the American Musicological Society*, *Popular Music and Society*, *American Music*, and the *New Grove Dictionary of American Music*, and he has co-edited two books. His current research focuses on drum kit performance practice. Baur is also an accomplished drummer with dozens of recordings and hundreds of live performances to his credit.

adam patrick bell is Associate Professor of Music Education in the School of Creative and Performing Arts at the University of Calgary, Canada. He is the author of *Dawn of the DAW: The Studio as Musical Instrument* (Oxford University Press) and editor of *The Music Technology Cookbook: Ready-Made Recipes for the Classroom* (Oxford University Press). bell has written several peer-reviewed articles and chapters on the topics of music technology in music education and disability in music education. Prior to his career in higher education, he worked as an elementary music teacher by day and music producer by night.

Matt Brennan is Reader in Popular Music at the University of Glasgow. He has served as Chair of the UK and Ireland branch of the International Association for the Study of Popular Music (IASPM), and has authored, co-authored, and edited several books in the field of popular music studies. His latest book, *Kick It: A Social History of the Drum Kit* (Oxford University Press), establishes the drum kit's central role in shaping the history of music over the last 150 years. His previous monograph, *When Genres Collide* (Bloomsbury), was named as one of Pitchfork's 'Favourite Music Books of 2017' and was awarded the IASPM Canada Book Prize.

Bill Bruford enjoyed a long and fruitful career as a musician and teacher before stepping back out of practice to investigate aspects of creativity and performance psychology. He is an unaffiliated early career scholar, having acquired his doctorate from the University of Surrey, UK (2016). He has given lectures and seminars at multiple European and North American institutions. His academic writing includes journal articles, book reviews, book chapters, and his most recent book, *Uncharted: Creativity and the Expert Drummer*. Dr Bruford was inducted into the Rock & Roll Hall of Fame as a member of the group Yes in 2017.

Daniel Gohn is a faculty member at the Department of Communication and Arts of the University of Sao Carlos, Brazil. His research interests include the use of technology in music education, popular music, and processes for the teaching and learning of percussion instruments. He is the author of *In the World of Drumming* (Hudson Music Digital) and other titles published in Portuguese only: *Music Education and Distance Learning: Approaches and Experiences* (Cortez Editora), *Digital Technologies for Music Education* (EdUFSCar), *Music Self-learning: Technological Alternatives* (Annablume), and *Yamaha's Percussion Book* (Ricordi).

Nat Grant is a multi-skilled artist and researcher: performer, sound artist, and composer working on unceded Wurundjeri country in Melbourne, Australia. Grant has created original music for theatre, dance, film, and live art; holds a PhD in composition from the Victorian College of the Arts; and in 2018 received the Age Music Victoria Award for Best Experimental/Avant-Garde Act. A podcaster and programmer for 3CR community radio, he is interested in the power of sound and music as storytelling tools. A co-curator for the weekly experimental performance series the Make it Up Club, Grant is invested in creating and maintaining community around sound making.

Scott Hanenberg is an instructor of music theory and music technology at Virginia Polytechnic Institute and State University. His research uses corpus analysis and positional listening to study meter and groove in popular music. Hanenberg's recent work has investigated the role of the drum kit in shaping listener interpretations of irregular meters.

Patrick Hernly is Lead Faculty of the Music Industry / Recording Arts program at St Petersburg College, where he teaches drum set and hand percussion, music theory, and critical listening for music production, and directs the Rock and R&B ensembles. He has been an active performer across multiple genres for the past two decades, recording and touring in North America, South America, Europe, and Asia. He earned a master's degree at Indiana University and a PhD in Music Education at the University of South Florida. His research on international music education has been presented in national and international conferences and publications.

Cornel Hrisca-Munn is a disabled musician (with no lower arms, and an above-knee right leg amputation), who has played drums and bass guitar in live, recorded, and television settings across the globe. He has a Master of Arts from the University of Oxford in Philosophy and Theology, and has conducted research in the fields of disability, philosophy, and theology in preparation for doctoral study. Hrisca-Munn manages successful online music platforms, playing multiple instruments, recording his playing, and providing online resources for drummers. He has delivered talks internationally, and has written articles regarding drums, disability, and testing musical equipment for manufacturers.

Brett Lashua lectures on the sociology of media and education in the Institute of Education, University College London. His scholarship is concerned primarily with youth leisure, popular music, cultural histories and heritage, and urban geographies. He is author of *Popular Music, Popular Myth and Cultural Heritage in Cleveland: The Moondog,* and *The Buzzard and the Battle for the Rock and Roll Hall of Fame* (Emerald), and co-editor of *Sounds and the City: Popular Music, Globalization and Place* (Palgrave) and *Sounds and the City: Volume 2* (Palgrave). A drummer for more than 35 years, he currently collaborates with the Patternbased collective.

Margaret MacAulay, PhD, is a postdoctoral research fellow at the Stigma and Resilience Among Vulnerable Youth Centre (SARAVYC) at the University of British Columbia's School of Nursing in Vancouver, BC. Her research and teaching focuses on the connections between sexuality, gender, new media, health, and culture. Her work has appeared in outlets such as *Critical Studies in Media and Communication*, the *Canadian Journal of Communication*, and *Signs: Journal of Women in Culture and Society.*

Pedro Ojeda Acosta is a musician, drummer, percussionist, composer, and music producer from Bogotá, Colombia. He has served for the past seventeen years as a university professor at various Colombian universities. He currently has several musical projects with which he has published several albums and has toured globally such as Romperayo, Los Pirañas, and Chupame El Dedo, among others. He also has a documentary project called *Los Propios Bateros*, about Colombian drummers from the fifties, sixties, and seventies.

Joseph Michael Pignato is Professor of Music at the State University of New York, Oneonta, where he teaches music industry courses and beat production, and directs ensembles that perform experimental music and improvised rock. He has published on music composition, improvisation, music teaching and learning, music technology, and drumming. Pignato is a principal investigator for and co-author of *The Music Learning Profiles Project* (Routledge) and leader of the critically acclaimed avant jazz collective Bright Dog Red, which records for Ropeadope Records.

Ben Reimer is a 'genre-bending wiz' (PuSh) and a performer of 'stunning virtuosity' (Ludwig-Van Mtl). Collaborations with composers Nicole Lizée, Eliot Britton, Vincent Ho, and Lukas Ligeti have produced a new repertoire for contemporary classical drum kit. His debut album Katana of Choice is an exhilarating musical ride (WholeNote) and a modern classic (I Care If You Listen). Further recordings include Kickin' It 2.0 (Land's End Ensemble), Bookburners (Nicole Lizée) and A Menacing Plume (Rand Steiger). He holds a Doctor of Music (McGill University), is a member of Architek Percussion and Park Sounds and is a Sabian, Yamaha Canada, and Vic Firth artist.

Juan David Rubio Restrepo is a drummer/percussionist, improviser, composer, conductor, multimedia artist, and scholar. His creative practice goes from the acoustic to the digital in traditional, non-traditional, and multisite-telematic collaborative settings. Rubio Restrepo has collaborated with bands 1280 Almas and Asdrubal, and saxophonist Antonio Arnedo in Colombia. In the United States, he has performed with artists like flutist Nicole Mitchell, trombonist Michael Dessen, and double-bassist Mark Dresser. His current academic research deals with issues of alterity, media industries, and nationhood in Latin America. He holds a BM from Pontificia Universidad Javeriana (Bogotá, Colombia), an MFA in music in Integrated, Composition and Technology from UC Irvine, and a PhD in Music with a focus on Integrative Studies from UC San Diego. He is currently Assistant Professor of Music and Chicano Studies, The University of Texas at El Paso.

Carlos Xavier Rodriguez is Associate Professor of Music Education at University of Michigan. He holds a BA from Pitzer College, an MA from UCLA, and a PhD from Northwestern University. He was previously appointed at University of South Florida, University of Iowa, and The Ohio State University. He teaches secondary general methods, introduction to music teaching, student teaching seminar, music technology, and international perspectives of music education. A leading authority on popular music and music education, he has published and lectured worldwide on musicality, creativity, and popular music and culture. He has recently edited the book *Coming of Age: Teaching and Learning Popular Music in Academia* (Maize Books).

Mandy Smith is Director of Education at the Rock and Roll Hall of Fame. She oversees all pre-kindergarten through college onsite and online learning as well as The Garage, the Rock Hall's interactive musical instrument exhibit. She earned a PhD in Musicology from Case Western Reserve University, an MA in Musicology from California State University, Long Beach, and a BA in History of Rock and Roll Music from Indiana University. Smith has drummed in punk, metal, alternative, and prog rock bands since the early 1990s. She recently had the honour of jamming with Kirk Hammett and Robert Trujillo of Metallica.

Gareth Dylan Smith is Assistant Professor of Music (Music Education) at Boston University. He is a board member of the International Society for Music Education, a founding editor of the *Journal of Popular Music Education*, and a drummer. Smith's 2013 monograph, *I drum, therefore I am: being and becoming a drummer*, was the first scholarly book-length study of kit drummers. His research interests include drum kit performance, aesthetic experience, distributed telematic performance, punk pedagogies, and eudaimonia. Smith plays drums with Stephen Wheel, Build a Fort, and Black Belt Jesus. He is currently working on two monographs about playing the drums.

Daniel Akira Stadnicki is a SSHRC Postdoctoral Fellow at McGill University and former Vanier Canada Graduate Scholar at the University of Alberta, where he also taught courses in both world and popular music studies. An award-winning drummer, scholar, and educator, Stadnicki was recently the principal drumming instructor at the Sarah McLachlan School of Music in Edmonton. He has presented at numerous international conferences, published articles in drumming trade magazines, as well as in the *Journal of Popular Music Education*. With Matt Brennan and Joseph Michael Pignato, Stadnicki is co-editing a special issue for the *Journal of Popular Music Education* on Drum Kit Studies in 2021.

Bryden Stillie is Senior Lecturer in Music and Head of Learning and Teaching in the School of Creative Industries at Edinburgh Napier University, Scotland. Stillie graduated from the prestigious BA Applied Music programme at The University of Strathclyde, Glasgow, in 1999, and continues to work as a professional drummer. His teaching specialisms are in drum kit performance, music technology, music education and musicianship skills. His current research interests focus on the areas of electronic drum kit pedagogy, supporting music student transitions into higher education, and effective use of blended and online learning in music.

Paul Thompson is a drummer and professional recording engineer who has worked in the music industry for more than 15 years. He is currently Reader at Leeds Beckett University in the School of the Arts and his research is centred on record production, audio education, popular music learning practices, creativity, and cultural production in popular music. His book *Creativity in the Recording Studio: Alternative Takes* was published in early 2019 by Palgrave MacMillan.

Introduction

MATT BRENNAN, JOSEPH MICHAEL PIGNATO, AND DANIEL AKIRA STADNICKI

Welcome to the *Cambridge Companion to the Drum Kit*. We are delighted to share this first of its kind text, an edited volume dedicated solely to scholarly consideration of the drum kit. This brief introduction to the *Companion* provides background on the work's origins, discussion of its potential import, an explanation of the volume's organization, introductions to the individual authors and chapters, and suggestions for how readers might use the text.

The *Cambridge Companion to the Drum Kit* has its origins in a collegial meeting at the 2016 Association for Popular Music Education conference in Boston, Massachusetts. Two of the editors, Daniel Akira Stadnicki and Joseph Michael Pignato, were enjoying a post-conference dinner with one of the contributing authors, Gareth Dylan Smith, all three avid drummers. The trio's discussion inevitably turned to drumming, the drum kit itself, and to the names of other drummers, scholars, and practitioners with similar interests.

Throughout the course of the conversation, a variety of fields, representing a wide swath of scholarship, drumming practices, and perspectives came to the fore. We recognized that the drum kit remains a remarkably underrepresented topic in music research despite growing interests in rhythmic and percussive phenomena across the humanities and social sciences. This interest includes significant studies and networks dedicated to understanding the dynamics of rhythm, groove, micro-timing, and entrainment. It dawned on the three that something was bubbling under the radar of existing conferences, established journals, and widely read texts, an emerging community of scholars concerned with the drum kit, the drummers who play them, and related issues.

This emerging community represents what Pignato has referred to as a 'community of response', or the gathering, intentional or by chance, of subcultural groups in response to a particular phenomenon.[1] According to Pignato, communities of response represent 'requisite first steps' to Lave and Wenger's 'communities of practice' and are worth noting because they often presage emerging movements, endeavours, or fields of activity.[2] This text then seeks to acknowledge that community of response, essentially to say, 'here it is. It is indeed a phenomenon unto itself, worthy of scholarly consideration'. By the time the ideas above reached the stage of a book proposal, Matt Brennan joined to round out the editorial team, and together they curated a collection of chapters that provides background on the drum kit as an historical phenomenon, identifies some nascent scholarship, and considers contemporary issues pertaining to drum kits and the drummers who play them. Authors contributing to this volume represent scholars, practitioners, and historically noted drummers hailing from four continents, North America, South America, Europe, and Australia.

The volume is organized in five discrete but connected parts: Part I, 'Histories of the Drum Kit', Part II: 'Analysing the Drum Kit in Performance', Part III: 'Learning, Teaching, and Leading on the Drum Kit', and Part IV: 'Drumming Bodies, Meaning, and Identity'. Each is highlighted in the subsequent paragraphs.

Part I, 'Histories of the Drum Kit', provides historical grounding for the text. Matt Brennan lays the foundation for Part I, and for the subsequent parts, offering historical and theoretical consideration of the drum kit. Paul Archibald considers how early sound recordings informed drumming practice and drummers' understanding of the instrument and its roles in bands and orchestras. Steven Baur considers the cultural history of the drum kit backbeat in sound recordings from the early twentieth century. Finally, Pedro Ojeda Acosta and Juan David Rubio Restrepo chronicle the drum kit in an historically specific application, that of Colombia's *Música Tropical Sabanera*.

Accordingly, Part II, 'Analysing the Drum Kit in Performance', considers specific and situated applications of the drum kit. Part II begins with an historically and geographically specific consideration, Daniel Gohn's history of the drum kit in Brazilian folkloric, popular, and jazz music. Ben Reimer highlights the ways in which the drum kit has been incorporated in contemporary classical music. Scott Hanenberg considers the increasingly complex approaches to meter and irregular rhythms present in contemporary drum kit performance. Daniel Akira Stadnicki provides a case study of drum kit aesthetics in the musical genre known as *Americana*. Part II ends with Brett Lashua and Paul Thompson's look at drum kits and drumming in contemporary recording contexts.

Part III, 'Learning, Teaching, and Leading on the Drum Kit', focuses on the ways in which drummers learn, teach, mentor, and lead from behind the drum kit. Bryden Stillie examines ways in which his students adapt to and learn from and with technologically augmented and hybrid drum kits. Carlos Xavier Rodriguez and Patrick Hernly examine timekeeping, often considered a perfunctory function of drum kit performance, through the lens of aesthetics. Joseph Michael Pignato engages jazz drummers Jack DeJohnette and Terri Lyne Carrington in a discussion of mentorship within jazz drumming tradition and culture. Finally, Bill Bruford considers leading from behind the kit, both the physical spaces behind the battery of drums and cymbals, as part of the backline, and from the conceptual space drummers occupy in music and in popular culture.

The final section, Part IV, 'Drumming Bodies, Meaning, and Identity', provides a capstone of meta-analyses of broad and complex issues posed by the drum kit and for the drummers who play them. Mandy J. Smith considers the example of John Bonham to illustrate how the corporeal experience of drumming reflects embodied experience unique to the drum kit. adam patrick bell and Cornel Hrisca-Munn consider the configurable nature of the drum kit as it relates to accessibility, ability, and notions of disability. Vincent Andrisani and Margaret MacAulay analyse representations of drumming culture on social media using the case study of Instagram, specifically as it pertains to and informs notions of gender and performance on the drum kit. Nat Grant offers an account of activist drum culture using the case study of *Hey Drums*,, an Australian initiative, founded by Grant, to offer female and non-binary drummers opportunities to play drums, connect with other drummers, and more fully participate in activities pertaining to the drum kit. Finally, Gareth Dylan Smith provides readers with considerations of drumming and identity, specifically on the deeply personal reason he became a drummer.

Notes

1 J. Michael Pignato. 'Situating Technology within and without Music Education' in A. S. Ruthmann and R. Mantie (eds.), *The Oxford Handbook of Technology and Music Education* (Oxford: Oxford University Press, 2017).

2 J. Lave and E. Wenger. *Situated Learning: Legitimate Peripheral Participation* (Cambridge: Cambridge University Press, 1991).

PART I

Histories of the Drum Kit

1 The Drum Kit in Theory

MATT BRENNAN

Introduction

What is a drum kit and how do we study it? There is a commonsense answer to this question: a drum kit is a musical instrument comprising an arrangement of drums, cymbals, and associated hardware, and it can be studied both formally (not just through private tuition but also prestigious music schools and academies) and informally (by practicing along to recordings, playing in bands, and so on). And yet this commonsense answer is deceptive because it hinges on taken-for-granted assumptions about the stability of the term 'drum kit' and the conventional ways of studying it. The problem, of course, is that musical definitions and conventions are not fixed, immoveable, or timeless; they are always in flux and in a constant process of being shaped by shifting historical and cultural contexts.

In fact, the definition of the drum kit – and consensus regarding its appropriate study – have changed dramatically over the course of the instrument's history. This chapter is a rough guide to unpacking that history, and in doing so it treats the drum kit not as a fixed object but as a theoretical concept. What follows is a discussion of the drum kit in theory divided into three parts: (1) the invention and changing status of the instrument; (2) the trajectory of drum kit studies within the wider field of musical instrument scholarship; and (3) a discussion of the 'drumscape' as a theoretical tool.

The Invention of the Drum Kit

The drum kit is a uniquely American instrument whose invention coincided with the birth of jazz at the turn of the twentieth century; or at least this is the prevailing origin story that we see reproduced in numerous popular histories of the instrument.[1] A typical version of the myth goes like this:

> The drum set is one of New Orleans' greatest gifts to American popular music. When the brass parade bands stopped marching and settled down in the riverboats to play – when the dances and comics in minstrel shows

> needed percussive accompaniment – when the blues came drifting off the plantations and mixed with Caribbean and African rhythms to make a new music called jazz, the drum kit was born.[2]

A similar account appears in a 2019 BBC documentary on the drum kit presented by Stewart Copeland. While being filmed on location in downtown New Orleans, Copeland holds up an enlarged photograph of the drummer Dee Dee Chandler, who played with the John Robichaux Society Orchestra at the tail end of the nineteenth century. Pointing to the bottom of Chandler's bass drum, Copeland informs the viewer that 'down here is one of the most important inventions in modern music', and then declares Chandler to be 'one of the first snare drum guys to play the bass drum at the same time ... by inventing a homemade foot pedal'.[3] To be fair to Copeland, the photograph of Chandler (taken circa 1896) is arguably the earliest surviving *photograph* of a drummer standing next to their bass drum pedal. But the viewer would be mistaken if they made the leap of assuming the photograph of Chandler was the first documented *evidence* of a bass drum pedal, or that it was unquestionably invented in New Orleans. Putting to one side the question of whether the hi-hat (which does not appear in drum catalogues until the mid-1920s) or separate tension tom-toms (which appear in the mid-1930s) are necessary core components of a drum kit, I will for the moment restrict my investigation specifically to the origin of the bass drum pedal.

Drummers have experimented with ways of playing more than one percussion instrument at once for centuries, if not millennia. To take a relatively recent historical example, it was common in the nineteenth century for both marching band and orchestral drummers to attach a cymbal to the rim of their bass drum so that they could play both at once.[4] Jayson Dobney has documented that this practice was also evident in the United States, noting that 'photographs taken during the Civil War often show a cymbal attached to a bass drum for use in a military band. After the war, this configuration could be found in many of the community and town concert bands that were gaining popularity throughout the country'.[5]

When theatre and symphonic orchestras attempted to represent the sounds of military marching band drumming indoors in cramped conditions and with fewer musicians, some inventive drummers began to place the bass drum on the floor so they could simultaneously play snare drum (often placed on a chair, since snare drum stands had not yet been invented) and bass drum (with cymbal often attached to the rim) – a performance practice which by the 1880s came to be known as 'double drumming'.

So when did foot-operated drum pedals arrive on the scene? This is not an easy question to answer. In order to illustrate the complexity of the problem, and the messiness of historical research more broadly, I will present *seven* potential candidates for the bass drum pedal's moment of origin, each with its own narrative advantages and disadvantages.

Option 1: bass drum pedals have existed from the early nineteenth century, but robust documentation proving their existence has not survived. As I document elsewhere in my book *Kick It: A Social History of the Drum Kit*, there are surviving illustrations from early nineteenth-century France that portray at least two different one-man bands using homemade beaters attached to their feet to play a drum with one foot, and a pair of cymbals with the other.[6] Based on this evidence, you could argue for the possibility that foot pedals for drums and cymbals were likely discovered by multiple people independently in different countries from at least the beginning of the nineteenth century onwards and probably earlier. Here we begin to see that choosing a particular origin narrative serves a particular agenda: this first version of the bass drum pedal origin story privileges (a) the international roots of the technologies that inform the drum kit as an instrument; and (b) a 'multiple discovery' (no one person is attributed) rather than a 'lone genius' (one person only is attributed) narrative of invention. This origin narrative also de-privileges (a) innovations that have documented widespread impact (e.g. a pedal design that was successfully mass-produced); and (b) the USA as the country of origin for the proto-drum kit.

Option 2: the oldest surviving example of a foot-operated drum pedal is located (somewhat surprisingly) in the Keswick Museum in England. (A full discussion of this unusual bass drum pedal can be found in a 2014 journal article by Paul Archibald.)[7] It was created by an inventor named Cornelius Ward for the novelty Richardson Rock and Steel Band. If we chose this as a moment of origin, it privileges (a) a single named inventor; (b) the role of drummers in novelty music (as opposed to jazz, for example); and (c) historical instruments in museum collections as a source of evidence.

Option 3: in the published memoir of Arthur Rackett, a long-time drummer for the John Philip Sousa Band, he recalled that 'in 1882 I settled in Quincy, Illinois. This was about the time that the first foot pedal came out. Dale of Brooklyn made it. Everybody laughed at the idea, but I sent for one and started to practice in the woodshed'.[8] This moment privileges oral history (Rackett's memory preserved in print) but ignores the need for material evidence (no catalogue or paper trail corroborate the memory survives).

Option 4: the oldest legal patent for a bass drum pedal dates back to 1887, when George Olney of St Louis, Missouri, was granted a patent for a design very similar to that of Dee Dee Chandler, but Olney's patent predates the photograph of Chandler by approximately nine years. This option privileges legal patents as documents of record, but de-privileges those who may have come up with a similar design but did not manage (or were somehow prevented) from patenting their idea.

Option 5: the earliest example I can find of a bass drum pedal being sold in an instrument catalogue is from 1893, when the German manufacturer Paul Stark published a catalogue to advertise his goods at the Chicago World's Fair. This option privileges commercial production and evidence from instrument catalogues, and de-privileges the USA as the accepted country of origin for the bass drum pedal.

Option 6: as mentioned above, the earliest photograph of a drummer next to his bass drum pedal is likely that of Dee Dee Chandler in New Orleans circa 1896. It privileges the city of New Orleans, African American culture (Chandler was black), photographic evidence, and the notion that the drum kit only coalesces as an instrument through a particular kind of musical performance practice (e.g. dance music influenced by New Orleans second line drumming). It de-privileges patents as evidence (i.e. Olney 1887), countries outside the USA, and popular music not rooted in the jazz tradition.

Option 7: arguably the most famous of all the candidates outlined so far is William F. Ludwig's 1909 patent for a highly successful and influential bass drum pedal design. This option privileges the overall impact a particular design has on the rest of drumming culture. From 1909 onwards Ludwig's design is not only successfully mass-produced and sold but also widely imitated by other manufacturers.

The point of outlining seven different possible origin moments for the bass drum pedal is not, in my view, to then select one of them as the definitive version. Instead, the point is to draw attention the *historiography* of the drum kit – in other words, to draw attention to the processes of inclusion and exclusion that must be made when writing the instrument's history. To investigate the origin of the drum kit, like any historical project, is necessarily to sift through a wide range of partial sources and piece together a story, which inevitably involves making judgments about what to leave in, and what to leave out of the story.

Put simply, there is frequently more than one way of framing the origin story of a musical instrument. The point here is that each of the possibilities above serves a particular ideological agenda, and to privilege one narrative necessarily excludes a host of equally important influences, inspirations, and voices. By giving attention to the multiple possible origin narratives and their implications, we can gain a better understanding of who and what we are including and excluding in the stories we tell, and why.[9]

The historiographical lesson learned from the bass drum pedal can also be applied to invention of the drum kit in full as a distinct instrument – there is more than one possible moment of origin. Does the first drum kit appear in 1906, when the Philadelphia-based instrument manufacture J. W. Pepper publishes a catalogue featuring a pre-bundled 'trap drummer's outfit' (comprising a bass drum, snare drum, cymbal, and bass drum pedal)? Or is it 1918, when Ludwig & Ludwig first advertise their own 'Jazz-Er-Up' outfit equipped with their signature bass drum pedal? Is it 1928, when a new accessory that we retrospectively recognize as a hi-hat pedal (produced and distributed by the Walberg & Auge company in Worcester, Massachusetts) begins appearing in multiple drum manufacturer catalogues? Or must we wait until 1936, when Gene Krupa collaborates with the Slingerland company to create the new 'Radio King' series of drum kits equipped with separate-tension tom-tom drums? To complicate matters further, what happens when electronic drum kits are introduced from roughly the 1980s onwards, or virtual drum kits from the 2000s onwards? Can a drum kit be acoustic, electronic, or virtual and still count as a drum kit? If this question causes even a modest amount of debate, then we have to assume that the meaning of a 'drum kit' is not fully stable. The pioneers of the acoustic drum kit could not have predicted that in the twenty-first century, debates around the meanings of a 'drum kit', 'drummer', and 'drumming' would include voices from computer software engineers and multinational corporations packaging virtual drummers into their digital audio workstations. Nevertheless, these actors significantly influence our contemporary understanding of what counts as a drum kit, drummer, or drumming performance.

To ask such questions is to point towards a broader question in the sociology of knowledge: what aspects of its design must stay the same in order for a drum kit to *remain* a drum kit over time? In the twenty-first century, when as many or more electronic drum kits are sold relative to acoustic drum kits – and when the sounds of multiple drum kits can be stored and deployed within a single software plugin – is the definition of what constitutes a drum kit categorically fixed? My argument is that it is not and never was, and this is what I mean when I say the drum kit is not a fixed object but a theoretical concept.

The History and Future of Studying the Drum Kit

Having now seen that the 'drum kit' is a contested concept whose meaning changes over time and across different contexts, it will come as no surprise that the same applies to *studying* the drum kit. William F. Ludwig published an essay in 1927 detailing his recollection of how drummers in the United States studied their instrument:

> The old timers of Chicago were practically all rudimental drummers . . . [and] all probably had the same experience in learning to drum as I had. My dad stepped into Lyon and Healy's store and simply said he wanted a drum book. [A book of military drum rudiments] was laid out on the counter and could be purchased for $1.00 each. It was the only drum book that [the store] had or recommended.[10]

With the advent of ragtime at the turn of the twentieth century, however, Ludwig observed that a new way of studying the instrument appeared: 'new beats were invented, new systems of playing the drum were invented and, in fact, ragtime methods of all sorts appeared on the market, each one different from the other. Originality seemed to be the main object'.[11] The ragtime and jazz eras fuelled a clash of musical cultures, specifically a tension between musicians who learned their instrument through reading and following notated sheet music versus those who learned to play through more informal methods and improvisation. In truth, learning to play the drum kit had always involved both formal and informal approaches, and even after the drum kit gained acceptance in institutions of higher education as part of university jazz programmes, drummers typically continued to study performance practice on their instrument using a mixed methods approach.

For most of the twentieth century, the practice of studying the drum kit could be divided into one of two categories: *construction* (how the instrument was designed and manufactured) or *performance* (how it was played). The study of the drum kit's physical construction can arguably be situated within the wider field of 'organology' – a term coined in 1933 to designate the academic study of the material and acoustic properties of musical instruments dating back to the nineteenth century; it should be noted, however, that the scope of organology was severely limited for many decades, and the drum kit was not considered worthy of serious attention until the late twentieth century (see, for instance, James Blades' 1970 landmark study, *Percussion Instruments and Their History*, which briefly contextualizes the drum kit's origins amidst the wider history of percussion).[12] Meanwhile, the study of drum kit performance can be situated with the broader field of 'performance practice' scholarship, which in the case of the drum kit made inroads into the academy with the gradual institutionalization of jazz in higher education over the second half of the twentieth century (Theodore Dennis Brown's 1976 doctoral dissertation, *A History and Analysis of Jazz Drumming to 1942*, is a milestone in this respect).[13]

The establishment of percussion education organizations are also relevant here, such as the Percussive Arts Society (created in 1961), which held its first International Convention (PASIC) in 1976.

While the practice of studying the drum kit has gradually crept into the academy, it is worth emphasizing that many of the most important early analyses of the drum kit's construction and performance were produced *outside* the academy. The publication of catalogues, newsletters, and periodicals about the drum kit are a useful example. The drum kit was a product aimed at a commercial market, and therefore the catalogues and newsletters produced by early drum kit manufacturers such as Leedy, Ludwig, and Slingerland are rich sources of information describing the latest innovations in the instrument; even though such descriptions were explicitly created to advertise the products of drum companies, they are nevertheless invaluable accounts of the drum kit's design and construction. In terms of performance practice, a plethora of 'method books' appeared following the dawn of jazz: notable examples include Carl Gardner's *Modern Drum Method* (1919) and Ralph Smith's *50 Hot Cymbal Breaks and 70 Modern Drum Beats* (1929), George Lawrence Stone's *Stick Control for the Snare Drummer* (1935), Jim Chapin's *Advanced Techniques for the Modern Drummer* (1948), and the list goes on.

Likewise, the vintage drum community that arose from the late 1980s onwards has produced numerous vital historical studies. While some of these were created with the primary aim of identifying, collecting, and restoring rare and potentially valuable drums and cymbals, others – including pioneering work by John Aldridge, Jon Cohan, Rob Cook, Chet Falzerano, and Geoff Nicholls, to name but a few – often included social history scholarship that provided insight into the cultural significance of the drum kit.[14] Long-standing special interest magazines such as *Modern Drummer* (first published in 1977) and *Not So Modern Drummer* (first published in 1988) also produced important articles on the instrument, key artists, and performance styles and techniques that predate much of the academic scholarship on the drum kit.

In recent years, a much wider range of approaches to researching the drum kit has flourished, arguably marking a shift from a paradigm of 'studying the drum kit' (concerned mostly with issues of construction and performance) to *drum kit studies* (a fully interdisciplinary field of inquiry). The emerging field of drum kit studies is distinctive for embracing insights from a variety of academic sources – including but not limited to philosophy, sociology, anthropology, psychology, education, race, gender and class studies – which are brought to bear on the drum kit, drummers, and drumming. Systems of cultural theory that have proved influential elsewhere in musical instrument scholarship – such as science and technologies studies (STS), social construction of technology (SCOT) theory, actor network theory (ANT), and material culture studies – can also be productively applied to enhance our understanding of the drum kit (more of which in the next section). Drum kit studies is not itself a discipline *per se*, but a loosely organized field of study, which is slowly showing signs of cohering (as evidenced by the publication of this *Cambridge Companion*). The point here, however, is not to define drum kit studies in opposition to earlier ways of studying the drum kit, but to build upon them. Nor is it to isolate drum kit studies inside the academy from those occurring outside the academy. The drum kit is a living instrument, and drum kit studies therefore can, and should, actively encourage interaction and engagement between all spheres of drum kit culture.

In an effort to explore the breadth of what drum kit studies can and should be, I propose unfolding the term 'drum kit' from its narrow, commonsense definition (described at the outset of this chapter) into a larger map of directions for further enquiry. Steve Waksman has previously argued that musical instruments can be understood in a multitude of ways: as commodities, material objects, visual icons, sources of knowledge, cultural resources, and of course, 'sound-producing devices, without which music could hardly be said to exist at all'.[15] Similarly, Kevin Dawe has shown how musical instruments create forms of meaning, 'changing soundscapes, affecting emotions, moving bodies, demarcating identities, mobilizing ideas, demonstrating beliefs, motioning values'.[16] Inspired by the above and other recent work in musical instrument research, I propose that through the lens of what one might call the *drumscape* (which I will outline in detail in the following section), drum kit scholars can add the sum of these multiple perspectives together and make steps towards understanding not just how the drum kit, drummers, and drumming relate to the wider world – but how they impact upon it.

The Drumscape as a Theoretical Tool

The concept of the 'soundscape' is a twentieth-century invention. One of its key proponents, the composer and naturalist R. Murray Schafer, once theorized that 'modern man is beginning to inhabit a world with an acoustic environment radically different from any he has hitherto known', arguing that the soundscape of the world required careful study 'in order to make intelligent recommendations for its improvement'.[17] Similarly, the anthropologist Arjun Appadurai introduced further concepts like 'mediascape' and 'technoscape' to make sense of the intangible forces that shape the global cultural economy. More recently, Kevin Dawe has put forth the term 'guitarscape' in an effort to theoretically frame the guitar as 'a large-scale musical-cultural-social occurrence that merits serious and ongoing academic study'.[18] I suggest that if we are comfortable using terms like 'technoscape' and 'guitarscape', drum kit scholars might also benefit from the concept of a *drumscape*.[19]

The drum kit in all its forms (acoustic, electronic, physical, virtual, and symbolic) participates in the drumscape. (By virtue of its name, the drumscape can also encompass other instruments in the percussion family.) Such an approach encourages the study of the drum kit not just as a physical object or a performance practice, but as a symbol (encompassing both physical and virtual forms) whose meanings are determined by cultural use. In short, the drumscape is a macroscopic lens through which to understand drums, drummers, drumming, and the meanings and impacts they produce.

To once again borrow from and modify Kevin Dawe's thoughtful discussion of the guitarscape, I suggest that the drumscape is a lens through which to consider (a) how the drum kit has been written about, thought about, and talked about; (b) the power and agency of the drum kit in culture and society; and (c) what kind of experience it is to play the drum kit (an experience involving both the mind and the body).[20] Moreover, the drumscape is not simply a concept through which to analyse the drum kit as a phenomenon: it is also a process in itself. In other words, we can interrogate a multitude of events when *drumscaping* occurs: in the sound mixing of a recording or a live concert; in the transistorized drum machine sounds emanating from the car speakers of a moving vehicle, or the wireless headphones connected to a mobile device; in a performance by a busker in a city park; in a religious service as a gospel drummer entrains a congregation towards a spiritual experience; or in a clothing store as market researchers study whether adjustments in the BPM of a four-on-the-floor kick influence the speed with which customers shop. Drumscaping need not even be sonic in nature: it could be present in the logic of a conversation between band members over how songwriting royalties should be divided, and whether the drummer's role merits a percentage (and if so how much); or the visual mapping of virtual music-making interfaces in a digital audio workstation that is informed in some way by an acoustic or electronic drum kit. All of these moments are both a part of the drumscape as a concept, and act as particular examples of drumscaping as a process.

Building on earlier theorizations of instruments by Simon Frith, Emily Dolan, and John Tresch, I propose that viewed through the lens of the drumscape, the seemingly simple term 'drum kit' can be understood from at least four different but related perspectives: the drum kit is a *technology*, an *ideological object*, a *material object*, and a *social relationship*.[21] I will examine each in turn.

To understand the drum kit as a technology is to approach it as the application of an accumulated field of human knowledge (i.e. instrument-building) resulting in the creation a new music-making device. The technology of the drum kit not only solves particular problems of labour and space – allowing a single musician to play multiple percussion instruments at once – but also opens up new and extends the possibilities for musical expression. However, understanding the drum kit as a technology is not to artificially separate it from its social interaction and cultural use, as may science and technology studies (STS) scholars have observed. As Timothy Taylor once put it, for instance, music technology is 'not separate from social groups that use it, it is not separate from the individuals who use it; it is not separate from the social groups and individuals who invented it, tested it, marketed it, distributed it, sold it, repaired it, listened to it, bought it, or revived it. In short, music technology . . . [is] always bound up in a social system'.[22] Approaching the drum kit as a technology is not synonymous with treating it as an object either. The technology of the drum kit could easily be understood, for example, not as a thing made up of wooden shells, skins, and cymbals, but as a spatial arrangement or conceptual interface. The drum kit is a form of software as well as hardware. Non-drummers might initially puzzle over the following arrangement of abstract shapes, but any drummer would immediately be able to identify its meaning and implied use (see Figure 1.1).

The diagram below implies an overhead view of a typical setup for a righthanded drummer: a rectangular shape represents a bass drum, four dark grey circles from left to right represent a snare drum, two mounted toms, and a floor tom; and three light grey circles to represent from left to right a hi-hat, crash cymbal, and ride cymbal. This interface, even in abstract symbolic form, would be familiar enough to a drummer to imply

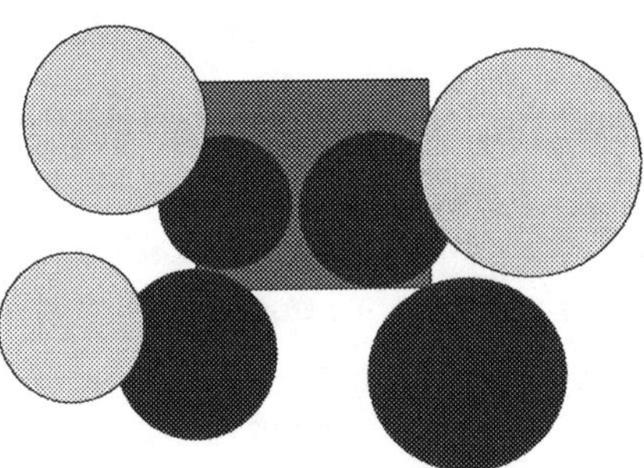

Figure 1.1 The drum kit as an abstract interface

not just a particular arrangement of drums and cymbals but also a rich set of performance practices – an amalgam of embodied techniques to coordinate one's feet, hands, and body and enable a particular kind of music making. But of course, the implied sounds and uses need not be fixed in an open interface. Conceived as software, the drum kit allows for new codes to be written upon it: whether in the form of an electronic kit or displayed on a computer screen, drummers could happily (and routinely do) assign new voices and instruments to each element of the interface, or indeed add or remove elements entirely. The drum kit interface allows for the mixing, matching, and manipulation of sounds and performance techniques; the drum kit is a musically rich instrument precisely because drummers frequently borrow and repurpose its symbols and techniques in unexpected ways. A competent and creative drummer understands the instrument's scripts but also subverts and rewrites them – navigating expressive pathways and possibilities that are musically distinct from other instruments.

Whether conceived of as an abstract interface or a concrete instrument, the drum kit as technology affords certain kinds of use and discourages others. It has the power to both enlarge and restrict the activity of music making. Understood from this standpoint (in other words, through the framework of actor network theory, or ANT), the drum kit is not a passive object, but an *object with agency*: it acts upon a drummer as much as a drummer acts upon it. The drum kit as technology encourages the user to experience music in a certain way (a very different way than, say, a guitar or woodwind instrument).

As an ideological object, the drum kit can be understood as a set of self-reinforcing ideas and values. The extent to which there is consensus surrounding these values informs social agreement of the drum kit's function and purpose, and how it should and should not be used. The ideology of the drum kit contains received wisdom about its history, tradition, the accepted canon of significant drummers as artists (and the criteria by which they are judged to be significant), and its status as a sonic and visual icon. The ideology of the drum kit can also challenge prevailing music ideologies: from the perspective of drum kit culture, West African musical performance practices might be near the top of a hierarchy of musical value, while they might be located further down the value hierarchy embedded into the ideology of, for instance, a European instrument like the harpsichord or piano. There are also multiple and conflicting ideologies of the drum kit. In jazz drumming culture, for example, it might be taken for granted that an acoustic drum kit is a 'real' or 'authentic' drum kit, and an electronic or software drum kit is not; in electronic dance music culture, by contrast, this distinction might not matter at all. None of these ideas and values are absolute truths, but some sets of ideas have historically gravitated towards the orbit of the drum kit and the genre worlds surrounding it, while others have been repelled. And as ever, these ideologies shift and change over time.

As a material object, the drum kit can be understood as being made of particular elements and having particular physical and acoustic properties. Elsewhere I examine how the changing materials of the drumscape are mirrored by a wider shift in the materials used for commodity goods as a whole. A political ecology of the drum kit could be divided into three overlapping historical eras, each grouped by the principal materials used to manufacture the drum kit as a product: (1) *renewable materials* (i.e. the wood and metal used in traditional acoustic drums and cymbals); (2) *non-renewable plastics and e-waste* (i.e. the electronic circuitry and synthetic materials used in electronic drum kits); and finally (3) *data* (used in drum replacement and augmentation software).[23] How this categorization plays out in detail represents an avenue for future research. Furthermore, the drum kit as a material object takes part in a global commodity industry, and is implicated in various commercial and industrial processes. Here the study of the drum kit could productively align with material culture studies more broadly.

As a social relationship, the drum kit only becomes a drum kit when it is used as such (in other words, when it is played) and when a relationship is established between the instrument and the person playing it.[24] As Gareth Dylan Smith has observed, a drum kit can play a powerful role in shaping a drummer's social identity.[25] According to this approach, drum kits are not merely aids to the activity of drumming, but also powerful forces acting in relationship to their users, shaping drumming and its meaning in the process; and as it is woven into the texture of everyday existence (to paraphrase cultural theorist Langdon Winnner), the drum kit sheds its tool-like qualities and becomes part of our very humanity.[26]

Conclusions

To summarize, 'what is a drum kit and how do we study it?' is not a question where a short and simple answer will suffice. But this is a good thing. The drum kit is a living, mutable concept, and to study it properly is not a short exercise, but a lifelong inquiry that requires the establishment of a community of scholarship with constituents from both inside and outside the academy. In offering a few provocations concerning the historiography of the drum kit, the trajectory of drum kit studies, and the theorization of the drum kit, I do not claim to have fully answered any of the questions posed in this chapter, nor do I see a concept like the drumscape as a unified theoretical approach for drum kit studies as a whole. These are simply some tools to add to the toolbox, and it is my hope that the reader will find other useful tools to understand the drum kit, drummers, and drumming in the rest of this book.

Notes

1 See, for example, M. Hart, F. Lieberman, and D. A. Sonneborn. *Planet Drum: A Celebration of Percussion and Rhythm* (New York, Harper San Francisco, 1991); A. Budofsky. *The Drummer: 100 Years of Rhythmic Power and Invention* (Cedar Grove, NJ: Modern Drummer Publications, 2006).

2 J. Cohan. *Star Sets* (Milwaukee: Hal Leonard, 1995), p. 2.

3 *On Drums . . . Stewart Copeland!* Television programme, 59 minutes. BBC Four, aired 13 January 2019.

4 H. MacDonald. *Berlioz's Orchestration Treatise: A Translation and Commentary* (Cambridge: Cambridge University Press, 2002), p. 280.

5 J. Dobney. The Creation of the Trap Set and Its Development before 1920', *Journal of the American Musical Instrument Society*, 30 (2004), p. 25.

6 M. Brennan. *Kick It: A Social History of the Drum Kit* (Oxford: Oxford University Press, 2020), pp. 34–35.

7 P. Archibald. 'Searching for the First Bass Drum Pedal: Rock Harmonicas to Viennese Pianos', *Popular Music History* 9:3 (2014).

8 A. H. Rackett. *Fifty Years a Drummer* (Elkhorn: Self-published, 1931), p. 10.

9 Brennan, *Kick It*, p. 51.

10 Quoted in C. Bolton (ed.) *The Ludwig Drummer: April 1926 to Spring 1948* (Anaheim Hills: Centerbrook, 1999), p. 63.

11 Bolton, *The Ludwig Drummer*, pp. 8–9.

12 J. Blades. *Percussion Instruments and Their History* (London: Faber & Faber, 1970).

13 G. R. Rognoni. 'Organology and the others: a political perspective', presented at Galpin Society/ AMIS Conference (3 June 2017).

14 J. Aldridge. *Guide to Vintage Drums* (Milwaukee: Hal Leonard Corporation, 1994); J. Cohan. *Zildjian: A History of the Legendary Cymbal Makers* (Milwaukee: Hal Leonard Corporation, 1999); R. Cook. *The Complete History of the Leedy Drum Company* (Fullerton: Centerstream, 1993); R. Cook. *The Ludwig Book* (Rebeats Press, 2003); Chet Falzerano. *Gretsch Drums: The Legacy of 'That Great Gretsch Sound'* (Hal Leonard Corporation, 1995); G. Nicholls. *The Drum Book: A History of the Rock Drum Kit* (Milwaukee: Hal Leonard Corporation, 2008).

15 S. Waksman. 'Reading the Instrument: An Introduction', *Popular Music and Society* 26:3 (2003), p. 252.

16 Kevin Dawe. 'The Cultural Study of Musical Instruments', in M. Clayton, T. Herbert, and R. Middleton (eds.) *The Cultural Study of Music: A Critical Introduction* (Abingdon: Routledge, 2003), p. 195.

17 R. Murray Schafer. *The Soundscape: The Tuning of the World* (Rochester: Destiny Books, 1994), pp. 3–4.

18 Kevin Dawe. *The New Guitarscape in Critical Theory, Cultural Practice and Musical Performance* (Ashgate Publishing, Ltd., 2010), p. 41.

19 This discussion develops an argument I first made in *Kick It: A Social History of the Drum Kit*, pp. 316–317.

20 Brennan, *Kick It*, pp. 45–46.

21 Here I draw from and modify Simon Frith's theorization of musical instruments outlined in S. Frith, M. Brennan, and N. Prior, 'Towards a new understanding of musical instruments', presented at Royal Musical Association Music and Philosophy Study Group conference, 14 July 2017; J. Tresch and E. I. Dolan. 'Toward a New Organology', *Osiris* 28, 2013, pp. 278–298.

22 T. D. Taylor. *Strange Sounds: Music, Technology, and Culture* (New York: Routledge, 2001), p. 7.

23 See M. Brennan, 'The environmental sustainability of the music industries', in K. Oakley and M. Banks (eds.), *Cultural Industries and the Environmental Crisis: New Approaches for Policy* (Springer, 2020). See also K. Devine. *Decomposed: A Political Ecology of Music* (Cambridge: MIT Press, 2019).

24 Thanks again to Simon Frith for this formulation, which first appeared in S. Frith, M. Brennan, and N. Prior 'Towards a new understanding of musical instruments', Royal Musical Association Music and Philosophy Study Group conference, 14 July 2017.

25 G. D. Smith. *I Drum Therefore I Am* (Farnham: Ashgate, 2013).

26 L. Winner. *The Whale and the Reactor* (Chicago: University of Chicago Press, 1986), pp. 6–12.

2 Historically Informed Jazz Performance on the Drum Kit

PAUL ARCHIBALD

Since jazz is an improvisational music, recordings offer perhaps the only valid way of its preservation. MARTIN WILLIAMS, *THE SMITHSONIAN COLLECTION OF CLASSIC JAZZ: GUIDE*, 1976.[1]

I asked Chauncey Morehouse 'do drummers really play that way, as we hear on the recordings?' and he said 'Absolutely not. Absolutely not.' VINCE GIORDANO, BANDLEADER OF NIGHTHAWKS ORCHESTRA, 2014.[2]

Misrepresented from the Beginning?

Recordings of interest concerning the drum kit began around 1913, when record companies began to take notice of dance crazes that were sweeping across the country.[3] Yet, fourteen years later in 1927, an advert from *The Talking Machine World*, titled 'Drum Notes Not Only Heard – But Identified!',[4] advertised a new home speaker, promising that 'thousands of radio listeners will now realise for the first time that radio orchestras have drums when they hook up this new, improved Crosley Musicone'. While it is dubious as to just how clear the drum parts would have been on this new device, what is clear is that, to some extent, audiences were not used to hearing the drum kit on record at this time, as its newfound clarity was used as a point on which to market this new technology.

Recorded music is utilised in many different ways: most obviously, as entertainment for the general listener; profit-making commodity for the producer, or record label; and often, an object of study for the performing musician seeking to learn from these captured moments in musical history. On this last point, the opening quotations to this chapter demonstrate both the importance and the danger of these recordings for the aspiring drum kit player.

Historically Informed Performance (HIP) is an approach to the performance of Western art music, most commonly from the Medieval, Renaissance, and Baroque eras. At its most basic level, it means performing music with special attention given to the performance conventions and technology present when the piece of music was composed. Taruskin's collected essays on his critique of HIP music, *Text & Act*, is telling of his primary complaint with early music performers: that they give authority to a preserving text.[5] 'Central to this concept', Taruskin explains, 'is an idealised notion of what a musical work is: something wholly realised by its creator, fixed in writing, and thus capable of being preserved'.[6] This, he argues, leads to HIP practitioners placing too much value on objects, and not enough on the people performing them, and insists that the ultimate authority rests with the interpreters rather than the texts, 'for texts do not speak for themselves'.[7] Performers seeking to recreate the styles of early jazz (or 'HIJP' performers, if I may insert the word 'jazz'), often replace scores with early recordings made in the 1910s and 1920s. This chapter argues that, while this may prove beneficial for musicians studying the clarinet, trumpet, trombone, and the like, the drum kit may not be adequately represented in such a way. Perhaps drummers, more than other instrumentalists, have reason to doubt the validity of what Taruskin describes as 'the text'.

My own experiences in performance, as a drummer playing early jazz music, have led me to reconsider what it is to play in this style, and where to look for my 'text'. The role that early recordings play in jazz history determine how this music is interpreted today. This chapter will explore how drummers were represented on record, how this differed from their colleagues, and how HIJP performers today can balance the importance of recorded music with these considerations.

Drummers Disadvantaged in Early Recordings: Acoustic Age

From the introduction, the 'Crosley Musicone' demonstrates that playback equipment during the 1910s through the 1920s was ill-equipped to reproduce the sounds of early drum kits. However, playback equipment was not the only reason for this, as the problem began in the studio itself.

There is an abundance of primary sources describing the need to remove drums from the acoustic recording studio (pre-electric recording technology, between 1890 and 1925). Even in the final year of acoustic recording (1924) *Variety* magazine reports the apocryphal claim that 'a drum has never been reproduced on wax'.[8] While this is an exaggeration, they certainly were not reproduced well. Tales of bass drums making the recording needle 'jump' are well known, but every component part of the drum kit came under attack in the early recording studio. One of the earliest sources comes from early audio-enthusiast publication *The Phonoscope*, in 1899. It recommends that, while the studio should accommodate the snare drum, sound engineers should 'omit the bass drum. It is likely to spoil the effect, as it does not record well'.[9] Three years later, this was repeated in similar journal (*The Phonogram*), but with an additional piece of advice: 'The bass drum and cymbals should be left out entirely, as they do not record at all well'.[10] In 1903 one publication described the recorded bass drum fidelity as 'disappointing',[11] and that same year the *Edison Phonograph Monthly* went further: 'In making a band record bass drums are never used, as these blur or "fog" the record; cymbals are seldom used and snare drums in solo parts only'.[12] As late as 1914 the same journal reported that the snare drum was no longer a solo instrument in terms of recording: 'a trio of banjo, piano and drum, is worthy of special attention, as it is the first time these three instruments have been successfully recorded in combination by us'.[13] This problem seemed to persist throughout the 1910s, as the advertising manager of the English division of Columbia Records recalled that in 1911 'the big drum never entered a recording room'.[14] In 1914 *Talking Machine World* states 'bass drums and cymbals should never be used, as they have a tendency to fog the record'.[15] This advice was followed right from the 1890s and carried through to the 1920s; a photograph of the Original Memphis Five taken in 1922 shows them as a 'recording unit', with drummer Jack Roth seated at nothing but a snare drum (see Figure 2.1).

Figure 2.1 shows drummer Roth's bandmates pictured with their complete instruments: trumpet, trombone, clarinet, and grand piano. Many parts of Roth's instrument – which in 1922 would feature a bass drum, multiple cymbals of different sizes and timbres, and an array of traps – are missing. Here, Roth played on a snare drum only. Replicating these recordings today necessitates choices about what to include and what to omit, complicating the accuracy or validity of the historic interpretation.

Figure 2.1 Original Memphis Five, 1922: drummer Jack Roth on a snare drum only. Originally published in *Record Research*

Moving later through the 1920s, an article from *Melody Maker* describes the conditions of a drummer in an acoustic studio as late as 1926:

> Drums are the one set of instruments which cannot be used in recording in anything like the same manner as they are when playing to an audience. This is because the notes of these instruments induce a sound wave, the vibrations of which are so long that they have little or no effect on the sensitive diaphragm which is the ear of the recorder. The Bass Drum does not record at all at least, it merely gives a dull rumbling sound nothing like it really is, and the side-drum, although recordable for solo work (such as is found in such numbers as 'Toy Drum Major') only succeeds in blurring the general rhythm when used in conjunction with other instruments. When recording all the drummer has to do is fill in the cymbal beats and now and again perhaps add a few effects such as clog-box, chimes and such like. I know of a drummer who drew his recording fee five guineas in this case for playing just one beat on a cymbal, and if ever they stop using pianos in syncopated bands I shall try to be a drummer at least when the band is playing for the discs.[16]

Recollections from studio musicians of the time tell a similar story, though contradict on what parts of the drum kit were preferred. Drummer Chauncey Morehouse (1902–1980) and bandleader Paul Whiteman (1890–1967) are reported to have not used bass drums in the acoustic studio.[17] Cornetist Wild Bill Davidson (1906–1989) recalls his recordings with the Chubb-Steinberg band in 1924–1925: 'Drums couldn't be used on the recordings, because the needle used in the process would jump the grooves when a drum beat; cymbals were used instead'.[18] Abbey 'Chinee'" Foster (1900–1962) recalls his 1925 recordings as a similar experience, only adding woodblock to the mix.[19]

While photographic evidence of bands in the acoustic studio are scarce, those that exist show an inconsistent picture, and almost never a full drum kit. One studio, Gennett Records, had a fortunate habit of photographing its many bands, albeit only bands comprising of white members, that passed through its doors through the first half of the 1920s. These images, all taken by photographer William Dalbey, captured each band in the same room, position, and theme (musicians pictured with their instruments), making for an informative comparison.[20] Of these eight photographs, taken between 1923 and 1928, five of these show drummers Stan King, George Gowans, Doc Stultz, Tom Gargano, and Earl McDowell playing on nothing more than a 'trap rack' with minimal traps (one cymbal, one woodblock), with no drums used at all. The recording made in this session, Davenport Blues, is of poor audio quality, but what percussion there is to hear supports what is in the picture; there is a prominent muted cymbal rhythm but little else. This setup was described by New Orleans Musician Charlie Bocage (1900–1963), who recalled that in his recording experience with drummer Louis Cottrell and the Piron band, these were the only drums allowed.[21] One photograph shows drummer Vic Moore using what would be a full drum kit (Chinese cymbal, Turkish cymbal, cowbell, woodblock, and snare drum) if it were not for the fact that there is no bass drum. His snare drum is heavily dampened with cloth or rubber (much like today's practice silencers that we place on acoustic kits), which would have greatly affected the performance. It is this photograph,[22] along with another depicting drummer Gargano[23] that led some to the conclusion that it was a matter of space that kept the bass drum at the studio door;[24] however, this can't be the case, as there are two photographs that show Hitch's Happy Harmonists showing drummer Earl McDowell using a bass drum with his full set-up (which includes cymbal and Chinese tom-tom).[25] A snare drum is likely present, obscured behind the bass drum. Unfortunately this isn't reflected in the corresponding recordings; the full set of drums depicted here cannot be heard any more than the recordings that came out of the other depicted sessions. It is, of course, possible that this was brought in merely to showcase the band's logo on the drum head, knowing a photograph was to be taken on those sessions.

The status of the drum kit in the studio is, at best, complicated and inconsistent; one can find evidence of bass drums present on early recordings (the famous 1917 Original Dixieland Jass Band sessions shows remarkable clarity from the bass drum). Strangely, this is often more common with earlier records from the late 1910s than the 1920s, and speaks to the infancy of the recording process itself: inconsistencies are likely explained by the engineer one had on the day; while some would indeed take risks, many, perhaps most, did not.[26]

It wasn't just the engineers that held the fate of the drummer's sound – at this time, everything was in the hands of the 'A&R' manager ('artist and repertoire' manager, sometimes referred to as the 'recording master'). One such A&R manager was Eddie King, involved in making records from as early as 1905, before moving to Victor Records, then leaving for Columbia Records in 1926.[27] A well-known authoritarian, an A&R executive like King could have serious consequences for the drum kit in the studio. Drummer Chauncey Morehouse recalls that King only allowed his own drum equipment to be used. An ex-drummer himself in the John Phillip Sousa Band, King had meticulously experimented with his various percussion items, and had his pre-approved house cymbals which he insisted every drummer use.[28] Musician Nat Shilkret (1889–1982), who remembers King as a good drummer in his day, recalls that King had a cymbal he was fond of, which he brought to Victor's recording studios, and that he would go into the recording room and hold the cymbal himself 'ready to strike it at spots at which he thought it would help'. Shilkret remembers that he and the other younger engineers were tired of this, and began hitting the cymbal themselves unbeknown to King, to chip away at the cymbal until King was compelled to throw it away.[29]

Drummers Disadvantaged in Early Recordings: Electric Age

It was radio broadcasting, and the revolutionary technology it employed, that grudgingly dragged the recording industry out of the acoustic era. Radio's superior electric technology was able to record drum kits clearer than ever before, years before the recording studio caught up. Figure 2.2 shows two bands in the radio studio using full drum kits in broadcasts from 1922. These are among the earliest photographs of a microphone being used to capture a full drum kit performance.

However interesting it is to see full drum kits on radio broadcasts as early as 1922, it remains unclear what one actually heard at the other end of an early radio broadcast. A report on the drum kit's sound over radio that year casts doubt that this greatly improved on the acoustic method: 'traps carry well over the radio because of their sharp, clearly defined characteristics. The bass drum is too low and slow'.[30] In 1925, *Radio Age* describes the conditions of radio recording as being similar to what we have heard of the acoustic studio: 'the drums are eliminated entirely'.[31] One year later *Radio Broadcast* wrote of the state of drums on radio: 'Perhaps in 95 per cent of the radio receivers in use to-day, it is impossible to hear a note as low as that given by a drum'.[32]

Similarly, when the recording industry followed radio and went electric in 1925, this was by no means an overnight change for the drum kit. The last half of the 1920s were an 'adjustment period' for this technology, and while good reports of drum kit recordings start to appear, inconsistencies remain. Clarinettist Barney Bigard (1906–1980) recalls a recording session with Duke Ellington in 1928 – almost certainly recorded in an electric studio, considering the date – where drummer Sonny Greer turned up but had to sit out because the studio simply could not record the drums.[33]

It is true that electrical recording rapidly improved as recordings moved into the mid-1930s, though by this time this technology brought with it a new swing style, and it was too late for the early jazz bands to immortalise their sound with clear fidelity. Early drummers did appear in later years on clear recordings demonstrating their techniques – most notably, Baby Dodds (1898–1959),[34] who made recordings discussing his 1920s drumming style – though these musicians could not unhear the different styles they had adopted since the days of when they used techniques they were purporting to demonstrate.

Figure 2.2 Top: An unknown band broadcasting from the Detroit News Auditorium, 1922. Bottom: Ted Lewis and his band broadcasting from the Union Trust Co.'s radio station in Cleveland, Ohio, at seven o'clock p.m. on Tuesday, 24 October 1922.

The power that recording technology, and the way it developed, had over a band is demonstrated by a 1925 *Billboard* article commenting on the switchover from acoustic to electrical recording, and how this would have consequences, not just on clarity and fidelity, but on what instruments would be favoured to the downfall of others:

> Much is being said for and against the new electrical recording process with which a few of the larger phonograph laboratories are experimenting. Altho [sic] many improvements over the old system are noted, there is no question . . . that many more changes will have to be made before the new way can be said to be perfect. For the first time in recording history, the piano is distinctly heard on the finished record when the electrical process is used. But it is observed that the banjo, an important factor in recording due to the piano's comparative silence, provides a clash under the new system, and so leaders who have been anxiously watching results have, in many cases, decided to eliminate banjos from future dates. Also, drums, never before used on dates, will enjoy an unusual vogue now, as they will be able to be heard to distinct advantage.[35]

Drums 'in' or 'out of vogue', as described above, were determined by the technology that could or could not capture them. Rather than merely adding fidelity, early electrical recording technology complimented some instruments to the disadvantage of others. Today some listeners regard the banjo as an old-fashioned sound in jazz – perhaps its demise was due to changes in recording techniques. This seems possible, given that it also predicts the rise of the saxophone in jazz music, as saxophonists 'will find electrical recording a boon . . . Thus many saxophonists formerly unable to plan dates will now be able to enjoy an extra source of revenue'. The article continues: 'Recording orchestras are busy figuring out new recording combinations under the new plan. As previously mentioned, instruments formerly neglected will be put in and others now used may have to be cut out, temporarily at least'.[36]

Beyond the Record

Clearly the recording process, and its restrictions, represented drummers in a way that was not indicative of the way they played on stage. In terms of not being able to record certain components of the drum kit, leaving parts at the studio door. This omission can rightly be described as restrictive and certainly drummers have therefore been misrepresented on record. Perhaps players today interested in HIJP should ignore or place less importance on these records than other members of the band. However, these studio restrictions ultimately changed the way that drummers played on their instrument (as a whole, or whichever parts were allowed in). When we consider these changes in style that recording necessitated (or perhaps we should say, facilitated?) perhaps what may be thought of as 'restrictions', could instead be viewed as part of the drum kit's story. Much like other forces that shaped the drum kit (as an instrument, and in terms of performance practice), perhaps recording restrictions, and the measures that drummers took accordingly, could be embraced by the HIJP performer today. Once we examine what performance practices came out of these restrictions, it becomes obvious that these carried through to live performance outside of the studio.

One such studio influence was how drummers dealt with the volume of their instrument. Drummers were encouraged to give unequal weighting to parts of the drum kit, such as sharp-sounding traps (e.g. woodblocks, cowbells, rims of the drum) to cut through and be heard, or to play with brushes where they would not have otherwise, in order to avoid saturating the recording horn. Baby Dodds speaks of this:

> When I first began to record, I was with the Oliver band . . . It was then I began to use wood blocks, the shell of the bass drum and cymbals more in the recording than I usually had, because they would come through. Bass drum and snare drum wouldn't record very well in those days and it was my part to be heard.[37]

Dodds also recorded with Jelly Roll Morton, on the famous Hot Pepper sessions. Dodds recalls of Morton: 'Because he wanted the drum so very soft I used brushes on *Mr. Jelly Lord*. I didn't like brushes at any time but I asked him if he wanted me to use them and he said "Yes"'. How many drummers since have wanted to sound like Baby Dodds, and mimicked a sound that Dodds himself did not enjoy? Similarly, Dodds discussed playing the washboard on some of his recordings for his brother Johnny.[38] Ed Allen (1897–1974) recalls 'washboard was a good substitute for drums, as bass drums wouldn't record in those days anyway'.[39] The drum kit and the way it is played, has been partially shaped by its own volume, and the way recording studios and acoustic bands reacted to this volume. Volume is something that has hampered, influenced, and inspired drum kit performance. It continues to be an issue when performing, practicing, and discussing the drum kit's place in popular music today.[40]

How many of these studio habits were brought forward into live playing? Would brush playing be as prominent in jazz today if it were not so encouraged amongst drummers in the early days of recording (and during this crucial stage of the instrument's development)? We associate washboard playing with the early jazz of this era, but not from reading about it – from listening to it. Practitioners of HIJP would benefit from considering the bigger picture, beyond the record: the studio, its restrictions, and its influence. Our contemporary understanding of jazz history reflects the practices of those bands captured on recording, as opposed to the bigger picture of jazz practice – in and out of the studio – at any given time of recording.

A Cycle of Influence

The picture becomes blurred as to what is considered 'live' and 'studio' performance when one considers the far-reaching influence these records have on subsequent generations of drummers. Jazz recordings have been, from their beginnings through to today, an essential teaching tool for musicians learning and developing the genre.[41] For example, Bix Beiderbecke is said to have taught himself trumpet by listening to the recordings of Original Dixieland Jass Band.[42] Cornetist Jimmy McPartland (1907–1991) describes his experience, as his friends heard, for the first time, recordings of the New Orleans Rhythm Kings: 'We stayed there from about three in the afternoon until eight at night, just listening to those records one after another, over and over again. Right then and there we decided we would get a band and try to play like these guys'.[43] The influence of early recordings was the inspiration for the formation of many bands. The next stage was using these recordings to learn the style, which McPartland then describes:

> What we used to do was put the record on . . . play a few bars, and then get all our notes. We'd have to tune our instruments to the record machine, to the pitch, and go ahead with a few notes. Then stop! A few more bars of the record, each guy would pick out his notes and boom! We would go on and play it. It was a funny way to learn, but in three of four weeks we could finally play one tune all the way through.[44]

Records were often a way for other drummers listening to develop their own styles. However, while clarinettists and trumpet players could learn the solos and licks on the records that would appear in the ephemeral setting of a nightclub note-for-note, the aspiring drummer was not so fortunate. Drummers either would not be able to hear the parts they wished to learn, or if they could, would they want to? And, the important question for HIJP performers today: should they? As recorded jazz music began to circulate throughout the United States and beyond, this affected the way in which a new generation of jazz musicians would learn the drum kit, and interpret their role in live performance. These musicians would then record the next generation of jazz records, and a cycle of influence would be born. During the spring of 1948, Baby Dodds travelled to Europe with Mezz Mezzrow's band, and commented on how his drumming had been interpreted by Europeans listening to his records:

> While abroad I came into contact with quite a few of the European jazz bands. A fellow named Claude Luter has a little band in France and he's got the same instrumentation that King Oliver had . . . He plays a lot like my brother because he learned to play by listening to his records. They studied the old records very carefully and tried to get everything down as perfectly as they could. Since they only had the records to teach them they played on the style of our music. Of course on the records they could hear only the cymbals and wood blocks and that is what they mostly used, since they couldn't hear the snares and bass drum as distinctly.[45]

When HIJP drummers today play early jazz, just where are they taking their technique from? Recordings have undoubtedly provided the most interesting, informative, and rewarding tool when researching how this music was played, yet in the early recording studio not all instruments were created equal. The representation of drummers on record should be considered in order to project an accurate picture of what was really played in dancehalls in the late 1910s and throughout the 1920s, but also in order to consider how and why drummers are represented and portrayed the way they are today.

Conclusion

What is it to record: events, opinions, music? In order to record, we need a mediator between past and present. Just as one cannot remove the historian from the history, technology is the inevitable barrier between what was played then, and what is heard now. This chapter began by implying that the drum kit was comparatively disadvantaged by this technology, and misrepresented, but perhaps this is a weighted statement. It certainly was most affected; the effects ranged from a culling of the instrument's component parts (and in this sense records perhaps shouldn't be used so stringently by the aspiring HIJP drummer) to legitimate performance considerations that have defined the sound of early jazz to modern listeners. We may wish that drummers were given an equal footing from the start, but the fact is that the sound of early jazz – the sound we may wish to replicate or recreate – is defined by these early studio restrictions, and they should add to the balance of considerations the HIJP drummer must make in their performance practice.

Notes

1 M. T. Williams *The Smithsonian Collection of Classic Jazz: Guide*. Smithsonian Collection of Recordings [LP], 1973.

2 V. Giordano, interview with the author (29 December 2014).

3 R. Gelatt. *The Fabulous Phonograph, 1877–1977* (London: Cassell, 1956), pp. 188–189.
4 Advertisement. 'Drum Notes Not Only Heard—But Identified', *The Talking Machine World*, 23:6 (June 1927), p. 109.
5 R. Taruskin. *Text and Act: Essays on Music and Performance* (Oxford: University Press, 1997).
6 Ibid, p. 277.
7 Ibid, p. 185.
8 Anon. 'Old Method Recording', *Variety*, LXXVI:7 (1 October 1924), p. 34.
9 Anon. 'The Secret of Making Phonograph Recordings', *The Phonoscope*, III:5 (May 1899, 2), pp. 1–2.
10 C. W. Noyes. 'Making a Record of a Band or Orchestra', *The Phonogram*, V:1 (May 1902), pp. 10–11.
11 A. Williams and T. W. Corbin. *The Romance of Modern Invention* (Philadelphia: Lippincott, 1903), p. 61.
12 Anon. 'Moulded Records for Phonographs', *Edison Phonograph Monthly*, 1 pp. 11–13, (August 1903).
13 Anon. 'Blue Amberols for August', *Edison Phonograph Monthly*, XII:8 (June 1914), p. 95.
14 'Rideout 1940' in R. Gelatt. *The Fabulous Phonograph, 1877–1977* (London: Cassell, 1956), p. 180.
15 Anon. 'Making a Band Record for the Phonograph', *The Talking Machine World*, 10:8 (1914), p. 30.
16 P. Mackay. 'Gramophone Record Making', *Melody Maker*, 1:2 (2 February 1925, 2), pp. 24–25.
17 Giordano; P. Whiteman and M. M. McBridge. *Jazz* (New York: J. H. Sears and Co., 1926), p. 225.
18 B. Davidson, interview by J. Steiner, transcript, Hogan Jazz Archive, Oral History (Tulane University, November 1961).
19 A. Foster, interview by W. Russell, Hogan Jazz Archive, Oral History (Tulane University, 29 June 1960).
20 The Gennett photographs I found and compared consist of:

Art Landry's Call of the North Orchestra. Taken at Gennett studios, Richmond, Indiana, 2 June 1923. Stan King, drums. Taken from the cover of C. B. Dahan and L. G. Irmscher. *Gennett Records and Starr Piano*, (Charleston: Arcadia Publishing, 2016).
Hitch's Happy Harmonists. Taken at Gennett studios, Richmond, Indiana, 23 February 1924, recording Ethiopian Nightmare (Gnt 5402). Earl McDowell, drums.
The Wolverine Orchestra Taken at Gennett studios, Richmond, Indiana, 18 February 1924. Vic Moore, drums.
Guy Lombardo and his Royal Canadians. Taken at Gennett studios, Richmond, Indiana, 10 March 1924. George Gowans, drums.
Charlie Davis and his Orchestra. Taken at Gennett studios, Richmond, Indiana, 24 October 1924. Doc Stultz, drums. In B. A. Hardy. 'Charlie Davis, Copenhagen, and the musical culture of the 20s', *Storyville*, 62 (December 1975–January 1976), pp. 55–66.
Bix Beiderbecke and his Rhythm Jugglers. Taken at Gennett studios, Richmond, Indiana, 26 January 1925. Tom Gargano, drums.
Hitch's Happy Harmonists. Taken at Gennett studios, Richmond, Indiana, 19 May 1925. Earl McDowell, drums.
Miami Lucky Seven. Taken at Gennett studios, Richmond, Indiana, sometime between March 1922 and January 1928. Earl McDowell, drums. In C. B. Dahan, L. G. Irmscher, 2016.
The majority of these photographs have since been compiled and presented in M. Brennan. *Kick It: A Social History of the Drum Kit* (New York: Oxford University Press, 2020).

21 C. Bocage, interview by Richard Allen, transcript, Hogan Jazz Archive, Oral History (Tulane University, 18 July 1960).
22 The Wolverine Orchestra, 1924.
23 Bix Beiderbecke and his Rhythm Jugglers, 1925.
24 Most notably Brown, in his detailed and important work on the early drum kit: T. D. Brown. 'A History and Analysis of Jazz Drumming to 1942', unpublished PhD thesis, The University of Michigan (1976), p. 94.
25 Hitch's Happy Harmonists, 1924; Hitch's Happy Harmonists, 1925.
26 Brown, 'A History and Analysis of Jazz Drumming to 1942', pp. 94–95.
27 T. Gracyk and F. W. Hoffmann *Popular American Recording Pioneers, 1895–1925* (New York: Haworth Press, 2000), p. 299.

28 Giordano.
29 N. Shilkret, N. Shell, and B. Shilkret *Nathaniel Shilkret: Sixty Years in the Music Business* (Lanham, MD: Scarecrow Press, 2005), p. 68.
30 Anon. 'Broadcasting of Voice and Musical Instruments', *The Talking Machine World*, XVIII:8 (15 August 1922), p. 51.
31 Schonemann. 'New Waves from the Domain of Radio: How Isham Jones Records Radio', *Radio Age* (April 1925), pp. 32–70.
32 J. H. Morecroft. 'The March of Radio', *Radio Broadcast*, I:2 (June 1926), p. 211.
33 B. Bigard and B. Martyn. *With Louis and the Duke: The Autobiography of a Jazz Clarinetist* (London: Macmillan, 1987), p. 59; J. H. Morecroft. 'The March of Radio', *Radio Broadcast*, I:2 (June 1926), p. 211.
34 B. Dodds. *Talking and Drum Solos*, Audio Recording (Chicago: Atavistic Worldwide, 1946, re-released 2003).
35 Anon. 'Electrical Recording and Instrumentation', *Billboard*, 30 May 1925.
36 Ibid.
37 B. Dodds, unpublished interview by W. Russell, Historic New Orleans Collection (1955).
38 A. Hodes and C. Hansen. *Selections from the Gutter: Jazz Portraits from 'The Jazz Record'* (Berkeley: University of California Press, 1977), p. 101.
39 E. Allen, interview by R. Allen and W. Russell, transcript, Hogan Jazz Archive, Oral History (Tulane University, 14 January 1961).
40 G. D. Smith. 'Actually, I am NOT playing too loud, and we're not doing this one at "rehearsal volume": (in)authentic drum kit performance practice in collegiate popular music ensemble settings' in *Make It Pop! Advancing Popular Music Education* (Berklee College of Music, 1–4 June 2016). Association for Popular Music Education Annual Conference.
41 M. Katz. *Capturing Sound: How Technology Has Changed Music* (Berkeley: University of California Press, 2010), pp. 77–81.
42 J. E. Berendt and G. Huesmann. *The Jazz Book: From Ragtime to the 21st Century* (Chicago: Chicago Review Press, 2009), p. 91.
43 K. McPartland, in N. Shapiro and N. Hentoff. *Hear Me Talkin' To Ya: The Story of Jazz by the Men Who Made It* (New York: Rinehart, 1955), p. 119.
44 McPartland, *Hear Me Talking To Ya*, p. 120.
45 B. Dodds and L. Gara. *The Baby Dodds Story as Told to Larry Gara.* (Baton Rouge: Louisiana State University Press, 1992), p. 91.

3 Towards a Cultural History of the Backbeat

STEVEN BAUR

Introduction

In a fiery 1956 sermon captured on grainy, black-and-white film, Reverend Jimmie Snow explains to his Nashville congregation why he preaches against rock and roll. 'I know how it *feels*', he intones, 'I know the evil feeling that you feel when you sing it. I know the lost position that you get into in *the beat.* Well, if you talk to the average teenager of today and you ask them what it is about rock-and-roll music that they like, the first thing they'll say is *the beat, the beat, the beat*!'[1] Like many social leaders who condemned rock and roll, Snow located the allure and impact of this music, commonly called 'beat music' or simply the 'big beat', in its powerful percussive accompaniment. The central and most distinctive feature of the rock-and-roll beat was its emphatic, relentless snare drum accents on 'two and four', the conventionally 'weak' beats of the measure – the so-called backbeat. Shocking though it was to many in the 1950s, the backbeat soon became and remains one of the single most prevalent features of Western popular music. This chapter explores the origins of the backbeat, charts its early history on record from the 1920s to the 1950s, and considers how it has functioned as a meaningful musical signifier and cultural agent.

For the purposes of this chapter I limit my discussion to backbeats that are exclusively rhythmic in nature, serving no harmonic or other musical function. Thus, neither the weak-beat piano, banjo, or guitar chords common in nineteenth-century songs and dance music, ragtime, early jazz, country, and blues, nor the slap-back bass in swing, Western swing, and rockabilly will be considered. Rather, I focus on the emergence of the backbeat as a convention in drum kit performance practice, typically played on the snare drum. The distinctive, piercing 'crack' (or 'whack', 'slap', 'spank', etc.) of the snare drum and its potential for extreme volumes make the drum kit backbeat different in kind from the off-beat piano, banjo, guitar, or bass rhythms cited above.

Backbeating As Signifyin(g) Practice

Reverend Snow was among many who linked the rock-and-roll backbeat to juvenile delinquency and violence. Justifying the ban on rock-and-roll shows in Jersey City in 1956, Mayor B. J. Berry asserted 'this rock-and-roll rhythm is filled with dynamite, and we don't want the dynamite to go off in Roosevelt Stadium'.[2] Critics also blamed rock and roll for promoting lascivious dancing and sexual promiscuity, claiming that its beat replicated the rhythms of sex. Condemnations of beat music commonly resorted to racist language associating the 'primitive' rock-and-roll beat with the 'savage' instincts of 'inferior' races. Few were more forthright than Asa Carter of the White Citizens Council of Alabama, who asserted 'rock-and-roll music is the basic, heavy-beat music of the Negroes. It appeals to the base in man, brings out animalism and vulgarity'.[3] As Steven F. Lawson summarizes, 'the language used to link rock with the behaviour of anti-social youths was couched in ... racial stereotypes. *Music Journal* asserted that the "jungle rhythms" of rock incited juvenile offenders into "orgies of sex and violence" ... The *New York Daily News* derided the obscene lyrics set to "primitive jungle-beat rhythms"'.[4] As late as 1987, conservative critics could assert that rock's 'notorious', 'evil' backbeat 'is very dangerous since it owes its beginnings to African demon worship'.[5]

Kofi Agawu has deconstructed the myth of 'African rhythm' – the notion that 'blacks ... exhibit an essential irreducible rhythmic disposition' – exposing it as a white invention often deployed in the justification of racial hierarchy.[6] As Ronald Radano notes, 'the primitivist orthodoxy of "natural rhythm"' can also serve as 'a means of affirming positive identities in an egregiously racist, nationalist environment'.[7] For instance, as Isaac Hayes recalled, 'it was the standard joke with blacks, that whites could not, cannot clap on a backbeat. You know—ain't got the rhythm'.[8] Similarly, blues musician Taj Mahal interrupted a 1993 performance to chide his German audience for clapping on the downbeat. 'Wait, wait, wait ... This is schwarze [black] musick', he instructs the crowd. 'Zwie, vier! One, TWO, three, FOUR!'[9]

The affirmative potential of such strategic essentialism notwithstanding, reducing the backbeat to an inbred racial trait is profoundly limiting and, like all essentialisms, has dangerous ramifications. This is borne out by the fierce backlash against rock and roll, 'the heavy-beat music of the Negroes', part of a larger racist backlash in the age of Brown vs. the Board of Education, the Little Rock Nine, and Emmett Till. Far from being an inbred musical predisposition of black people, the backbeat emerged as a strategic cultural response to specific social, historical, and musical conditions. Understanding this history requires that we consider the practice of backbeating before the development of the drum kit during the first decades of the twentieth century. Indeed, as all drummers know, one does not need a drum kit to perform the multi-limb rhythmic beating that is the essence of drum kit performance practice.

Samuel Floyd has traced various elements common in African-American music – including call-and-response patterns, pitch-bending, and unflagging off-beat rhythms – to the ring shout, a ritual adapted from West African sacred traditions.[10] Participants sing and chant over the rhythms of their shuffling feet, hand claps, and other body percussion. As Floyd explains, the ring shout also exemplifies the practice of 'signifyin(g)' central to West African and African-American expressive culture, as participants extemporaneously expand on traditional texts with additional verses, embellishments, commentary, and so forth. Theorized by Henry Louis Gates, Jr, signifyin(g) involves the interpretive elaboration on received ideas, narratives, texts, etc., often as a means of resisting or inverting dominant ideologies and power relationships, and it underlies much African-American vernacular culture, from ragging tunes to rap battles.[11] As a signifyin(g) practice, backbeating is a means of responding to and reinterpreting the conventional 'strong' downbeat of Western music – of simultaneously acknowledging and resisting it, of playing with and working against it, of inverting it, enhancing it, and making it groove.

Incarceration, Hard Labour, and the Backbeat

In ways both metaphorical and real, backbeating has functioned as a meaningful response by African Americans to the brutal oppression of slavery and the long, violent aftermath of the Civil War. For many black southerners, conditions scarcely changed after abolition. Laws targeting black people fed a network of prisons that effectively replicated the conditions of slavery. Trivial offences or bogus charges could land black citizens in labour camps such as the notorious Angola State Penitentiary in Louisiana, Parchman Farm in Mississippi, or the Darrington State Prison Farm in Texas. Each are known for their brutal conditions, but also for field recordings conducted by John and Alan Lomax beginning in 1933.

These recordings establish African-American prison songs as one of earliest repertories on record that commonly features emphatic backbeat accompaniments. For example, 'Long John' (1933), sung by a group of prisoners led by 'Lightning' Washington, is based on a story from antebellum black folklore. Representative of the trickster hero central to many signifyin(g) texts, Long John is a fugitive slave who leads a nationwide chase, outwitting his would-be captors at every turn. Washington lines out the tale, lacing it with Biblical references, and the group repeats each line to the accompaniment of axes striking on the backbeat.[12] As is common in trickster tales, Long John uses cunning and wit to subvert established power structures, just as the backbeat subverts conventional notions concerning 'strong' and 'weak' beats.

In their percussive accompaniments, these prisoners transform the tools of their oppression into musical instruments, making them potential tools of liberation. By signifyin(g) on the downbeat, the prisoners transform the rhythms of forced labour into compelling grooves, creating the possibility of experiencing the body, not only as a site of violent oppression, but also as a potential site of creativity and pleasure. Here backbeating constitutes a strategy for survival and resistance, providing historical precedent for John Mowitt's assertion that the rock-and-roll backbeat 'define[d] the substance of a modest, but tenacious pedagogy of the oppressed . . . a practical wisdom about how to "strike back" and "make do" under conditions of adversity and cynical humiliation'.[13]

The Lomaxes also recorded songs performed during the inmates' few leisure hours, such as 'That's All Right, Honey' (1933) by Mose 'Clear Rock' Platt. Platt boasted to Lomax of his various jailbreaks and his powers of evasion. In an audacious display of storytelling (and signifyin[g]), he explains that he ran so fast that the 'splat-splattin'' of his feet was mistaken for the sound of motorcycle engine, and that his shirttail had caught fire, which was mistaken for a taillight. 'Dey calls me "Swif-foot Rock" 'cause de way I kin run', he explains, adding 'white man say he thought I mus' have philosophies in my feet'.[14] Platt's philosophical feet can be heard, faintly tapping downbeats during his singing of 'That's All Right, Honey', each foot-tap answered by a much louder clapped backbeat. Platt sings line after line of affirmative lyrics over the up-tempo 'stomp-CLAP' groove, celebrating freedoms that, 'sho 'nuff', will be his. Platt's exuberant performance testifies to the uplifting power of backbeating; such a spirited performance within the confines of a system designed to break the spirit constitutes a powerful act of resistance, of beating back.

Backbeating in Pentecostal Worship

Body percussion had long been practiced in Western Africa, described by European explorers as early as 1621.[15] It took on greater significance in the United States, where drumming among slaves was feared and outlawed in many places. While slave holders could ban drums, they could not ban the bodies that sustained their economy, and accompaniments to sacred song and dance moved from drums to African-American bodies. As Jon Michael Spencer explains, 'To the African the drum was a sacred instrument possessing supernatural power that enabled it to summon the gods into communion with the people . . . [and] percussiveness produced the power that helped move Africans to dance and into trance possession . . . With the drum banned, rhythm . . . became the essential African remnant of black religion in North America … It empowered those who possessed it to endure slavery by temporarily elevating them … to a spiritual summit'.[16]

Among Christian denominations, African-American Pentecostal and Holiness (also called Sanctified) churches took up body percussion most fervently. Pentecostalism emphasizes spirit possession, achieved through rhythmic song and dance, and dozens of recordings from the 1920s demonstrate the centrality of backbeating to Pentecostal worship. In Memphis alone, Bessie Johnson and Her Memphis Sanctified Singers, Elder Lonnie McIntorsh, and the Holy Ghost Sanctified Singers made recordings with consistent handclapped backbeats that fuel impassioned vocal performances as in, for example, Johnson's 'Keys to the Kingdom' (1929). Another remarkable example, 'Memphis Flu' (1930) by Elder Curry and His Congregation, is a proto-rock-and-roll song, replete with Little Richard-style eighth notes hammered out on the piano's high, percussive register to solid, communal backbeating. Such congregational backbeating is the audible presence of community; all participants contribute to a unifying, thoroughly embodied groove, which constitutes the primary vehicle for spiritual communion. No wonder Pentecostal preachers like Reverend D. C. Rice would defend percussive worship music, insisting that 'people need to feel the rhythm of God'.[17]

Pentecostal music was not only a form of praise, but often a means of protest, with statements of resistance embedded in religious contexts. Most explicit are the various 'Egypt' songs, wherein the deliverance of Israelites from Egyptian captivity is understood to prophesy the deliverance of black people from racist oppression in the United States. The earliest vocal recording I have found with consistent backbeating throughout (excepting the introduction) is 'Way Down in Egypt Land' (1926) by the Biddleville Quintette. The song confronts the darkest depths of slavery, '*waaaaaay* down in Egypt land', but the exuberant, rhythmically charged performance, driven by handclapped backbeating, makes clear that this is a celebration of deliverance. Perhaps the earliest *drummed* backbeating on a vocal record occurs on Elder J. E. Burch's stirring 'Love Is My Wonderful Song' (1927), fuelled by emphatic snare backbeat accents over driving bass drum quarter notes.

A fairly direct line connects Pentecostal backbeating to 1940s rhythm and blues. Prolific gospel recording artist Sister Rosetta Tharpe collaborated with the equally prolific Lucky Millinder on several recordings. Millinder had been leading bands on record since 1933, when he took over the Blue Mills Rhythm Band, but none of his recordings feature prominent backbeats until his work with Tharpe.[18] Their 1941 collaboration, 'Shout Sister, Shout', features Pentecostal-style congregational backbeating placed at the forefront of the mix during choruses. Millinder would again foreground clapped backbeats on 'Who Threw the Whiskey in the Well', a gospel parody describing a worship service that evolves into a spirited, boozy bash. Recorded in 1944 with vocalist Wynonie Harris, the record was a massive hit, spending eight weeks atop the 'race' chart in 1945 and crossing over to #7 on the pop chart. Handclapped gospel backbeats propelled Harris's next hit, 'Good Rockin' Tonight' (1948), a cover of Roy Brown's 'Galveston Whorehouse Jingle'.[19] Whereas backbeats accompany only the choruses of 'Shout Sister, Shout' and 'Who Threw the Whiskey in the Well', handclapped backbeating accompanies the entirety of 'Good Rockin' Tonight', excepting the introduction, where drummer Bobby Donaldson plays emphatic snare backbeats thickened by loose, 'dirty' hi-hats, which, along with wah-inflected trumpet growls and insinuating saxophone squeals, set a steamy scene for the entry of gospel clapping. Here the sacred and the secular, the spiritual and sexual meet on two and four.

Sex and the Backbeat

Euphemistic references to sex such as 'rocking' were commonplace well before the rise of rhythm and blues, especially in a strain of the blues, sometimes called 'hokum' blues, built around clever double entendres and thinly veiled references to sex. Hokum blues songs often address the world of prostitution, and many were performed in brothels and bawdy dance halls, where musicians entertained and played music for dancing, particularly the kind of dancing that might encourage subsequent assignations.[20] No other strain of the blues from the 1920s and 1930s features as flagrant backbeating as the hokum blues, where the 'rocking' celebrated in the lyrics finds a parallel in the back-and-forth motion between bottom-heavy downbeats and penetrating backbeats.

For instance, Margaret Webster's 'I've Got What it Takes', recorded in 1929 with Clarence Williams's Washboard Band, features salacious lyrics set over an infectious, backbeat-based shuffle groove played on the washboard by drummer Floyd Casey. Among the most prolific recording artists of the 1920s and 1930s, Williams recorded with Bessie Smith, Louis Armstrong, Fats Waller, among others, in addition to numerous recordings under his own name. I credit some of his success to the compelling percussive accompaniments provided by Casey. As these records demonstrate, the washboard was well suited to the recording technology of the day, offering a variety of percussive timbres, from the deep 'thump' of the wooden frame to the piercing, metallic scrape in the high register. Here the washboard constitutes a kind of miniature drum kit that produced better results in the studio than could be achieved easily with drums. Like the axes and other tools that accompanied prison songs, the washboard represents an instrument of labour that was radically repurposed and deployed in the celebration of freedoms.

Allusions to prostitution are common in the songs of Memphis Minnie, the influential blues singer, songwriter, and guitarist, who, like many musicians of her era, played at brothels and often 'entertained' in more ways than one.[21] At a remarkable 1936 session, Minnie recorded seven sides, each featuring an unidentified percussionist playing stark, consistent backbeats on either a washboard or woodblock. Most of these songs address sexual politics, some making direct references to prostitution, such as 'Black Cat Blues' with the refrain 'everyone wants to buy my kitty', Minnie's saucy swagger punctuated by pulsating backbeats. These are perhaps the earliest recordings to feature backbeating in the context of guitar-based blues, establishing Memphis Minnie as a rhythm-and-blues pioneer.

As Hazel Carby, Shayna Lee, and others have shown, in such songs women performers reclaimed female sexuality from the objectifying male gaze and projected empowering representations of female agency and desire.[22] In this context, the backbeat is an apt metaphor for sex, rollicking between steady downbeats and penetrating backbeat accents, imparting an embodied experience that renders these assertions and celebrations of sexuality all the more compelling. Not surprisingly, some of the most influential drummers in the development of rock and roll, including prolific session drummers Earl Palmer and Hal Blaine, and Elvis Presley's drummer D. J. Fontana – all early masters of the backbeat – started out playing in strip clubs providing rhythmic accompaniments to steamy floor shows.

Shout Choruses, Afterbeats, and the Kansas City School

Earl Palmer has often been noted for his role in standardizing the rock-and-roll beat. He played drum kit on Fats Domino's 'The Fat Man' (1949), an early hit that features consistent backbeats, and his recordings with Little Richard were among the earliest to feature the backbeat in conjunction with straight eighth-note hi-hat or ride cymbal patterns (as opposed to the swung or shuffled accompaniments typical of rhythm and blues and early rock and roll). Palmer identified the Dixieland 'shout chorus' as the inspiration for his earliest use of a consistent backbeat.[23] In the shout chorus, the ensemble takes up boisterous figures while the rhythm section plays heavy 'weak' beat accents. For instance, drummer Andrew Hilaire plays emphatic snare backbeats during the last chorus of 'Black Bottom Stomp', recorded in 1926 with Jelly Roll Morton's Red Hot Peppers. As an isolated, deliberately 'unruly' section, the shout chorus stands out as exceptional, as a moment of abandon during which the normal rules do not apply, or rather, in carnivalesque fashion, are inverted.

As early as the 1920s, then, drum-kit backbeating was associated with the kinds of excess and disorder critics would impute to the rock-and-roll beat decades later. The term 'shout' chorus alludes to the kind of spirited performances associated with black sacred music, but I have come to think of such choruses in instrumental jazz and later rhythm and blues as 'cut-loose' choruses, a metaphor with particular resonance for black people contending with the legacy of bondage. Typically, these backbeat-driven choruses support and impel particularly intense solos that transgress the dynamic, scalar, and timbral restraints in place during 'regular' choruses.

Emphatic backbeats would remain exceptional in jazz drumming, reserved for occasional, particularly boisterous choruses. By the early 1930s, the conventional swing pattern ('ding ding-da ding ding-da') had established itself as the central component of jazz drumming. A secondary convention, the 'afterbeat', was standardized during the 1930s and emerged in conjunction with a major technological innovation, foot-operated cymbals. Designs from the early 1920s, including the 'low boy' (also known as 'sock cymbals') and the 'snow shoe', led to the hi-hat, which drummers began incorporating into their kits in the late 1920s.[24] Bringing two cymbals together via the foot pedal could create a variety of sounds, the most serviceable proving to be the light 'chick' produced when the cymbals are brought together and held closed to prevent reverberation. Drummers typically placed the 'chick' on the weak beats, either in alternation with bass drum half notes ('boom-chick-boom-chick') or over bass-drum quarter notes. The convention of playing left-foot afterbeats was well enough established by 1928 that Slingerland would introduce the 'Duplex After Beat Drum' to meet drummers' evolving needs (Figure 3.1). The advertisement suggests that the ideal afterbeat is 'just loud enough to be heard without prominence'. As Duke Ellington often explained, the jazz afterbeat was part of a 'cool' sensibility that eschewed aggression and provocation in favour of stylized restraint, inciting nothing more than head tilts and finger snaps. 'Of course, one never snaps one's fingers *on* the beat', he states, 'it's considered aggressive. You don't push it. You just let fall. If you'd like to be conservatively hip, . . . tilt your left earlobe on the beat and snap the fingers on the afterbeat'.[25] Though clearly related, the unobtrusive 'conservatively hip' jazz afterbeat was a far cry from the explosive big beat that inspired such fear and fury in the mid-1950s.

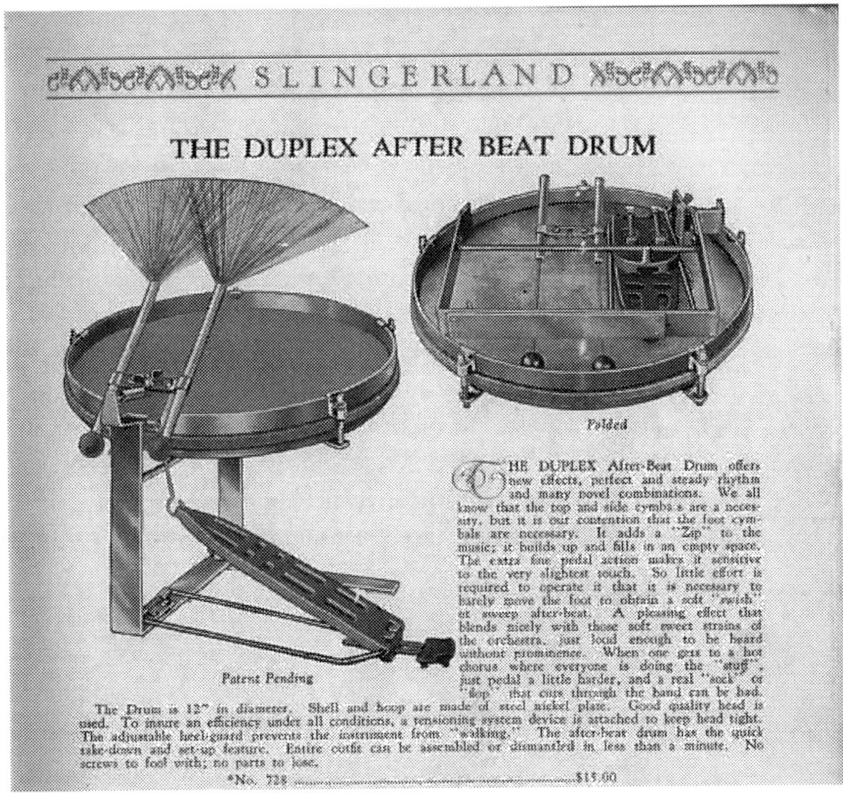

SLINGERLAND

THE DUPLEX AFTER BEAT DRUM

Folded

THE DUPLEX After-Beat Drum offers new effects, perfect and steady rhythm and many novel combinations. We all know that the top and side cymbals are a necessity, but it is our contention that the foot cymbals are necessary. It adds a "Zip" to the music; it builds up and fills in an empty space. The extra fine pedal action makes it sensitive to the very slightest touch. So little effort is required to operate it that it is necessary to barely move the foot to obtain a soft "swish" or sweep after-beat. A pleasing effect that blends nicely with those soft sweet strains of the orchestra. Just loud enough to be heard without prominence. When one gets to a hot chorus where everyone is doing the "stuff", just pedal a little harder, and a real "sock" or "flop" that cuts through the band can be had.

Patent Pending

The Drum is 12" in diameter. Shell and hoop are made of steel nickel plate. Good quality head is used. To insure an efficiency under all conditions, a tensioning system device is attached to keep head tight. The adjustable heel-guard prevents the instrument from "walking." The after-beat drum has the quick take-down and set-up feature. Entire outfit can be assembled or dismantled in less than a minute. No screws to fool with; no parts to lose.

*No. 728 ....$15.00

Figure 3.1 Slingerland 1928 catalog, page 31

The backbeat *was* central to one exceptional school of jazz drumming. Famed for extended jam sessions, Kansas City jazz musicians of the 1920s and 1930s, cultivated a groove-based aesthetic that distinguished it from the arrangement-based styles preeminent elsewhere. As Ross Russell recounts:

> Kansas City had a reputation for the longest jam sessions in jazz history. [Pianist] Sam Price . . . recalls dropping in at the Sunset Club one evening around 10:00 P.M. A jam session was in full swing.
> After a drink, Prince went home to rest, bathe, and change clothing.
> He returned to the club around one . . . and the musicians were playing the same tune. They had been playing it uninterrupted for three hours.[26]

Period recordings suggest that backbeat-based drumming sustained these legendary all-night jams. 'South', recorded by Bennie Moten's Kansas City Orchestra in 1924, is the earliest recording I have yet found featuring strong, consistent backbeats as the primary percussive accompaniment for the entirety of the recording. Willie Hall, like most drummers in the age of acoustic recording, was denied his drum kit in the studio, opting instead

Figure 3.2 Bennie Moten Radio Orchestra, 1922 (Willie Hall, drums; from the 'Goin' to Kansas City' Collection, courtesy of Herman Walder and the Kansas City Museum)

for a woodblock, a standard component of the early drum kit and the most common replacement for the snare drum in the studio. Hall lays down consistent woodblock backbeats on all twelve recordings he made with Moten in 1924 and 1925 (Figure 3.2).

Hall left Moten's band after the 1925 sessions, but the backbeat remained a distinguishing feature of the ensemble. Their 1926 recording of 'Thick Lip Stomp' is a clinic in backbeating. Drummer Willie McWashington plays stark backbeats through the first six choruses but varies the treatment throughout, moving from choked cymbal crashes, to the woodblock, and then to the snare. He starts each of the next four choruses with tasteful four-measure solos, setting up dramatic stop-time ensemble backbeating. The whole band rests on the downbeats and plays emphatic percussive accents on beats two and four (excepting the soloist, of course, and occasionally Moten's piano) in the style of a Dixieland shout chorus, but for four full choruses.

McWashington placed backbeating at the center of his rhythmic accompaniments on nearly all fifteen recordings he made with Moten in 1926 and 1927, before gradually moving towards hi-hat and ride-cymbal-based swing accompaniments on subsequent records. 'New Tulsa Blues' (1927) is among several remarkable recordings that feature robust back-beats over well-recorded bass drum downbeats. During the introduction,

McWashington plays a shuffle groove that rollicks between heavy bass drum downbeats and shuffled tom-tom eighth notes on two and four:

||: Boom BAA-da Boom BAA-da :||

McWashington maintains propulsive bass-drum downbeats throughout the recording, each kick answered by a forceful 'whack', played variously on a snare drum, tom-tom, choked crash cymbal, or woodblock, often in combination. The relentless rocking between heavy downbeats and piercing backbeats, sometimes with subtle, syncopated embellishments, is entrancing, and helps explain why Kansas City musicians were inspired to extend jams to such unprecedented lengths.

The Backbeat in 1940s Rhythm and Blues

The Kansas City school notwithstanding, heavy, consistent backbeats remained rare in jazz through the swing era. With the rise of bebop in the 1940s, jazz drummers further undermined any sense of a regular backbeat, peppering the conventional swing ride pattern with unpredictable snare ornaments and accents and dropping bass drum 'bombs' with designed irregularity. A more commercially oriented offshoot of swing that also emerged in the 1940s, jump blues, has often been considered a 'missing link' between swing and rock and roll. Longtime *Rolling Stone* contributor, J. D. Considine, credits 1940s jump blues artists such as Louis Jordan with popularizing the backbeat, introducing the crucial element that would define rock and roll.[27] Similarly, legendary composer, producer, and executive Quincy Jones claimed that 'Lionel Hampton and Louis Jordan were probably the first rock-and-roll bands that were really conscious of what we call the big beat ... [Jordan] did shuffle boogie with backbeats and everything else that were all the elements of rock and roll'.[28] But the backbeat does *not* figure prominently on any of Jordan's recordings until 1949, by which time other artists had been making records with far more emphatic backbeats.

Most of Jordan's 1940s hits feature an even four-beat boogie-woogie groove alongside a walking quarter-note bass line. The drum kit accompaniments (usually played by Joe 'Chris Colombo' Morris or Shadow Wilson) are consistently light and typically feature a snare drum played with brushes, comping a groove based on quarter-note and shuffle patterns over faint four-on-the-floor bass-drum quarter notes, often with light hi-hat afterbeats (as on 'Caldonia', 'Choo Choo Ch'Boogie', 'Ain't Nobody Here But Us Chickens', and others). Jordan's drummers sometimes play swing hi-hat accompaniments, with downbeat accents on open hi-hats ('SHEE Chick-cha SHEE Chick-cha SHEE') obliterating any sense of a backbeat (as on 'Saturday Night Fish Fry' and 'Is You Is Or Is You Ain't'). While hi-hat and brushed snare afterbeats are common on Jordan's recordings from the 1940s, they project a sense of cool restraint similar to the 'conservatively hip' afterbeating Ellington endorsed, rather than the aggressive, unrestrained big beat.

The Jordan recording from the 1940s that comes closest to the rock-and-roll backbeat is 'Beans and Cornbread' (1949), wherein Jordan invokes the sermonic tone of gospel music. Columbo uses drumsticks rather than the lighter brushes used on most Jordan records, playing a swing ride-cymbal pattern with light snare backbeats, scarcely audible over the hi-hat afterbeats. By contrast, Joe Morris's version of the song recorded a month later features emphatic backbeats throughout (excepting stop-time sections) as drummer 'Philly' Joe Jones doubles loud snare backbeats with explosive cymbal crashes. Ensemble handclaps amplify the boisterous backbeating on Morris's version of 'Beans and Cornbread' and reinforce the gospel allusion. The raucous backbeating imbues the brawl described in the lyrics with far greater turbulence than Jordan's more humorous version. As such a comparison shows, the backbeating on Jordan's records through the 1940s more closely resembles the swing afterbeat than the rock-and-roll backbeat.

Jones is on firmer ground with Lionel Hampton, who does foreground backbeats on several 1940s recordings. On 'Central Avenue Breakdown' (1941), a heavy boogie-woogie romp fuelled by a dual-piano attack, drummer Al Spieldock drives the groove with emphatic snare backbeats. 'Hamp's Boogie Woogie' (1944) and 'Hey-Ba-Ba-Re-Bop' (1946) feature backbeats during extended instrumental sections. On both, drummer Fred Radcliffe supports the soloists (and vocalist on the latter) with light, even, four-beat shuffle grooves for most of the song but kicks the band into a different gear with forceful backbeating during boisterous, cut-loose choruses.

While recordings from the 1940s tend to reserve consistent backbeat accents for exclusively instrumental recordings or instrumental sections of vocal numbers, there are exceptional cases of drummers accompanying entire vocal recordings with emphatic backbeats, the most remarkable being those on Buddy Johnson's 'Walk 'Em' (1945), played by Teddy Stewart, and Rabon Tarrant's brushed, but penetrating, backbeat swats on 'Ooh Mop' (1945) by Jack McVea's All Stars. These exceptions notwithstanding, the vast majority of recordings made during the 1940s by jump blues artists, including Amos Milburn, Roy Brown, Joe Liggins, Ivory Joe Hunter, and Roy Milton featured light afterbeat drum kit accompaniments, occasionally with loud backbeats during isolated instrumental choruses. This started to change around 1949, after which most of the artists just named began to incorporate consistent backbeat accompaniments.

This is true as well for other strains of 1940s rhythm and blues. Records by leading blues shouters such as Big Joe Turner, Jimmy Rushing, Jimmy Witherspoon, Wynonie Harris, and Tiny Bradshaw eschew consistent backbeats until after 1949. For instance, Big Joe Turner released dozens of recordings during the 1940s, but his earliest record with consistent backbeats is 1950's 'Jumpin' at the Jubilee', and even so, the strong handclapped gospel backbeats overpower the unknown drummer's snare drum. By 1953, however, Turner's records commonly featured heavy snare backbeats, which are particularly emphatic and up front of the mix on his biggest hits, 'Honey Hush' (1953, Alonzo Stewart, drums), 'Shake, Rattle, Roll' (1954, Connie Kay, drums), and 'Flip, Flop, Fly' (1955, Connie Kay, drums).

We have already encountered the hand-clapped gospel backbeats on Wynonie Harris's 'Who Threw the Whiskey in the Well' and 'Good Rockin' Tonight'; however, neither feature drum-kit backbeats for the entirety of the song, nor do any pre-1949 recordings by Harris, which typically feature even four-beat shuffle grooves similar to those on Jordan's recordings. Starting with 'All She Wants to Do Is Rock', a paean to a sexually voracious girlfriend recorded with Joe Morris's band (Kelly Martin, drums) in 1949, strong backbeats figure prominently on many of his records. For instance, 'Lovin' Machine' (1951) features drummer William Benjamin playing heavy backbeats accompanied by a swing pattern played on slightly opened hi-hats. As in the introduction to 'Good Rockin' Tonight', reverberating, loose hi-hats produce a noisy, 'dirty' tone (as opposed to the crisp, 'clean' tone of tightly closed hi-hats) that – along with the emphatic backbeats, growling horns, and honking saxes – provide a raunchy backdrop to Harris's sexually charged lyrics.

Garry Tamlyn traces a similar trajectory with blues instrumentalist-singers of the 1940s. Backbeats are rarely featured for an entire track on recordings by artists such as Muddy Waters, Eddie Boyd, 'Big' Bill Broonzy, Floyd Dixon, and others throughout most of the 1940s, but become increasingly common from roughly 1949 onwards.[29] Notable exceptions include Jazz Gillum's 'Roll Dem Bones' (1946) and Muddy Waters's 'Hard Day Blues' (1946), both featuring drummer Lawrence 'Judge' Riley, a fixture of the Chicago blues scene. On the former, Riley accompanies the entire tune, excepting stop-time sections, with some of the heaviest, most consistent backbeats recorded during the 1940s. The latter features solid, if relatively subdued, backbeats throughout, but, following several verses decrying a life of frustration, Riley explodes with emphatic backbeats that erupt from beneath the musical surface, blowing the lid off of the recording's dynamic restraints and impelling a fiery James Clark piano solo.

The Big Beat Takes Over

Pioneer that Riley was with his heavy, albeit often sporadic, backbeats on recordings by Arthur Crudup, 'Big' Bill Broonzy, Muddy Waters, and others, it is not likely he had a profound impact beyond the Chicago blues scene before 1950. None of his backbeat-based recordings cracked the charts, nor was there a proliferation of backbeats on record after he started employing them in 1946. But there would be after 1949, most likely due to the cumulative impact of several enormously successful, backbeat-based recordings from that year (in addition to 'The Fat Man', mentioned above, and 'Good Rockin' Tonight' from the previous year).

Wynonie Harris points to one of them in 'All She Wants to Do Is Rock', when he boastfully proclaims:

> *My baby don't go for fancy clothes, high class dinner, and picture shows,*
> *All she wants to do is stay at home and hucklebuck with daddy all night long.*

Harris's use of the term 'hucklebuck' as a euphemism for sex is a reference to the biggest rhythm-and-blues hit of 1949, 'The Huckle-Buck' by Paul Williams and His Hucklebuckers, an instrumental track based on Charlie Parker's 'Now's the Time' (1945), now outfitted with a backbeat-based groove anchored by Reetham Mallett. During statements of the main theme (starting at :35 and 1:54), Mallett swats the backbeat more forcefully and drops heavy bass drum bombs that anticipate selected downbeats, boosting the allure of Parker's slinky melody with insinuating low-end bumps, an early instance on record of the backbeat played in conjunction with a prominent, syncopated bass drum part. The effect proved irresistible, and 'The Huckle-Buck' spent a record-breaking fourteen weeks atop the R&B chart.[30]

The same day Williams's band recorded 'The Huckle-Buck' (15 December 1948) in New York City, Big Jay McNeely's All Stars recorded 'Deacon's Hop' in Los Angeles, which also topped the R&B chart in 1949, fuelled by a heavily percussive, backbeat-based accompaniment. The recording opens with McNeely soloing to the accompaniment of nothing but loud swing hi-hats and handclaps that double the swing rhythm with accents on two and four. The stark saxophone-percussion texture alternates with full band sections, during which drummer William Streetser lays down heavy backbeats, fattened by loud, loose hi-hat hits. The title 'Deacon's Hop' implies the same comingling of the sacred and secular we encountered with Harris's 'Good Rocking Tonight.' Sonically,

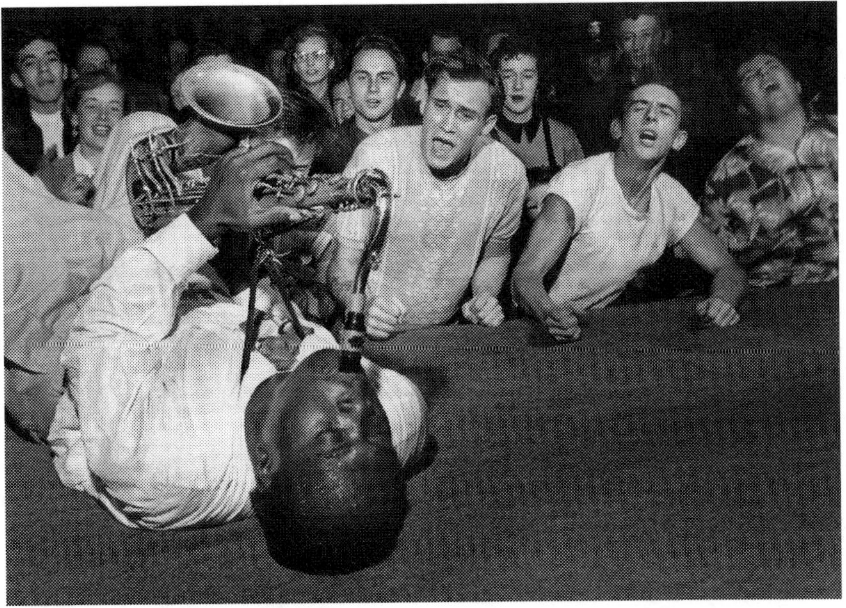

Figure 3.3 Big Jay McNeely, Olympic Auditorium, Los Angeles, 1951 (used with permission of © Bob Willoughby, mptvimages.com)

the handclaps evoke the world of worship, while the emphatic backbeats and 'dirty' reverberating hi-hats match McNeely's bawdy honking, moaning saxophone. Documenting a McNeely performance, photographer Bob Willoughby apparently snapped one of his shots precisely on the backbeat as audience members pound the stage and snap their fingers in unison (Figure 3.3). The image captures the power of communal back-beating and illuminates why it was so threatening to conservative leaders in the 1950s; enraptured male fans beat the stage violently with clenched fists while a white female fan snaps her fingers, just visible between McNeely's legs as he writhes suggestively and wails on the saxophone to the intense delight of the crowd.

One of the most impactful backbeats of the early 1950s appears on 'Sixty-Minute Man', the Dominoes' massive 1951 hit. Like other early backbeat-driven hits, 'Sixty Minute Man' fuses the sacred with the sexual, as a vocal harmony group of the gospel tradition offers a graphic celebration of swaggering male sexuality. The backbeat, played by a drummer whose name went unrecorded, is bolstered by gospel handclaps, both placed high in the mix of a sparse arrangement. The 'in-your-face' back-beat at the song's moderate tempo projects the erotic rocking that Allan Bloom would decry as 'the beat of sexual intercourse'.[31] It helped drive 'Sixty-Minute Man' to the top of the R&B chart, where it stayed for fourteen weeks (matching the record set by 'The Huckle-Buck'), crossing over to #17 on the pop chart, astounding for a song with such graphic lyrics. By 1952, the backbeat was a well-established convention common in all strains of rhythm and blues. It would require a white performer to bring the backbeat into the living rooms of white, middle-class Americans nationwide.

On 5 June 1956, Elvis Presley caused a sensation with his controversial hip-shaking performance of 'Hound Dog' on the *Milton Berle Show.* Towards the end of the performance, Presley dramatically cues his unsuspecting bandmates to stop, before leading them in a slow, grinding reprise of the tune, conducted largely by Presley's thrusting pelvis. As drummer D. J. Fontana remembers:

> All of a sudden, he decides he's going to go into this blues thing. That was the first time he had done it anywhere, and we all looked at each other, 'What do we do now?' . . . I went back into my roots playing strip music actually . . . and I just figured well I better catch his blues licks and his legs and arms and do everything I can.[32]

Fontana's roots in 'strip music' apparently involved hard, spanking backbeats, which he ably deploys at Presley's slowed down tempo, impelling the singer's pelvic gyrations. As Matt Brennan explains, it was Fontana who introduced Presley to the backbeat and inspired his famous stage moves.[33] Fontana's backbeat and Presley's pelvis caused an uproar, exhilarating and outraging viewers in equal measure, and inspiring the kinds of condemnations of beat music I cited at the beginning of this chapter.

Conclusions

Of course, there was far more at stake than the prudish sensibilities of the white middle class in 1950s America. The 'vulgar' performance of Presley and his band reinforced the notion that rock and roll was primarily about 'disorder, aggression, and sex: a fantasy of human nature, running wild to a savage beat'.[34] Most alarmingly, Presley's performance – profoundly and unashamedly influenced by African-American music and dance – represented a shocking case of cultural desegregation and an imminent threat to a white supremacist ideology entrenched since the nation's founding. And it did so backed by the interpellating force of the backbeat, a musical idiom deeply rooted in African-American signifyin(g) practices and strategies of resistance. By the end of the 1950s the backbeat had become firmly established as a primary convention, not only of rock and roll, but of popular music more broadly, and has since become so ubiquitous that its early history has been obscured.

I believe this history helps explain why the backbeat has proven to be so compelling and why it posed such a threat in the mid-1950s. Now a central convention of most popular music genres, drummers, engineers, and producers have dedicated enormous effort to crafting effective treatments of the backbeat, from the conga doubling that gives 'Let's Stay Together' and other Al Green hits their distinctively deep, warm backbeat to the tambourines, tire chains, and wall scrapes used to enhance the backbeats behind the Motown sound, from the celebrated 'delayed' backbeat cultivated at Stax Records to the massive, electronically contrived backbeats in some strains of popular music since the 1980s. Reverend Snow was right to consider the backbeat a powerful cultural force, and we are only beginning to recognize its profound impact on American cultural history.

Notes

1 Snow's sermon and all of the recordings mentioned in this chapter, can be accessed at the YouTube playlist 'Baur, Backbeat Examples, Cambridge Companion to the Drum Kit' at: www.youtube.com/playlist?list=PLbOWiapgBhv90tvHlhGcbERcWcr71OHSh
2 Mayor Berry's statement was delivered at a filmed press conference and can be viewed at: www.youtube.com/watch?v=hN67c_t5xSI (accessed 14 December 2019).
3 'White Council vs. Rock and Roll', *Time* (18 April 1956), available at: http://umsl.edu/virtualstl/phase2/1950/events/perspectives/documents/rocknroll.html (accessed 1 March 2020).
4 S. F. Lawson. *Civil Rights Crossroads: Nation, Community, and the Black Freedom Struggle* (Lexington: University Press of Kentucky, 2003), p. 245.
5 S. Lawhead. *Rock of this Age: The Real and Imagined Dangers of Rock Music* (Downer's Grove: Intervarsity Press, 1987), p. 54.
6 K. Agawu. 'The Invention of "African Rhythm"', *Journal of the American Musicological Society* 48 (1995), pp. 380–395.
7 R. Radano. 'Hot Fantasies: American Modernism and the Idea of Black Rhythm' in R. Radano and P. V. Bohlman (eds.), *Music and the Racial Imagination* (Chicago: University of Chicago Press, 2000), p. 459.
8 Quoted in G. Hirshey, *Nowhere to Run: The Story of Soul Music* (New York: Times Books, 1984), p. 184.
9 J. Rudinow. *Soul Music: Tracking the Spiritual Roots of Pop from Plato to Motown* (Ann Arbor, Michigan: University of Michigan Press, 2010), p. 121.
10 S. Floyd. 'Ring Shout! Literary Studies, Historical Studies, and Black Music Inquiry', *Black Music Research Journal* 22 (2002), pp. 49–70.
11 H. L. Gates, Jr. *The Signifying Monkey: A Theory of African-American Literary Criticism* (New York: Oxford University Press, 1988).
12 The backbeat on "Long Gone" is a half-time backbeat. Rather than accents on the second and fourth beats of each measure, there is a single backbeat on the third beat of each measure. Other prison recordings with emphatic backbeats played with work tools include 'Good God Almighty' ('Lightning' Washington and Group, 1933), 'Jumpin' Judy' (Unidentified Shelby County Workhouse Prisoners, 1933), 'No More, My Lawd' (Henry 'Jimpson' Wallace, 1948), 'Old Alabama' (Dan 'B.B.' Barnes and Group, 1948), 'Black Gal' (Dan 'B.B.' Barnes and Group, 1948), and 'Early in the Morning' (Walter 'Tangle Eye' Jackson and Group, 1947).
13 J. Mowitt. *Percussion: Drumming, Beating, Striking* (Durham and London: Duke University Press, 2002), pp. 118–119, 162.
14 Quoted in R. Cohen (ed.), *Alan Lomax: Selected Writings, 1934-1997* (London and New York: Routledge, 2005), p. 23.
15 D. J. Epstein. *Sinful Tunes and Spirituals: Black Folk Music to the Civil War* (Urbana and Chicago: University of Illinois Press, 1977), pp. 141–144.
16 J. M. Spencer. *Protest and Praise: Sacred Music of Black Religion* (Minneapolis: Fortress Press, 1990), pp. 135–136.
17 Reverend D. C. Rice quoted in G. D. Wardlow, 'Rev. D. C. Rice, Gospel Singer', *Storyville* 23 (1969), p. 167.

18 Most of the Blue Mills Rhythm Band's recordings feature a light afterbeat, played with brushes on the snare drum and/or by the left foot closing the hi-hat cymbals. Below I distinguish between the afterbeat, which is prevalent on recordings from the 1930s and 1940s, and the backbeat, which does not become prevalent until after 1949.

19 P. Lauterbach. *The Chitlin' Circuit and the Road to Rock 'n' Roll* (New York: W. W. Norton, 2011), p. 140.

20 Dale Cockrell has shown that work in houses of prostitution played a much larger role in the professional life of musicians in the early twentieth century than has been acknowledged. See D. Cockrell, *Everybody's Doin' It: Sex, Music, and Dance in New York, 1840–1917* (New York and London: W. W. Norton & Company, 2019).

21 See P. Garon and B. Garon. *Woman with Guitar: Memphis Minnie's Blues* (San Francisco: City Lights Books, 2014), pp. 177–204. J. Dickerson emphasizes her side gig turning tricks in *Goin' Back to Memphis: A Century of Blues, Rock 'n' Roll and Glorious Soul* (New York: Schirmer, 1996), pp. 40, 48.

22 H. Carby. 'It Jus Be's Dat Way Sometime: The Sexual Politics in Women's Blues', *Radical America* 20 (1986), pp. 9–24; S. Lee. *Erotic Revolutionaries: Black Women, Sexuality, and Popular Culture* (Lanham, Maryland: Hamilton Books, 2010).

23 P. Perrone. Earl Palmer Obituary, *The Guardian* (23 September 2008), available at: www.theguardian.com/music/2008/sep/23/popandrock.usa (accessed 27 March 2020).

24 See Matt Brennan's profoundly insightful social history of the drum kit for a more thorough account of the development of the hi-hat and other components of the drum kit. M. Brennan. *Kick It: A Social History of the Drum Kit* (Oxford and New York: Oxford University Press, 2020).

25 The quotation is taken from a compilation of film clips of Ellington discussing the afterbeat available at: www.youtube.com/watch?v=nPcZ5ex2t-g (accessed 17 January 2020).

26 R. Russell. *Jazz Style in Kansas City and the Southwest* (Berkeley, Los Angeles, and London: University of California Press, 1971), p. 27.

27 J. D. Considine. 'The Missing Link in the Evolution of Rock and Roll: Jump Blues', *The Baltimore Sun* (5 December 1993), available at: www.baltimoresun.com/news/bs-xpm-1993-12-05-1993339172-story.html (accessed 11 January 2020).

28 Quincy Jones, interviewed in *The History of Rock 'n' Roll*, Time-Life Video & Television and Warner Bros. Entertainment (1995).

29 G. Tamlyn. 'The Big Beat: Origins and Development of the Snare Backbeat and other Accompanimental Rhythms in Rock 'n' Roll', unpublished PhD dissertation, University of Liverpool, (1998).

30 S. Danchin. *Earl Hooker, Blues Master* (Jackson: University Press of Mississippi, 2001), p. 272. The lyrics to Jimmy Preston's 'Rock the Joint', another backbeat-driven hit from 1949 and perennial candidate for 'first rock and roll song' also make reference to the hucklebuck.

31 A. Bloom. *The Closing of the American Mind* (New York: Simon and Schuster, 1987), p. 73. In his critique of Bloom, Theodore Gracyk takes Bloom too literally and sets out to prove that the rock beat 'has no special "sexual" aspect'. Indeed, there is nothing *essentially* sexual in the backbeat, but in certain contexts, it can be suggestive of sex and invite erotic movement. Gracyk puts forward a straw man argument, selecting examples of rock beats far removed from such contexts. See T. Gracyk. *Rhythm and Noise: An Aesthtics of Rock* (Durham: Duke University Press, 1996), pp. 125–48.

32 D. J. Fontana, interviewed for the documentary *Rock & Roll* (BBC and WGBH/Boston, 1995), WGBH Open Vault website available at: http://openvault.wgbh.org/catalog/V_E1BD21C33F73416A9A585F30CD5718B8 (accessed 11 January 2020).

33 Brennan, *Kick It*, p. 186. Presley and his band's performance exemplifies well what Susan McClary has called the 'phallic backbeat'. As we have seen, female performers were equally adept at engaging the backbeat's erotic potential. See S. McClary. *Feminine Endings: Music, Gender, and Sexuality* (Minneapolis: University of Minnesota Press, 1991), p. 154.

34 J. Miller. *Flowers in the Dustbin: The Rise of Rock and Roll, 1947–1977* (New York: Fireside, 1999), p. 88.

4 Historicizing a Scene and Sound

The Case of Colombia's 'Música Tropical Sabanera'

PEDRO OJEDA ACOSTA AND JUAN DAVID RUBIO RESTREPO

Over the last two decades, there has been a surge in English academic literature on the musical style known as *cumbia*. This scholarship has traced cumbia in local and transnational scenes, focusing mostly on its sociocultural dynamics.[1] Cumbia is a polysemic signifier, referring to a wide variety of musics, dances, and expressive cultures taking place across the American continent and, at the time of this writing, worldwide. Nevertheless, little attention has been given to its musical and rhythmical aspects.[2] However intricate cumbia's origins may be, they are traceable to the Colombian Northwest and Panamá and the second half of the nineteenth century.[3] While the wide array of music practices grouped under this single genre are heterogenous, cumbia's distinctive rhythmic structures constitute one of the few musical traits present in most of its manifestations. This chapter offers an account of various Colombian grooves, some of which came to be circulated transnationally since the 1940s under the single denomination cumbia.

Focusing on a generation of Colombian drummers active in the 1950s and 1960s, we unpack the percussive lexicon that provided this music with its unique sound. Cumbia was a product of complex networks of music cosmopolitanisms and a generation of talented, creative, and savvy drummers. These artists were influenced by local and foreign sounds. The drummers we discuss and the specific recordings we study coincided with a moment where the Colombian national recording industry was booming. This surge, we argue, was concomitant with a dynamic and creative music practice/industry in which composers, performers, and producers were tuning in their ears to their audiences. Therefore, the musics we consider in this chapter develop between the encounter of a raising modernity that brought the emergence of transnational media industries and rural music practices. We discuss the work of four drummers and five rhythmic structures in Colombian tropical music; Pompilio Rodriguez's *merecumbé*, Cecil Cuao's *cumbia*, Nicolás Cervantes's *porro*, and José María Franco's *gaita* and *fandango binario*.

The style, technique, and instrumentation of these drummers illustrate their cosmopolitan drumming practice. Instrumentally, they used a hybrid drum kit that syncretized variations of the set developed and standardized in the United States (kick, hi-hat, toms, snare, and cymbals) with the timbales, cowbells, and clave found in Afro-Cuban musics. Their style was also influenced by musics coming from these countries, mostly swing and guaracha, respectively. However, a set of local music practices composed the very core of their aesthetic practice. Evidencing exceptional musicianship, these drummers took a series of grooves played by local ensembles and adapted and developed these grooves to be played on the drum kit. In the process, they created a vibrant aesthetic practice. These drummers' intimacy with local rhythmic structures, evidenced in the way they crafted their grooves and the sense of technique they had, made their sound idiosyncratic. We identify two indigenous ensembles that were particularly influential: *millo* ensemble and *banda pelayera*.[4]

We use *música tropical sabanera* to refer to the wide array of musics we address. This categorization derives from merging the categories *música tropical* and *música sabanera*. Música tropical is an umbrella term used throughout the Spanish-speaking Americas that, broadly speaking, groups musics mostly of Afro-Colombian, Afro-Cuban, and Afro-Dominican descent, considered danceable.[5] In the Colombian context, música sabanera refers to musics emanating from the savannahs (thus the 'sabanero' denomination) of inland Caribbean territories. Importantly, the 'sabanero' category alludes mostly to brass and accordion-based musics.[6] Música tropical sabanera groups a diverse set of styles that originated in these same territories and that were actively produced and marketed as danceable musics, but that used a 'jazz band' instrumentation *without* accordion. Though deeply local in its inception, música tropical sabanera and the drummers behind it were the product of complex networks of music cosmopolitanism.

A Cosmopolitan Drumming Practice

In Colombia, música tropical sabanera (and most types of popular music) was recorded and produced in the city of Medellín, located in the northern Andes. As scholars have shown, in the early decades of the twentieth century, Medellín rose as Colombia's most prominent industrial economy.[7] Medellín saw the golden days of Colombia's recording industry and the dawn of its radio industry. However, the origins of música tropical sabanera and the local recording industry are to be found in the Caribbean cities of Cartagena and Barranquilla.[8]

The colonial city of Cartagena de Indias was one of the 'official' ports through which enslaved African people entered the Spanish-occupied territories. It was in its peripheral territories where colonists, *cimarrones* (marrons), and indigenous people met, giving birth to a plethora of miscegenated cultural expressions, some of which run deep in the musics we discuss. Barranquilla, not being a colonial post, rose as Colombia's most prominent port in the Atlantic – a distinction it continues to hold – in the 1920s. In an era of rising modernization across Latin America, Barranquilla became a node through which foreign performers and imported commodities entered the country; this included recordings, musical instruments, and recording gear. On top of this, radio sets in cities such as Barranquilla were capable of tuning in to Cuban radio stations, by then one of the major players in the transnational music market.[9] The city was then a cosmopolitan hub. During the first half of the twentieth century, Barranquilla and Cartagena received the most current international sounds. This included jazz, tango, bolero, guaracha, and mambo, among many others.

Cartagena and Barranquilla were also among the first cities with 'modern' music industries. Three developments were significant in this regard: the opening of performance venues and the emergence of local radio stations and record labels. In the 1930s, tea rooms, dance halls, and social clubs became meeting points were middle- and upper-class audiences congregated for a time of leisure.[10] These establishments offered live entertainment for well-to-do families, employed local talent, and hosted international staples such as the Cuban Trio Matamoros and the Orquesta Casino de la Playa.[11] These visiting artists, plus the music local musicians were listening to through radio and recordings, were fundamental in shaping local jazz bands.[12]

Colombian jazz bands were equally influenced by local ensembles such as the aforementioned millo ensemble and banda pelayera. While the drummers we study did not perform in these indigenous ensembles, they were directly influenced by them. Since at least the 1940s, bandas pelayeras regularly travelled from nearby towns such as Monteria, Sincelejo, and San Pelayo to perform in Cartagena's main square.[13] In the case of Barranquilla, the millo ensemble has been an integral part of the city's soundscape, particularly of its iconic Carnaval de Barranquilla. Therefore, while both of these local ensembles originated in peripheral areas, they were constantly listened to in the coastal cities.

Radio stations and record labels were also key agents. *La Voz de Barranquilla* and the *Emisora Atlántico* began operations in 1929 and 1934, respectively. In Cartagena, *La Voz de Laboratorios Fuentes* opened in 1934, directed by polymath Antonio Fuentes.[14] Many of these stations broadcasted live music in radio-theatres. Antonio Fuentes's record label

Discos Fuentes was key in establishing música tropical sabanera. Bands that pioneered this sound such as Peyo Torres's Orquesta Granadino (based in Sincelejo) and Simón Mendoza's Sonora Cordobesa (based in Monteria) recorded for Discos Fuentes as early as 1952.[15] Once in Cartagena, the musicians of these bands were hired to perform and record in other projects.[16] This further illustrates the fluid musical circuit that existed between the coastal cities and their peripheries.

The high demand for jazz bands established this ensemble as a long-standing phenomenon. It was in the midst of this dynamic, cosmopolitan, and diverse context, that the drumming style we study emerged and developed. Knowledgeable of the rhythmic language behind transnational staples such as swing, mambo, and tango, but also deeply rooted in the wide array of local musics around them, the drummers we profile built the rhythmic foundation of what would eventually become a Pan-American phenomenon.

On Rhythms and Entextualization

The onto-epistemological implications of transcribing musics outside the Eurocentric canon have been dealt with at length by ethnomusicologists worldwide. As Ochoa Gautier has argued, *entextualization,* that is 'the act of framing the musical object to be studied through multiple modes of "capturing" it', has been essential in making non-Western musics 'objects of knowledge'.[17] While we acknowledge this, we also situate the musics we study as another instance of what Ochoa Gautier, following Garcia Canclini, calls Latin America's 'unequal modernity'. Being in a liminal space between the dynamics of media capitalism and rural cultural practices, música tropical sabanera is the product of such unequal modernity. Recordings constitute in themselves a form of entextualization.

While the musics we study were influenced by and used techniques derived from Eurocentric knowledge, i.e., orchestration and arrangement techniques, instruments, performance settings, etc., we locate their percussive elements in a space of in-betweenness. Local rhythmic structures intertwined with foreign ones. Importantly, this percussive lexicon existed outside Eurocentric music textualities. The transcriptions below and their respective analysis are then approximations of a rich, fluid, and highly improvisational practice and they constitute themselves an act of entextualization.

Merecumbé, Cumbia, and Porro: The Colombian 'Tropical' Sound

The 1950s saw the boom of the Colombian recording industry. Modernized iterations of cumbia (from accordion as well as millo ensembles) and porro pelayero – musics previously deemed as rural and racialized – rose to the national sphere. First emerging in the private clubs, radio stations, and recording studios of Barranquilla and Cartagena, cumbia and porro eventually made it to similar spaces in the Andean cities of Medellín and Bogotá. This was indicative of a major shift in the nation's aural politics. Such moves came along significative aesthetic changes. Presenting a sophisticated demeanour, the bands leading this charge were those of Edmundo Arias (1925–1993), Antonio María Peñaloza (1916–2005), Francisco 'Pacho' Galán (1906–1988), and Luis Eduardo 'Lucho' Bermúdez (1912–1994). Such demeanour was matched by the music's composition. Fully notated arrangements for jazz band ensembles, occasional solos with background accompaniment, and a playful yet controlled rhythmic section were salient characteristics.

Following Wade, scholars have used the concept of *whitening* to theorize this transition from rural sounds to national soundtrack.[18] Proposing a 'modernist teleology' suggesting that bands such as those of Galán and Bermúdez diluted the music's rhythmic complexity, wore formal garments, and portrayed an aura of sophistication in order to appeal to a middle- and upper-class bourgeois sensitivity, Wade argues that these aesthetic and socio-cultural shifts were concomitant with a racialized perception white mestizos (broadly speaking, miscegenated yet predominantly racially, and most importantly ethnically, white populations) had of these rural musics. Adapting music techniques and production values derived from the Euro-American canon was thus an aesthetic manifestation of these whitening racial dynamics.

We nuance this argument by suggesting that these bands' percussive aspects complicate such a claim. Put differently, we find in the rhythmic lexicon we study a rich, inventive, and intricate drumming technique that, although not 'traditional', is also not 'modern' in the teleological sense the whitening concept presupposes.[19] Furthermore, we find in this music practice a delicate balance between creativity and media industries. Record labels, composers, band leaders, performers, venues, and consumers were all part of a network of distributed agency.

Similar to Euro-American dance crazes such as the charleston or the twist, in the 1950s, Colombian band leaders sought to establish novel dance rhythms in the market. Bermúdez's *gaita* and Galán's *merecumbé* were among the few that achieved national (and international) relevance. Created by Pacho Galán in collaboration with drummer Pompilio Rodriguez (1929–2007), the merecumbé – its creators argued – was a combination of *merengue* and cumbia (as performed by millo ensembles).[20] In 1929, Rodriguez's father Francisco Tomás Rodriguez founded the orchestra Nuevo Horizonte. Pompilio toured with his father since age twelve, performing a wide array of styles. By the time he started working in Galán's orchestra in 1956, he was a veteran. Rodriguez explains that, in creating the merecumbé, he was inspired by Galán's brass arrangements.[21] According to Rodriguez, Galán asked him to build a groove that would fit the genre's self-proclaimed originality.

The merecumbé became a major hit, prompting Galán to record entire albums in this style.[22] Compared to other structures in this chapter, merecumbé is less improvisational. In the track 'Rico Merecumbé', released in 1958 by the label Ondina, Rodriguez built three variations of the groove (Example 4.1) that match Galán's arrangement. We transcribe the basic structure of each variation and number them using Arabic numerals. Variation number one is the merecumbé proper. With it, Rodriguez accompanied the only sung section of the piece; a chorus intercalated with a call and response arrangement between the saxophones and trumpets. Importantly, the actual merecumbé groove (variation one) only appears when the chorus sings 'hay que rico merecumbé', making the connection between Rodriguez's rhythmic structure and the genre explicit.

In the track, Rodriguez used most timbres of his hybrid drum kit composed of kick, snare, and cymbals with timbales and cowbells. The cowbell, that only appears at the beginning of the cycle, marks a 'broad downbeat', becoming an anchor point for an otherwise syncopated structure. The transition from cáscara to timbal high and low was designed to counterpoint Galán's merecumbé-style brass arrangement.[23] The resolution on the second off-beat of the second bar is characteristic of cumbia as performed by millo ensembles. While in traditional formats this accent is played on the indigenous bass drum– like *tambora*, Rodriguez used the timbal low to emulate the instrument's low-pitched sonority. In variation two, he 'opened up' the groove into the crash cymbal playing the constant off-beat stylistic of traditional banda pelayera and millo ensemble. In jazz band formats, this off-beat is played by the hand-held cymbal doubled by the maracón rattle. The one-quarter-note-two-eighth-notes pattern found in most musics called cumbia appears in variation three. In both the second and third variations, Rodriguez added ornaments. The syncopated eighth note he placed in between the main line (second beat of bars 1 and 2 of variation two, and the first beat of the second bar of variation three) gives the groove more drive.

Example 4.1 Four stages of Pompilio Rodriguez's *merecumbé* groove in Pacho Galán's 'Rico Merecumbé'

Along with cumbia and merecumbé, porro was the most popular type of música popular sabanera in the 1950s and 1960s. In fact, porro arrived in México before cumbia.[24] While musically distinct, all of these rhythms were circulated outside Colombia under the single name cumbia.[25] Being one of the most transnationally successful bandleaders of this scene, Lucho Bermúdez's porro composition 'Arroz con Coco' is illustrative of this style's rhythmic structures.[26] Recorded in 1956 for the label Silver, the track features Nicolás Cervantes on drums. Brother of drummer Reyes Cervantes, Nicolás was part of the Barranquilla-based Emisora Atlántico Jazz Band.

In variation one, Cervantes held a strong downbeat on the cowbell (sometimes doubling it with the kick) and phrased in a fluid and syncopated fashion with his other hand. The one-hand roll (bar 1) and eighth note phrasing (bars 2, 3, and 4) illustrate Cervantes's mindful equilibrium. On the one hand, Cervantes held the downbeat with the cowbell to provide the dancer with a clear sense of beat. On the other hand, Cervantes played fluidly on the timbales, keeping the groove fresh and engaging. In variation two, Cervantes transitioned from half notes to the quarter-note-eighth-note rhythm on the cowbell in a more soloistic fashion. We transcribe a passage of these variations in Example 4.2. Moving between kick, floor tom, and snare, Cervantes shows great dexterity. While on some occasions Cervantes used the kick to support the downbeats, he also used it to orchestrate the improvised phrases built around the cowbell pattern.

Example 4.2 Two stages of Nicolás Cervantes's *porro* groove in Lucho Bermúdez's 'Arroz con Coco'

The Cuao family deserves a special mention in the history of música tropical sabanera. Formed by brothers Wilfredo (Lucho Bermúdez's drummer for several years), Cecil (also known as 'Ciser' or 'Calilla'), Tomás ('El Mono'), and Juan Carlos ('Juancho'), all born in the city of Santa Marta, the Cuao drumming dynasty was deeply influenced by Panamanian drummer Ruben Dario Romerín. Romerín arrived in Santa Marta with a jazz band, eventually settling there. His influence speaks of the crucial role Panamá and Panamanian musicians have had in the history cumbia. We focus on Cecil Cuao's rendition of the cumbia 'La Pollera Colorá', composed by Juan Bautista Madera and Wilson Choperena. Cecil Cuao recorded this version in 1960 with the orchestra of Pedro Salcedo

(1910–1988). This track contains several of the rhythmic structures that became staples of cumbia, as performed by these formats, especially its opening section. In it, Cuao focuses on the timbal low and cáscara playing a series of breaks (Example 4.3, variation one).

Example 4.3 Three stages of Cecil Cuao's *cumbia* groove in Pedro Salcedo's 'La Pollera Colorá'

Following the local terminology, we call these *repiques*. We do so to stress the geopolitical specificity of this drumming practice and avoid faux homologies with Euro-American counterparts such as 'fills' or 'comping'. Repiques are passages where the basic groove is ornamented, leaving the main rhythmic structure altogether at times. Deeply rooted in local drumming practices, repiques are an expression of enjoyment and virtuosity. Although common in transitional parts of the structure, repiques can happen at any time and with different intensities.

In 'La Pollera Colorá', Cuao's repiques derive from the rhythmic structures of the tambora as performed in millo ensembles. These structures are fundamental to set the tone of the track. We include the *llamador* hand drum in the transcription (replaced on this track by a conga) to show the polyrhythmic quality of the groove. The phrasing constantly driving towards, and often resolving on, the second off-beat (bars 2 and 4 of variation one) is particularly stylistic. After the introduction, Cuao added the cáscara, using flams that emulate the tambora sound and technique (bars 1 and 3 of variation two). In variation two, Cuao used a mixture of rim shots and repiques to accompany the instrumental melody. Finally, when the voice appears, Cuao played a bare-bones version of the tambora cumbia groove in variation three.

Gaitas and Fandangos Binarios: José Mariá Franco and the Rural-Cosmopolitan Sound

José María Franco was one of the most creative drummers of música tropical sabanera. His work with Orquesta Emisora Fuentes, Orquesta

A No. 1, Sonora Curro, and band leaders Pedro Laza (1904–1980) and Rufo Garrido (1896–1990) are particularly salient. The sound of these bands has been characterized as 'rootsy'.[27] Arguably, this notion has been constructed in relation to Lucho Bermúdez's and Pacho Galán's bands. The latter presented a more sophisticated image and a sound more in line with the Latin American dance bands of the era. In contrast, Laza's and Garrido's bands were less stylized. Showing a more direct connection to banda pelayera, their performers displayed a sense of technique and sound quality mostly unconcerned with Eurocentric standards. Under the guidance of Discos Fuentes' owner Antonio Fuentes, Pedro Laza made the connection explicit by naming his band Pedro Laza y sus Pelayeros.

Drumming-wise, José María Franco's style was improvisational and deeply rooted in rural traditions. Using a hybrid drum kit composed of snare, kick, hi-hat, cymbals, and timbales, Franco adapted the distributed percussion traditionally performed in banda pelayera (snare, hand-held cymbals, and bass drum) into a single kit. In 'La Compatible', Franco performed four variations of the groove (Example 4.4). In the introduction (variation one), eighth notes on the cáscara are overlaid by a constant off-beat on the timbal low, a common trait in the gaita style. During the brass melody (variation two), Franco 'opened up' this syncopated feel into the crash cymbal, ornamenting on the timbales. The one-quarter-note-two-eighth-notes cumbia pattern appears with the clarinet melody/solo (variation three), played on the cáscara with some important variations we consider below. For the trombone solo (variation four), Franco 'closed up' the groove, avoiding variations and transitioning from cáscara to woodblock/cha cha bell (also called 'coquito'), playing straight eighth notes at times and making the overall texture more articulated.

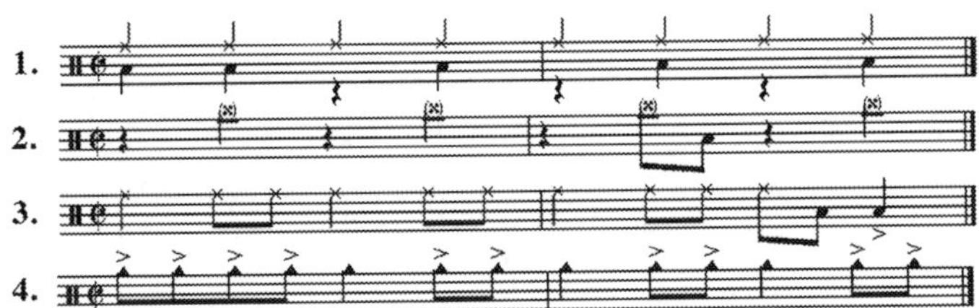

Example 4.4 Four stages of José Franco's *gaita* groove in Pedro Laza's 'La Compatible'

The excerpt from Franco's repique in La Compatible we transcribe in Example 4.5 illustrates the music's improvisational nature and rhythmic style. The eighth-note-to-quarter-note rhythmic resolution towards the second off-beat (bars 1 and 8) and the dotted eighth notes transitioning between downbeats and off-beats (bars 2 to 6), all of them in the timbal's low register, are stylistic of traditional cumbia as performed by tambora in millo ensembles.

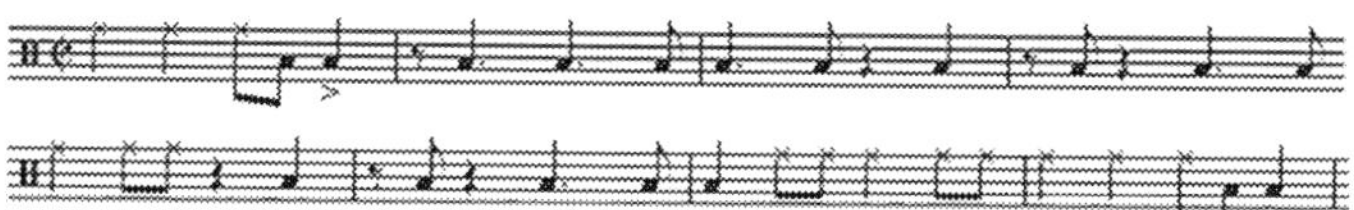

Example 4.5 José Franco's *repiques* in Pedro Laza's 'La Compatible'

In 'El Arranque', also recorded in 1960 for Discos Fuentes and released in the album Fandango, Laza and Franco elaborated on the traditional style of *fandango* as performed by banda pelayera. While the traditional fandango is ternary, El Arranque's subdivision is mostly binary. Due to the fact that the track is called a fandango in the record but that it is binary, we use the denomination *fandango binario*. Using a similar drum kit configuration, Franco kept a steady line on the kick throughout (Example 4.6). The structure he used in variation one is found in musics across the Americas; it is commonly known as the *Cuban tresillo* (♩. ♩. ♩).This cell is also found in several musics of the Colombian-Caribbean. Importantly, the rhythmic feel of the figure is neither binary nor ternary. This probably has to with the track's fast tempo, but also with Franco's familiarity with these percussive languages. In particular, the second dotted eighth note falls in a rhythmic space non-quantizable under Eurocentric standards. This is crucial in building the overall character of the track.

Example 4.6 Four stages of José Franco's *fandango binario* groove in Pedro Laza's 'El Arranque'

As Franco held this figure on the kick, he phrased on the snare. The technique and style are deeply influenced by banda pelayera. The unarticulated rolls and sudden and syncopated rim-shot accents with a three-against-two feel are stylistic of this tradition. The maracón, playing a constant figure departing from the off-beat and landing on the downbeat, created a polyrhythmic, syncopated, and 'ahead-of-the-beat' feeling. In the second variation, Franco transitioned to the cha cha bell in 'coquito' style. In variation three, Franco doubled the maracón. However, on this occasion, Franco muted the crash cymbal on the downbeat, a common technique used in música tropical sabanera.

In Franco's style, and particularly in his collaborations with Pedro Laza and Rufo Garrido, we find a language deeply influenced by banda pelayera.

However, cosmopolitan influences are also salient. The use of timbales and Franco's orchestration on the cáscara and cowbells shows a strong link to Afro-Cuban musics, especially to guaracha. As a matter of fact, the bands of Garrido and Laza recorded several 'Colombian guarachas'. On top of that, the fact that a drum kit was used and that these local musics were being performed by jazz band ensembles signals a strong connection to US swing music. We observe similar influences in the drumming techniques employed by all the drummers considered in this chapter.

Closing Remarks

We have used the term música tropical sabanera to group a wide variety of sociocultural contexts and music practices. On the musical side, two characteristics connect them; the jazz band format and an aesthetic practice that syncretized rural musics of the Colombia-Caribbean with transnational ones such as swing and guaracha. The emergence of these musics was concomitant with the advent of the Colombian music industry in the twentieth century.

This process of commercialization and syncretisation does not imply a teleology in which music continuously evolved to reach Euro-American (read *white*) standards – what we have called modernist teleology. The aesthetic practices and racial dynamics of música tropical sabanera tell a much more nuanced story. While the music of Pacho Galán, Lucho Bermúdez, and Pedro Salcedo did portray a more sophisticated aura, its percussive lexicon was anything but 'diluted' or 'simplified' (adjectives often used to describe these musics vis-à-vis the style of millo formats). The rhythmic structures we have analysed tell us about a creative, exciting, and idiosyncratic music practice. Signalling a different aesthetic practice, the bands of Pedro Laza and Rufo Garrido developed a sound more influenced by local practices, particularly banda pelayera. For all practical purposes, the idea of whitening forwarded by Wade and other scholars accounts for the fact that, while Bermúdez, Galán, Edmundo Arias, and Pedro Salcedo rose to transnational prominence, Pedro Laza, Rufo Garrido, Clímaco Sarmiento, Peyo Torres, and bands such as La Sonora Cordobesa did not. Bermúdez, in particular, toured transnationally in México, Cuba, and Argentina, performing his arrangements with local orchestras. These tours were important – though not the only – agents in circulating cumbia across Latin America. In this light, the drummers behind these rhythmic structures are the unsung heroes of a sound that spread throughout an entire continent.

As fundamental as these drummers are, their stories and legacy continue to be mostly unknown, even for Colombian drummers studying traditional musics. While the turn of the millennium brought a renewed interest for rural musics by academically trained musicians, the drumming practices of música tropical sabanera have fallen under their radar. Ignoring that such a process already took place half a century before them, contemporary drummers go back to banda pelayera and millo ensembles and re-adapt these rhythms to the drum kit, thus reinventing the proverbial wheel. Be that as it may, the music created by these drummers continues to resound through an entire continent and, nowadays, with cumbia's international prominence, the entire world.

Notes

1 P. Wade. *Music, Race and Nation: Música Tropical in Colombia* (Chicago: University of Chicago Press, 2000); A. L. Madrid. *Nor-tec rifa!: Electronic Dance Music from Tijuana to the World* (New York: Oxford University Press, 2008); H. Fernández L'Hoeste and P. Vila. *Cumbia!: Scenes of a Migrant Latin American Music Genre* (Durham: Duke University Press, 2013); G. Baker. '"Digital indigestion": Cumbia, Class and a Post-Digital Ethos in Buenos Aires', *Popular Music* 34:2 (2015); J. Tucker. 'Peruvian Cumbia at the Theoretical Limits of Techno-Utopian Hybridity' in A. R. Alonso-Minutti, E. Herrera, and A. L. Madrid (eds.), *Experimentalisms in Practice: Music Perspectives from Latin America* (New York: Oxford University Press, 2018).

2 There are exceptions in Spanish literature. L. Convers and J. S. Ochoa, *Gaiteros y Tamboleros: Material Para Abordar El Estudio De La Música De Gaitas De San Jacinto, Bolívar (Colombia)* (Bogotá: Pontificia Universidad Javeriana, 2007); F. O. Escobar. *El Libro De Las Gaitas Largas: Tradición De Los Montes De María.* (Bogotá: Pontificia Universidad Javeriana, 2013); J. S. Ochoa, C. J. Pérez, and F. Ochoa. *El Libro de las Cumbias Colombianas* (Medellín: Fundación Cultural Latin Grammy, 2017). None of these studies have focused on cumbia's drum kit lexicon.

3 While most literature situates the origins of cumbia in the Colombian northwest and its inland territories (particularly along the Magdalena river), cumbia predates the modern Colombian nation. Historical documents have traced the emergence of cumbia to the second half of the nineteenth century. Panamá separated from Colombia in 1903. Furthermore, the flute-like gaita (one of the iconic instruments of 'traditional' cumbia) is derived from indigenous instruments still used by the Cunas, and indigenous community that lives across the Panamá-Colombian border. Panamá continues to have a rich cumbia tradition. While we shortly address the contributions of Panamanian musicians to the modern percussive cumbia lexicon, the systematic process of erasure Panamá has endured in cumbia scholarship begs for further inquiry.

4 The millo ensemble is named after the *flauta e' millo, caña e' millo*, or *pito atravesao*, a flute-like reed instrument indigenous to Colombian Atlantic coast that takes its name from the millo plant from which it is built. The ensemble that accompanies this instrument is called 'conjunto de millo' (millo ensemble). It is traditionally composed by flauta e' millo, alegre hand drum, a smaller version of it called llamador, tambora (a bass drum–like instrument), and maracón or guache (rattle-like ideophones). Banda pelayera is a marching band–type ensemble. The pelayero appellative alludes to the town of San Pelayo in the Córdoba state. This city hosts the annual Festival Nacional del Porro. Both the millo and pelayero ensembles play a wide array of music genres with distinct rhythmic structures. F. Ochoa Escobar. 'Las Investigaciones Sobre La Caña De Millo O Pito Atravesao', (*Cuadernos de Musica, Artes Visuales y Artes Escenicas* 7:2 (2012), pp. 159–178).

5 In *Music, Race, and Nation*, Wadeuses the música tropical as an umbrella term grouping a wide variety of musics that originated in the Colombian-Caribbean and its peripheries, and that developed into a wide array of music practices once they were mediated by the local recording industry.

6 In his study of Medellín's music industry in the 1960s, Juan Sebastián Ochoa uses the adjective 'sabanero' to refer to a group of accordion-based musics from the Colombian Caribbean and pelayero-style jazz bands such as those of Clímaco Sarmiento and Perdo Laza. J. S. Ochoa. *Sonido Sabanero y Sonido Paisa: La Producción de Música Tropical en Medellín Durante Los Años Sesenta* (Bogota: Editorial Pontificia Universidad Javeriana, 2018).

7 P. Wade, Music, Race and Nation*; C. Santamaría Delgado.* Vitrolas, Rocolas y Radioteatros: Hábitos de Escucha de la Música Popular en Medellín, 1930–1950 (Bogotá: Editorial Pontificia Universidad Javeriana, 2014); J. S. Ochoa, *Sonido Sabanero y Sonido Paisa.*

8 Antonio Fuentes founded his label and radio station in Cartagena in the 1930s. He moved to Medellín in 1954. O. Peláez and L. F. O. Jaramillo. *Colombia Musical: Una Historia – Una Empresa* (Medellín: Discos Fuentes, 1996).
9 During the first decades of the twentieth century, radio sets in Barranquilla were capable of tuning in to Cuban radio stations CMQ, Radio Progreso, and La Cadena Azul that broadcasted the latest danzón, bolero, and son hits. During this time, Cuban artists were in contact with Mexican musicians and audiences. This illustrates the complex networks of music cosmopolitanism that were in motion at the time. Ochoa, *Sonido Sabanero y Sonido Paisa*, p. 76.
10 Wade, *Music, Race and Nation*, p. 77.
11 Ibid.; Ochoa, *Sonido Sabanero y Sonido Paisa*.
12 Local jazz bands from the1920s to 1940s included the Lorduy Jazz Band, Sosa Jazz Band, Orquesta Emisora Atlántico Jazz Band, and Atlántico Jazz Band among others. The standard jazz band ensemble was composed by: 2/3 trumpets, 2 saxophones, 1/2 trombone(s), drum kit, congas, maracas/maracón/guache, double-bass, and piano (with banjo sometimes substituting it). L. E. Muñóz Vélez. *Jazz en Colombia: Desde los Alegres Años 20 Hasta Nuestros Días* (Barranquilla: Fundación Cultural Nueva Música, 2007).
13 We based this on the testimony of drummer Guillermos Navas who recalls seeing bandas pelayeras performing at Cartagena's Plaza de la Aduana (the city's main square) as a child. Born in 1930, Navas performed with bands such as Orquesta A No. 1, Jazz Band Unión, and Panamanian bandleader Marcos Guilkes. Banda pelayera scholar William Fortich Díaz has argued that porro first emerged in Cartagena. Fortich Díaz – born in San Pelayo and one of the founders of the Festival Nacional del Porro in 1977 – suggests that porro was initially played by traditional ensembles during the nineteenth century. This style was then reappropriated by military-type bands in towns such as San Pelayo in the early twentieth century. W. Fortich Díaz. 'Así Nació el Porro y su Festival' *Postivia Alamedas*, available at: http://positivaalamedas.co/region/cultura/asi-nacio-el-porro-y-su-festival/ (accessed 27 January 2020).
14 Wade, *Music, Race and Nation*, pp. 91–92.
15 While Orquesta Granadino was Peyo Torres's most renowned band, Torres made his first recording for Discos Fuentes using the name Orquesta Rítmo de Sabanas, coined by Antonio Fuentes. They recorded El Culebro in 1952, a porro originally published on a 78 rpm. The track has a rural porro pelayero feel performed by a jazz band ensemble. Torres's orchestra was one of the pioneers of this sound.
16 For instance, Orquesta Emisora Fuentes, Orquesta A No. 1, and Pedro Laza y Sus Pelayeros were formed by a mixture of performers from the coastal cities and the peripheries.
17 A. M. Ochoa Gautier. 'Sonic Transculturation, Epistemologies of Purification and the Aural Public Sphere in Latin America', *Social Identities* 12:6 (2006), pp. 803–825.
18 Wade, *Music, Race and Nation.*
19 We agree with Ochoa who also argues against Wade's teleological account of música tropical in Colombia. J. S. Ochoa, *Sonido Sabanero y Sonido Paisa.*
20 While a rhythm by the name of merengue exists in accordion and gaita ensembles, it is unrelated to its Dominican homonym. The merengue played by accordion-based ensembles is ternary, the one performed by gaita ensembles is binary. It is still unclear to which merengue Galán alluded to in his merecumbé.
21 First recorded in 1954, the original version of 'Hay Cosita Linda', recorded by Cartagena-born drummer Manuel Gómez 'El Negrito Viroli', had a porro feel.
22 Wade, *Music, Race and Nation*, p. 156.
23 Rodriguez composed his merecumbé groove in a 'responsorial' fashion; that is, in a contrapuntal fashion in relation to the horn section. It is also worth noting that Rodriguez 'flipped' the groove at times by dropping the cowbell one bar after vis-à-vis the rest of the band.
24 Colombian singer Luis Carlos Meyer popularized porro in México in the late 1940s. Meyer recorded porros and cumbias with a Mexican orchestra led by Rafael de Paz. These recordings constitute one of the earliest contacts Mexican audiences had with Colombian musics. Eventually, these musics were grouped under the single denomination cumbia.
25 In Colombia, most listeners do differentiate between porro and cumbia. This is not the case for the bulk of American countries.
26 Although 'Arroz con Coco' is widely known as a porro, it was categorized as a gaita in the compilation album Burucuca, edited by Polydor in 1961.
27 Wade, *Music, Race and Nation*, p. 158.

PART II

Analysing the Drum Kit in Performance

5 The Drum Kit beyond the Anglosphere

The Case of Brazil

DANIEL M. GOHN

Since its origins in the United States, the drum kit has been adopted around the world by many cultures that have employed it in different ways. Based on the rich traditions of their own countries, drummers have developed particular voices by applying phrasings and sonorities that came from diverse palettes of established musical practices. One of such case is Brazil, where the vast array of national rhythms ranges from *samba* and *baião* to *maracatu* and many others. Brazilians emulate percussion instruments such as *pandeiro*, *tamborim*, *surdo* and *zabumba* on the drum kit in order to simulate full percussion ensembles, creating sonic environments that are distinctly connected to their musical heritage.

Very often, drum kit scholarship focuses on jazz and rock music, ignoring genres outside of those realms. Drum kit culture was originally formed in English speaking nations and that seems to direct scholars' main focus of research. As a consequence, one frequently finds generalizations about musics from other genres, without taking into account all the subtleties that differentiate them and labelling them in broad terms such as 'Latin' or 'World Music'. Beyond the anglosphere, a growing body of academic work has developed over the early twenty-first century. Studies considering Brazilian drumming present clear examples of a valuable body of non-English scholarship. Research has revealed the intricacies of drummers such as Edison Machado (1934–1990), Airto Moreira (1941), Dom Um Romão (1925–2005), Márcio Bahia (1958), Wilson das Neves (1936–2017), Hélcio Milito (1931–2014) and Luciano Perrone (1908–2001), among others.[1] In spite of the recentness of this scientific effort, this area has been competently mapped out and now can be scrutinized by scholars around the world.

Organized in two sections, this chapter presents research in the Portuguese language: Historical Overview and Technical Characteristics of Brazilian Drum Kit Playing. Through the lenses of scholars that explored the subject, there are indications of drummers with significant contributions and a short discussion on some of the aspects involved in what became known as 'the Brazilian feel'. In no way do I intend for this chapter to be fully comprehensive, given the extent of the matter and the enormous collection of names and details involved. Ultimately, my aim is to display some of the academic achievements in the area, serving as a prelude to more in-depth studies on Brazilian music.

Historical Overview

Pioneer Players

The arrival of the drum kit in Brazil took place during the 1920s and, unfortunately, documentations about drumming pioneers in the country are scant. Nevertheless, there are names from that time frequently mentioned as relevant. Among those pioneering figures are Valfrido Silva, Joaquim Tomás, João Batista das Chagas Pereira ('Sut'), and Luciano Perrone.[2] The latter, although certainly not the first one, is known as a 'father figure' for Brazilian drummers.[3] Perrone brought the drum kit into prominence with his groundbreaking work, which included the first recorded drum kit solo in Brazil.[4]

Luciano Perrone started playing in orchestras that accompanied silent movies and soon was applying elements of rhythms such as samba, baião and *maxixe* to the drum kit. He was the drummer for the first recording of 'Aquarela do Brazil' in 1939, composed by Ary Barroso and arranged by Radamés Gnattali, with whom he performed for more than fifty years. Together, Perrone and arranger Gnattali faced the challenge of adapting ensembles comprised of eight or more percussionists into the playing of a single musician, filling all the spaces left.[5] When they began working at the *Rádio Nacional* in Rio de Janeiro, the drum kit was the only form of percussion available to handle all the arrangements. Those circumstances demanded exploration of the instrument's sonic possibilities.[6] Establishing a connection between the informal universe of samba playing, classical maestros, and arrangers, Perrone was pivotal in defining the development of his instrument.[7]

Luciano Perrone and his fellow peers made efforts to reproduce the sound of samba percussion instruments on the drum kit. One example is his playing on the snare drum with snares off, holding a stick with one hand while the other hand would play directly on the drum.[8] The resulting muffling was very characteristic of *atabaque* or tamborim patterns.[9] Perrone also was known for his samba *cruzado* (crossed samba), a style in which the right hand plays on the snare and the left crosses over to play the surdo figures on the floor tom, with a muffled strike on beat one and an open sound on beat two.[10]

During the 1930s and 1940s jazz bands proliferated throughout Brazil, performing regularly in nightclubs within major cities and thus jazz music was mixed with a diverse pool of rhythms such as samba, *marcha-rancho*, maxixe and the Argentinian *tango*.[11] Along with the orchestras that emerged when television arrived in the early fifties, those bands set the scene in which Brazilian rhythms took form on the drum kit. The great success of Luiz Gonzaga, composer and accordion player from the north-east of Brazil, brought the rhythms baião and *xote* into the common repertoire.

The aforementioned samba cruzado is an example of samba *batucado*, which means it was played mainly on drums with minimal cymbal work. Cymbals were used for punctuating rhythmic figures and signalling section changes but not for 'riding the rhythm'. Educator and drummer Oscar Bolão, who lived closely to Luciano Perrone for many years and was his student and disciple, noted that for Perrone 'Brazilian music was about drums' (rather than cymbals).[12] In Perrone's approach, even the hi-hat played with the foot was sporadic.[13] The samba batucado was firstly played with both hands on the snare drum only and later there was a development, in which the left hand (for right-handed drummers) crossed over to play the toms. The snare drum invariably was the central component of the kit whereas the toms completed rhythmic ideas. That was the norm from the 1930s up to the 1950s, when US influences and technological progress led to new scenarios in the Brazilian musical landscape. Economic development and the strengthening of infrastructure became primary objectives in Brazil and everything related to the cutting edge was greatly cherished and valued.[14]

A new way to play samba became identified with innovation and modernity samba *no prato* (samba on the cymbal).[15] The ride cymbal took on a central role, with sixteenth note riding patterns as well as a variety of broken syncopated patterns. The bass drum then was played with an ostinato (dotted eight note followed by a sixteenth note, hi-hat on the upbeats), substituting the simpler patterns previously used (most times only a quarter note on the second beat, with a rest on the first beat). That new pattern was known as *bumbo a dois* (two on the bass drum). Two drummers often get the credit for being the first to play in this new style of samba no prato, during the mid-1950s: Hildofredo Alves Correa and Edison Machado.[16] What is certain is that Edison Machado was the one to popularize the novelty and eventually reap respect and recognition. Those new trends were not only stylistic changes, they represented the contrast of the new (samba no prato) against the old (samba batucado). That dichotomy was entangled in a larger discussion, one that included nationalist discourse, safeguarding the 'authentic' Brazilian music, and groups that believed Brazil should be open to the influences coming from the United States. The former considered samba batucado as the only genuine approach for the drum kit, the latter was listening to jazz and struggling for experimentation and freedom.

Bossa Nova and Samba Jazz

Within the context presented above, at the end of the 1950s bossa nova emerged as a prominent Brazilian genre. Displaying highly sophisticated melodic and harmonic lines, this music had a strong impact on Brazilian culture. The 1959 recording of 'Chega de Saudade' by João Gilberto was particularly influential, leading ears and eyes around the world to the music of Brazil. This was especially true after 1963, when Gilberto recorded the seminal album *Getz / Gilberto* with saxophone player Stan Getz. Jazz and Brazilian music were effectively blended. In 1962, Brazilian musicians went to perform a concert at Carnegie Hall in New York and stayed in the United States after that, beginning an era of collaborative work between musicians of both countries. At that time rock and roll had landed in Brazil, engendering *jovem guarda* and subsequently taking part in *tropicalismo*. Jovem guarda was heavily influenced by The Beatles' music, irreverent behaviour and clothing style. Tropicalismo was a mix of a myriad of elements, including Brazilian rhythms (especially from northeast Brazil), American and British rock, and symphonic string arrangements.

Drummers were striving to keep up with all this newness. For instance, before bossa nova they usually played brushes just like drumsticks, striking drumheads in their batucadas. Within the delicate ambiance of bossa nova there was a demand for more intricate brush activity, including more of the swishing motions that were traditional for jazz drummers. Often bossa nova drummers played with a stick in one hand and a brush in the other.[17] That approach required playing softer and with a smoother touch. Milton Banana (1935–1998) was the drummer for João Gilberto in both *Chega de Saudade* and *Getz/Gilberto* albums. To cope with Gilberto's requests for gentle sounds, Banana had to delve into more advanced brushes technique.[18] Helcio Milito also became a master with brushes, developing a particular style in which his left hand played sixteenth notes sweeping the drumhead (with a light accent on the third note of each beat) and his right hand played those same sixteenth notes, but tapping and accenting phrases (another possibility for the right hand would be to play only the accents, especially at fast tempos).[19]

The 1960s were a prolific era for instrumental trios (piano, bass and drums). Examples include Tamba Trio, with Helcio Milito on drums; Bossa Três and Rio 65 Trio, both with Edison Machado; Copa Trio, with Dom Um Romão; Sambalanço Trio and Sambrasa Trio, both with Airto Moreira; and Zimbo Trio, with Rubens Barsotti; among many others.

There were also larger groups, such as the Copa 5 quintet, led by J.T. Meirelles and with Dom Um Romão and later Edison Machado on drums; and the Bossa Rio sextet, led by Sérgio Mendes and that had Edison Machado as well. These musicians pushed their artistic boundaries and were paramount in the development of Brazilian drumming on the drum kit. Those in Rio de Janeiro would gather at the Beco das Garrafas (Alley of the bottles) for jam sessions,[20] where instead of a featherweight style the drums were played hard.[21] With intense and substantial doses of jazz improvisation, the resulting music became known as samba jazz.

Samba jazz gave leeway to drummers to shine with their individual musical voices. With the samba no prato approach, they could phrase the left hand freely on the snare drum and toms accordingly to the soloist's ideas, in a similar concept to jazz drummers comping. Edison Machado was the main purveyor in the diffusion of this new conception, having reached it through sheer fortuity. According to Machado, he started playing this way, playing on the ride cymbal, when his drumhead broke during a show.[22] Machado's bass drum technique was described by drummer Tutty Moreno as 'velvety' even at very fast tempos.[23] Keeping the bumbo a dois solid, steady and effortless was fundamental to handling the syncopated rhythms that took place on the cross-stick and on the ride cymbal. In slow and medium tempos Machado usually played sixteenth notes with the right hand and a fixed pattern with the left (two eight notes on the first beat and the second sixteenth note of the second beat). In fast tempos, he abandoned the sixteenth notes and played both hands together with tamborim patterns, very syncopated and with irregular metrics.[24] Machado's artistry was best portrayed in his only recording as a band leader, entitled *É Samba Novo* (1963), with polyrhythmic perspectives, melodic lines on the toms, and intense interaction with improvisers.

Dom Um Romão was another influential drummer that emerged along with samba jazz. Romão often also employed samba no prato and bumbo a dois but with distinctive features on his left hand such as the *raspadeira* (scraper). That was the act of, before playing a cross-stick, quickly striking the rim of the high tom, resulting in a flam.[25] When playing the snare and toms, Romão would emulate typical patterns of Afro-Brazilian percussion instruments such as surdo, pandeiro, tamborim, *reco-reco*, *caixa*, *cuíca*, *repinique* and *chocalho*, looking not only for the rhythms but also for the sonic singularities of those instruments.[26] For instance, his recurrent use of the *telecoteco*[27] and other syncopated patterns on the cross-stick alluded to tamborim figures whilst his rimshots on the snare drum implied the sound of the repinique.[28]

Dom Um Romão's playing was fierce and energetic, but he had a delicate touch when the situation demanded, notable on his recording with Frank Sinatra and Antonio Carlos Jobim. The same could be observed in Edison Machado, who also had to restrain his dynamic gamut when he recorded the first Jobim solo album.[29] These musicians ventured into uncharted territory with samba jazz but absolutely knew how to navigate in the calm waters of bossa nova. They were the two jazzier players in Brazil at the time and had prowess and finesse to perform at any musical circumstance.[30]

Technical Characteristics

The 'Brazilian Feel'

In 1965 Dom Um Romão moved to the United States and three years later Airto Moreira did the same. Both musicians were, first and foremost, drum kit players but became successful musicians in the United States as percussionists.[31] Playing a rich spectrum of timbres with their instruments, Romão and Moreira were responsible for the spreading of the *berimbau* outside Brazil. Both drummers were sought after due to the varied musical palette represented by their approaches and because they added the 'Brazilian feel' to their groups, a special quality that can be identified with the idea of 'swing' in jazz. Though a difficult concept to pinpoint, the 'Brazilian feel' can be explained in technical terms and understood by careful listening to specialist drummers such as Moreira.

Asked what was the best music he had ever played, Moreira points to Quarteto Novo, a group that mixed rhythms from north eastern Brazil with jazz improvisation and that grew to be a major reference for future generations of Brazilian musicians.[32] The only record produced by this group dates from 1967 and in it, Moreira was already using different percussion instruments added to his drum kit, searching for 'colours' and 'textures' that later became his personal mark. Moreira also started emulating the sounds of the zabumba on the snare drum and of the triangle on the hi-hat, widening his vocabulary with new ideas. Unlike the other great Brazilian drummers of the sixties (Romão, Machado, Milito, Banana, etc.) that kept their playing within the samba terrain, Airto Moreira expanded his boundaries by pursuing new rhythms such as *frevo*, *coco*, *xaxado* and baiao.[33] Moreover, Moreira brought different time signatures into rhythms that were usually played in 2/4, including sambas in 7/8 and 3/4.[34]

During the 1970s, especially in solo recordings Airto Moreira was playing drum kit and percussion, sometimes one after the other, sometimes putting it all together through the use of overdubs. That combination had a strong influence on many players that were focusing mainly on the drum kit, such as Robertinho Silva (1941), Nenê (1947), and Tutty Moreno

(1947).[35] Improvements in recording technologies made possible for various layers of percussion to be stacked on top of each other, and as a result drum kit parts were simplified, to 'make room for other instruments'.[36] The same simplification was happening to drummers who were working heavily in studios in Brazil, such as Wilson das Neves. Instead of his sambas with bumbo a dois and lots of cross-stick syncopations, he recorded many songs with only hi-hat and bass drum on the second beat.[37] Das Neves is another name that embodies the Brazilian feel through the whole of his career, despite the fact that he moulded his playing in consonance to many different musical scenarios.[38] Whatever the genre, these musicians always employed a considerable dose of *ginga*, the Portuguese word that corresponds to swing.

Music notation has its limitations to accurately capture the ginga of Brazilian rhythms. As Wilson das Neves has explained, 'you can't write down the swing of a person'.[39] Understanding ginga with a physics lexicon, there are rhythmic fluctuations in a flexible net, in which the elasticity makes possible the existence of some basic structures, but not in metronomic perfection.[40] Considering the question musically, one way to look at it is to ask: how successful is this drum kit player in the reproduction of various percussion instruments, including basic rhythmic structures and transitional sounds?[41] Part of the challenge in answering that question stems from the interpretation of sixteenth notes, the 'elementary pulse' for samba[42] and for other Brazilian rhythms as well.

The 'elementary pulse' is played with irregular spacing between the sixteenth notes as they do not each get twenty-five per cent of the beat. There are continuous variations in the distribution of these notes from measure to measure so any attempt to register 'a definite notation for samba' is likely to be ineffective.[43] The nuances in dynamics also are hardly captured by music notation. Analyses of snare drum samba patterns have shown four levels in the accents played, with consecutive fluctuations in their disposition.[44] Disparately, drum technique books usually display samba as an oversimplified pattern of four sixteenth notes, with accents on the first and on the fourth.

Facing all these subtleties in dynamics and note placement, it becomes evident that simply playing a samba pattern 'as written' is not enough to perform it authentically. Research on micro-rhythms has confirmed this discrepancy demonstrating that notation is a 'virtual reference structure' while the 'actual sounding event' often results from deviations from that presumed form.[45] Hence samba comes alive from musicians' use of expressive micro-timing, in the same manner that swing occurs in jazz.[46] Just like jazz ride patterns rarely align perfectly on the beat, whether the 'beat' is provided by a metronome click or another instrument, samba drummers are *playing* with the beat, rather than playing *with* the beat.[47]

A dichotomy arises for drum kit players when working on stick technique and Brazilian rhythms. Traditionally, technique is developed through the study of rudiments, but that results in a paradoxical situation: when practicing rudiments there is a goal of perfect balance between hands in regards to sound qualities, dynamics and note placement. When playing Brazilian rhythms on the drum kit, however, hands often have to sound different for an authentic feel and note placement occurs within the above-mentioned flexible net and its fluctuations. As a consequence, when performing Brazilian rhythms one must 'forget' some of the equilibrium that was emphatically aimed for during technique practice. For those who have practiced rudiments for a long time and are first playing Brazilian drum kit rhythms, it might be difficult to abandon the rigidity and give in to elasticity in note placement. On the other side, those who were raised amidst Brazilian culture possibly have learned those rhythms aurally and might know their sounds, but then to evolve as a drum kit player there is a need to work on rudiments for the development of muscle memory and stick control.

Modern Brazilian Drumming

Those distinctive sixteenth notes fluctuations prompt a difficult task when playing samba no prato in fast tempos. There are alternatives of using broken patterns with hands in unison or in combinations of phrases, but many Brazilian drummers have risen to the challenge of playing the non-stop flow of sixteenth notes. That approach is inevitably burdensome and special techniques have been developed to cope with that demand in tempos over 130 bpm.[48] For instance, renowned drummer Kiko Freitas plays sixteenth notes using what he denominates *ação e reação* (action and reaction), derived from the Moeller technique.[49] This enables him to emulate the sound of the repinique, which is traditionally played with a stick in one hand (playing the first three notes of each beat) while the other hand plays directly into the drum (the fourth note), but using only his right hand to ride his samba rhythms.[50]

As part of a long lineage of players, Freitas is a symbol of modern Brazilian drumming. Between Freitas and Luciano Perrone, many others have carried on the traditions and taken them to new heights. Newer generations are in constant exposure to modern drumming concepts through communication technologies and the diffusion of hybrid styles, from influential musicians that have flourished since the 1970s. Examples are plentiful. Marcio Bahia came with a progressive rock background, and after jazz studies and classical percussion training, spent more than thirty years of intense work with Hermeto Pascoal, exploring an ample spectrum of Brazilian music. Bahia played rhythms such as *choro*, maxixe, samba, baião, xote, xaxado, frevo, and maracatu in odd times, orchestrated around the drum kit with great dexterity and four-way coordination.[51] Because of the pluralism in experiences prior to joining Hermeto's group, Bahia was able to adapt to multiple situations, sometimes improvising freely in complex structures and other times reading note per note dense and intricate written arrangements.

Before Marcio Bahia, two other prominent drummers had played with Hermeto Pascoal: Zé Eduardo Nazário and Nenê. Nazário acknowledges Edison Machado and Dom Um Romão as his foundations and understands that his generation took their work a step further.[52] Realcino Lima Filho, best known as Nenê, replaced Airto Moreira in Quarteto Novo when Moreira left for the United States. Both Nazário and Nenê had the right skills and musical tools to embark on Hermeto's artistic journey during the 1970s, just like they both did for multi-instrumentalist Egberto Gismonti in later years. Along with Paulo Braga, Pascoal Meirelles, Duduka da Fonseca and many others, these musicians shaped Brazilian drum kit drumming to modern times, building ideas that younger musicians are now fusing with past approaches, current techniques and twenty-first century drum sounds.

Conclusion

The influence of Brazilian drum kit drumming on global popular music has been immense and cannot be underestimated. It has been especially evident in the popularity of samba and bossa nova, as genres popular in their own right, but even more so in the influence of those genres on contemporary drumming in jazz and popular music throughout the world. Therefore, Brazilian drum kit drumming has been essential in the cultural flows that informed the development of the drum kit. As much as Brazilian musicians look for references within jazz and rock, the rhythms that emerged from Brazil are nowadays deemed to be a core part of the skillset for jazz drummers and players of other genres.

The fine details of what makes Brazilian drum kit drumming unique and special are yet to be explored thoroughly. Definitely the concept of ginga is a distinguishing element, in which musicians play around the rhythmic fluctuations and characteristics of the music. The verb *gingar* is also related to body movement and is used to describe the motions in capoeira, another cultural manifestation that vividly represents the essence of Brazilian people. In other words, gingar intrinsically means the expression of being Brazilian both musically and in the way dancers move. That idea resonates with 'the fact that different microrhythmic designs appeal to (and signify differently for) different audiences'.[53] Even though any rhythm may be deconstructed and mathematically analysed, that remains an ineffable and ethereal trait of all the drummers mentioned in this chapter.

Besides this intangible quality of ginga, Brazilian drum kit drumming comes from adaptations of percussion instruments, opening singular pathways for musical creativity. Drummers might emulate the sound of a pandeiro on the hi-hat and then make the snare drum have earmarks of a repinique; they might use the floor tom like a zabumba or bring tamborim patterns into life on the ride cymbal bell. They also often weave colours from assorted rhythms of the Brazilian plate, forging new combinations of ideas. Thus the 'Brazilian feel' keeps evolving, well grounded in its roots but open for innovation, establishing a fertile field for new music and for scientific investigation.

Notes

1 L. Barsalini. 'As sínteses de Edison Machado: um estudo sobre o desenvolvimento de padrões de samba na bateria', unpublished master's dissertation, University of Campinas (2009); G. Dias. 'Airto Moreira: do samba jazz à música dos anos 70 (1964–1975)', unpublished master's dissertation, University of Campinas (2014); G. Favery. 'O idiomatismo musical de Dom Um Romão: um dos alicerces da linguagem do samba jazz na bateria', unpublished master's dissertation, University of Campinas (2018); F. Bergamini. 'Marcio Bahia e a Escolar do Jabour', unpublished master's dissertation, University of Campinas (2014); L. Sanitá. 'A trajetória musical do baterista Wilson das Neves', unpublished master's dissertation, University of Campinas (2018); L. Casacio. 'Hélcio Milito: levantamento histórico e estudo interpretativo', unpublished master's dissertation, University of Campinas (2012); T. Aquino. 'Luciano Perrone: batucada, identidade, mediação', unpublished doctoral thesis, University of São Paulo (2014) and A. Damasceno. 'A batucada fantástica de Luciano Perrone: sua performance musical no contexto dos arranjos de Radamés Gnattali', unpublished master's dissertation, University of Campinas (2016).

2 Other drummers that could be pointed are Carlos Blassifera, Babi Miranda, Jorge Aires, Faísca, Plínio Araújo and Juquinha, among many others.

3 The term has been used in O. Bolão. *Batuque é um privilégio. A percussão na música do Rio de Janeiro* (Lumiar Editora, 2003), p. 135 and U. Moreira. *A história da bateria. Da idade da pedra ao século XXI* (Self-publication, 2005), p. 100.

4 The term 'solo' here does not mean a long stream of musical ideas on the drum kit, but fills of two measures played only with drums on Faceira, composed by Ary Barroso and recorded in 1931. In Aquino, 'Luciano Perrone', p. 48, the importance of that recording is compared to the impact caused by Gene Krupa with 'Sing, Sing, Sing' in 1935.

5 L.Barsalini.'Modos de execução da bateria no samba', unpublished doctoral thesis, University of Campinas (2014), p. 73.

6 Aquino, 'Luciano Perrone', p. 38.

7 Aquino, 'Luciano Perrone', p. 134. Luciano Perrone's legacy is represented by his two solo records, *Batucada Fantástica* (1963) and *Batucada Fantástica Vol. 3* (1972). Aquino underlines that each track of these records is didactically titled after a rhythm or percussion instrument, and thus they serve as 'business cards' to present Brazilian rhythms around the world.

8 Bolão, *Batuque é um privilégio*, p. 140.

9 Barsalini, 'Modos de execução', p. 51 and Damasceno, 'A batucada fantástica', p. 27.

10 Moreira, *A história da bateria*, p. 100.

11 Moreira, *A história da bateria*, p. 101.

12 Aquino, 'Luciano Perrone', p. 26.

13 Aquino, 'Luciano Perrone', p. 87.

14 J. R. Tinhorão. *Música Popular:Um tema em debate* (Editora 34, 1997), pp. 48–50. Tinhorão points out US cultural influences in Brazil since the 1920s. There was a period of strong influence subsequently to the First World War and then another right after the Second World War.
15 Edison Machado used to call this 'the new samba'. That became the title of his solo record, *É samba novo* (It's new samba).
16 That discussion appears in Moreira, *A história da bateria*, pp. 103–104; Barsalini, 'As sínteses', p. 175; and Favery, 'O idiomatismo musical', p. 149.
17 One common example was the brush playing sixteenth notes on the snare (either tapping the drumhead lightly or using the swishing motion) and the stick playing phrases on the rim (cross-stick).
18 R. Castro. *Chega de Saudade. A história e as histórias da bossa nova* (Companhia das Letras, 1990), p. 173. Castro mentions concerts when Milton Banana had to play so soft that he could barely be heard. João Gilberto was known for complaining of drummers that played 'too loud'.
19 Casacio, 'Hélcio Milito'.
20 That name made reference to the bottles thrown by residents of the buildings nearby on the nightclub's frequenters, because of the noise they made at late hours. Castro, *Chega de Saudade*, p. 285.
21 In Castro, *Chega de Saudade*, p. 287 there is a quotation of jazz columnist Robert Celerier, who called the music played at Beco das Garrafas 'hard Bossa Nova'. He also speculates that, if João Gilberto had heard some versions of his own compositions played there, he would be very upset with the heaviness on the drums. Castro states that Beco das Garrafas was to bossa nova players the equivalent of what Minton's Playhouse (jazz club in Harlem, New York) represented for be-bop in the early 1940s.
22 Barsalini, 'As sínteses', p. 84. In analysis of Machado's first recordings, Barsalini observed that he frequently played sixteenth notes on the snare drum first (samba batucado) and then started riding on the cymbal or hi-hat for sonic variations in different song sections or to highlight featured soloists.
23 Barsalini, 'As sínteses', p. 85.
24 Barsalini, 'As sínteses', pp. 98–101.
25 Drummer Pascoal Meirelles surmises that Romão developed his raspadeira technique listening to Art Blakey, jazz drummer who was very influential among Brazilians in the 1960s. In Favery, 'O idiomatismo musical', p. 110.
26 Favery, 'O idiomatismo musical', p. 152.
27 The telecoteco name is onomatopoeia of common tamborim patterns. The syllables te and le are played with a stick on the tamborim and the syllable co is played with the medium finger of the hand that holds the instrument, from underneath. Examples of the sequence are teco-teco-teco-teleco-teco-teco-teleco in Damasceno, 'A batucada fantástica', p. 56 and teco-teleco-teleco in Aquino, 'Luciano Perrone', p. 136.
28 Another example is the rhythmic figure of sixteenth note followed by eight note and sixteenth note, called by Mario de Andrade as 'the characteristic syncopation'. Favery, 'O idiomatismo musical', pp. 153 and 173–174.
29 Castro, *Chega de Saudade*, p. 416. Dom Um Romão recorded seven songs for the album Francis Albert Sinatra & Antonio Carlos Jobim in 1967. He had a pillow inside his bass drum and 'was playing as soft as Milton Banana used to play with João Gilberto'. Edison Machado recorded Jobim's *The Composer of Desafinado Plays* in 1963.
30 Ibid.
31 Romão played percussion with jazz fusion group Weather Report (replacing Airto Moreira) from 1972 to 1976 and performed with many rock, pop, and jazz artists including the band Blood, Sweat and Tears. Moreira also played percussion with an extensive list of significant musicians, including Weather Report, Miles Davis and Return to Forever, although with the latter he performed primarily on the drum kit.
32 Dias, 'Airto Moreira', p. 32.
33 Dias, 'Airto Moreira', pp. 88–102.
34 Dias, 'Airto Moreira', pp. 116 and 126. An example for 7/8 is Misturada, from the Quarteto Novo record, and for 3/4 is Return to Forever, from the record of same name.
35 Dias, 'Airto Moreira', pp. 163 and 171.
36 Dias, 'Airto Moreira', p. 168. Quotation from Moreira.
37 Sanitá, 'A jornada musical', p. 142.
38 Ibid. Wilson das Neves's recording career had elements from candomblé, bossa nova, traditional samba, samba jazz, funk and rock, among others.

39 H. Cunha, 'Linguagem e interpretação do samba: aspectos rítmicos, fraseológicos e interpretativos do samba carioca aplicados em estudos e peças de caixa clara', unpublished master's dissertation, University of Campinas (2014), p. 36.
40 T. Pinto, 'As cores do Som: Estruturas sonoras e concepção estética na música afro-brasileira', *África* 22–23 (2004), pp. 99–105.
41 In Cunha, 'Linguagem e interpretação', p. 32 that question is framed with the idea of transitional sounds as part of the samba texture. Those sounds are not as strong as the basic rhythms that all the instruments reinforce and they sometimes can be inaudible, but are key in the concept of ginga. Examples are the click sounds with the drumstick on the surdo rim, the platinelas (metal jingles) of the pandeiro, the hands that play rhythms directly on the shell of various drums, etc.
42 Pinto, 'As cores do Som', p. 92.
43 Pinto, 'As cores do Som', pp. 99–100. Pinto points to constant fluctuations between the rhythmic figure of sixteenth note followed by eighth note and sixteenth note, and triplets.
44 Cunha, 'Linguagem e interpretação', p. 68.
45 A. Danielsen. 'Introduction: Rhythm in the Age of Digital Reproduction' in A. Danielsen (ed.), *Musical Rhythm in the Age of Digital Reproduction* (Ashgate, 2010), p. 6.
46 M. Butterfiled. 'The Power of Anacrusis: Engendered Feeling in Groove-Based Musics', *Music Theory Online* 12:4 (2006).
47 J. A. Prögler. 'Searching for Swing: Participatory Discrepancies in the Jazz Rhythm Section', *Ethnomusicology* 39:1 (1995), pp. 21–54.
48 Barsalini, 'Modos de execução', p. 198 mentions Erivelton Silva, Celso de Almeida and Ramon Montagner as current references in that aspect.
49 V.C. Baschera. 'Ação e reação: a catalogação de uma nova técnica de mãos, suas vertentes e possibilidades', unpublished master's dissertation, Instituto Politécnico do Porto (2016), p. 30.
50 For two other examples, see A. Smith. 'O baterista. Contemporary Brazilian Drum-Set: Afro-Brazilian Roots & Current Trends in Contemporary Samba-Jazz Performance Practice', unpublished doctor's thesis, Indiana University (2014), p. 60. Edu Ribeiro mixes different techniques, including using his fingers only, controlled wrist strokes and side to side motions. Ramon Montagner employs a push-and-pull technique with which he gets two articulations per hand motion.
51 Bergamini, 'Marcio Bahia'.
52 T. Braga. 'A caixa clara na bateria: Estudo de caso de performances dos bateristas Zé Eduardo Nazário e Marcio Bahia', unpublished master's dissertation, Federal University of Minas Gerais (2011), p. 40.
53 Danielsen, 'Introduction', p. 9.

6 Drum Kit Performance in Contemporary Classical Music

BEN REIMER

Introduction

The drum kit, an instrument deeply rooted in popular music traditions, is a defining element of many popular music styles. Since the early twentieth century, generations of drummers have explored new musical and technical possibilities of the instrument and, recent years, the drum kit has emerged in contemporary classical music settings as a solo instrument with prescribed notation. In this chapter, contemporary classical music refers to music being written now, or in the past few decades by composers operating within the framework of Western classical music notational traditions. While there is a growing interest in this repertoire today, composers have drawn inspiration from the drum kit since the early developmental stages of the instrument in the early twentieth century. I will present an overview of composed works starting with Darius Milhuad's *La Créations du Monde* from 1923 and ending with Nicole Lizée's *Ringer* from 2009. I will show that early approaches to drum kit composition began as an assimilation of existing popular music styles with little progression in performance techniques and expression for the instrument. In recent years, many composers have approached drum kit composition by balancing contemporary classical music techniques with the drum kit's rich traditions, grooves, and styles to make something progressive and new. Through my own commissioning, performances, and research I have contemplated the elements that led to this confluence in contemporary classical drum kit music.

Personal Background

In 1988, I began taking drum kit lessons in my hometown of Winnipeg, Manitoba, Canada. Thanks to the exceptional drum instruction of my teacher David Schneider, I embraced a wide range of styles and playing traditions. I went on to play in a variety of bands ranging from punk, progressive rock, and reggae styles. After highschool I decided to pursue a music degree, but I chose to focus on orchestral and concert percussion instead of drum kit. I received a Bachelor of Music degree from McGill University in Montréal and a Master of Music degree from the State University of New York in Stony Brook, both in contemporary classical percussion performance. No longer receiving drum kit instruction, and with little time for playing in bands, I was quickly distinguishing myself as a classical percussionist rather than a drummer.

After my Master's degree, I returned to Manitoba where I began teaching percussion at Brandon University and playing regularly with the Winnipeg Symphony Orchestra. Around this time, I began to consider if the drum kit could have a greater role in my life of contemporary classical performance. I knew of a few composed works for drum kit such as Frank Zappa's 'The Black Page' and Louis Cauberghs's 'Halasana', and I wanted to expand on what I saw as a limited amount of repertoire. In 2006, I sought out and was successfully awarded my first commission of the solo *Train Set* by composer Eliot Britton.

In 2007, I met composer Nicole Lizée while performing her chamber work *This Will Not Be Televised* with members of the Winnipeg Symphony Orchestra. Pleased with my performance, Lizée invited me to play drum kit for various works on her debut album *This Will Not Be Televised,* released by Centrediscs in 2008. That same year, with the support of the Canada Council for the Arts, I commissioned Lizée's first solo for drum kit, *Ringer.* Encouraged by these new experiences, in 2010 I returned to McGill University in Montréal to complete a Doctor in Music degree where I wrote my dissertation 'Defining the Role of Drumset Performance in Contemporary Music'. As of today, through collaborations with composers from around the world I have premiered an extensive collection of contemporary classical drum kit solos, chamber works and concertos. My solo drum kit album *Katana of Choice – Music for Drumset Soloist* was called 'a modern classic' by I Care If You Listen and the title track by Nicole Lizée was nominated for a JUNO (Canadian music award) for best classical composition in 2019. When I consider my broad range of musical training and performance experience it seems natural that I am drawn to an artistic practice that crosses between genres. I draw from this personal experience to articulate broader points about the place of the drum kit in the classical world and the unique skill sets required when approaching the drum kit in contemporary classical music.

Drummer or Multiple Percussionist?

In contemporary classical music practice, the term 'multiple percussion' is associated with a body of repertoire for the solo percussionist, which incorporates several instruments played by a single performer. As drum kit repertoire appears increasingly alongside works for multiple percussion, there is a tendency to place such performers and repertoire in the same categories. Drummer Max Roach was said to have brought 'dignity to an instrument long misunderstood and assaulted by the ignorant' and set a precedent by referring to himself as a multiple percussionist in album liner notes.[1] At the time, this reflected his elevation of drum kit performance and the desire to be considered equal to the other instrumentalists.

As solo drum kit repertoire in contemporary classical music has increased, the discussion of its inclusion in college percussion pedagogy has led some authors to still justify its existence and continue the comparison to multiple percussion. The 2012 dissertation by Kevin Nichols called 'Important Works for Drum Set as a Multiple Percussion Instrument' provided an introduction and unique performance perspective to composed drum kit solos such as *The Sky is Waiting . . .* (1977) by Robert Cucinotta, *One for Solo Drummer* (1990) by John Cage, *Brush* (2001) by Stuart Saunders Smith and others. He noted the lack of studies or method books which 'investigate the literature for drum set as a multi-percussion instrument' and expressed his 'desire to encourage solo drum set performance and composition by making this music and these concepts more widely known and understood'.[2] Murray Houllif's 'Benefits of Written-Out Drum Set Solos' encouraged solo repertoire for students as 'an effective means to learning improvisation'.[3] In 'Drum Set's Struggle for Legitimacy', Dennis Rogers argued that written recital pieces can demonstrate that the 'drum set is a legitimate instrument that is quite acceptable in the percussion curriculum'.[4]

In this chapter, I use the term drum kit without association to multiple percussion. I do so to distinguish the drum kit as an instrument worthy of its own legitimate considerations, apart from earlier efforts to elevate the instrument's status. The label of multiple percussion places an unwanted shadow over the popular music styles and the associated players, techniques, and instruments that are the foundation of the instrument.

What, then, clearly distinguishes drum kit from other contemporary or multiple percussion performance? The *Encyclopedia of Percussion* says that the drum kit is 'a set of drums, usually bass drum, snare drum, tom-toms, hi-hat, and cymbals'.[5] James Blades describes drum kit performance as 'the advancement of counter rhythms and independence'.[6] Jazz drummer Kenny Clarke described his use of multiple limbs as 'coordinated independence'.[7] Combining these ideas, I suggest that the definition of drum kit performance is: the use of coordinated independence of multiple limbs on a collection of drums and cymbals, including but not limited to, bass drum with pedal, snare drum and hi-hat, set up for convenient playing by one person.

Early Drum Kit Composition Via Jazz Assimilation

La Création du Monde (1923) by Darius Milhaud

The earliest approach to drum kit composition appeared in Darius Milhaud's ballet, *La Création du Monde,* premiered on 19 October 1923. Like many European composers of the time, Milhaud assimilated the sounds, instruments, and performance practices of the exciting new popular music style from the United States called jazz. Milhaud drew inspiration from the words of the artist Jean Cocteau. In his manifesto, *Le Coq et l'Arlequin* (1918), Cocteau called for a new sound in French music, dismissing the more 'Russian-inspired impressionism' of past composers such as Claude Debussy.[8] 'Enough of clouds, waves, aquariums, waterspirits, and nocturnal scents; what we need is a music of the earth, every-day music'.[9] Cocteau encouraged composers to draw inspiration from the new sounds of jazz, bringing together the 'low-art' of the cafés and dance halls and exoticism of African culture into a new French modernist approach.

Author Bernard Gendron described Milhaud as a 'modernist flâneur' who was 'more akin to the tourist, the slummer, and the fashion plate, than to the ethnomusicologist', and Milhaud's 'adventures in curiosity and assimilation' resulted in a very limited reflection and understanding of jazz and along with this, the drum kit.[10]

The limited understanding of jazz music assumed the term to include a variety of styles and techniques including blues, ragtime, the Original Dixieland Jazz Band's popular take on ragtime known as Dixieland, Tin Pan Alley songs from New York City and, generally, any music played by dance bands at the time. The drum kit was at the centre of this style.

Despite the confusion during these early days, there was at least one common musical meaning when people in France invoked the term *jazz*: it meant rhythm and the instruments used to make it. Above all, the drums – *la batterie* – were not only the most prominent instrument but their mere presence, many believed, made any band into a jazz band.[11]

Milhaud toured through the United States in 1922 where he searched for what he called the 'authentic' elements of jazz.[12] Immediately upon returning to Paris, Milhaud began to work on the music for the ballet, *La Création du Monde* for seventeen instrumentalists including drum kit. The drum kit included snare drum, bass drum with foot pedal, woodblock and cowbell. The '*grosse caisse à pied, avec cymbale*', meaning 'kick drum with cymbal' referred to the 'clanger', a predecessor of the hi-hat.[13] Milhaud indicated in the music when to activate or deactivate the clanger against the mounted cymbal.[14] Ragtime rhythms common in the twenties were imbedded in the music with written out triplet figures, and instructions for rim shots and other jazz idioms were found throughout.

To appreciate how Milhaud assimilated the style, I recommend listening to Baby Dodds's 1946 recording on Folkways Records for reference of period ragtime performance. Having remained committed to the drum kit instrumentation of the twenties (Dodds never took up the hi-hat, for example) the recorded solo *Spooky Drums* in particular is a window into early drumming and gives an authentic reference to ragtime rhythms and their placement around the drum kit.

Milhaud was not the only composer to assimilate jazz and, as a result, drum kit elements into the contemporary classical setting. Here is a brief list of other works that followed: George Gershwin, *Rhapsody in Blue* (originally for the Paul Whiteman Jazz Orchestra, 1924); Mátyás Seiber, *Jazzolettes* (1928); Igor Stravinsky, *Preludium for Jazz Band* (1936 / 37); William Walton, *Façade*, Second Suite (1938); Gunther Schuller, *Studies on Themes by Paul Klee* (1959); and Leonard Bernstein, *Symphonic Dances from West Side Story* (1960). While these composers included popular elements of early jazz and, along with it, the drum kit into a contemporary classical work of the 1920s, the music often suffered the fate of the limited understanding of the style. Milhaud himself bemused that 'the critics decreed my music was frivolous and more suitable for a restaurant'.[15] With works such as *La Création du Monde* we were given an early glimpse of a search for legitimacy of jazz in a classical setting and a hope that the new 'everyday music' would provide inspiration and new approaches to composition. It is a familiar theme when exploring the history of compositions for the drum kit and one we know still exists in recent discussions about percussion pedagogy. Jazz did not benefit from being placed in the concert hall, just as the drum kit did not need to be called multiple percussion.

Drum Kit Composition as Homage

Bonham (1989) by Christopher Rouse

Written for drum kit and percussion ensemble, *Bonham* by American composer Christopher Rouse was 'an ode to rock drumming and drummers, most particularly Led Zeppelin's legendary drummer, the late John ("Bonzo") Bonham'.[16] The work was for eight players: one drum kit and seven other percussionists. It was premiered in 1989 by the Conservatory Percussion Ensemble, conducted by Frank Epstein, at the New England Conservatory of Music in Boston.

In *Bonham,* the drum kit opened, and continued throughout much of the piece with an ostinato (repeating pattern) that quoted the iconic John Bonham groove from the song 'When the Levee Breaks' from *Led Zeppelin*

IV (1971). The 'Levee' groove had been highly sampled by other popular artists such as Bjork, The Beastie Boys, Depeche Mode, Dr Dre, Coldcut, and Eminem. In *Bonham,* fragments of other Led Zeppelin songs such as 'Custard Pie', 'Royal Orleans', and 'Bonzo's Montreaux' appeared in aspects of the drum kit music as well as throughout the entire ensemble, but it is the 'Levee' groove that defined the piece.

In the case of *Bonham,* the performer had to become familiar with the elements that made John Bonham's sound iconic. Rouse recommended in the score that the drummer 'use the fattest possible sticks to reproduce as closely as possible throughout the entire work the beginning of "When the Levee Breaks", recorded by Led Zeppelin'.[17] This referenced the legendary drummer's reputation for being a powerful, dynamic player – so powerful, in fact, that he is often credited for being an early influence on the heavy metal drumming that would follow him. Jon Bream in *Whole Lotta Led Zeppelin* said, 'no drummer ever created such a monstrous sound, and in Bonham's force field of rhythm there ranks the basis of the sound now called heavy metal'.[18]

The drum kit performer should have not only adhered to Rouse's suggestion of heavy sticks, but must have looked further into the characteristics of John Bonham that resulted in such a powerful sound. For example, Bonham played on large size drums associated mostly with his Ludwig Amber Vistalite set made from acrylic which was being commercially produced as 'Plexiglas' in the seventies. Another contribution to Bonham's unique sound was the experimental recording techniques used by engineer Andy Johns and the band. While some variations on specifics exist, the basic concept was that the drums were placed at the bottom of a staircase, with microphones placed above, one or two floors up. This was 'distant from the Beatlesque, cloth-covered drumhead sound that was de rigueur at the time', which produced more clarity and articulation.[19] Instead, the drums were given room to resonate while the microphones captured the natural power of John Bonham's performance style.

The John Bonham sound on 'When the Levee Breaks' was a combination of the drummer's distinct power and feel combined with his choice of instrument and the groundbreaking recording techniques that captured it all. Christopher Rouse's suggestion for the 'fattest possible sticks' could not alone reproduce this complex sound. The drummer approaching *Bonham* should rather be educated in the important elements described above that formed the Bonham sound and draw from as many influences as possible to even come close.

The popularity and success of Rouse's work, *Bonham,* was rooted in the adoration and idolization of a drumming icon that is common among generations of musicians. Placing Bonham grooves within the classical percussion ensemble context was an homage to this drummer and the music of Led Zeppelin. This type of composition remains popular within the classical percussion ensemble community because it allows players to explore drummers and styles that often have been separated from the typical focus in Western classical music. Similar approaches for drum kit and percussion ensemble include John Beck's *Concerto for Drum kit and Percussion Ensemble* (1979), written for 'Tonight Show' drummer Ed Shaughnessy, and Larry Neeck's *Concerto for Drum kit and Concert Band* (2005) featuring a rock groove in the style of Sandy Nelson, a jazz-waltz influenced by Joe Morello and a Gene Krupa, up-tempo swing.[20]

While recorded history has endless examples of drum solos, the drum kit as concerto soloist was indeed a new role found in the above works. What kept these works tied to their predecessors such as Milhaud is that the music was still copying styles and therefore not exploring new performance practices of the drum kit. The only thing new for drum kit was the performance context itself. We still ran the risk of displaying the traits that Gendron described in Milhaud's case as 'his excessively formalistic approach ... his underestimation of performance at the expense of composition ... his simplistic schemes of classification, and his virtual ignorance of the cultural and social context'.[21] In the case of *Bonham,* the limitation was in the impossibility of recreating the drumming style of John Bonham. By placing such a reproduction of an iconic groove into the formula of contemporary percussion ensemble composition we have missed the true significance and brilliance of the original performance of John Bonham with Led Zeppelin and run the risk of sounding like a gimmick or simplifying the greatness of this performance.

As I have stated before, it is the drum kit's roots in popular music and its rich traditions, iconic players, grooves, and styles that remain tied to the instrument at all times. It is what the previous composers were counting on as they quoted jazz or rock tradition. It took an artist equally versed in rock and contemporary classical music to create the first drum kit solo that seemed to be progressive rather than repeating the past.

Genre Cross-Over in Drum Kit Composition

The Black Page (1976) by Frank Zappa

The legendary rock bandleader Frank Zappa was able to cross over to contemporary classical traditions by writing chamber works for Ensemble Intercontemporain and conductor Pierre Boulez, among others and was said to 'somehow manage to work with these many, many influences ... for many composers this would be a really big danger, to get lost in all those things you could do . . . but he's really original at using all these influences'.[22] Zappa did not approach writing with regards to labels and class and he 'refused to rank his own works or engage in debates regarding the difference between "popular" and "serious" music. It was all one to him'.[23]

Written for drummer Terry Bozzio, *The Black Page* was an ambitious solo expressing the melodic potential of the drum kit featuring an excessive use of nested polyrhythms and complex patterns demanding unusual crossing of limbs and rapid movement around the drum kit. The typical function of the bass drum foot changed. No longer the timekeeper and foundation, the bass drum was equally involved with the hands in the thematic and melodic material. While not indicated in the score, Bozzio added a constant quarter note pulse with the hi-hat foot in the original recording, a feature adopted by all future performances, and one that has remained standard practice today.[24] This simple addition created a stable, familiar framework for the rhythmic complexity. Even with these complexities the solo still had an accessibility through an overall sense of groove that never strayed too far from the familiar. The performer and listener can hear a connection to the iconic drum solos of the past such as Gene Krupa's solo in 'Sing Sing Sing', Max Roach's 'The Drum Also Waltzes' or John Bonham's many live solos with Led Zeppelin.

Because of the notational complexity and technical challenges mixed with rock sensibilities, *The Black Page* was a true crossover work and demonstrated a confluence between musical influences and new potential for drum kit composition. Just as important, the solo encouraged a new level of performer equally comfortable in contemporary classical music notation and rock-based drumming. Terry Bozzio described his progression since working with Frank Zappa and *The Black Page*:

> Apply theory, harmony, and melody orchestration . . . to the modern drum kit, because it has evolved to the point where we can do those things. I see no difference between an organist who plays lines with his feet and four different voices with his two hands and the contrapuntal possibilities that are extant on the modern drum set.[25]

Complexity in Drum Kit Composition

Ti.re-Ti.ke-Dha (1979) by James Dillon

James Dillon was born in Glasgow, Scotland in 1950, and spent considerable time living in London. As a teenager in the sixties, he was drawn to rock and played in a rhythm and blues band called Influx.[26] Dillon eventually pursued post-modern composition, but he did so on his own terms, receiving formal education at a university level for only two years before leaving disillusioned. Even so, by the mid-seventies Dillon was considered a part of the New Complexity school of composition and his music was described as 'close to if not beyond the limits of performability, justified by reference to the fearsome intellectual discourse which is said to lie behind those torrents of notes'.[27] While this style of composition often held a reputation of being elitist or overtly formalist, Dillon said that composing in the seventies was a time 'to claw my way back to where music still has meaning and not present some kind of second-hand experience'.[28]

In 1979, Dillon wrote *Ti.re-Ti.ke-Dha* in celebration of the 'International Year of the Child'.[29] It was premiered by percussionist Simon Limbrick in South Bank, London, 1982.[30] The complete list of instruments in *Ti.re-Ti.ke-Dha* extended beyond the common drum kit to form a massive setup with additional suspended cymbals (one screwed tightly and struck only at the dome), cowbells, hi-hat (with a collection of sleigh-bells attached to top), log drums, snare drum, three timbales, five tom-toms, bass drum with pedal, tam-tam and a bellstick (Figure 6.1). Balancing efficiency and playability with the unusual instrumentation and complex polyrhythmic material resulted in one of the most challenging works in contemporary drum kit repertoire. How each individual interpreted and solved these challenges is part of what made a performance

Figure 6.1 Recommended *Ti.re-Ti.ke-Dha* setup with bongos, conga and purpleheart. Image created by the author.

unique. To illustrate, the following section presents two examples of setup challenges and recommended solutions.

The timbales had a far greater involvement in the music than the traditional tom-toms (which only enter at measure 82). Dillon's recommended layout in the score recognized that they needed to be easily reached, placing them directly in front of the player with the tom-toms to the right. The timbales' size and inability to be mounted on traditional drum kit hardware posed logistical issues. Also, the timbales had similar timbres to the tom-toms causing some difficulty in making a distinction between the two voices. As shown in Figure 6.1, replacing the timbales with a set of bongos and a travel conga offered a bright, short attack, distinct from the thunderous, resonant tom-toms. Not only sonically effective, they were compact and fit efficiently onto the drum kit.

Dillon also specified two log drums, each producing a single pitch. Generally placed on a flat surface, such as a trap table, the log drums did not attach to any type of hardware. Balance was also a problem since the log drum characteristically featured a 'warm sonority with limited carrying power'.[31] Since Dillon specified the use of snare drumsticks throughout the piece the sound produced from attacking the log drum was lacking in tone and volume. Shown in Figure 6.1, the solution was to attach a piece of 'purpleheart' wood onto, and extending beyond, each log drum to allow for a resonant attack area and mount each on a snare drum stand. A thoughtfully chosen setup improved efficiency of motion around the drum kit and clarified some of the dense layers of complexity which Dillon placed into his work.

Dillon employed three common hi-hat practices: loud foot attacks that splashed the cymbals together, dryer foot closing 'chick' sounds and playing the hi-hat with sticks. Traditionally used as a time keeping device or for accentuating the pulse, Dillon extended these techniques to be part of the upper layers of thematic material and linear movement (Figure 6.2). The constant execution of these complex foot techniques combined with polyrhythms was an exercise in multiple limb independence, polyrhythmic proficiency and physical balance. A drummer relies on a basic balance when performing and as Grammy-award winning drummer Paul Wertico stated, 'it's usually easier to feel balanced when playing simpler exercises. Grooves that require complex counterlines and polyrhythms can sometimes make you feel as if you're going to fall over'.[32]

While large drum kits, foot variations and polyrhythmic playing were all common tools of the modern drummer, James Dillon put these elements to the extreme in *Ti.re-Ti.ke-Dha*. Challenges with the setup, notational complexity and even basic balance demanded a unique combination of performance skill, much like *The Black Page* did a few years prior. Also

Figure 6.2 Foot techniques: closed HH with foot (✻); open HH with foot (𝒫𝑒𝑑.); HH struck with stick (**Λ**); repeating bass drum pulse, mm. 1 and 2. James Dillon: *Ti.re-Ti.ke-Dha*. Edition Peters No.7242 © 1982 by Peters Edition Limited, London.
Reproduced by kind permission of the publishers. J. Dillon. *Ti.Re-Ti.Ke-Dha*, 2nd ed. (London: Hinrichsen Edition, Peters Edition Ltd., 1979, 1982)

similar is Dillon's ability to combine New-Complexity style notation (more common with contemporary percussion performance practice than drum kit) with advanced drum kit techniques and fundamentals.

Recontextualization in Drum Kit Composition

Ringer (2009) by Nicole Lizée

Canadian composer Nicole Lizée has been commissioned by a wide range of artists such as Kronos Quartet, So Percussion, and BBC Proms. Her music has often involved unorthodox instruments such as the Atari 2600 video game console, omnichords, stylophone, and karaoke tapes. Lizée's music has shown her pervasive interest in the drum kit and its connection to time, groove, popular music styles, and iconic performers. In her works for drum kit, she has expanded upon traditional performance practices through what she called recontextualization:

> Referring to the past (or other contexts) but twisting, manipulating to create something new, vital, and meaningful to me (and to the 'now'), without losing trace of its origins, place in history, functions, etc. but reinterpreting, filtering and distorting all of these – and placing it in a new context.[33]

I commissioned and premiered the drum kit solo *Ringer* by Nicole Lizée in 2009. It was recorded for my album *Katana of Choice – Music for Drumset Soloist* in 2017 and has been performed by other contemporary

Figure 6.3 Drum kit setup for *Ringer*. Image created by the author.

drum kit players around the world. Lizée referred to iconic drum kit grooves (such as John Bonham's in 'When the Levee Breaks') as 'classic drumset paradigms'.[34] The solo *Ringer* for drum kit was a recontextualization of such paradigms in which 'the end result is intended to be at once familiar and alien'.[35] This involved the emulations of drum machines and samplers behaving erratically, fragments of classic grooves characteristic of electronica and dance music warped and iconic drummer Steve Gadd's paradiddle grooves reimagined as rhythmic and melodic themes.

The drum kit in *Ringer* included kick drum with double pedals, hi-hat and remote hi-hat with pedal (placed to the right of the main kick drum pedal), snare drum, cabasa, cymbals (ride, splash and sizzle) and glockenspiel (Figure 6.3). The arrangement came from personal discussions with Lizée while trying samples of the material during the composers writing of the work and during preparation of the premiere.

The glockenspiel was placed where the snare drum typically is on a drum kit. By doing so 'the glockenspiel overtakes or replaces . . . the snare. In place of what would usually be pitchless accents and articulations, melodic fragments are formed'.[36] This was most obvious in the section constructed around drummer Steve Gadd's paradiddle grooves. Since the seventies, Steve Gadd has been considered one of the greatest drummers of all time, and he has changed how players approach the drum kit and even how the instrument was made. Endorsed by Yamaha since 1976, Gadd's Yamaha Recording Custom drum kit defined the drum sound of the eighties.[37] Gadd also established a signature groove commonly referred to as the 'Gadd Paradiddle' based around the sticking of the paradiddle rudiment (R-L-R-R, L-R-L-L) and its multiple variations. In *Ringer*, the

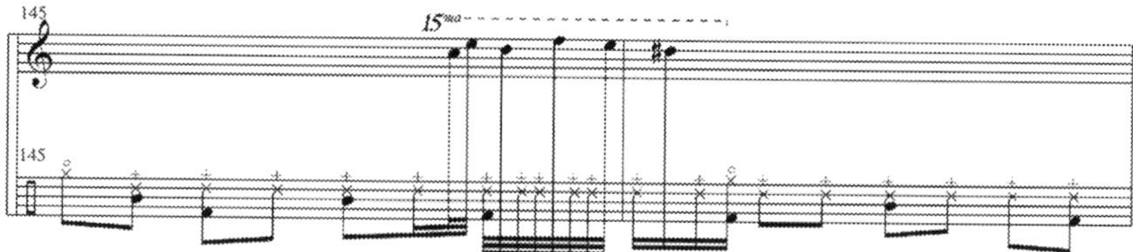

Example 6.1 The Steve Gadd paradiddle in *Ringer*, m. 145–46.
Image made available by Nicole Lizée

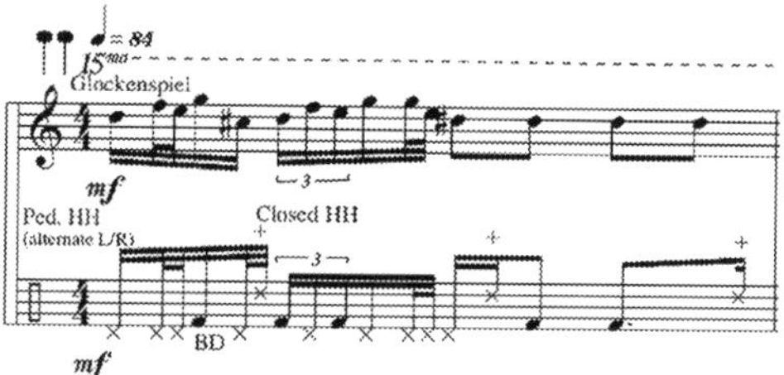

Example 6.2 Unison feet and hands in *Ringer*, m. 1. Image made available by Nicole Lizée.

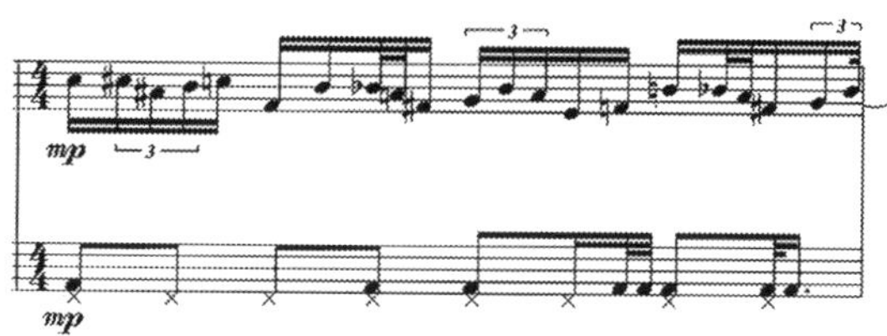

Example 6.3 Independent feet and hands in *Ringer*, m. 202.
Image made available by Nicole Lizée.

Gadd Paradiddle was morphed and extended around the drum kit, most notably the glockenspiel. *Ringer* required advanced double bass pedal technique and double hi-hat pedal technique in rhythmic unison with hands (Example 6.2) or completely independent (Example 6.3). Example 6.1 shows 'melodic fragments' that were formed on the glockenspiel in replace of snare drum.

Just as James Dillon merged contemporary percussion complexity with drum kit techniques, in *Ringer* Nicole Lizée showed a confluence between various influences, or a 'fusing of roles' where 'groove and melody synthesize and become one'.[38] The inclusion of advanced melodic and rhythmic patterns on the glockenspiel emphasized the performance traditions of a classical percussionist. Typically, such player would have the most experience navigating this instrument since it has appeared most commonly in symphony orchestra repertoire and contemporary classical ensemble settings. Fused into the framework of the drum kit, the performer must be equally experienced in advanced foot techniques and other common drum kit techniques. The presence of rock icon paradigms such as Steve Gadd's paradiddle required a deep appreciation and understanding of where the material came from and how it was originally played. Then when recontextualized into the new setting for which *Ringer* presents, the performance still has feeling and groove.

Conclusion

By studying this broad range of works together, I see consistent elements that are required when approaching the drum kit in contemporary classical composition. These are original thought, meaningfulness, and the knowledge of history. Of course, placing the drum kit in the context of the concert hall or within a string orchestra is an exciting premise, but without meaningfully connecting purpose with concepts that move drum kit performance to new places musically, technically, and artistically, the result, as discovered by Milhaud, will be 'frivolous'.

Today, the drum kit has become a more common addition to ensembles such as Bang On A Can, So Percussion, Alarm Will Sound, my own quartet Architek Percussion, and many others who are performing and commissioning works which blur the boundaries between popular and contemporary classical music. Composers of the past few decades have had a greater opportunity through publications, recordings, online tutorials, and performance footage to learn about the rich history of the drum kit. Since I premiered *Ringer* in 2009, I have collaborated with a multitude of composers interested in writing for the drum kit. These collaborations have resulted in drum kit performances and recordings by such composers as Lukas Ligeti, John Psathas, Vincent Ho, Rand Steiger, Nicole Lizée, Eliot Britton, John Luther Adams, and many others. Performing this music links an individual to iconic players, grooves, and musical styles that should remain at the core of interpretation, appreciation and, ultimately, performance. It celebrates the evolution of the drum kit, the expressive potential that is possible today, and suggests that new ideas are still to come. I currently teach percussion at McGill University and I am seeing a new generation of players versatile in drum kit and classical percussion performance. I am regularly being introduced to players from around the world promoting the growing interest in this repertoire.

Notes

1 B. Korall. *Drummin' Men, The Heartbeat of Jazz: The Bebop Years* (New York: Oxford University Press, 2002), p. 104.

2 K. A. Nichols. 'Important Works for Drum Set as a Multiple Percussion Instrument', unpublished thesis, University of Iowa (2012), p. 3.

3 M. Houllif. 'Benefits of Written-Out Drum Set Solos', *Percussive Notes,* (February 2006), p. 12.
4 D. G. Rogers. 'Drum Set's Struggle for Legitimacy', *Percussive Notes* 32:3 (1994), p. 28.
5 J. H. Beck. 'Alphabetical Listing of Percussion Instruments and Terms', in *The Encyclopedia of Percussion* (New York and London: Taylor Francis Group, 1995), p. 34.
6 J. Blades. *Percussion Instruments and Their History* (London: Faber and Faber Limited, 1970), p. 462.
7 M. Hennessey. *Klook: The Story of Kenny Clarke* (London: Quartet Books Limited, 1990), p. 27.
8 B. L. Kelly. *Tradition and Style in the Works of Darius Milhaud 1912–1939* (Aldershot: Ashgate Publishing Limited, 2003), p. 5.
9 J. Cocteau. *A Call to Order,* R. H. Myers translator (London: Faber and Gwyer, 1918–1926), p. 19.
10 B. Gendron. *Between Montmartre and the Mudd Club: Popular Music and the Avant-Garde* (Chicago: University of Chicago Press, 2002), p. 91.
11 Jackson. *Making Jazz French: Music and Modern Life in Interwar Paris* (Durham: Duke University Press, 2003), p. 29.
12 D. Milhaud. *Notes Without Music,* R. H. Myers, ed., D. Evans, translator (London: Dennis Dobson Ltd., 1952), p. 118.
13 D. Milhaud. *La Création Du Monde* (Paris: Éditions Max Eschig, 1929).
14 Ibid.
15 D. Milhaud, *Notes Without Music,* p. 50.
16 C. Rouse. *Bonham* (Hendon Music Inc., a Boosey & Hawkes Company, 1989; 1996), score, program notes.
17 Ibid.
18 J. Bream. *Whole Lotta Led Zeppelin: The Illustrated History of the Heaviest Band of All Time* (Minneapolis: Voyageur Press, 2008), pp. 42–43.
19 A. Liu-Rosenbaum. 'The Meaning in the Mix: Tracing A Sonic Narrative in "When the Levee Breaks"', *Journal of the Art of Record Production* 7 (November 2012).
20 W. B. Parker. 'The History and Development of the Percussion Orchestra', unpublished thesis, Florida State University (2012), p. 25.
21 Gendron, *Between Montmartre and the Mudd Club,* p. 91.
22 R. Rense. 'Frank Zappa, The Yellow Shark', compact disc booklet liner notes. (Ryko Records, 1993).
23 D. Menn. 'Frank Zappa, Strictly Genteel', compact disc booklet liner notes (Ryko Records, 1997).
24 First released on *Zappa in New York* (Discreet, 1978).
25 Ibid.
26 K. Potter. 'Contemporary British Composers 3: James Dillon: Currents of Development', *The Musical Times* 131:1767 (1990), p. 253.
27 Ibid.
28 Potter, 'Contemporary British Composers 3', p. 255.
29 J. Dillon. *Ti.Re-Ti.Ke-Dha,* 2nd ed. (London: Hinrichsen Edition, Peters Edition Ltd., 1979, 1982).
30 James Dillon. 'Percussion', *Edition Peters,* available from: www.edition-peters.de/cms/front_content.php?composer_id=81&changelang=2&lang=2&idcatart=25 (accessed: 16 September 2013).
31 Beck, 'Alphabetical Listing of Percussion Instruments and Terms', p. 55.
32 P. Wertico. 'A Question of Balance', *Paul Wertico: Articles,* available from: www.paulwertico.com/articles/aquestionofbalance.php (accessed 1 September 2019).
33 Nicole Lizée, email conversation, 24 April 2013.
34 Ibid.
35 'Ringer for Solo Drumkit', *Canadian Music Centre,* available from: www.musiccentre.ca/node/33923 (accessed 1 September 2019).
36 'Ringer for Solo Drumkit'.
37 G. Nicholls. *The Drum Book: A History of the Rock Drum Kit* (Backbeat Books, 2008), p. 75.
38 'Ringer for Solo Drumkit'.

7 Theorizing Complex Meters and Irregular Grooves

SCOTT HANENBERG

Introduction

Music-theoretical writing about the drum kit often stresses the instrument's role in shaping listener experiences of musical time. Much of this work concerns the backbeat, whether establishing its prevalence in specific rock and pop genres,[1] detailing a range of expressive microtiming feels,[2] or contrasting the pattern with other characteristic rhythms.[3] Study of the drum kit offers an effective point of contact between the sort of syntactic concerns central to much music-analytical writing and the experiential world occupied by performers and listeners.[4] Inquiry into the explanatory potency of the drum kit – what it tells the listener, how it communicates, and how to best interpret its intimations – is still rapidly evolving.

One question that remains to be explored in detail concerns the role of the drums within metrically irregular grooves, which are incompatible with the paradigmatic backbeat pattern often heard in Euro-American popular music. I argue that listener understanding of such grooves is acutely reliant on the guidance of the drums. To investigate this claim, I have analysed the drumbeats of grooves with large irregular cycles, ranging from ten to over sixty beats or pulses. In this chapter, I theorize a typology of additive successions well suited to the analysis of such cycles – I classify patterns as either *punctuated* or *split*. Punctuated grooves arise when an established meter is interrupted at regular intervals by isolated measures in another meter. Split grooves comprise cycles with two or more subsections of approximately balanced lengths. My research forges connections between drum-kit practice, theories of rhythm and meter, and cognitive models of listener entrainment.[5]

In comparing irregular drumbeats with cycles of different durations, an important distinction must be drawn between two types of listener engagement. Listeners can easily entrain to shorter repeating cycles, developing an immediate, intuitive connection to a groove. With progressively longer temporal spans, the ability to entrain is attenuated.[6] I posit that, as entrainment loses its efficacy, some listeners may choose to track irregularity through different means – either by counting, or by chunking and shifting between metric expectations.[7] Where the entrainment model is colloquially described as *feeling* the groove, the other strategies could be described as *thinking* the groove. The boundary between the two modes of attending is fluid and will vary for each listener; differences in tempo complicate matters further.[8]

Moreover, in transcribing grooves with larger repeating cycles, there is often more than one viable arrangement of measures and time signatures.[9] Whereas much music with a drum kit (rock, jazz, hip-hop, electronic, etc.) fits unproblematically into a 4/4 meter, even grooves with modest irregularities confound the straightforward mapping between meter and time signature that is often taken for granted in score-based musical traditions. Indeed, even the distinction between compound duple (6/8) and simple triple (3/4) meters can be difficult in the absence of a score.[10] The transcriptions in what follows are all my own; most could be re-barred and some admit alternative beat-levels (e.g. my 11/4 may be another listener's 11/8 or vice versa). My use of traditional European notation follows the practice of commercially available transcriptions of this music and that seen in private instruction common to neighbourhood lesson studios and institutions of higher education. Nevertheless, it remains a coarse shorthand for representing the sonic texts in question – not (as in the case of the classical score) the text itself. The best way to engage with my analysis involves finding and listening to the songs; this work is based on the original, studio-recorded album versions of each song, almost all of which can be found and heard online.

Regarding the repeating cycles under consideration, my criteria are as inclusive as possible: a groove is understood as any pattern of musical sounds that establishes a cyclic structure, and the cycles in question may be long enough to demand multiple meter changes. For example, I include a repeating pattern of sixty-one eighth notes in Radiohead's 'Paranoid Android' (1997), but I would never transcribe the passage in 61/8 time – I hear four measures of 4/4, three of 7/8, and one of 4/4. In what follows, I often employ nested brackets to represent the subdivision structures of complex spans.[11] The 'Paranoid Android' groove would be ((8,8)(8,8))((7,7)(7,8)). This method has the advantage of leaving certain potentially ambiguous features of the groove (e.g. beat level or time signature) open to interpretation.

In the songs analysed – mostly rock but admitting several outliers – the snare backbeat is often the most salient drumbeat cue and its metric role is the most codified of any drum-kit function, indeed, perhaps of any musical utterance. In 4/4 grooves, I hear the backbeat as exemplifying what Christopher Hasty calls 'metric continuation': an articulation that simultaneously extends the duration of an earlier counterpart, while itself demarcating a point of metric salience.[12] In metrically irregular grooves, the snare retains this metric-functional role, aiding listeners in parsing the unfamiliar structure. Often this happens by imitating the familiar 4/4 backbeat as closely as possible within the irregular metric context. Less frequently the alternation of 'forebeat' (commonly articulated by the kick drum) and snare backbeat is more radically reimagined, or else the drumbeat abandons the backbeat trope altogether. I found one other common drumbeat option: undifferentiated articulation (i.e. using the same drum) of the beat or pulse level, or of a salient rhythmic pattern.

Punctuated Irregular Cycles

I refer to patterns in which one meter predominates, interrupted at regular intervals by measures in a second meter, as punctuated irregular cycles. Without exception, the interrupting change of meter comes at the end of the repeating cycle (or, put differently, exceptions to this trend are so rare that they foster ambiguity). The language that Scott Murphy uses in his discussion of Platonic-Trochaic successions is well suited to my analysis: both projects concern cycles made up of a *run* (a stable repeating pattern) and a *comma* (an interruption that punctuates that pattern).[13] A heavy 11/4 groove in Tool's 'Right in Two' (see Example 7.1) demonstrates a relatively simple punctuated structure, in which a single two-beat group punctuates an otherwise triple metric fabric (i.e. 3+3+3+2). In Murphy's terms, the run comprises three groups of three, and the comma is the final two-unit group. I have transcribed the groove as comprising alternating measures of 6/4 and 5/4 time, approximating the measure lengths found in a familiar 4/4 backbeat, but there are other plausible alternatives. A transcription showing three measures of 3/4 and one of 2/4 would highlight the punctuated nature of the cycle, while a consistent 11/4 meter would reflect the regular patterning at the deeper hierarchical level of the phrase.

The drums are crucial in expressing the structure of this groove: an alternation of kick and snare stretches the standard backbeat to accommodate the three-beat spans, delaying the snare until every third beat. When the more familiar, two-beat backbeat alternation arrives at the end of the cycle, it expresses power and confidence, propelling the groove forward. The cymbals also participate in distinguishing the two-beat punctuation, switching from hi-hat eighths to emphatic quarter-note crashes.

Example 7.1 A punctuated 11/4 groove in Tool's 'Right in Two' (2006): 5:20

Table 7.1 lists forty-one grooves with punctuated irregular cycles, organized according to drumbeat. Some songs contain more than one such groove. In the column that gives the cardinality of each cycle, I use an Asterix (*) to denote a sub-tactus pulse (i.e. at the eighth-note level or the quarter note in a double-time groove) and a double-sword (‡) to denote the level below that (usually that of the sixteenth note).

The most common subdivision structure for punctuated patterns retains the intuitive preference for quadruple hypermeter observed in most Euro-American music, rock and otherwise. Large-cardinality irregular grooves that follow this trend often comprise three measures in the initial meter followed by one in a new meter. Two variants of this three-plus-one hypermetric configuration are (1) a seven-plus-one patterning, as in Tool's 'Forty Six & 2', and (2) cases in which the comma is better expressed by two measures, as in Muse's 'Animals'.

Thirty-three of the grooves analysed are based on a backbeat or a modified version of it, with the snare drum expressing metric continuation. In twenty-one of these, a 4/4 groove with a traditional backbeat serves as the primary meter. The punctuated elements of such grooves are sometimes based on the same backbeat, admitting subtle metric deletions or expansions to fit the punctuating meter. In the verse groove of Metallica's 'Master of Puppets', every fourth measure can be heard as a distorted 4/4 with metric deletions within the first and third beats (i.e. the snare articulations retain their full quarter-note durations). Although the band's practice of never recording to a click track makes it difficult to say with certainty, I hear an internal structure of (2,4)(1,4) at the sixteenth-note level. While commas that vary the backbeat are not uncommon, the prevailing strategy is to mirror the structural interruption to the meter with a stylistic interruption in the drumbeat – a fill. In the second verse of Dream Theater's 'Metropolis Part 1: The Miracle and the Sleeper' (around 2:35), every third measure is abbreviated by an eighth note; drummer Mike Portnoy uses subtle fills to drive across these metric deletions to the downbeats of the following 4/4 measures. In this groove, the 4/4 backbeat is also modified in a way that prepares the recurring 7/8 measures. The second snare of every 4/4 measure is delayed by an eighth note, placing them in the final eighth-note position of those measures, recalling the placement of the final snare in many 7/8 backbcat variants.[14]

When 4/4 is not the primary meter, drummers usually retain the backbeat as much as possible within the metrically irregular context. Cycles that modify a compound quadruple (e.g. 12/8) feel, with the drummer marking the dotted eighth note with alternating kick and snare, account for five examples. Tori Amos is especially fond of stretching compound beats to form novel grooves. Larger cyclic patterns are found

Table 7.1 *Examples of punctuated irregular cycles*

	Drums	Meter: Run	Meter: Comma	Meter: Cardinality	Artist—Song (year)
Kick-Snare Alternation	Backbeat; run has simple subdivision	4 (×2)	3	11*	Devo—'Blockhead' (1979)
		2 (×5)	1	11	King Gizzard & the Lizard Wizard—'Gamma Knife'(2016)
		4 (×2)	5	13	King Crimson—'Starless' (1974)
		2 (×5)	3	13*	Dream Theater—'Metropolis Part 1: The Miracle and the Sleeper' (1992)
		4 (×3)	3	15	TTNG—'Gibbon' (2008)
					Yes—'Siberian Khatru' (1972)
			5	17	TTNG—'Panda' (2008)
		4 (×4)	3	19‡	Dream Theater—'Scene Six: Home' (1999)
					Frank Zappa—'Keep it Greasy' (1979)
					Mahavishnu Orchestra—'Celestial Terrestrial Commuters' (1973)
			5	21*	UK—'In the Dead of Night' (1978)
			7	23*	Dream Theater—'Metropolis Part 1: The Miracle and the Sleeper (1992)
		4 (×6)	5 (×2)	34‡	Dream Theater—'Metropolis Part 1: The Miracle and the Sleeper' (1992)
		4 (×7)	5	33*	Phish—'Split Open and Melt' (1990)
		4 (×12)	(2,4)(1,4)	61‡	Metallica—'Master of Puppets' (1986)
		5 (×2)	7	17	Tool—'The Grudge' (2001)
		5 (×3)	3 (×2)	21	Muse—'Animals' (2012)
			(3,3,2)	23	Tool—'Hooker with a Penis' (1996)
		7 (×3)	8	29*	Dream Theater—'Scene Six: Home' (1999)
					Nine Inch Nails—'March of the Pigs' (1994)
		4+5 (×3)	4+4	35	Dream Theater—'The Count of Tuscany' (2009)
	Backbeat; run has compound subdivision	3 (×4)	3	15*	Queens of the Stone Age—'I think I Lost My Headache' (2007)
		3 (×6)	8	26*	Tori Amos—'Virginia' (2002)
		3 (×7)	2	23*	Radiohead—'You' (1993)
			4	25*	Tori Amos—'Carbon' (2002)
					Tori Amos—'Spark' (1998)

	Backbeat Variant; triple run	3 (×3)	2	11	Allman Brothers—‘Whipping Post’ (1971)
					Tool—‘Right in Two’ (2006)
	Backbeat Variant; irregular run	5 (×4)	(2,2,2)	26*	TTNG—‘26 is Dancier than 4’ (2008)
		5 (×7)	7	42‡	Tool—‘The Grudge’ (2001)
		7 (×7)	9	58*	Tool—‘Forty Six & 2’ (1996)
		(3,3,2) (×3)	(3,3,3)	33*	Hail the Sun—‘Eight-Ball, Coroner’s Pocket’ (2012)
		5+4 (×2)	3	21‡	Frank Zappa—‘Keep it Greasy’ (1979)
Undifferentiated		3 (×3)	2	11	Hail the Sun—‘Eight-Ball, Coroner’s Pocket’ (2012)
			4	13(*)	Ben Folds—‘Bastard’ (2005)
					Egg—‘I Will Be Absorbed’ (1970)
					Tool—‘Undertow’ (1993)
					Tori Amos—‘Carbon’ (2002)
		5 (×2)	4	14*	Dream Theater—‘A Nightmare to Remember’ (2009)
		4 (×5)	5	25‡	OSI—‘Memory Daydream Lapses’ (2003)
		8 (×2)	(3,4,3)	26‡	Mahavishnu Orchestra—‘One Word’ (1973)

*Denotes probable sub-tactus pulse; ‡ denotes probable sixteenth-note pulse.

in 'Carbon', 'Spark', and 'Virginia' (see also 'Datura' in Table 7.2).[15] Drumbeat patterns such as that seen in 'Right in Two', in which the alternation of kick and snare is played out every three beats, as opposed to the slower (five-, six-, and seven-beat) spans just described, suggest triple meter more readily than compound meter. The Allman Brothers' 'Whipping Post' is another such example.

Other primary meter options typically modify simple-time (4/4) backbeats trough deletion, as in 7/8 measures, or expansion. An example of the latter is the outro groove of TTNG's '26 is Dancier than 4', with a run comprising four repetitions of a 5/8 pattern followed by a six-pulse comma. The internal articulation of each subsection in the run is a quarter-note kick followed by three snares – a sixteenth, an eighth, and a dotted eighth. The first and third snare articulations are structural, resulting in a (4,3,3) pattern for each 5/8 measure.

Only eight of the punctuated grooves I surveyed eschew the backbeat possibilities just detailed, instead supporting a prominent rhythmic pattern with an undifferentiated articulation (i.e. playing the entire pattern on the same drum). The snare drum is the most common in this role, paralleling its importance in modified backbeat grooves. Many of the rhythmic succession represented in this category likewise have counterparts with modified-backbeat drum patterns (see e.g. Hail the Sun, 'Eight-Ball, Coroner's Pocket', and Egg, 'I Will Be Absorbed'); however, some successions are limited to this category. An instrumental near the three-quarters point in Dream Theater's 'A Nightmare to Remember' has a pattern of (3,2,3,2,2,2), which I parse as a run of ten pulses (5,5) and a comma of four. In a recurring instrumental passage in OSI's 'Memory Daydream Lapses' the ride cymbal subdivides a twenty-five-pulse cycle as (4,4,4,4,4,2,3) – a run of twenty and a comma of five. The initially even pulse is in a comfortable quarter note, making the five-sixteenth note comma especially jarring on early hearings. Some listeners may also entrain at the half-note level, parsing the pattern as (8,8,9).

Before moving on to split cycles, I consider a case where punctuated, large-cardinality groupings occupy regular metric frameworks. The rhythmic acrobatics of Swedish metal group Meshuggah are theorized by Jonathan Pieslak and Olivia Lucas, both of whom note the band's penchant for cyclic irregular riffs, punctuated to fit phrase and formal boundaries based on 4/4 meter and foursquare hypermeter.[16] What is remarkable about the band's handling of these grooves is the functional promiscuity of the snare drum. Whereas the irregular cycle is almost always given by the guitars and bass, supported by the kick drum, and whereas the cymbals are almost always responsible for maintaining a steady quarter-note beat, allowing entrainment to the overarching foursquare organization of the groove, the snare is free to ally itself to either stratum. In my habit of hearing the snare as the leading metric cue in this music, the patterning of

Table 7.2 *Examples of split irregular cycles*

<table>
<tr><th colspan="2">Drums</th><th colspan="2">Meter</th><th>Artist—Song (year)</th></tr>
<tr><th colspan="5">Backbeat Modifications</th></tr>
<tr><th>Type</th><th>Snare Placement</th><th>Card.</th><th>Split</th><th></th></tr>
<tr><td>Simple-meter Backbeat</td><td>- 2 - 4 |- 2 - |1 2 - 4</td><td>11</td><td>4 | 3 | 4</td><td>Dionne Warwick—'I Say a Little Prayer for You' (1967)</td></tr>
<tr><td></td><td>- 2 - 4 ° |- 2 - 4 ° °</td><td></td><td>5 | 6</td><td>Dream Theater—'A Nightmare to Remember' (2009)</td></tr>
<tr><td></td><td>- - 3 - 5 - 7 - 9 - 11</td><td></td><td>5 | 6 or 3 | 4 | 4</td><td>Esperanza Spalding—'Crowned and Kissed' (2012)</td></tr>
<tr><td></td><td>- 3 - - |- 2 - 4 - 6</td><td>11*</td><td>5 | 6</td><td>Van Der Graaf Generator—'Man-Erg' (1971)</td></tr>
<tr><td></td><td>- 2 - 4 - 6 |- 2 - 4 - 6 7</td><td>13</td><td>6 | 7</td><td>Genesis—'Turn it on Again' (1980)</td></tr>
<tr><td></td><td>- 2 - - 5 - 7 | - 2 - 4 - 6</td><td></td><td>7 | 6</td><td>Radiohead—'Sail to the Moon (Brush the Cobwebs out of the Sky)' (2003)</td></tr>
<tr><td></td><td>- 3 - |- 3 - - |1 - ° °</td><td>13*</td><td>4 | 5 | 4</td><td>Fromuz—'13th August' (2008)</td></tr>
<tr><td></td><td>- 3 - - |- 3 - 5 - -</td><td></td><td>6 | 7</td><td>Dream Theater—'Metropolis Part 1: The Miracle and the Sleeper' (1992)</td></tr>
<tr><td></td><td>- 3 - - ° |- 3 - ° °</td><td></td><td>7 | 6</td><td>Nine Inch Nails—'The Becoming' (1994)</td></tr>
<tr><td></td><td>- 2 - - 5 - |- 2 3 - - 6 - -</td><td>14</td><td>6 | 8</td><td>Tool—'Vicarious' (2006)</td></tr>
<tr><td></td><td>- 2 - 4 - 6 - |- 2 - 4 - 6 - 8</td><td>15</td><td>7 | 8</td><td>Pretenders—'Tattooed Love Boys' (1979)</td></tr>
<tr><td></td><td></td><td></td><td></td><td>Toadies—'Possum Kingdom' (1994)</td></tr>
<tr><td></td><td>- 2 — — — |- 2 - 4 - 6 -+</td><td></td><td>8 | 7</td><td>Soundgarden—'Spoonman' (1994)</td></tr>
<tr><td></td><td>- 3 - - 7 |- 3 - - 7 -</td><td>15*</td><td>7 | 8</td><td>Incubus—'Make Yourself' (1999)</td></tr>
<tr><td></td><td></td><td></td><td></td><td>Soundgarden—'The Day I Tried to Live' (1994)</td></tr>
<tr><td></td><td></td><td></td><td></td><td>Tool—'Ticks & Leeches' (2001)</td></tr>
<tr><td></td><td>— 3 - — ° | — 3 - — ° ° °</td><td>16*</td><td>7 | 9</td><td>TTNG—'Baboon' (2008)</td></tr>
<tr><td></td><td>- -+ — — 7 - |— 3 - — — - -</td><td>17</td><td>8 | 9</td><td>Björk—'Crystalline' (2011)</td></tr>
<tr><td></td><td>— 3 - — 7 - - |— 3 - — 7 -</td><td></td><td>9 | 8</td><td>The National—'I Should Live in Salt' (2013)</td></tr>
<tr><td></td><td>1 - - 4 |- -+ - 4 |- - 3 |- - 3 | - -+ - 4 |° ° ° °</td><td>22</td><td>8 | 6 | 8</td><td>Tori Amos—'Police Me' (2009)</td></tr>
<tr><td></td><td>- - 3 - - 6 - - 9 - 11 - 13 |- - 3 - - 6 - ° ° °</td><td>23</td><td>13 | 10</td><td>TTNG—'Rabbit' (2008)</td></tr>
<tr><td></td><td>- 2 - 4 - 6 7 |- 2 - 4 - 6 7 | - 2 - 4 - 6 - 8 |- 2 - 4 - 6 7</td><td>29</td><td>14 | 15</td><td>Fu Manchu—'Pick-Up Summer' (1992)</td></tr>
<tr><td></td><td></td><td>30</td><td>14 | 16</td><td>TTNG—'26 is Dancier than 4' (2008)</td></tr>
</table>

Table 7.2 (*cont.*)

<table>
<tr><th colspan="2">Drums</th><th colspan="2">Meter</th><th>Artist—Song (year)</th></tr>
<tr><th colspan="5">Backbeat Modifications</th></tr>
<tr><th>Type</th><th>Snare Placement</th><th>Card.</th><th>Split</th><th></th></tr>
<tr><td></td><td>- -+ — - -+ - |- -+ - - 5 — |
- -+ — - -+ - |- -+ - - 5 - 7 - 9</td><td></td><td></td><td></td></tr>
<tr><td></td><td>— 5 - - - — - |— 5 - - - — — - - -</td><td>33‡</td><td>14 | 19</td><td>The Matt Savage Trio—‘Blues in 33/8’ (2006)</td></tr>
<tr><td></td><td>— 3 - — 7 - — 11 - 13 |
— 3 - — 7 - — 11 |
— 3 - — 7 |— 3 - ° ° °</td><td>38*</td><td>24 | 14</td><td>National Health—‘Tenemos Roads’ (1978)</td></tr>
<tr><td></td><td>— 5 - - — 13 - |— 5 - - — - - - |—
5 - - — 13 - |— 5 - - — 13 - -</td><td>59‡</td><td>29 | 30</td><td>Dream Theater—‘The Count of Tuscany’ (2009)</td></tr>
<tr><td>Compound-/triple-meter Backbeat</td><td>1 - - — |- 3 - —
1 - - — |1 - - —</td><td>13*</td><td>6 | 7</td><td>Tool—‘Schism’ (2001)</td></tr>
<tr><td></td><td>- 3 - - 7 |- 3 - 6</td><td></td><td>7 | 6</td><td>Mutant-Thoughts—‘Odd Boy’ (2019)</td></tr>
<tr><td></td><td>— 4 - — — 12 - - 15 - -</td><td>17*</td><td>5 | 6 | 6</td><td>Noisia—‘The Hole Pt. 1’ (2019)</td></tr>
<tr><td></td><td>° ° ° - 5 6 - 8 9 |° ° ° - 5 6 - 8 9 10</td><td>19*</td><td>9 | 10</td><td>The Beatles—‘Happiness is a Warm Gun’ (1968)</td></tr>
<tr><td></td><td>— 4 - — 9 - - |— 4 - - — 10 -</td><td>22*</td><td>11 | 11</td><td>Dream Theater—‘A Nightmare to Remember’ (2009)</td></tr>
<tr><td></td><td>— 4 - - — 10 - - - |
— 4 - - — 10 - - - |</td><td>27*</td><td>13 | 14</td><td>Tori Amos—‘Datura’ (1999)</td></tr>
<tr><td></td><td>— 4 - - — ° ° ° ° |
— 4 - - — — 13 ° ° °</td><td>29*</td><td>13 | 16</td><td>Tool—‘Intolerance’ (1993)</td></tr>
<tr><td></td><td>— 4 - - — 10 - - ° ° ° |
— 4 - - — 10 - - ° ° ° ° ° °</td><td>33*</td><td>15 | 18</td><td>Dream Theater—‘The Count of Tuscany’ (2009)</td></tr>
<tr><td></td><td>— 4 - - — 10 ° ° ° |— 4 - -
— 10 ° ° ° | — 4 - - — 10 ° °
[complicated throughout by toms]</td><td>38*</td><td>13 | 13 | 12</td><td>Tori Amos—‘Carbon’ (2002)</td></tr>
<tr><td></td><td>— 4 - - — 10 .+ - - |— 4 - - —
10 - .+ ° ° ° |— 4 - - — 10 .+ - - |
— 4 - - — 10 - .+ - -</td><td>55*</td><td>28 | 27</td><td>Tori Amos—‘Datura’ (1999)</td></tr>
</table>

<table>
<tr><td>Mixed Subdivision</td><td>— 4 - ° ° |– ° °</td><td>11*</td><td>7 | 4</td><td>Tool—‘Right in Two’ (2006)</td></tr>
<tr><td></td><td>– 3 - - |– – 5 - -</td><td>12*</td><td>5 | 7</td><td>Tool—‘Schism’ (2001)</td></tr>
<tr><td></td><td>– .+ .+ - .+ .+ - |- - 3 - - 6 - - 9</td><td>17*</td><td>8 | 9</td><td>Hail the Sun—‘Eight-Ball, Coroner’s Pocket’ (2012)</td></tr>
<tr><td></td><td>– 3 - – 7 - |- - 3 - - 6 - - 9 - - 12</td><td>20*</td><td>8 | 12</td><td>Radiohead—‘Go to Sleep (Little Man Being Erased)’ (2003)</td></tr>
<tr><td></td><td>– – 5 - - - |– – 5 - - 8 - –</td><td>20*</td><td>9 | 11</td><td>Tool—‘The Patient’ (2001)</td></tr>
<tr><td></td><td>– – 5 - – |– - 4 - - - - 10 - -</td><td>20‡</td><td>8 | 12</td><td>Nine Inch Nails—‘Just Like You Imagined’ (1999)</td></tr>
<tr><td></td><td>— 4 - - — 10 - - — 16 - - |
– – 5 - - - - - 15 - - 19 -</td><td>38*</td><td>18 | 20</td><td>Soundgarden—‘Rusty Cage’ (1991)</td></tr>
<tr><td colspan="5">Undifferentiated Articulations</td></tr>
<tr><th>Type</th><th>Succession</th><th>Card.</th><th>Split</th><th></th></tr>
<tr><td>Undifferentiated Articulation Throughout</td><td>3,2,3,3</td><td>11‡</td><td>5 | 6</td><td>Tool—‘Right in Two’ (2006)</td></tr>
<tr><td></td><td>2,2,3,2,2,2,2</td><td>15*</td><td>7 | 8</td><td>Penguin Cafe Orchestra—‘Perpetuum Mobile’ (1987)</td></tr>
<tr><td></td><td>3,2,2,3,3,2,3</td><td>18*</td><td>7 | 11 or
10 | 8</td><td>Dream Theater—‘The Count of Tuscany’ (2009)</td></tr>
<tr><td></td><td>(3,3,2,2)(3,3,4,2)</td><td>22‡</td><td>10 | 12</td><td>Hail the Sun—‘Testostyrannosaurus’ (2012)</td></tr>
<tr><td></td><td>(3,3,2,2)(3,3,2,2,2)</td><td></td><td></td><td>Incubus—‘Adolescents’ (2011)</td></tr>
<tr><td></td><td>(3,3,2,2,2)(3,3,2,2)</td><td></td><td>12 | 10</td><td>Tool—‘Swamp Song’ (1993)</td></tr>
<tr><td></td><td>(2,2,2,3)(2,2,3,3)(2,3,3)</td><td>27*</td><td>9 | 10 | 8</td><td>Tool—‘Jambi’ (2006)</td></tr>
<tr><td></td><td>(3,3,3,2,2)(3,3,3,2,2,2)</td><td>28*</td><td>13 | 15</td><td>Tool—‘Undertow’ (1993)</td></tr>
<tr><td></td><td>(3,4,4,4)(3,3,4,3)</td><td>28</td><td>7 | 8 | 6 | 7</td><td>Tori Amos—‘Star of Wonder’ (2009)</td></tr>
<tr><td></td><td>(2,2,2,2,2,2,)(3,3,3,3,3)</td><td>29*</td><td>14 | 15 or
12 | 5 | 12</td><td>Hail the Sun—‘Eight-Ball, Coroner’s Pocket’ (2012)</td></tr>
<tr><td></td><td>(16)(3,3,8)</td><td>30‡</td><td>16 | 14</td><td>Emerson, Lake & Palmer—‘Karn Evil 9 1st Impression, Pt. 1’ (1973)</td></tr>
<tr><td></td><td>5/4 (x3) | 6/8 (x4)</td><td>54*</td><td>30 | 24</td><td>Queen—‘Innuendo’ (1991)</td></tr>
<tr><td>Some Backbeat</td><td>4,3,3,4</td><td>14</td><td>7 | 7 or
4 | 6 | 4</td><td>Of Monsters and Men—‘Crystals’ (2015)</td></tr>
<tr><td></td><td>(3,3,3,3)(4,4,4,4)</td><td>28*</td><td>12 | 16</td><td>Tool—‘Schism’ (2001)</td></tr>
<tr><td></td><td>(4,4,4,4)(3,3,2,4,2,4,2,2)</td><td>38‡</td><td>16 | 22</td><td>Emerson, Lake & Palmer—‘Karn Evil 9 1st Impression, Pt. 1’ (1973)</td></tr>
<tr><td></td><td>(4,4,4,4)(5,5,4)(5,5)</td><td>40‡</td><td>16 | 14 | 10</td><td>Dream Theater—‘A Nightmare to Remember’ (2009)</td></tr>
</table>

Example 7.2 A split fifteen-beat cycle in the verse of Soundgarden's 'Spoonman' (1994): 0:18

this drum has a decisive influence on my interpretation of Meshuggah's various grooves. Thus, in the opening groove from 'Stengah' (Pieslak's Example 7.3), where the snare supports an 11/8 riff on the third and sixth articulations in a (3,4,3)(3,4,5) sixteenth-note structure (until five repetitions lead to a 9/8 comma), that irregular organization is the dominant metric structure in my hearing. Conversely, in the opening of 'Lethargica' (Lucas's Example 7.2), where the snare marks a slow half-time backbeat against the displaced 23/4 riff, I find it easier to move with the available underlying 4/4.

Split Irregular Cycles

Grooves of the split type are based on a cycle with two or more subsections, the lengths of which are approximately balanced. In the clearest split patterns, subsections are easily differentiated by a change in pulse grouping (e.g. shifting from 2s to 3s). Radiohead's 'Go to Sleep (Little Man Being Erased)' exemplifies this strategy, alternating measures of 4/4 and 12/8.[17] The change in meter is reinforced by a change in drumbeat, from standard backbeat in the 4/4 measures to a snare on every third eighth note in 12/8. Split patterns of this sort invite the listener to keep two metric schemas available at all times, shuttling between them as necessary.

When no change of grouping occurs, cues in phrasing or arrangement are typically required to support a split interpretation. This is the case in Soundgarden's 'Spoonman' (see Example 7.2). The repeating pattern of fifteen beats could be parsed as (4,4)(4,3) – suggesting a punctuated logic – but two features of the arrangement contradict this analysis. The first is the long instrumental pause through the second measure. In the absence of a continuous groove in any part of the rhythm section, the re-entry in the cycle's third measure is marked as a new beginning, paralleling the first measure. Such parallelisms often indicate a split pattern, though they are seldom so clear. The second feature of 'Spoonman' that supports a split structure is the (3,2,3) grouping of the first half: the short drum fill marks beat three as closing a measure and the vocal phrasing establishes a more local parallelism between the first and sixth beats of the pattern (a transcription in 5/4 + 3/4 would better reflect the structure of the vocals, while my version prioritizes the drums). Without the stability of an ongoing 4/4 meter to connect the first two measures with the third, the punctuated possibility is untenable.

Table 7.2 catalogues fifty-nine split cycles. The most consistent trend within these grooves is the prevalence of two-part organization at the highest level, though three-and four-part structures are not uncommon. As with punctuated cycles, drumbeats derived from the backbeat predominate, accounting for forty-three groves. Twelve of the other sixteen use undifferentiated articulations, and the remaining four combine the two approaches.

Within split cycles with a backbeat-variant drumbeat, more than half (twenty-six grooves) are directly based on the 4/4 archetype; a further ten modify a compound- or triple-meter framework; and in the remaining seven irregularity is pervasive enough that comparison to a regular meter is less useful than simply considering the particulars at hand. With those rooted in the 4/4 backbeat model, the most common approach is a two-part split alternating between a septuple group and a quadruple one (the latter may require two measures, depending on hierarchical level). The first part invariably ends with a metric deletion, balanced by a second part without deletion. Examples include 'Tattooed Love Boys' by the Pretenders and 'Make Yourself' by Incubus. Fu Manchu's 'Pick-Up Summer' expands the pattern, using a septuple sub-cycle as the base meter with only occasional 4/4 measures to begin the second part of the split: (7,7)(8,7) or (4,3)(4,3)|(4,4)(4,3) at the beat level. Björk's 'Crystalline' demonstrates a related but distinct situation, leading with a measure of 4/4 and expanding the second part by an eighth note: (8,9) or (4,4)(4,5) in eighth notes.

Examples based on a compound-meter archetype include some of the longest, most complex cycles I have found. In an extended instrumental in the introduction of Dream Theater's 'The Count of Tuscany', a four-part structure arises through the alternation of compound duple measures and larger compound options triple in the first part, quadruple in the second. The structure is (6,9)(6,12) or a compound (2,3)(2,4). The drums enter after the cycle is established by other instruments, at first with long fills through the triple and quadruple measures, marking these spans as independent units and driving towards the downbeats of the more stable duple measures. Portnoy then shifts to a modified backbeat, alternating kick and snare in the first two compound beats of each measure, retaining shorter fills through the remaining beats of the longer measures: Kick – Snare | Kick – Snare – [fill] | Kick – Snare | Kick – Snare – [fill] – [fill].

Not all compound-meter grooves are restricted to pure compound beat divisions. Eleven- and thirteen-pulse options are often used to vary an otherwise 6/8 or 12/8 metric fabric. Not surprisingly, Amos is responsible for some of the most involved manipulations of this sort. At its most complex, 'Datura' is based on a process of metric alternation that extends upward through three hierarchical levels. The measure level comprises an alternation of 6/8 and larger measures, the two-bar level alternates between thirteen (6,7) and larger cardinalities, and the four-bar level alternates between twenty-eight (13,15) and twenty-seven (13,14). The drums are an indispensable aid for any listener wishing to hear their way through these complexities, consistently marking the fourth pulse of every measure with a snare backbeat. Drum fills stretch the metric fabric to accommodate the longer measures. Another notable example is a recurring instrumental in Tool's 'Intolerance' that expertly balances elements of compound and 4/4 meters. The two-part (13,16) structure juxtaposes what seems like an expanded 12/8 (or 12/16) measure against a double tresillo (3,3,3,3,2,2), most commonly understood as a syncopated expression of a 4/4 meter. By marking the fourth sixteenth note of each measure with the snare, the drumbeat only weakly directs the listener towards a compound hearing, leaving interpretation open.

Ambiguous and Mixed Cases

While the structures of most of the larger patterns I have identified are best described as either punctuated or split, there exist several ambiguous cases as well as some cycles large enough to employ both strategies at different hierarchical levels. Table 7.3 summarizes eight relevant examples. The ((8,8)(8,8))((7,7)(7,8)) groove in Radiohead's 'Paranoid Android', noted in my introduction, exemplifies the mixture of punctuated and split strategies. At a high level, the cycle is a two-part split. The first part remains consistently in 4/4 time, while the second punctuates a 7/8 run with a single 4/4 measure. The drums maintain a backbeat or close variant, peppered with fills that do not destabilize the established meter. Frank Zappa's 'Catholic Girls' contains a more complex instrumental – more changes of meter, using meters that are less common (see Example 7.3). Nevertheless, apart from the inversion of the hierarchical relationship between split and punctuated strategies, the structural principles at work in 'Catholic Girls' are essentially the same as in 'Paranoid Android'. As the example shows, the better part of the groove alternates between pairs of measures in 9/16 (2,2)(2,3) and 7/16 (4,3), establishing a split cycle of four

Table 7.3 *Examples of ambiguous irregular cycles*

Drumbeat Description	Meter: Structure Description	Meter: Card.	Artist—Song (year)
	Ambiguous Grooves		
Backbeat variant with second of three snare hits displaced	Split (3/4 + 4/4) or punctuated (3,3,3,3)(2)	14*	Tool—'Schism' (2001)
Compound-meter backbeat with extended, hemiola fills	Split (9/8 + 3/4) or punctuated (3,3,3) (2,2,2)	15	Dream Theater —'The Count of Tuscany' (2009)
Undifferentiated kick	No clear/consistent subdivisional structure; synth sometimes groups sub-beats as ((2,2)(2,2))((3,2)(2,2))	17*	Björk—'Hollow' (2011)
Backbeat or half-time backbeat (simple grouping); fills (compound)	Split (8,6,9) or punctuated (2,2,2,2,2,2,2)(3,3,3)	23*	TTNG—'Baboon' (2008)
Backbeat and backbeat variant	Four-part split: 3/4, 7/8, 3/4, 4/4 or (6,7)(6,8); but punctuated texture—3x similar guitar riff + fourth measure of chordal texture	27*	Better than Ezra —'King of New Orleans' (1996)
Some slow compound-meter backbeat; some compound-meter undifferentiated kick	Mostly 6/4; isolated 4/4 measure but not the final measure of the cycle (i.e. not quite 'punctuated') 6/4 (×3); 6/4, 4/4; 6/4 (×2)	40	Radiohead—'The Tourist' (1997)
	Grooves that Mix Punctuated and Split Structures		
Mixed – see Example 3	Deep four-part punctuated (32,32,32,22‡); run comprises split structures (9,9|7,7) 9/16 (×2) | 7/16 (×2)—all ×3; 11/16 (×2)	118‡	Frank Zappa —'Catholic Girls' (1979)
Backbeat and backbeat variant + fills	Deep two-part split (4mm. + 4mm.); second part punctuated (7,7)(7,8) 4/4 (×4) | 7/8 (×3), 4/4	61*	Radiohead —'Paranoid Android' (1997)

Example 7.3 A combination of punctuated and split structures in the instrumental in Frank Zappa's 'Catholic Girls' (1979): 1:38

duple measures. At a deeper (fourteen-measure) level, a run comprising three repetitions of this split cycle is punctuated by two measures of 11/16, modeled on a triple meter with a deletion of the final sixteenth note (4,4,3). The full cycle is thus ((9,9)(7,7))((9,9)(7,7))((9,9)(7,7))(11,11). The drums are confined to undifferentiated tom and cymbal work through much of the groove, reinforcing the surface-level subdivisions of the melodic line. However, a few emphatic snare articulations are definitive in directing listener attention. For example, a backbeat articulation in the first 7/16 measure clarifies the duple nature of that measure and confirms the irregularity of the overall passage (otherwise, it might be possible to hear the (9,9)(7,7) span as a syncopated 4/4 groove). The snare drum also renders the triple structure of the 11/16 measures unambiguous.

Unlike the complex but clear metric structures just discussed, other examples listed in Table 7.3 are less well defined, often due in part to the absence of a backbeat variant in the drums. I consider one example in detail to highlight some relevant considerations when analysing ambiguous cases. The opening groove of TTNG's 'Baboon' presents a mild conflict between an undifferentiated quarter-note snare rim knock through the first two thirds of the cycle and a dotted rhythm in the guitar through the last two thirds (see Example 7.4(a)). The twenty-three eighth notes are most likely grouped as (8,6,9), and the first and last groups almost certainly recommend simple and compound subdivision, respectively. What is less clear is the subdivision of the six-pulse group: when I follow the snare, I hear a measure of simple triple meter, whereas the guitar suggests compound duple time, anticipating the following compound triple group.

Example 7.4 Two drumbeats suggest different interpretations of the same guitar riff in TTNG's 'Baboon' (2012): (a) 0:00, (b) 0:47

The compound-meter interpretation is reinforced by vocal articulations throughout the first verse, likely leading first-time listeners to hear an alternation of 4/4 and 15/8 measures – a clear split structure.

New complications arise in the second verse, despite the shift to a traditional backbeat through the first two measures of the cycle (see Example 7.4(b)). The same two conflicting metric layers remain present but, because of the emphatic nature of the backbeat, I find that it requires a concerted effort to entrain to the compound-meter option as early in the cycle as in verse one. Moreover, the final seven pulses do not group together to punctuate a straightforward run of two 4/4 measures. Rather, the compound feel in the final beats is supported by the drums beginning with the final snare backbeat of the second measure, suggesting either an extension followed by a compound duple measure (8,9,6) or an elision of 4/4 and 9/8. This latter interpretation is reflected in my transcription through my use of the 3/4 time signature, which does not denote a true measure of simple triple time (most often articulated with snares on beats two and three) but rather an abbreviated 4/4 measure.

The drumbeat changes again in the third verse, now articulating a half-time backbeat for the first seven beats of the cycle. This option undercuts the early compound grouping even more decisively than the standard backbeat in the second verse. The shift to compound time is clarified through its contrast to the initial half-time feel: the drums support an unambiguous 9/8 measure, interrupting the second would-be 4/4 measure. But what is the logic of the resulting (4,4)(4,2)(3,3,3) structure? Is it split – either in two parts with differing subdivisions, seven duple and three triple units, or in three parts like the first verse (8,6,9) – or is it a simple-meter run punctuated by a compound-meter comma? One issue concerns the relative proportions of the groups involved: eight, six, and nine are about as well balanced as fourteen and nine, making it difficult to intuitively hear either grouping structure as preferable. Put differently, while the nine-pulse group is undoubtedly small enough to satisfy the definition of a comma, it is not so small as to compel that interpretation (unlike, for example, a three- or even a six-pulse group). The same question of balance characterizes the ambiguous grooves in Dream Theater's 'The Count of Tuscany' and Tool's 'Schism'.

Conclusions

The drum kit shapes listener interpretations of metric structures in several ways. The perceptual salience of most drum-kit articulations lends the instrument a welcome clarity within demanding musical soundscapes such as those presented above. At the musical surface, this clarity aids in the task of beat identification. Changes in sub-tactus grouping (below the level of the quarter note), for instance, are often open to multiple interpretations, or would be without some direction from the drums. At the measure level, backbeat variants are by far the most common approach taken by drummers when navigating irregular grooves. For listeners, these drumbeats afford ready analogy to the archetypal 4/4 backbeat, clarifying which beats and sub-beats serve the role of metric continuation within an irregular cycle. Also following their use in regular meters, drum fills in irregular metric contexts are typically deployed at phrase boundaries. In punctuated cycles the comma is often marked by a fill – sometimes modifying the drumbeat only modestly, to accommodate the change of meter, other times employing more assertive means to draw listener attention away from the metric irregularity and refocus it towards the impending downbeat. In split cycles fills may indicate subgroup boundaries, most commonly with larger cycles.

In this chapter, analysis of the drum kit has revealed a great deal of syntactic detail within the recordings analysed. Attending to the syntax of drum-kit performances decodes irregular metric patterns, which in turn shape the temporal experience of grooves. While this syntactic treatment of the music has been my primary focus, I hope to have drawn attention to the importance of performance practice in shaping recorded music, and to the ultimate subjectivity endemic to listener interpretation. Regarding performance practice, this study would have been impossible without understanding the backbeat and its role in rock drumming. Further investigation of drumming performance (e.g. sticking patterns or teacher lineages) would enhance my analysis. Regarding listener interpretation, these analyses are limited insofar as they remain my own. To fully understand the interaction of drumming and meter at an intersubjective level will require cognitive studies pooling hundreds of listeners' metric interpretations. Ultimately, the theory of punctuated and split metric structures that I have sketched here demonstrates the centrality of drum-kit syntax to the performance, perception, and analysis of metrically irregular rock music.

Notes

1 See G. Tamlyn. 'The Big Beat: Origins and Development of Snare Backbeat and other Accompanimental Rhythms in Rock'n'Roll', unpublished thesis, University of Liverpool (1998), pp. 54–60; M. Mauch and S. Dixon. 'A Corpus-Based Study of Rhythm Patterns', *13th International Society for Music Information Retrieval Conference* (2012), pp. 163–168; N. Biamonte. 'Formal Functions of Metric Dissonance in Rock Music', *Music Theory Online* 20:2 (2014).

2 See M. W. Butterfield. 'The Power of Anacrusis: Engendered Feeling in Groove-Based Musics', *Music Theory Online* 12:4 (2006), following J. A. Prögler. 'Searching for Swing: Participatory Discrepancies in the Jazz Rhythm Section', *Ethnomusicology* 39:1 (1995), pp. 21–54. See also

A. Danielsen (ed.), *Musical Rhythm in the Age of Digital Reproduction* (Burlington: Ashgate Publishing, 2010).

3 See M. Butler. *Unlocking the Groove: Rhythm, Meter, and Musical Design in Electronic Dance Music* (Bloomington: Indiana University Press, 2006); I. Chor. 'Cognitive Frameworks for the Production of Musical Rhythm', unpublished thesis, Northwestern University (2010); and N. Biamonte.

4 An eloquent injunction to seek out such points of intersection between 'the rigour by which scientific work is judged' and 'the experience that is music' is found in A. F. Moore, 'Listening to the Sound Music Makes' in C. Scrotto, K. Smith, and J. Brackett (eds.), *The Routledge Companion to Popular Music Analysis: Expanding Approaches* (New York: Routledge, 2019), p. 48.

5 In particular, I follow F. Lerdahl and R. Jackendoff. *A Generative Theory of Tonal Music* (Cambridge: MIT Press, 1983);C. Hasty. *Meter as Rhythm* (New York: Oxford University Press, 1997); D. Temperley. *The Cognition of Basic Musical Structures* (Cambridge: MIT Press, 2001); J. London. *Hearing in Time: Psychological Aspects of Musical Meter*, 2nd ed. (New York: Oxford University Press, 2012); and the extensive experimental work of Mari Riess Jones, Edward Large, and Caroline Palmer.

6 London, *Hearing in Time* suggests that metric entrainment has an upper limit of 1.8–2 seconds, summarizing experimental findings.

7 On chunking see, e.g. I. Neath and A. M. Surprenant, *Human Memory: An Introduction to Research, Data, and Theory*, 2nd ed. (Belmont: Wadsworth, 2003).

8 On tempo see, e.g. J. London, B. Burger, M. Thompson, and P. Toiviainen. 'Speed on the Dance Floor: Auditory and Visual Cues for Musical Tempo', *Acta Psychologica* 164 (2016), pp. 70–80.

9 Fundamental issues in transcribing recorded music are outlined by C. Doll. 'Some Practical Issues in the Aesthetic Analysis of Popular Music' in C. Scrotto, K. Smith, and J. Brackett (eds.), *The Routledge Companion to Popular Music Analysis: Expanding Approaches* (New York: Routledge, 2019), pp. 7–9, which treats rhythmic interpretation.

10 See T. de Clercq. 'Measuring a Measure: Absolute Time as a Factor for Determining Bar Lengths and Meter in Pop/Rock Music', *Music Theory Online* 22:3 (2016); R. Cohn. 'Meter' in A. Rehding and S. Rings (eds.), *The Oxford Handbook of Critical Concepts in Music Theory* (Oxford: Oxford University Press, 2019); and C. Doll, 'Some Practical Issues in the Aesthetic Analysis of Popular Music'.

11 This and other systems of numerical shorthand for describing metric subdivisions are summarized in M. Gotham. 'Meter Metrics: Characterizing Relationships Among (Mixed) Metrical Structures', *Music Theory Online* 21:2 (2017), pp. 2–5.

12 See Hasty, *Meter as Rhythm*, p. 105.

13 See S. Murphy. 'Cohn's Platonic Model and the Regular Irregularities of Recent Popular Multimedia', *Music Theory Online* 22:3 (2016).

14 I discuss the relevant drumbeat patterns in Chapter 4 of 'Unpopular Meters: Irregular Grooves and Drumbeats in the Songs of Tori Amos, Radiohead, and Tool', unpublished thesis, University of Toronto (2018). And in 'Using Drumbeats to Theorize Meter in Quintuple and Septuple Grooves', *Music Theory Spectrum* 42:2 (2020).

15 Drummer Matt Chamberlain is an indispensable asset in bringing life to these metric irregularities, but it seems that Amos is their originator. Examples of the same sort of metric play are found as early as *Under the Pink* (1994), before Amos began working with Chamberlain (see, e.g. 'Past the Mission', 'Icicle', and 'Yes, Anastasia').

16 See J. Pieslak. 'Re-casting Metal: Rhythm and Meter in the Music of Meshuggah', *Music Theory Spectrum* 29:2 (2007), pp. 219–245; O. R. Lucas. '"So Complete in Beautiful Deformity": Unexpected Beginnings and Rotated Riffs in Meshuggah's obZen', *Music Theory Online* 24:3 (2018).

17 A transcription can be found in B. Osborn. *Everything in Its Right Place: Analyzing Radiohead* (New York: Oxford University Press, 2017), p. 67.

8 Shake, Rattle, and Rolls

Drumming and the Aesthetics of Americana

DANIEL AKIRA STADNICKI

So correct me if I'm wrong. Americana is folk music with drumset. COMMENT FROM ATOMICORGANIC ON DRUMFORUM.ORG[1]

Since its emergence as a radio format in the mid-1990s, the Americana genre has provided a unique venue for drummers to participate in a folk musical context – a space seldom reserved for percussive accompaniment, especially on modern drum kits. Closely associated with several genre categories – most notably American Roots music, as well as alt.country, jazz, rock, blues, and many others – Americana inherited a mixture of drumming traditions, each with their own percussive codes, conventions, legacies, and repertoires. These range from 'drumless' bluegrass to iconic rock albums and bands of the 1960s and 1970s; 1990s post-punk aesthetics; early blues and rock and roll; and the more recent revitalization of the African-American string band tradition. Much like the genre itself, 'Americana drumming' is difficult to pin down, but certain ideas have developed around conventionalized sound palettes, instrumentation, and performance techniques that speak to a shared aesthetic discourse. Software companies have even released drum sample packages that fetishize the timbral qualities of calf skin drumheads, citing their legendary preference among top drummers in the genre, including Jay Bellerose and iconic forerunner Levon Helm.[2] Apple's *GarageBand* offers pre-assigned and genre-specific drummers such as 'Mason': a bearded (and possibly plaid-wearing) avatar silhouette found under the 'Songwriter' category who is 'inspired by Americana and classic R&B artists' and plays 'loose, swaggering beats on a vintage kit'.[3] Such notions permeate descriptions of drumming in the genre, where the intersection of material culture, ideal drum tones, and time-feels coalesce.

As such, this chapter will explore some of the aesthetic and discursive dynamics of drumming in Americana, focusing on the work of celebrated session drummer Jay Bellerose. I argue that Bellerose's performances help unpack some of the genre's stylistic and temporal ambiguities, as his drumming confers both a sense of contemporaneity and, paradoxically, a proto-Modernity that spans the history of drumming in American popular music. While I will not be able to provide an in-depth overview of Americana and all of its variegated streams and influences, this chapter will explore drums and percussion in the broader scope of Americana to help contextualize different approaches, sounds, instruments, and how they correspond to shared generic concepts.[4] Following ethnomusicologist Simon Keegan-Phipps and his description of tradition as 'a *way* of engaging with material', Americana similarly functions as a sign-vehicle for drummers to musically participate in a given genre by engaging in its shared aesthetic resources.[5]

Drumming Americana, Accompanying the Folk

Sometimes criticized as the symbolic encroachment of commercial, mass-produced, or popular music styles, the drum kit rarely signifies 'tradition' in ways that would resonate with many folk musicians and fans. Debates surrounding the appropriateness and integrity of adding drums to various folk musics continues to circulate online, though it is certainly not new. This includes the bluegrass music scene[6] – a genre that is often unaccompanied by the drums and whose rhythmic texture (i.e. its characteristic 'boom-chick' backbeat) is already achieved between the upright bass, mandolin, acoustic guitar, or 'chop' of the fiddle. For instance, editor of *Bluegrass Today* John Loveless recently published an April Fool's article detailing how the *International Bluegrass Music Awards* (IBMA) will have a new 'Drummer of the Year Award'. It noted how Ringo Starr celebrated the announcement since The Beatles always wanted to be recognized as a bluegrass band (but stuck to rock and roll because of their controversial use of the kit). Continuing, Loveless described other IBMA events, such as a 'round-the-clock *Will the Drum Circle Be Unbroken* jam to run in the lobby of the Marriott City Center in Raleigh from 9:00 a.m. Tuesday morning through Sunday morning 9:00 a.m.'[7] While such hackneyed jokes have been around for centuries, they repeat longstanding controversies surrounding the use of drums in more traditionally-coded musical contexts.[8]

Similarly, online drum forums share advice about achieving ideal Americana sounds, pinpointing records with vintage kits, analogue recording equipment, preferences for simplified or 'appropriate' drum parts, and often emphasizing the importance of 'tone over attack'.[9] According to one blogger, 'every song needs a "rhythm beat" of some sort, but it doesn't always have to come from a five-piece drum-kit', recommending that other drummers should emphasize 'pulses, not beats' to support Americana compositions.[10] Session drummer Stephen Belans also describes a simple 'heartbeat' as the foundational groove in most Americana contexts, since 'there's only so much space you can take up as a drummer in this kind of music and have it work out'. While admitting that there isn't one type of Roots/Americana sound, Belans describes it as a 'natural sound' on record: 'It doesn't sound gated, it doesn't sound crazy squished, it doesn't have some ridiculous false reverb'. Instead, recorded Americana drums are meant to sound as if 'you're standing in the room' with the drummer.[11] As with many styles of drumming, the acoustic parameter of *timbre* – the 'multidimensional attribute of perceived sound comprising everything that is not pitch or loudness' – remains a critical factor in the sound profile and description of Americana drumming among practitioners;[12] articulating the profound impact of learning from recordings and the enmeshed interaction that occurs between aural emulation and applied techniques.

Americana's Fluidity: Mapping a Rhythmic Legacy

According to the Americana Music Association, the genre is defined as:

> contemporary music that incorporates elements of various American roots music styles, including country, roots-rock, folk, bluegrass, R&B and blues, resulting in a distinctive roots-oriented sound that lives in a world apart from the pure forms of the genres upon which it may draw. While acoustic instruments are often present and vital, Americana also often uses a full electric band.[13]

Reflective of the broad scope of the association's definition, there are a number of inter-related genre streams and industry trajectories that helped collectively lead to the formation of Americana. For better or worse, many of these terms are used interchangeably, or have become consolidated under the Americana banner. This includes alt.country, Outlaw Country, Hard Country, and Roots music[14] – the latter being one of the more ambiguous terms, applied as a qualifier for alt.country music scenes outside the United States (such as the 'Calgary Roots' community in Alberta, Canada),[15] or as a World Music marketing strategy for diverse folk and traditional musics that problematically 'resemble the source from which it sprang'.[16] There are also several other sub-genre categories and artists that have been folded into the Americana discourse, speaking to a legacy of 'alternative' folk and country artistry, including southern rock, country rock, folk rock, and neo-traditional country.[17] Many of these categories were defined largely in opposition to mainstream country and popular music, positioning artists as outsiders, firebrands, or forgotten icons working outside the Nashville music industry (in some cases, emplacing a Roots or Americana sound onto other cities, such as Austin, Texas).[18] Interestingly, Fabian Holt distinguishes American Roots music from Americana along the lines of institutional support, noting how films and initiatives sponsored by PBS, the Smithsonian Institute, and others positioned Roots music as 'an essentialist metaphor of timeless authenticity in the context of a common cultural history'.[19] Since Holt's publication, however, I would argue that distinctions between the two categories have overlapped further: blurring the lines between Americana's once youthful, hip 'citybilly' punk rock, or 'rock influenced country' marketability with Roots music's shared revivalism, the collapsing distinctions between folk and popular music, and the recontextualization of blues, gospel, and bluegrass as 'old and stable components of *the* national canon'.[20]

Accordingly, the catalogue of Americana artists and influential figures seems to grow with each passing year. Several 'best-of' album lists tend to distinguish alt.country albums from Roots, Outlaw, or Americana categories, but they often share many of the same names. *Paste Magazine's* alt. country overview included Gillian Welch, Wilco, Ryan Adams, Lucinda Williams, Uncle Tupelo, Johnny Cash, The Carolina Chocolate Drops, Lyle Lovett, k.d. lang, and Sturgill Simpson.[21] In their 'Story of Outlaw Country in 33 Songs' article, *Pitchfork* included contemporary acts such as Miranda Lambert, as well as early icons beginning with Willie Nelson, Kris Kristofferson, Townes Van Zandt, and Waylon Jennings.[22] *No Depression's* compilation albums and 'bookzines' include Johnny Cash's 'The Time of the Preacher' (featuring Members of Soundgarden, Nirvana, and Alice in Chains), tracks from Whiskeytown (Ryan Adams' early band), Neko Case, The Carter Family's original 'No Depression in Heaven',[23] country stars Patty Loveless and Keiran Kane,[24] and the chamber/folk music project Abigail Washburn and the Sparrow Quartet (featuring Bela Fleck).[25]

But what about the drums? From full-volume, rock-oriented rhythm sections to minimalist kick drum, snare, and/or tambourine set-ups (i.e. early Mumford and Sons, Shakey Graves, the Lumineers); the 'barnyard and junkyard' sounds of Tom Waits; or the subtle percussive accompaniment on Gillian Welch's recordings (*Revival*, 1996; featuring Jim Keltner and Buddy Harman), drums in the Americana genre have not coalesced into a definitive sound or approach.[26] There are, however, key precedents and signposts. Perhaps more than any other figure, Levon Helm's work with The Band is cited as *the* pioneering example of early Americana.[27] His drumming was characterized by a tasteful blend of R&B, soul, early rock and roll, country, second line, and gospel grooves, often on deadened tom-toms and muted cymbals (using tape or towels) using a 'lighter' cymbal articulation with the tip of the drumstick. Helm was, of course, famous for seamlessly incorporating vocals with his drumming, but he was also described as possessing a 'less is more' approach that 'play[ed] for the song'.[28] This created space for the other instruments, while also managing to produce an incredible in-between straight and swung time feel. Retrospective tributes to the late drummer described Helm as the centre of a 'ramshackle' Band sound that was a 'hybrid of blues shuffle and street-march, with a fat, whomping back beat that sat so far "behind" . . . that it nearly steps into the next bar'.[29] *Modern Drummer* magazine even described the seminal album *Big Pink* as 'the soundtrack of the American collective unconscious', focusing on 'the deep traditions of rural America, from mountain music to gospel to R&B, rockabilly, and especially the sounds of the deep South and folk music'.[30] In these contexts, Helm's straight/swung feel, vintage drum tones, Southern identification (a native of Arkansas), and The Band's hybrid folk, soul, and rock and roll endure in contemporary discussions of ideal Americana drumming.

On the other end of the spectrum, however, there exists a more timbrally complex and esoteric stream of drumming performance in Americana – one that gestures towards the sound and minimal instrumentation of early folkloric field recordings, even evoking the percussive sound worlds of Tom Waits (a progenitor of the genre). Waits' 'visionary chronicles of derelict America' have long exploited the narrative potential of timbre, including his use of 'non-instruments' (brake drums, chest drawers, rooster crows) and 'unusual textures, sounds, percussion, rhythms, and recording techniques'.[31] Taken together, these rhythmic and textural undercurrents reflect a shared 'sonic aesthetic' in Americana, one that 'emphasizes the humanity and materiality of music-making'. Here, Christine Steinbock writes how several Americana artists exploit the 'anomalies of human-made music and the unique sonic qualities that machines cannot replicate', such as 'the hand clap, knee slap body percussion in Gillian Welch's "Six White Horses"' or 'the abrasive attack in Justin Townes Earle's guitar playing'.[32] Focusing on the music of Welch and her collaborator Dave Rawlings, Steinbock explores how the artists 'disintermediate their relationship with listeners and express Americana's human-centred sonic aesthetic by providing a space for the anomalies of humanmade music to flourish', noting their penchant for recording live off the floor, as well as a 'general eschewing' of digital editing.[33] These 'anomalies' become authenticated, reflecting themes in Americana as offbeat, misunderstood, imperfect, and ultimately, humanized. While such concepts are linguistically tied to ideas about the more ambiguous dimensions of timbre, they lend themselves to drumming material culture and applied practice where metaphor translates into sonic palettes and performance techniques.[34] For drummers, what would be an otherwise straightforward backbeat groove can be texturally enriched by the addition (or substitution) of alternative percussive elements, generating a more 'sloshy' and complex time-feel. This sound is indicative of the characteristic grooves of Jim Keltner (John Lennon, The Travelling Wilbury's, T Bone Burnett, Ry Cooder), who often simultaneously performs with a variety of shakers and tambourines while on the kit. Today, several session drummers in the Roots and Americana scenes perform in this manner using prepared kits, bells, beads, tambourines, auxiliary percussion, and shakers, including Marco Giovino (Norah Jones, Robert Plant and the Band of Joy), Butch Norton (Lucinda Williams), among many others. This approach can sonically obfuscate the more conventional drum kit 'trinity' (i.e. the kick, snare, and hi-hat) through using alternate sound sources, revitalizing both the 'contraption' element that distinguished the design of early trap drum kits, as well as diverging from more conventional drum sounds and raucous volumes.

From a marketing standpoint, these atypical percussive sounds and textures often accompany a 'refined' and mature artist narrative, particularly among repackaged legacy artists who were originally marketed as rock, blues, or mainstream country, but have since been included in the Roots and Americana fold (such as Robert Plant, BB King, Elvis Costello, Johnny Cash). The sound and production value of these recordings reveal a unique discourse of aging, memory, and what Gillian Turnbull describes as 'the aesthetic of history'.[35] Here, an aching beauty resides under a worn and weathered patina, expressing notes of redemption, loss, mortality, and nostalgia, often through its use of acoustic instrumental timbres and references to multiple styles of American popular music. Though problematically re-articulating the fetish of 'liveness' in rock ideology where acoustic performance functions as a 'sign of the real', it is here where Joseph Kortarba considers Americana as providing 'musical experiences that are contemporary but not pop;[36] meaningful but in a way relevant to aging folks; and accessible to folks who do not like their music over-amplified and or directed to some other – younger – audience'.[37] A prime example is Johnny Cash's later work with producer Rick Rubin in the 1990s, which engaged in a creative discourse of genre temporality. In particular, Cash's posthumous release *Ain't No Grave* (2010) sonically bookended his career by providing an almost tongue-and-cheek 'necro-marketing' of his voice from the grave,[38] and the song's overdubbed 'percussive chains and footsteps' reiterated the singer's longtime associations with outlaws and prisoners.[39] In this sense, Americana recordings can re-situate legacy performers at the confluence of old and new, producing a *sense* of temporality – what Georgina Born writes as the 'outer time of cultural history' – by engaging with a humanized (and percussive) sonic aesthetic.[40]

Case Study: Jay Bellerose

One of the most prolific session drummers today, Jay Bellerose has collaborated with a who's who of contemporary artists (Ray Lamontagne, Rihannon Giddens, Alison Krauss, The Punch Brothers) and various legacy acts in the Americana genre (including Robert Plant, BB King, Ramblin' Jack Elliot, and Alain Toussaint). Far from suggesting that Bellerose's output can provide a stand-in for all forms of drumming in Americana, his work and ongoing collaborations with key tastemakers – most notably, producers T Bone Burnett and Joe Henry – situates him at the forefront of progressive folk and roots music in the United States. In recent interviews and magazine articles, the drummer has shared stories about his upbringing, key influences, as well as a fateful incident that happened while he was studying at the Berklee College of Music. The most distilled version of this narrative appears in his bio on Alison Krauss' website:

> While a student at The Berklee School of Music in Boston, Bellerose had his drum kit stolen, and it is hard to over-estimate the significance of the event on his future artistry: working from a hodge-podge of drums donated by friends, Jay began to discover new sonic possibilities by assembling mismatched kit configurations that varied from song to song, setting battered marching drums and bits of arcane, vaudeville-era hand percussion devices along side more conventional modern drums. The ever-changing results revealed a signature sensibility that finds Jay compared to impressionist painters as often as to drum luminaries like Sonny Greer.[41]

The stolen drum kit narrative is intriguing for its way of connecting Bellerose's playing to earlier (i.e. 'arcane') popular styles, coupling his drumming with the material and cultural histories of the kit, as well as symbolically shedding the weight of modern set-ups, timbres, and conventions in contemporary music. The event was significant (and potentially ruinous) for a session drummer in the 1980s, who, according to Bellerose, was expected to 'mute the drums as much as you can and hit them as hard as you can'.[42] The story was expanded upon in a podcast interview with Nashville-based songwriter and producer Steve Dawson. As Bellerose explained, his stolen kit was replaced by a friend's simple, beat up Ludwig bass drum, snare, and cymbal: 'This thing taught me so much about how many more sounds are in the few pieces of a drum set that a lot of people just overlook. I was using the whole animal, I was ringing it all out'.[43] Interestingly, Bellerose connected his newfound set-up with memories from his childhood, likening it to his early interests in 'pulling sound' out of household items, including tapping on boxes, washing machines, pots, and pans.[44] This self-styled mythology about his intuitive interests in everyday objects positions Bellerose as somewhat of an outsider, drumming against the grain of mainstream conventions, very much like the Roots and Americana musicians he often performs with. He experimented with various kit set-ups in his early career, even playing on what appears to be a djembe in place of a snare with Paula Cole in the 1990s.[45]

Kit Culture: On Gear

So much interest and attention has been placed on Jay Bellerose's collection of vintage kits that many descriptions of his playing seem to erase any boundaries between the man and the instrument. Inspired by the artistry and sounds of big band drummers such as Buddy Rich, Sonny Green, and Gene Krupa, Bellerose often uses larger drum sizes from the era. Not only does this allow him to project without playing as hard, but it coincides with a certain 'touch' he developed with wooden sticks that allows him to 'keep the energy, and play quiet, and *still rock*' (citing Charlie Watts as an influential example of a drummer 'pulling sound' from the kit without hitting too hard).[46] Bellerose is famously known for performing without a hi-hat, opting instead for a fistful of maracas, mounted tambourines, or tying bells and shakers to his left leg. His cymbal use is often sparse, leaving considerable room for the drum's bottom end to ring out prominently. While Bellerose's patterns are not necessarily complicated (especially when transcribed on paper), they are complex: nuanced with selective fill placements and grooves that evoke early jazz records, second-line drumming, Dixieland, as well as soul, R&B, and early rock and roll. And yet, his recordings achieve something else entirely, as if providing snapshots of drum kit performance through the aperture of its weathered and gnarled history; conveying a mood with a 'subliminal kind of tone' with rhythmic phrasing that is 'something you feel more than hear'.[47] Live, Bellerose shakes his kit in ways that exploit its jangly artifacts, including squeaky hardware; some of his calf skin drumheads are even patched together with pieces of leather. Fans of Bellerose are often surprised when they witness him perform, as a post from Steve Krugman on the *Hollywood Drum* website describes:

> It's difficult to separate hearing Bellerose play from seeing Bellerose play . . . As drummers, it's generally pretty natural to visualize a recorded performance in the mind's eye . . . Bellerose's approach to the instrument is singularly unfamiliar. To hear him without sight or see him without sound invites mystery.[48]

Krugman goes on to discuss the various maracas, mounted and shaken tambourines used during Bellerose's set at an LA venue with Jennifer

Figure 8.1 Jay Bellerose performing at *The York* in Los Angeles with Molly Miller (guitar) and Jennifer Condos (bass) in September 2019.
Image credit: Lawrence Buccat (screen shot of YouTube video, used with permission)
Source: L. Buccat. Molly Miller Trio, YouTube (2 May 2019), available from: www.youtube.com/watch?v=qpvFpTk7psY (accessed 15 April 2020)

Condos and guitarist Molly Miller (see Figure 8.1), noting his effortless brushwork, constantly switching out mallets and sticks, and 'blur[ring] the lines between conventional drumset and ensemble percussion, improvisation and orchestration'. Such observations are found elsewhere, primarily on Robert Plant and Allison Krauss' *Raising Sand* recording (2007), which received considerable attention for Bellerose's 'slinky grooves', unique drum sounds, vintage kit set-ups, and 'shakers strapped to his ankles'.[49] Fans the world over have fawned Bellerose 'loose and jangly', 'deep-but-dead' Americana drum sound, which collectively accounts for both time-feel and copious vintage set-ups.[50]

In particular, Bellerose's 1940s-era Slingerland 'Rolling Bomber' kit has achieved legendary status among collectors and fans. Known for its all-wood construction (including rosewood lugs and rims) due to metal rationing throughout WWII, the drums confer a strong sense of cultural capital, coinciding with an 'obsessive preference for "vintage" musical technology' among Americana and alternative country fans, both young and old.[51] Described as having a 'natural resonance' because of their construction, Bellerose's use of the kit has inspired several others to seek them out, including Norwegian jazz drummer Erland Dahlen and *Modern Drummer* writer Patrick Berkery, who interviewed Bellerose in 2008.[52] At the same time, widespread interest in the Rolling Bomber kit also points to an underlying trope of Pax Americana nostalgia: a sentiment for when the United States was truly 'great', which persisted in country music during the Gulf War and remained throughout the Americana genre post-9/11.[53]

Developing (and Producing) a Characteristic Drum Sound

According to Bellerose, the Rolling Bomber kit represents his broader interests in a more uncontrolled tuning aesthetic, as well as a willingness to adapt to changes in humidity, among other factors that affect the drums while on the road.[54] Admitting that he'd rather 'just change the drum' instead of tuning it, he claims that it is 'more about the character of the note and less about the pitch of the note. I love dissonance and overtones. Sometimes I like when things rub a little bit, and it doesn't sound perfect'.[55] Bellerose apparently developed this unconventional aesthetic from a process of listening to rare and discontinued vinyl (what he calls 'sonically-odd stuff'). This includes emulating Alan Lomax's field recordings and finding drums that similarly sounded as if they were 'distorted or . . . like they have reverb on them', comparing Lomax's recordings to 'a Tom Wait's record'.[56] Given his unique drum sound, vintage collection, and approach to the kit, one could read Bellerose's drumming at the primordial intersection of American popular music: a reimagined *drumscape*[57] that blends roots music from the pre-rock era (the 'legends of country music, blues, and the folk revival') with the sonic imprint of technological artifacts heard on early field recording devices.[58]

Of course, Bellerose's characteristic drum sound developed through collaborating with a long list of personnel, including record producers, engineers, mixing and mastering technicians. Eschewing the belief that he alone can recreate the 'T Bone' or 'Joe Henry' drum sound in the studio, Bellerose explains that it is 'more complex than just hiring one person from that camp, or hiring me to play drums. I mean, yeah, you're going to get shades of it. But there's a team'.[59] A key figure in this development is T Bone Burnett – leading authority and arbiter of American roots music, and whose work in film helped revive international interests in old time, bluegrass, and Americana (in particular, *O Brother Where Art Thou?* (2000)). In many ways, Burnett's approach to recording drums and percussion resonates with multiple facets of Bellerose's aesthetic, including his fondness for playing at quieter volumes. Burnett's interests in 'minimizing attack and maximizing tone',[60] for instance, focuses on room sound, reflective surfaces, and placing 'microphones so that they hear all of the tone and the overtones of the drums'.[61] There is also a diminished reliance on compression in Burnett's productions, which is achieved instead by playing very quietly, using calf skin drumheads, and tapping on the skins softly 'to get a much fuller sound'.[62] At the level of applied practice, Bellerose's atypical approach can even be connected to specific Burnett productions. For instance, the drummer recorded alongside Jim Keltner on BB King's 2008 album *One Kind Favor*, as well as on Burnett's solo record

True False Identity (2006) with both Keltner and Carla Azar. These multi-drummer sessions encouraged Bellerose to situate himself amongst the other rhythms, perhaps guiding his solo-drumming effort on *Raising Sand* (another Burnett production) with its prominent auxiliary percussive sounds and warm, deadened drum sounds – a 'third voice', perhaps, stepping out and taking centre stage. Furthermore, both Burnett and Bellerose like to challenge preconceptions about the 'imposed role on drummers' as timekeepers (Bellerose),[63] critiquing how conventionalized parts of the kit (such as the hi-hat) dictate 'proscribed time' in a way that 'can make the beat stiff' (Burnett).[64] Here, Burnett describes why they did not use hi-hats during the *One Kind Favor* sessions, opting instead for 'these big shakers . . . like 10 or 15 different gourds with beads in them or nuts . . . So it expands and broadens the beat'.[65] This affinity for alternative percussive textures coincides with Burnett's broader conception that all instruments are a drum of some sort,[66] articulating the possibility for any sound source to function as a type of percussion. In this context, backbeats do not have to necessarily occur on a snare drum (or any other conventionalized part of the kit), just 'as long as it's getting hit in the right place with the right meaning' – generating a low-end and esoteric sound world through instrumental substitution that sets up the rhythms and beats 'in the overtone structure, which creates a lot of mystery and a real sense of place'.[67]

Conclusions

This chapter investigated some of the aesthetic discourses surrounding drums and percussion in the Americana genre, including material cultures, performance techniques, collaborations, and key figures. Taken collectively, these dynamics 'make sense through their interrelatedness, not as isolated events' because 'genre can be viewed as a culture with the characteristics of a system or systemic functions'.[68] Rather than trying to define Americana drumming as a clear set of techniques and approaches, I highlighted how the realms of timbre and texture give rise to complex forms of percussive musicking; generating a discourse where vintage drums, 'warm' tones, and behind-the-beat time feels mutually convey at least a *rhythmic* understanding of something as ambiguous as Americana.

Notes

1 'Atomicorganic', *Americana Drums* (18 July 2011), available from: www.drumforum.org/threads/americana-drums.53678/page-3.atomicmorganic (accessed 12 March 2020).

2 'Organic Drum Loops: About', available from: www.organicdrumloops.com/about/ (accessed 12 March 2020).

3 'GarageBand for Mac: Choose Genres and Drummers', (9 August 2019), available from: https://support.apple.com/kb/PH24948?viewlocale=en_US&locale=en_US (accessed 12 March 2020).
4 There are several studies that have achieved this kind of work, including: P. Fox and B. Ching (eds.), *Old Roots, New Routes: The Cultural Politics of Alt. Country Music.* (Ann Arbor: University of Michigan Press, 2008); A. A. Fox. '"Alternative" to What? O Brother, September 11, and the Politics of Country Music' in C. K. Wolfe and J. E. Akenson (eds.), *Country Music Goes to War* (Lexington: University of Kentucky Press, 2005); F. Holt. *Genre in Popular Music* (Chicago: University of Chicago Press, 2007).
5 S. Keegan-Phipps. 'The Study of Digital Media and Creative Culture: Why the Folk Arts Are a Special Case (3) Innovation and Tradition' (5 April 2015), available from: https://simonkeeganphipps.wordpress.com/category/research-projects/ (accessed 12 March 2020).
6 r/Bluegrass. 'Drums: Yes or Nay?', available from: www.reddit.com/r/Bluegrass/comments/45hkgo/drums_yea_or_nay/ (accessed 12 March 2020).
7 J. Lawless. 'IBMA Announces New Award for Drummers', *Bluegrass Today* (1 April 2019), available from: https://bluegrasstoday.com/ibma-announces-new-award-for-drummers/ (accessed 12 March 2020).
8 See M. Brennan. *Kick It: A Social History of the Drum Kit* (Oxford: Oxford University Press, 2020).
9 *Americana Drums.*
10 B. Benediktsson. 'How to Create Rhythm without a Full Drum Kit', *Envato Tuts+* (13 April 2013) available from: https://cutt.ly/zgQYfuN (accessed 12 March 2020).
11 Ibid.
12 Z. Wallmark, M. Iacoboni, C. Deblieck, and R. A. Kendall. 'Embodied Listening and Timbre: Perceptual, Acoustical, and Neural Correlates', *Music Perception* 35:3 (2018), p. 332.
13 'What Is Americana Music?', *The Americana Music Association,* available from: https://americanamusic.org/what-americana-music (accessed 12 March 2020).
14 For more on alt.country, see B. Ching, . 'Going Back to the Old Mainstream: No Depression, Robbie Fulks, and Alt. Country's Muddied Waters', in K. M. McCusker and D. Pecknold (eds.), *A Boy Named Sue: Gender and Country Music* (Jackson: University Press of Mississippi, 2004), pp. 178–195; P.Fox and B. Ching, *Old Roots, New Routes.* On Outlaw Country, see T. D. Stimeling. 'Narrative, Vocal Staging and Masculinity in the 'Outlaw' Country Music of Waylon Jennings.' *Popular Music* 32:3 (2013), pp. 343–358. On Hard Country, see B. Ching. *Wrong's What I Do Best: Hard Country Music and Contemporary Culture* (Oxford: Oxford University Press, 2001). On Roots music, see M. F. DeWitt (ed.), *Roots Music,* 1st Edition (New York: Routledge, 2011); B. Mazor. *Ralph Peer and the Making of Popular Roots Music* (Chicago: Chicago Review Press, 2015).
15 G. Turnbull. '"Land of the In Between": Nostalgia and the Gentrification of Calgarian Roots Music', *MusiCultures* (11 February 2020), available from: https://journals.lib.unb.ca/index.php/MC/article/view/20245 (accessed 15 March 2020).
16 S. Redhead and J. Street. 'Have I the Right? Legitimacy, Authenticity and Community in Folk's Politics', *Popular Music* 8:2 (1989), p. 180; and Holt, *Genre in Popular Music,* p. 40.
17 On rock, see: J. T. Eastman. 'Rebel Manhood: The Hegemonic Masculinity of the Southern Rock Music Revival', *Journal of Contemporary Ethnography* 41:2 (2011), pp. 189–219; J. T. Eastman. *The Southern Rock Revival: The Old South in a New World* (Lanham: Lexington Books, 2017). On country, see: J. Einarson. *Desperados: The Roots of Country Rock* (New York: Copper Square Press, 2001). On folk, see: R. S. Denisoff. 'Folk-Rock: Folk Music, Protest, or Commercialism?', *Journal of Popular Culture* 3 (1969), pp. 214–230; R. G. H. Burns. 'Continuity, Variation, and Authenticity in the English Folk-Rock Movement', *Folk Music Journal* 9:2 (2007), pp. 192–218. On neo-traditional country, see: A. A. Fox, '"Alternative" to What? O Brother, September 11, and the Politics of Country Music', p. 168. Fox is referring here to Steve Earle and Randy Travis' country music releases of the mid-1980s.
18 Budofsky. Here, the author describes Austin as 'the rootiest of America's music towns'.
19 Holt, *Genre in Popular Music,* p. 39.
20 Holt, *Genre in Popular Music,* pp. 45–46, 40, and 49.
21 J. Jackson. 'The 50 Best Alt-Country Albums of All Time', *Paste Magazine* (4 August 2016), available from: www.pastemagazine.com/articles/2016/08/the-50-best-alt-country-albums-of-all-time.html (accessed 15 March 2020).
22 D. Cantwell, S. Deusner, B. McKenna, M. R. Moss, and S. Sodomsky. 'The Story of Outlaw Country in 33 Songs', *Pitchfork,* (29 October 2018), available from: https://pitchfork.com/features/lists-and-guides/the-story-of-outlaw-country-in-33-songs/ (accessed 12 March 2020).

23 *No Depression: What It Sounds Like Vol. 1*, (Dualtone, 2004).
24 *No Depression: What It Sounds Like, Vol. 2*, (Dualtone, 2004).
25 G. Alden and P. Blackstock (eds.), *No Depression: The Bookazine (Whatever That Is): The Next Generation* 76 (Austin: University of Texas Press, 2008).
26 S. Tchir. 'Tom Waits' Rain Dogs: Influences and Musical Genre', unpublished thesis, University of Alberta (2013), p. 73.
27 C. Harris. *The Band: Pioneers of Americana Music* (Lanham: Rowman and Littlefield, 2014), pp. 2 and 193.
28 J. Potter. 'Levon Helm May 26, 1940–April 19, 2012', *Modern Drummer* (November 2012), available from: www.moderndrummer.com/article/november-2012-levon-helm/ (accessed 12 March 2020); K. Micallef. 'Drummers: The Great Levon Helm', *Modern Drummer* (April 2008), available from: www.moderndrummer.com/2008/02/levon-helm/ (accessed 12 March 2020).
29 B. Wheeler. 'What Levon Helm Called Rock 'n' Roll Was Deep-bottomed American Music', *The Globe and Mail* (19 April 2012; updated 11 May 2018), available from: https://cutt.ly/OgQYuxF (accessed 12 March 2020).
30 Potter, 'Levon Helm May 26, 1940–April 19, 2012'.
31 C. Kessel. *The Words and Music of Tom Waits* (Westport: Greenwood Publishing, 2009), pp. 15 and 30.
32 C. Steinbock. 'Facing the Future with a Foot in the Past Americana, Nostalgia, and the Humanization of Musical Experience', unpublished thesis, Carleton University (2014), p. 19.
33 Steinbock, 'Facing the Future with a Foot in the Past Americana, Nostalgia, and the Humanization of Musical Experience', p. 64.
34 Z. Wallmark and R. A. Kendall. Describing Sound: The Cognitive Linguistics of Timbre in E. Dolan and A. Rehding (eds.), *The Oxford Handbook of Timbre* (Oxford: Oxford University Press, 2018). DOI: http://10.1093/oxfordhb/9780190637224.013.14.
35 Turnbull, 'Land of the In Between', p. 33.
36 P. Auslander. *Liveness: Performance in a Mediatized Culture* (London: Routledge, 1999), p. 98.
37 J. A. Kortaba. *Baby Boomer Rock 'n' Roll Fans: The Music Never Ends* (Lanham: Rowman and Littlefield, 2013), p. 119.
38 J. Stanyek and B. Piekut. 'Deadness: Technologies of the Intermundane', *TDR: The Drama Review* 54:1 (Spring 2010), pp. 14–38.
39 L. H. Edwards. 'Johnny Cash's "Ain't No Grave" and Digital Folk Culture', *Journal of Popular Music Studies* 28:2 (2016), p. 187.
40 G. Born. 'On Musical Mediation: Ontology, Technology and Creativity', *twentieth-century music* 2:1 (2005), p. 23.
41 'ALISON WILL BE PERFORMING WITH THESE FINE MUSICIANS', Alison Kraus website, available from: https://alisonkrauss.com (accessed 12 March 2020).
42 S. Dawson. 'Episode 25 (Jay Bellerose)', *Makers and Shakers Podcast* (31 August 2016), available from: www.stevedawson.ca/makersandshakers/episode-25-jay-bellerose, 49:52–50:00 min. (accessed 12 March 2020).
43 Dawson, 'Episode 25 (Jay Bellerose)', 38:54–39:13 min.
44 Dawson, 'Episode 25 (Jay Bellerose)', 47:45–48:30 min. (here, Bellerose explains that he learned how to pull tone out of household items); also, C. Weinmann. 'Jay Bellerose: Dancing Days', *Drumhead Magazine* 74 (August 2019), p. 19–20.
45 'What's for Afters? Paula Cole – Where Have All the Cowboys Gone (1997)', *YouTube* (25 March 2014), available from: www.youtube.com/watch?v=5u2DgN5uX80 (accessed 12 March 2020).
46 Dawson, 'Episode 25 (Jay Bellerose)', 53:25–54:00 min.
47 L. Sachs. *T Bone Burnett: A Life in Pursuit* (Austin: University of Texas Press, 2016), p. 212.
48 S. Krugman. 'Hittin': Jay Bellerose @ The York', *Hollywood Drum.com: The Latest News* (25 September 2019), available from: www.hollywooddrum.com (accessed 12 March 2020).
49 P. Berkery. 'Jay Bellerose: All In A Year's Work', *Modern Drummer* (March 2009), available from: www.moderndrummer.com/2009/02/jay-bellerose-2/ (accessed 12 March 2020).
50 S. Goold. 'Album of the Week, #19', *The Steve Goold Blog* (29 September 2009), available from: https://stevegoold.wordpress.com/category/jay-bellerose/(accessed 13 March 2020).
51 Fox, 'Alternative to What?', p. 171.
52 A. Carcu. 'Erland Dahlen: Rolling Bombers and Blossom Bells', *All About Jazz* (23 September 2014), available from: https://cutt.ly/pgQT8Jk (accessed 12 March 2020); P. Berkery. 'The

Backstory on My New Old Drums', *Patrick Berkery Blog* (19 December 2017), available from: www.patrickberkery.com/new-blog/2017/12/19/the-backstory-on-my-new-old-drums (accessed 12 March 2020).

53 Fox, 'Alternative to What?', pp. 171–176.

54 Weinmann, 'Jay Bellerose: Dancing Days', p. 20.

55 Ibid.

56 Dawson, 'Episode 25 (Jay Bellerose)', 13:58–14:00 min.

57 For an in-depth study of the drumscape, see Matt Brennan's Kick It (Conclusion).

58 Holt, *Genre in Popular Music*, p. 39.

59 Dawson, 'Episode 25 (Jay Bellerose)', 1:11:44–11:12:05 min.

60 L. Hutchinson. 'T Bone Burnett', *Performing Songwriter* (14 January 2013), available from: http://performingsongwriter.com/t-bone-burnett/ (accessed 12 March 2020).

61 J. Pareles. 'T Bone Burnett Wants to Make Music to Heal Shrinking Attention Spans', *New York Times* (10 April 2019), available from: www.nytimes.com/2019/04/10/arts/music/t-bone-burnett-invisible-light.html (accessed 12 March 2020).

62 Hutchinson, 'T Bone Burnett'.

63 Weinmann, 'Jay Bellerose: Dancing Days', p. 16.

64 S. Jennings-X. 'Interview: T Bone Burnett', *Mix Online* (1 October 2008), available from: www.mixonline.com/recording/interview-t-bone-burnett-366025 (accessed 12 March 2020).

65 Ibid.

66 See L. Hutchinson, S. Jennings and M. Keefe-Feldman. 'T Bone Burnett Inspires and Challenges Berklee Students at Campus Visit', *Berklee Now* (3 December 2015), available from: www.berklee.edu/news/t-bone-burnett-inspires-and-challenges-berklee-students-campus-visit (accessed 30 April 2020).

67 Hutchinson, 'T Bone Burnett'.

68 Holt, *Genre in Popular Music*, p. 23.

9 Drum Tracks

Locating the Experiences of Drummers in Recording Studios

BRETT LASHUA AND PAUL THOMPSON

Introduction: Setting Up, Counting In

The following chapter locates the social, spatial, and technological experiences of popular music drummers by 'tracking' their involvement in the creative processes of recording studio work. The kick drum or the snare drum might become the most prominent part of a finished recording but where the drummer belongs in the process of making a record is not always at the forefront. From a drummer's perspective, interactions with the rest of the band, and the various personnel involved in the recording process, can be alienating and foreign, as 'Derek' (age 46) described:

> I remember my first session, first thing: getting a level on my kick drum. It was taking forever, and I started worrying: 'something's wrong with how I'm doing this. It's taking too long.' The clock was ticking, money being wasted and the pressure was on, and we hadn't even started! Alone in the live room, I could see everyone talking in the control room, and only every once in a while would the talkback mic click on [in my headphones], just to be told to stop or start up again. I had no idea what they had been talking about! Meanwhile, the rest of the band were sitting around, impatient, and – since I was tracking drums alone to start – no one else could do anything. I wasn't given time to settle in, and my takes were nervous, stiff, uptight. The studio was a vast, dark, mysterious space full of alien technology – like a spaceship! I hated it at first; I felt I was supposed to set up, play my parts, and then sit in the corner for days while everyone else spent hours fussing with a new FX unit or making as many overdubs as needed. If I asked to change something – like, 'could you put more emphasis on that chord?' – it was like I'd crossed a line: *get back in the corner!* I didn't feel part of it until I learned to sit in the engineer's chair. Then I started treating myself, and the other drummers I worked with, the way I wanted to be treated – you know, *included.*

This opening description begins to illustrate some of the social, spatial, and technological relations and occlusions for drummers in recordings studios, as viewed from a drummer's perspective.

Recording studios are often closed worlds of privileged access, and most notably in commercial record production, can be hierarchical with established divisions of labour, power, and agency.[1] Although the drums are typically the first element to be captured during the production process, drummers' experiences in the studio are often characterised by the need to get tracks done quickly and efficiently, then to get out of the way for the rest of the band or group to record, overdub and experiment with their takes.[2] If they are acknowledged as part of creative studio processes at all, drummers are commonly seen as less musical than other participants within the process and largely supplemental to the successive creative practices of producing music in studios as their role is often 'functional'.[3] Smith argued that drummers are 'a part, and yet apart' in marginal positions within bands, groups or musical ensembles.[4] Brennan listed longstanding pejorative characterisations of drummers, widely circulated through 'drummer jokes' as non-musicians: dumb, noisy, illiterate, uncreative, broke, and replaceable.[5] Accepted belief systems have been described by Bourdieu as 'doxa', which is a universe of common opinions, popular ideas and undisputed beliefs that exist within a field of cultural production. Doxa appear as natural and self-evident; doxa 'goes without saying because it comes without saying'.[6] One example of doxa within the recording studio is the superficial division between art and craft. Bourdieu labels this division the autonomous and heteronomous poles of an art world, which can be seen in the depiction of 'art' based or autonomous practitioners, such as the vocalists or guitarists, and more 'craft' oriented or heteronomous musicians such as drummers (or studio personnel such as the engineer).[7] All are needed in the studio to create a recording, but from certain viewpoints, or the doxa of the field, some appear to be considered more artistic and creative than others (i.e. more than *drummers*).

Researchers have begun to deconstruct and contest the accepted beliefs about drummers.[8] Through our ongoing ethnographic research in studios,[9] this chapter draws from observational fieldnotes from sessions when both authors were acting as ethnographers and drummers ('drummer-as-ethnographer') and – in Paul's fieldwork – also as session engineer.[10] We also conducted semi-structured interviews with eight drummers. In our analyses, we identify and critique prevailing doxa by (re)centring the views and experiences of drummers in creative studio practices. In overview, we highlight (or count in): (1) the spaces of drummers in studios (i.e. *where* drummers 'belong', or not); (2) the production of social identities in studios (i.e. *who* drummers are in relation to power hierarchies of recording processes); and (3) the knowledge and involvement of drummers in creative processes (i.e. *what* drummers 'know' and are able to do with their knowledge in studios). These thematic sections are presented as 'takes' to intone the tracking and layering involved in studio production.

First Take: Drummers, Spaces, and Studio Practices

Our first analytical theme explores the social production of space for drummers in recording studios.[11] For Lefebvre, 'if space is a product, our knowledge of it must be expected to reproduce and expound the process of production. The "object" of interest must be expected to shift from *things in space* to the actual *production of space*'.[12] Lefebvre was interested in the ways that space both shapes, and is shaped by, social relations, and sought 'to consider struggles over the organization and meaning of space'.[13] The spatiality of recording studios – i.e. who is able to do what, and where – is revelatory in view of drummers' roles, agency, and identities. For example, in fieldnotes made during sessions with an Americana band, Brett repeatedly noted his peripherality as the drummer, especially after the band finished tracking: e.g. in the control room, 'I'm sat again in the seats farthest from the mixing desk' or 'I'm not involved in discussions of others' tracks, but the guitarist was very involved in critique during tracking the drums' and 'I stayed in the live room for almost the entire night, only popping into the control room at the end of the session to listen to a rough mix'.[14] These fieldnotes illustrate that studio sessions involve more than the production of music; it also involves the production of spaces: 'The production of social space is a process . . . social space incorporates social actions'.[15]

This spatialisation emerged in our interviews, where staying 'where they belong', spatially, was not only a part of where drummers were in the studio, physically, but also where they belonged in view of making contributions to the music being recorded – that is, within the doxa of studio practices. One drummer (Mike, age 20) commented on his 'place' in creative songwriting processes in the studio:

> What I'm quite good at is where there needs to be a break or a dynamic change. I can hear that a lot as a drummer. From that point, I can influence when we should put in, you know, 'rock star stops.' But I guess with other musical instruments I'd say probably not: you stay out of it. If you're doing a track and you know, you're done, your parts are down, and they're tracking the bassline or something like that, you don't say something like 'the bass tones are muddy. Maybe sharpen it up in the mix a little bit'? There's a role for the drummer in the group during the songwriting process or during rehearsals that is to contribute to – I'll say orchestrate – the song progression, the place for starts and stops and dynamics, but then, in the studio your role is less; it's just play your parts and then step out.

A similar view was shared by Jess (age 27), who enjoyed the efficient atmosphere of a professional recording studio but drew a clear line between her performance in the live room and the activities in the control room. As a hired session player, she was used to and preferred a degree of distance from the production processes beyond performing her parts:

> You're in and out a lot quicker; your engineers know what they're doing. The gear is all ready to go, you're not doing more takes than necessary. They can sort out all that stuff [e.g. production] in the other room, like, they're ready for you, you do your bit and then you're out. I prefer that. Not that I'm busy and I've got other places to be, but I just like to get it done.

Jess's view illustrates the doxa of drummers as efficient labourers best placed in the live room, but not entering into more artistic or technical spaces (i.e. the control room), or like Mike, staying out of broader involvement – 'social actions' – in the arts of the recording studio, and thus productive of drummer's spaces in creative studio practices.

Another drummer, Keith (early 30s) described the drummer's contributions to song creation:

> I like to think of the drummer as providing the perspective, you know? So if you want to think about it in a relation to painting, a painter might say 'oh I'm gonna paint this flower and we're gonna use these colours and we're gonna use this sort of paint', but I like to think of the drummers role as saying: 'well, how are you gonna paint that flower? Is it gonna be a profile? Is it gonna be from top down? Is it gonna be from the bottom up? Is it gonna look like this massive flower? Is it gonna be right inside? Is it gonna be like a Georgia O'Keeffe perspective and reflect some sort of like body eroticism'? . . . it is providing the perspective or the frame.

Note that in this view the drummer is not a painter or part of the painting, but rather the one who frames the creative work of others. This effectively positions drummers *outside* the creative processes, despite – we would argue – being an integral contributor *inside* songwriting and recording processes.

While most of the drummers spatialised – and marginalised – their involvement through phrases such as being the 'backbeat in the backseat', some drummers were assertive about claiming space: 'it has always been a battle; you have to fight your corner. Saying "I need to re-track that" or "before we move on, we need to edit this"; everyone groans when I say that, but giving me an extra take or an edit now will make them all happier later [when they track]' (Derek, age 46). Another drummer (Paul, age 37) recounted an experience where other session players weren't used to playing to a click track while working on a song that started with a bassline: 'Everybody rushed when the bass came in [following the bass] and it made me look like I couldn't play to the click track. They decided not to follow me either! Who's in the driver's seat?' These comments illustrate the active social production of space within studios: popular music drummers are positioned in social spaces that are seen as hierarchically lower in status, less artistic and less powerful in the relations that suffuse popular music recording; we read this positioning as manifest in the physical locations that drummers occupy.

Another part of this hierarchical 'backseat' positioning involves the broader relations between drummers and other studio personnel, such as engineers and producers, in the spatiality of studios. Echoing the experiences of Derek in the chapter's opening extract, Paul offered: 'engineers really don't understand what it feels like on the other side of the glass. They think it's really easy and it's not. It's a really pressured situation'. Against this, most drummers commented that it was not easy to act – against the grain, or counter to the doxa – to become involved in production using the technological affordances of the studio. Paul added:

> One of the reasons I think drummers make really good producers is because they sit at the back of the band, and that also teaches you how to arrange – not a string arrangement but arrange a song – where you're thinking about how all the parts work together. Richard Burgess is a really good example of that. There're tons of producers who are drummers and it's because that unofficial hierarchy of decision-making in the recording studio and you assume that drummers are at the bottom of that, but I think a lot of bands, if they respect their drummer they also respect the drummer's perspective.

In sum, our fieldnotes and interviews alerted us to the spatial circulation of power relations in recording studios: the production of music was also the production of space in which the doxa of drummers was also (re)produced. This spatialisation was manifest in the role of drummers in songwriting, in the physical spaces where drummers 'belonged' in studios, and in the contributions that drummers felt they could make to creative studio practices and production. We extend the idea of 'positioning' in relation to drummer's identities in our next take.

Second Take: Playing for the Song? Identities, Positionalities, and Habitus

One phrase repeated across our interviews was 'playing for the song'; this is a common trope in discourse about drummers: e.g. Ringo Starr was recently celebrated in *Drum! Magazine* for 'playing for the song', arguing he did so in a way that was more than 'just some thankless, mundane task'.[16] In this take, we critique 'playing for the song' as an insight into the doxa surrounding drummers' identities. For Stuart Hall, identities are 'always constructed through memory, fantasy, narrative and myth. Cultural identities are . . . not an essence, but a *positioning*'.[17] Drummers are not naturally or biologically predisposed to be wild or 'uncreative',[18] but rather these are 'points of identification that are made within the discourses of history and culture'.[19] That is to say, drummers' identity positions are produced, and drummers often assume stereotypical subject positions. One crucial arena where this production and positioning takes place – where its *mythification* occurs – is the recording studio. 'Playing for the song' is much a part of the mythification of drummers as 'simple' subjects.

Most of the drummers we interviewed shared views of 'playing for the song' by 'keeping things simple' and 'not over playing' or, as one respondent noted, 'creating a space to allow the other musicians to shine'. One interviewee offered: 'I'm the type of drummer who would rather hear another drummer play parts and grooves, parts for the song . . . I love the person off the street who serves the song'. Beyond an appeal to simplicity, this comment infers that popular music drumming is easy (and perhaps it is), but the critical point here is that these beliefs are already in circulation and are part and parcel of 'who drummers are' and 'what they are expected to do' in songwriting and recording.

When asked about his earliest experiences of recording, one drummer spoke about his home studio, and having to be the drummer, rhythm guitarist, and recording engineer. These multiple roles in formative experiences provide 'the reason why I'm not a very good drummer technically . . . because of my route into playing drums, it's always been about a collective thing for me. It's about playing with a band, rather than being amazing'. This inference that drummers are somehow rather less 'amazing' than other band members was echoed also by Jess: 'In the group, I felt like the drums are always the ones that need to sit back a little bit in the correct situations and let the people that are standing up at the front be front'.

The positioning of the drummer to 'sit back' raises questions of 'how far back'? in view of 'playing for the song'. Invited to a session to record a medley in homage to the late Americana musician Jason Molina, Brett's fieldnotes recount a process of repeatedly being told to simplify his drum lines to barest minimums, stripping out accents, fills and 'softening' his playing with each successive take. While this barebones aesthetic was in keeping with Molina's spare songwriting, for Brett it also felt like an exercise in which the other musicians in the session policed the notion of what it meant to 'play for the song' – a phrase Brett heard throughout the session. Returning to the studio for a second day to track one more song, he recounted:

> I'm waiting for the others to turn up (drummer cliché – I'm early; they're late!), I just learned [from the engineer] they had already finished the last

> song: the piano player had tracked the drums after I left last night! I'm not bothered about someone else tracking drums for the tune, but what he's played is so minimal as to be utterly faceless. Is that what they'd meant by 'playing for the song'? For me, such characterlessness means disappearing into the wallpaper. That's not playing for the song, is it? It's the erasure of the drummer.[20]

While perhaps an unusual example, Brett's fieldnotes raise further questions about the idea of 'playing for the song'. For Paul, it meant offering 'something slightly different or subtle, [or] interesting' in each part of a song. Yet, the doxa of 'playing for the song' often positions drummers as so simple (in Brett's fieldnotes) as to be 'replaceable', when (in Paul's words) playing 'just to facilitate the song'.[21]

These perceptions have indelible effects on the dispositions of drummers towards their bodies, behaviours, and identities. In Bourdieu's terms, what emerged from our fieldwork is a view of drumming 'habitus': the dispositions towards the body and the behaviours, actions and thoughts to which an individual (i.e. drummer) is *habituated*, through socialisation in families, schools, and – in popular music – in groups, bands, and in the social spaces of studios.[22] For Bourdieu, the habitus 'is a socialised body . . . which has incorporated the immanent structures of a world or of a particular sector of that world – a field – and which structures the perception of that world as well as action in that world'.[23] As Reay put it, habitus is both the body in the social world and the social world made manifest in the body.[24] For drummers, these bodily dispositions are revealed in comments about studio sessions. Derek recounted:

> Live, I felt like I was supposed to play like 'Animal' from the Muppets, or Keith Moon, you know, like a flailing wild man; my motto was 'if I didn't bleed, it wasn't a good show!' But then there was this total disconnect with how I felt I should play in the studio: tight, precise, clinical, simplified. It wasn't me. It never felt right and I don't think my playing ever translated to studio work.

Here Derek hints at a drumming habitus expressed through ways 'of standing, speaking, walking, and thereby of feeling and thinking' about drumming.[25] Habitus is made manifest in everyday actions and, for drummers, through all of the thoughts, actions, and gestures that encompass drumming. The myth of playing for the song, therefore, is part of the habitus of drummers' identities, as well as part of the positioning of drummers within the 'the discourses of history and culture' that are part of the doxa of drummers' worlds.[26] As Paul intoned in Take One, becoming involved in a wider world of creative studio practices also required engagement with a range of studio knowledge and personnel. We explore this expanded world and body of studio knowledge in our final take.

Third Take: Agency, Creative Practice, and Studio Knowledge

The third analytical theme that arose from interviews with drummers was that of agency within the recording or production process. Agency is a crucial element of creative activity because it is located within a drummer's ability to make choices, take actions or exercise their free will.[27] Giddens, for example, argues that: 'agency concerns events of which an individual is the perpetrator, in the sense that the individual could, at any phase in a given sequence of conduct, have acted differently'.[28] Agents are considered to be knowledgeable subjects who 'know how to act . . . know the rules of behaviour, and . . . know the sequences of actions'.[29] Giddens also asserts that: 'it is always the case that the day-to-day activity of social actors draws upon and reproduces structural features of wider social systems'.[30] This can be seen in the previous two takes where the activities of drummers inside the recording studio draw upon and reproduce existing hierarchies within studios and the art world of popular music production more broadly. In this sense drummers can be seen as constrained by the structures of the recording studio and the record production process but it is vital to underline that they are also enabled by these structures too.[31] Giddens labels this interdependence between agency and structure as 'structuration', which is 'an attempt to resolve the tension which exists between individual and society'.[32] Structuration acknowledges that 'all action, including creative and innovative action, arises in the complex conjunction of numerous structural determinants and conditions'.[33]

A drummer's ability to make particular choices in the recording studio and exercise agency is both enabled and constrained by the institutional boundaries of the cultural field in which they work. These boundaries include studio technologies, studio practices that implement that technology, and the limits that the current institution can assimilate.[34] A studio drum recording can be viewed as the complex result of economic and conceptual influences, which have been 'mediated through the formal structures of the text (literary or other), and owing its existence to the particular practice of the located individual'.[35] Our drummer-interviewees noted that their ability to exercise agency was most limited at the beginning of their career and in sessions where they were hired to perform on record. Tony (age 57) began drumming professionally in studios in 1982, working for a producer recording drums for jingles and advertisements. As in previous takes in this chapter, Tony was expected to record his parts and then get out of the way. However, two years later after joining a band signed to a record label, he began to have more agency in the recording process. He recounted recording sessions in Trident Studios:

> By now I'm starting to get more involved in not just working on the material but working on the sounds as well and I was allowed to do it. We had a producer called Pete Wilson, who'd done the Style Council, and he let me sort of get involved really and try and develop the sound to a more 'big band' style sound, which is what I'd always wanted to do. That was the first time I was really allowed to do that.

This involvement wasn't without constraints, as Tony explained:

> Studios are expensive and they wanted it done quickly. We were still a new band and I don't think they wanted to spend a ton of money on the studio, they wanted to spend the money somewhere else like on the marketing but it wasn't the pressure of that, it was more the pressure of trying to come up with something that Robert [the lead singer] liked because it was counterintuitive to the type of music that I was into at the time . . . I was always trying to play a bit tighter, a bit safer and in the pocket and he's not having it; he wanted it really raggedy and loose.

Drummers must balance the expectations of the multiple participants involved and exercising the agency they have within studio processes. A drummer's status within the cultural unit of a band is often related to the amount of agency they have in the recording studio. For example, Keith explained:

> I joined that band after they had two hit records so that's something I try to remember at all times. Of course it's possible for me to bring what I think are great ideas into the project, but it's important for me to remember that their success predated my involvement with them. So, I need to ensure I'm never offended if they don't want my input with songwriting or arrangement or production but at the same time feel confident enough to offer that stuff.

Session drummer Jess also acknowledged this:

> I wouldn't really get involved in the post [production] side of it. I would only say something if . . . for example, I always bring my snares in and if a guy in the studio in post was making my snare drum – which has cost a lot of money and that I know how I want it to sound – sound like crap, then I'd say something.

Across our interviews, drummers noted that as they became more experienced and developed their status – or in Bourdieu's terms accumulated cultural and symbolic capital – their abilities to exercise agency also changed. Some drummers were able to exercise greater agency inside the recording studio because of their knowledge and experience with recording technologies. As Tony was asked increasingly to work with click-tracks in the studio, he became determined to gain a greater understanding of technologies such as drum machines to the point where he thought of them 'as his friends'. His first experience of these technologies was when his original drum part was removed and replaced with a sampled, programmed part. Instead of viewing this as an imposition upon his agency, Tony appreciated the way in which it contributed to the overall production of the song, stating: 'Because of that, the band actually bought an SP-12 Sampler and I learned how to use it. The next album we did, there's no live drums on it; they're all programmed'.

Other drummers noted that developing experience and knowledge with recording technologies was linked to their agency as a drummer inside the recording studio too. Emre, an engineer, producer, and drummer, noted:

> I spent masses of time learning how to place parts on the grid so I don't have so much editing to do [laughs]. When people really want that 'beat detective' kind of feel, I've spent a long time learning how to pocket the drums right on the grid. I'm naturally looser and elastic when I play so that took a while to learn how to do that, and obviously playing with lots of session players who have perfect time, I thought 'right, I've got to learn how to do this because it's not what comes naturally to me'.

The interviewees also highlighted that working closely with other studio personnel was a crucial part of exercising agency over the ways in which their drums were captured on record as Paul explained: 'Because of my experience of engineering I was able to work with the engineer to set up the mics, get particular sounds, then also play the performances which were all done to a click, and then edit them myself'.

Mike reported a close working, creative relationship with the studio engineer during his first studio recording session at age sixteen. He described this relationship as 'the most immediate', with the engineer the 'pivotal person' in the creative process:

> Me and 'Bill' spent six hours on one single and we just stripped everything back and made everything simplistic for the record, in what I think sounds so much better, rewriting a track and just loving it. So, he had an engineer's and producer's role in it. I would play the section and then Bill would be like 'let's make a compromise; like let's take this out, or do you want to add this in?', and it was always up to me but obviously he knew what he was doing, and we changed the track to make it . . . it's like simplistic, like just very sturdy, and it was just like a classic rock track.

Recording a take, isolating and chopping up its components, and reconstructing a new track (similar to vocal 'comping', or creating an aggregated 'composite' track from a number of takes) shows a luxury of time and production not often afforded to drummers and drum takes. This example also evinces a high degree of alteration, and thus creative control, through editing and reconfiguring an overall track. Yet, by reducing the track and making it 'simplistic', like a 'classic rock track', this again demonstrates the doxa of workmanship and the identity positioning of 'playing for the song' as discussed in Take Two. It also highlights the ways in which agency operates inside the structures of the recording studio with the expectations of the social field (the fans, the media, the recording) always present within the decision-making process. The examples highlight the interrelationship between agency and structure in which both are necessary in order for drummers (and engineers and producers) to operate inside the recording studio.[36] Agency, or freedom, is therefore bound by the constraints, or the structures, that facilitate its operation. These constraints may include musical style, pre-written musical parts of a song, the technologies used, and the status of the drummer within the recording studio context. Drummers must navigate these multiple, competing concerns in exercising agency inside the recording studio.

Final Take: Concluding Thoughts

In conclusion, we offer a handful of take-aways as contributions to the growing body of knowledge about drummers and drumming. First, through sociological lenses, we have called for greater attention to drummers in the social worlds of recording studios. Here we echo Reay: 'the goal of sociological research is to uncover the most deeply buried structures of the different social worlds that make up the social universe, as well as the "mechanisms" that tend to ensure their reproduction or transformation'.[37] Second, the chapter contributes to the conceptualisations of the 'work' of drummers in creative recording environments across its central conceptual axes, or 'takes': spaces, identities, and agencies. Third, through ethnographic fieldwork and qualitative interviews, the chapter has sought to enhance the methodological richness of research about, and with, drummers, offering finer-textured and more deeply contextualised accounts of musicians' experiences – in this case, drummers – in recording studios.

Notes

1 E. R. Kealy. 'From Craft to Art: The Case of Sound Mixers and Popular Music', *Sociology of Work and Occupations* 6:1 (1979), pp. 3–29; E. Bates. 'What Studios Do', *Journal on the Art of Record Production* 7:2 (2012), www.arpjournal.com/asarpwp/what-studios-do/; P. Thompson.*Creativity in the Recording Studio: Alternative Takes* (Basingstoke: Palgrave Macmillan, 2019).

2 B. Lashua. 'The Beat of a Different Drummer: Music-Making and Leisure Research', in R. Mantie and G. D. Smith (eds.), *Oxford Handbook of Music-Making and Leisure* (Oxford: Oxford University Press, 2017), pp. 427–449.

3 B. Bruford. *Uncharted: Creativity and the Expert Drummer* (Ann Arbor: University of Michigan Press, 2018).

4 G. D. Smith. *I Drum Therefore I Am* (Farnham: Ashgate, 2013), p. 45.

5 M. Brennan. *Kick It: A Social History of the Drum Kit* (Oxford: Oxford University Press, 2020), pp. 1–6.

6 P. Bourdieu. *Outline of a Theory of Practice* (Cambridge: Cambridge University Press, 1977), p. 167.
7 P. Bourdieu. *The Rules of Art: Genesis and Structure of the Literary Field* (Stanford: Stanford University Press, 1996).
8 Brennan, *Kick It*; Bruford, *Uncharted*; J. Mowitt. *Percussion: Drumming, Beating, Striking* (Durham: Duke University Press, 2002); Smith, *I Drum Therefore I Am.*
9 B. Lashua and P. Thompson. 'Producing Music, Producing Myth? Creativity in Recording Studios', Iaspm@journal 6:2 (2016), pp. 70–90; P. Thompson and B. Lashua. 'Getting It on Record: Issues and Strategies for Contemporary Ethnographic Practice in Recording Studios', *Journal of Contemporary Ethnography* 43:6 (2014), pp. 746–769; Thompson, *Creativity in the Recording Studio.*
10 Lashua, 'The Beat of a Different Drummer'.
11 H. Lefebvre. *The Social Production of Space*, D. Nicholson-Smith translator (Oxford: Blackwell, 1991).
12 Lefebvre, *The Social Production of Space,* pp. 36–37 (original emphasis).
13 R. Shields. 'Knowing Space', *Theory, Culture and Society* 23:2–3 (2006), p. 149.
14 Fieldnotes (5 September 2017).
15 Lefebvre, *The Social Production of Space,* pp. 33–34.
16 J. Bosso. 'Beatles History: Ringo Starr's 10 Greatest Recorded Moments'. *Drum! Magazine* 267 (Spring 2019), https://drummagazine.com/beatles-history-ringo-starrs-10-greatest-recorded-moments/.
17 S. Hall. 'Cultural Identity and Diaspora' in J. Rutherford (ed.), *Identity: Community, Culture, Difference* (London: Lawrence and Wishart, 1990), p. 226 (original emphasis).
18 Brennan, *Kick It.*
19 Hall, 'Cultural Identity and Diaspora', p. 226.
20 Fieldnotes (6 September 2017).
21 Brennan, *Kick It.*
22 P. Bourdieu. *Distinction* (London: Routledge, 1984).
23 P. Bourdieu. *Practical Reason* (Cambridge: Polity Press, 1998), p. 81
24 D. Reay. '"It's All Becoming a Habitus": Beyond the Habitual Use of Habitus in Educational Research', *British Journal of Sociology of Education* 25:4 (2004), pp. 431–444.
25 P. Bourdieu. *The Logic of Practice* (Cambridge: Polity Press, 1990), p. 70.
26 Hall, 'Cultural Identity and Diaspora', p. 226.
27 J. Wolff. *The Social Production of Art* (London: MacMillan, 1981); A. Giddens. *The Constitution of Society: Outline of the Theory of Structuration* (Berkeley: University of California Press, 1984); Bourdieu, *The Rules of Art.*
28 Giddens, *The Constitution of Society,* p. 9.
29 L. B. Kaspersen. *Anthony Giddens: An Introduction to a Social Theorist* (Oxford: Blackwell, 2000), p. 35.
30 Giddens, *The Constitution of Society,* p .24
31 Ibid.
32 Kaspersen, *Anthony Giddens,* p. 32.
33 Wolff, *The Social Production of Art,* p. 9.
34 H. S. Becker. *Art Worlds* (Berkeley: University of California Press, 1982).
35 Wolff, *The Social Production of Art,* p. 139.
36 Giddens, *The Constitution of Society.*
37 Reay, 'It's All Becoming a Habitus', p. 431.

PART III

Learning, Teaching, and Leading on the Drum Kit

10 Studying Hybrid and Electronic Drum Kit Technologies

BRYDEN STILLIE

Introduction

The drum kit exists as a result of significant technological innovations and developments that have influenced the design and manufacture of its constituent parts. The drum kit can be defined as a technology in itself, in that it is a device that exists and functions as a direct result of 'the practical ... use of scientific discoveries'.[1] The technological developments of the traditional acoustic drum kit have been recorded and described in articles in periodicals such as *Modern Drummer* (Modern Drummer Publications) and *Rhythm Magazine* (Future plc), and are comprehensively charted in Matt Dean's book, *The Drum: A History*.[2] Additionally, Matt Brennan (Chapter 1 in this book) provides a short historiography of the technological development of the drum kit in which he states that the definition of the drum kit is continually 'in flux'; arguably, this has never been more true considering recent developments in electronic drum kit technologies and how they are used in performance by drummers.[3]

In this chapter, however, I have chosen to be mindful of the use of the word *technology* when discussing the modern drum kit setup, as the description of the drum kit as a technology may not be recognisable to many contemporary drummers. My choice is predicated on the growing use of the word technology to describe the electronic devices that permeate our every-day life. In this chapter the word technology will only be used in the context of the electronic technologies used to augment, or replace, the acoustic drum kit. 'Technology has vastly extended the drummer's sonic palette' and in many cases, technology has also augmented the role of the drummer within their performance settings.[4] These technologies include percussion controllers, sample pads, triggers, and music creation software(s) that are now commonly used to augment, or even replace, the traditional drum kit setup.[5]

This chapter seeks to open the discussion about how drum kit educators might embrace drum kit technologies as an exciting and highly relevant part of their curricula. Through examination of the experience of students studying my own drum kit technologies course, this chapter will propose ways in which educators might consider supporting their students to explore these technologies and develop valuable skills and knowledge by situating them at the heart of their student's creative music making.

Situating the Drum Kit in Popular Music Education

This chapter is firmly situated in Popular Music Education, an emerging and expanding field of music research.[6] Courses in popular music in higher education (HE) have only existed for around three decades and as such, educators are still developing teaching approaches that provide recognisable, valuable, effective, personalised and authentic experiences for their learners.

Drum kit is taught across a range of popular music performance courses at HE level, with tutors drawing on a series of long-standing approaches and methods to teach the instrument.[7] However, the learning opportunities drummers might experience during their studies may vary based on: (1) the level at which they are studying; (2) the tutor with whom they are studying; and (3) the course they have selected to study. Most drum kit curricula have been designed based on what the tutor decides is valuable with some degree of personalisation for each student.[8] Some courses will teach drum kit as an ensemble instrument with no, or limited, one-to-one tuition. On other courses students may receive a weekly one-to-one lesson, and in some cases, drum kit is taught to groups using electronic drum kits which have the same setup and layout as an acoustic drum kit, with each drummer wearing headphones.

From my own experience working as a drum kit specialist in HE, it is rare that drum kit curricula include teaching the creative use of drum kit technologies. In this chapter, I examine student perceptions of learning these technologies as part of their undergraduate studies at Edinburgh Napier University, Scotland. I explore the benefits of studying this course, the challenges students encountered, and discuss the implications of these findings for future course and technology development.

Teaching Electronic Drum Kit Technologies

Since 2008, I have been running a compulsory course that teaches drum kit technologies to drummers in Year 3 of the BA Popular Music degree programme at Edinburgh Napier University, Scotland. Drummers

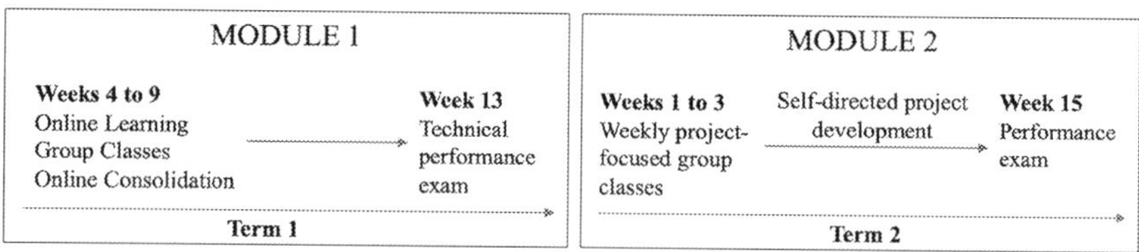

Figure 10.1 The arrangement of the drum kit course within the two-performance module structure

embarking on this course are performing at approximately London College of Music Diploma level, have studied at least two modules in music technology and have developed skills in music analysis.[9] This prior experience equips students with the prerequisite skills to engage effectively with the learning on the course. The course has been designed to explore the full affordances of drum kit technologies, to provide students with a skill set that will support their creative and musical activity, and to produce versatile graduate drummers who have increased chances of employment in the music industry.[10] From a music industry perspective, it is now commonplace for drummers to integrate technologies into their setup, therefore it is important that students have the opportunity to develop knowledge and understanding of drum kit technologies to enable them to perform the production-led music they aspire to play.

The course straddles two modules (Figure 10.1). In Term 1 students learn the functionality of the technologies then engage in a series of practical tasks and creative performances.[11] The initial section of the course occurs across a six-week block. The curricular content is delivered using a flipped classroom methodology.[12] Each week, students engage in online learning prior to class, participate in practical face-to-face group workshops, and engage in online individual and group consolidation activities. The primary drum kit technology used on this course is the Roland SPD-20 percussion controller.[13] There are a number of reasons for this selection:

- the simplicity of the user interface;
- the ability to layer two MIDI notes on different MIDI channels on each pad; and
- the controller is prevalent in contemporary popular music, the focus of the BA Popular Music programme.

In the initial weeks, students cover the following topics: accessing and editing sounds; acoustic and electronic drum triggers; the MIDI functions of the percussion controller; and connecting the controller to computer-based music software to access sampler instruments.[14] At the end of the first term students are assessed on their performance of a set work for solo hybrid drum kit.[15]

In the second term students develop a solo performance to be played using only drum kit technologies and music software. The process of developing these performances requires students to:

1. analyse and describe their chosen song;
2. record, program, produce, and deconstruct the arrangement they will perform;
3. learn a new notation method and produce a score of their performance; and
4. develop a different approach to coordination that is driven by the complexity of musical arrangement which embraces both the affordances and the limitations of the technology.

Stages 1 and 2 above require students to analyse the music they are creating from multiple perspectives including melody, harmony, rhythm, texture, timbre, and from a music production standpoint. To successfully analyse and reproduce the music they want to perform, students need to understand the stylistic characteristics of the music, and the production techniques employed in the recordings. At this stage students are also analysing timbre – 'all that is left after pitch and dynamic level'.[16] The students deploy analysis skills to examine timbre to then accurately recreate sounds and produce quality reproductions of their chosen songs. Tutor support is offered at this stage, but in line with observations made by Tobias, students on this course regularly develop their production skills through researching and viewing online videos.[17]

Drivers for This Current Research and Method

Module-level feedback has always highlighted that students value the opportunity to learn these technologies as part of their studies. However, the feedback rarely provided detail, depth, or context on the learning experience. I chose to conduct qualitative research to gain a deeper understanding of the student experience on the course to ensure that the learning experience was relevant, valuable, and delivered effectively. I conducted semi-structured interviews with twelve drum kit students (two female and ten male) from Year 3 and 4 of the BA Popular Music course. Seven students studied the drum kit technologies course in 2017–2018 and five students studied the same course in 2018–2019. Three students had never used these technologies before and of the remaining nine students, the majority had used electronic drum kits as a direct substitute for an acoustic drum kit. All students had experience of using Logic Pro X, the music software used in this course. Interviews were recorded (with permission) and were fully transcribed. I scrutinised the transcripts and conducted a thematic analysis to identify emergent themes.

Research Findings and Discussion

The analysis of the transcripts exposed the following four themes:

1. The learning and teaching experience
2. Working with notation and developing coordination
3. Employability
4. Desired course developments

Learning and Teaching Experience

The findings indicate that participants valued the opportunity to learn drum kit technologies. The student learning experience in Term 1 can be categorised into four distinct learning activities: (a) online class preparation; (b) face-to-face groupwork in class; (c) online consolidation activities; and (d) the preparation and completion of a summative assessment. In particular, participants felt that the flipped classroom approach used to structure and deliver learning experiences was of significant benefit to their engagement and understanding of the weekly topics.[18] The online learning activities enabled students to prepare for class, increasing their confidence in the use of these unfamiliar technologies.

> It meant that you could do it [learn] at your own pace so you could pause videos instead of taking up class time . . . if you watched all the videos everything you needed to know was all in those videos . . . It also meant that if you forgot something, then you could go back. Participant 4 (Year 3)
>
> It was like having a one-on-one lesson with you [the tutor] that never ended because we were able to go back and double check everything. If there was a bit that we didn't understand, we were able to rewind . . . It gave me the knowledge on a one-to-one basis at a time and place, and pace that suited me best. Participant 6 (Year 3)

The comments received in relation to the preparatory activities highlight that the use of video demonstration was highly effective in enabling learners to develop a deep understanding of how the technologies function. This approach mirrors the way in which many instrumentalists use online video streaming services such as YouTube or Vimeo, or specialist instrumental education sites such as Drumeo, or video created by their tutor in formal, non-formal and informal contexts.[19] The asynchronous nature of this online delivery had a positive impact on student learning, enabling students to study and review materials at their own pace, at a time that suited their schedule.[20]

Traditional acoustic drum kit tuition does not suit group teaching settings for a variety of reasons, for example, only one person can play the kit at a time and the volume and space considerations of having more than one kit in a room. These issues are somewhat mitigated when using drum kit technologies as their volume can be controlled, the equipment often occupies a smaller physical space, and if resources allow, multiple drummers can be playing and learning in the same space.[21] This approach can be seen in many institutions where rooms are filled with electronic drum kits set up in rows facing the teacher. However, this approach does not necessarily support what Lave and Wenger describe as a 'community of practice' or promote collaborative learning, since the drummers are working individually.[22] In this setting, the in-class activity is not predicated on sharing or co-creating knowledge, or collective problem-solving. A significant difference in the way my course is delivered is that there is very little tutor direction in group workshops. Students collaborate to complete a series of tasks and share their learning and understanding in the group. This enables the students to enter what Vygotsky describes as the 'zone of proximal development' i.e. the collaborative learning environment enables students to develop a deeper understanding of the equipment compared to completing the tasks individually.[23]

> They [group classes] were really good in terms of other people coming up with questions . . . all of us basically are teaching each other and learning from each other's mistakes and problems. Participant 3 (Year 3)
>
> I really enjoyed it because it was collaborative . . . If one of us figured something out, the environment was tailored to enable us to share that . . . it tended to be that someone would experience a problem, and once we found the solution, the whole class would know. Participant 12 (Year 4)

Following workshop classes students engage in a range of online consolidation tasks, some of which are used to develop a community of inquiry.[24] The tasks included: sharing videos that demonstrate the skills developed in the previous class; writing research-led collaborative blogs to explain the functionality of certain technologies to the class; and sharing research into drummers who use technology in live performance. Students recognised that by completing each task they deepened their knowledge and increased their confidence in using these technologies.

> It was like a recap on what we had gone through in class. It obviously gave you [the lecturer] confidence knowing that we could do it [in class] and then go away and do it again. Participant 9 (Year 4)

> It was very important that the tasks we were set were determined on what we had learned in class . . . and being able to show what you had done in your own time to everyone else was pretty cool. Participant 7 (Year 4)

Working with Notation and Developing Coordination

Approaches to scoring music for hybrid drum kit so far have negated to include directions for coordination and assume that the learner will be able to 'work it out'.[25] This may be the case if the coordination required to trigger the electronic sounds is an obvious substitution for elements of an original groove. For example, Example 10.1 shows notation of a simple hybrid performance. The pad strike in bar 2 is played using similar coordination to that used in bar 1.

Most drummers would be familiar with the coordination required to play the groove in Example 10.1, and the process of substituting a different sound source on beat one is similar to the coordination used to play the crash cymbal when introducing a new section of an arrangement. However, if the coordination is not clearly mapped for the learner, there is always a chance that the coordination they apply will not be the most straightforward or efficient. In Figure 10.2, the coordination used to perform the pad strike may seem obvious – for a right-handed drummer the pad could be played by the right hand in substitution for the hi-hat. However, it could just as easily be performed with the left hand allowing the drummer to also play the hi-hat on beat 1 of the second bar. Clear signposting of the required coordination is vital to ensuring economy of motion and to allow as much of the existing or underlying groove to be maintained.

A key feature of this course is that drummers learn a notation system specifically for electronic drum kit technologies. This notation system can represent the coordination, rhythmic phrasing, and the pad numbers that are to be struck to activate sounds (Figure 10.2 and Example 10.2).

This notation method has been highly effective in supporting the process of learning and sharing music, so much so that students have learned the notated performances without actually practicing on the technology. Students often use a piece of paper with the SPD-20 layout drawn

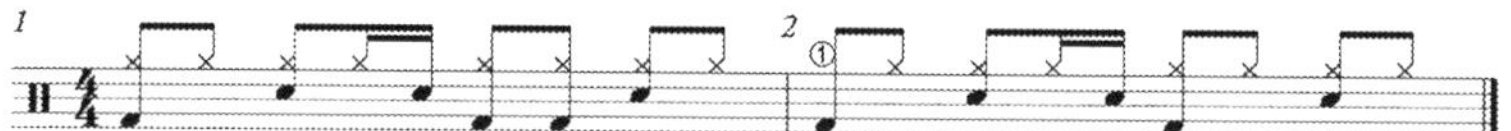

Example 10.1 Hybrid drum kit notation showing pad strike substitution for the hi-hat in bar 2

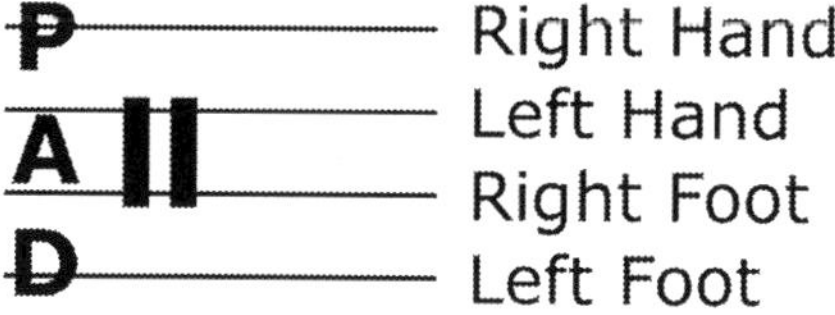

Figure 10.2 The PAD notation clef and legend

Example 10.2 Notation of a hybrid performance. The left hand is used to trigger the electronic elements of the performance

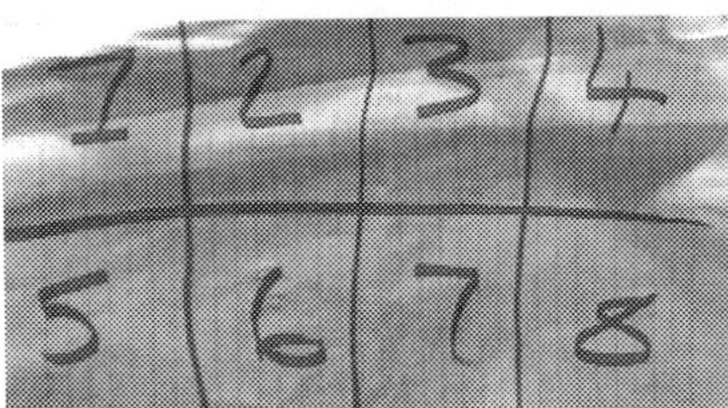

Figure 10.3 The hand-drawn layout of an SPD-20 used by a student to learn a hybrid performance

on it and learn the coordination required by tapping the numbers in the grid to familiarise themselves with the patterns (See Figure 10.3).

Using the PAD notation, students were able to quickly learn the coordination required to perform new pieces.

> I really liked it. I thought it was brilliant, I have never seen anything like it. It's unique. I think each limb having its own line on the stave really works. Participant 9 (Year 4)

> It was quite easy to read, it also just . . . makes sense. I hadn't seen any pad notation before, it was good. Participant 10 (Year 4)

When we examine the educational publications that focus on developing coordination and dexterity, almost all are predicated on developing these skills in relation to the acoustic drum kit setup.[26] Hybrid and fully electronic performances provide an alternative way of developing coordination. Cameron suggests coordination, and creative performance, can be developed through reallocating patterns with grooves to different limbs on the traditional drum kit.[27] When drummers use drum kit technologies to activate melodic, harmonic and/or rhythmic elements of a piece, performances will require non-standard coordination that will rarely be recognisable as a groove or fill. In fully electronic performances any limb can activate any sound which greatly enhances the opportunity to manipulate and develop coordination. For example, to increase challenge, drummers might make significant use of their non-dominant hand to trigger parts of the arrangement. Additionally, increasing the rate at which sounds are triggered can make the performance more difficult. Changes made to these variables can pose significant challenges to the coordination of drummers who have only learned patterns on acoustic kit. For many, integrating electronics often feels like playing two instruments (or more) at a time. During the interviews it was clear that students recognised that their coordination was challenged and that it improved as a result of performing the set work.

> The conceptual challenge of playing drum kit differently, or of utilising technology for performance, which I don't think any of us had previously done, changes the way you think about your parts. Suddenly you are not thinking about drum beats you are thinking about musical parts that have to be played and from a coordination standpoint technically you are changing what you do with your body. Participant 12 (Year 4)

> The coordination was probably the hardest part for me . . . It definitely got you used to wrapping your head around the completely different way you have got to approach actually playing . . . Once you have got your head around the coordination, playing grooves whilst playing the added sounds in amongst that, you are kinda set to do anything you want when you are just solely [playing] on the electronics. Participant 3 (Year 3)

Employability

Although electronic drum kit technologies emerged in the late 1970s, they have only recently started to feature in the kit setups of a significant number of drummers. Several factors have influenced this growth, such as: lower relative cost of purchasing equipment; the greater choice of products available to drummers; an increased expectation that highly produced sounds are replicated in live performances so that artists 'sound like the album'. As an educator based in the HE sector, there is significant pressure to produce employable graduates.[28] This expectation greatly influenced the development of this course. Students felt that the course enhanced their employability and furnished them with vital skills for their future career.

> I've been hired to perform as part of a pit band for a musical and the whole premise is that I will be using a sample pad alongside the kit I'm playing the kit, percussion, sound effects or samples that they need. It just gives you another notch on your belt. It's another bullet point on your CV . . . in the modern climate of what music is, electronics are very important. Participant 6 (Year 3)

> It's done a lot for it [employability]. Every band that you see playing anywhere there's not a drummer who doesn't have a sample pad or trigger here and there. I think it's vital for drummers going forward to be able to use this stuff . . . not being able to program something stops you from being able to play almost every song that is in the charts right now. Participant 4 (Year 3)

Desired Course Developments

The current course expects students to demonstrate their use of the technologies in solo performance settings. A number of students discussed their desire to explore the use of technologies in band settings. Using solo performances with technology as the focus for the course ensures that the learners understand, explore and demonstrate the technology's full potential. However, it is understandable that students would want to learn to use it in settings where they will most likely use it in the future.

> It might be worth . . . using it [percussion controller] in more of a live setting . . . having like a hybrid acoustic kit and then triggering clicks and samples . . . I feel like the Spitfire piece in the first trimester probably benefited me more than the second trimester piece that we had to do, only because I have not been in a situation where I have had to use it [SPD-20] as a MIDI controller and make all my own stuff [samples] even though I think it is so beneficial. Participant 2 (Year 4)

While the notation method used to communicate the physical coordination, rhythmic phrasing and pad numbers is clearly effective and enables students to learn pieces quickly, students described their experience of checking the accuracy of their own PAD scores using the notation software as challenging.

> The only thing I wish is that you can actually hear [the samples produced by Logic X] . . . when you are playing it [the score] in Sibelius, it was crazy . . . If you could choose each of the numbered sounds even if it wasn't what you were actually programming. If you could choose something that was kinda close I think that would be really useful cause you had no idea if you had put it all in right just by looking at this page of numbers. Participant 1 (Year 3)

The problem experienced by this student defines one of the key challenges associated with the scoring and playback process. Traditional scoring software provides a visual representation of programmed MIDI information. The software uses MIDI information to play back the specific pitch or tone that is notated (melodic or harmonic), or mapped (drums and percussion), i.e. each piece of notation links to a specific pitch or sound for the duration of the score. The numbering system used in the PAD notation only gives a visual representation of the pad to play, the coordination to be used and the rhythmic phrasing. The score does not produce MIDI information that maps directly to the sounds used across an entire performance as the sounds that need to be activated are constantly changing based on the patch.

The PAD score has to be generated by typing in the pad numbers on the music scoring software. Currently it is impossible to capture a live performance that will automatically map directly onto the PAD music notation in the scoring software. This is because the additional information needed to produce the score, pad number and the limb it is played with, is not represented by a MIDI message and therefore cannot be recorded in the scoring software.

Reflection

Based on the research findings presented, this course is clearly deemed as valuable by students in that they feel they are learning important skills that will support their future career. Much of the music that these students play and listen to is production-led and many of them are turning to technology to extend the sonic palette available to them, recreate sounds produced in the studio, and in turn, enhance their role within their bands. Students recognised that the tasks set for summative assessment posed significant challenge and encouraged them to learn and make use of the technology in ways that stretched their abilities as a drummer, producer, and arranger of music. It is evident that they feel the learning experience is valuable not only in terms of their development as a drummer, but also in terms of the development of wider skill sets relating to group work, autodidactic learning practices and problem solving. The learning and teaching methods used to support the delivery and consolidation of core knowledge have motivated and enthused learners to engage with complex and somewhat abstract concepts. The course has provided an opportunity to explore these concepts to a deep level within a structured curriculum that scaffolds learning and provides opportunities for personalization.[29] The learning experiences in Term 1 enable students to develop an understanding of, and familiarity with, the PAD notation system. This approach ensures that when students create their own PAD scores, they are able to accurately capture the coordination and pad positions required to recreate a performance of their chosen song.

Performances using drum kit technologies in hybrid and fully electronic settings pose significant challenge to the coordination that these students have developed on the traditional acoustic drum kit. This is an exciting finding, as this alternative approach to teaching and developing coordination may provide a new avenue for drummers to develop what Cameron describes as 'multi-dexterity' and freedom of movement that can affect improvement in all areas of their drum kit performance.[30] The change of mindset students experienced when performing in hybrid settings where they are now playing a *new* instrument is an interesting finding that requires further examination and research.

Student responses identified opportunities to further develop the course and explore other ways of using the drum kit technology. In particular, the findings suggested that two parts of the course need to be examined: (1) the setting of performance tasks that mirror how the technology is commonly used by drummers in industry and (2) how the PAD notation might be manipulated to activate the correct sounds in the music software.

Point 1 is straightforward to address through course revision. It is clear that students are keen to explore ways in which they might use the technology in more recognisable performance settings that might enable what Joseph Pignato describes as 'identity expression' and 'idiosyncratic purposeful creation', where students have the freedom to use the technology in their own desired musical setting.[31] Reflecting on the feedback, providing an opportunity to explore how student choice can be factored into the course design is an exciting prospect. Performing with technology in a band setting has been largely neglected based on the assumption that by studying the course as is, and through developing the advanced skills required to address the needs of the solo hybrid and fully electronic performance assessments, students will have covertly developed the skills to use the technology in an ensemble.

Point 2 presents a set of more significant challenges. Firstly, capturing a performance through the recording of MIDI information would not be possible as the MIDI note that is recorded for a single pad varies based on the active patch. Therefore, the scoring software would represent the pad differently each time the patch changed. The information that needs to be captured by the software is the pad number and the limb to be used to activate it. However, this problem poses an exciting challenge as no manufacturer currently offers a feature that enables the pad number to be captured by the software during recording. If this problem could be overcome, the information captured during a MIDI-based recording would be an accurate representation of the performance.

Secondly, the challenge of being able to check the accuracy of a PAD score presents a complex, but not insurmountable, problem. If there was a way to use the programme change information to alter the MIDI notes output by the software, then it would be possible to play back the correct sounds using the PAD software score. This could be achieved through the use of an intermediary software program that enables MIDI note information to be remapped to a different note number based on Program Change information (Figure 10.4).

The drum kit has evolved and extended to meet the needs of the musics in which it is used. Drum kit technologies now enable drummers to accurately replicate the sounds heard in recordings and to extend the creative and musical possibilities of the instrument. With any development

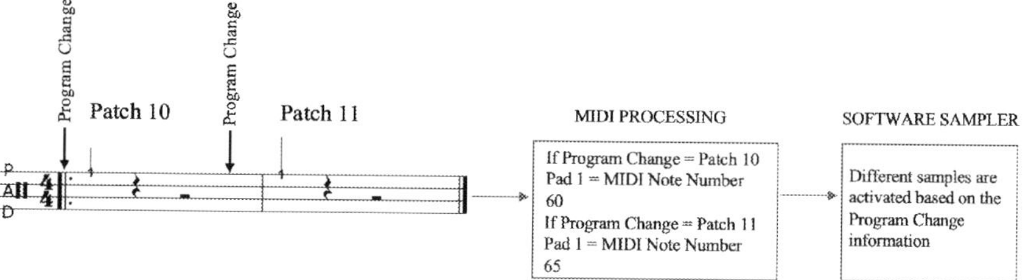

Figure 10.4 How MIDI signals generated by a software score could be processed to activate the correct samples in a software sampler

of the drum kit, we witness an advancement of the technique(s) associated with said development; for example, the development of the bass drum pedal has spawned techniques such as heel down, heel up, slide, swivel and heel-toe. The associated pedagogies then follow, with educators developing methods of teaching and sharing said techniques. We are now in an era where teaching the fundamentals of technique and musicianship are still central to a drummer's development, but as educators responsible for training and mentoring the next generation of drummers, drum kit technologies provide a new and exciting area of study to explore in our curricula.

Notes

1 'Cambridge Online Dictionary', *Cambridge Dictionary online*, available at: https://dictionary.cambridge.org (accessed 6 September 2019).
2 M. Dean. *The Drum: A History* (Plymouth: Scarecrow Press, 2012).
3 M. Brennan. 'The Drum Kit in Theory' in M. Brennan, J. Pignato, and D. Stadnicki (eds.), *Cambridge Companion to the Drum Kit* (Cambridge: Cambridge University Press, 2021).
4 B. Bruford, *Uncharted: Creativity and the Expert Drummer* (Ann Arbor: University of Michigan Press, 2018)
5 Percussion controllers would include Roland SPD-20, MIDI KAT, Alesis Performance Pad Pro. Sample Pads would include the Roland SPD-SX, Yamaha DTX 12 Multi, Alesis Sample Pad Pro. Triggers are defined as either stand-alone pads, or piezo/force sensitive resistant devices, that enable a stick strike on either a pad or drum to be converted into a signal to trigger a sound. Music creation software could include software packages such as Logic Pro X, Pro Tools, or Ableton Live.
6 For further detail see, G. D. Smith, Z. Moir, M. Brennan, S. Rambarran, and P. Kirkman. 'Popular Music Education (R)evolution', in G. D. Smith, Z. Moir, M. Brennan, S. Rambarran and P. Kirkman (eds.), *The Routledge Research Companion to Popular Music Education* (Abingdon: Routledge, 2017), pp. 4–13.
7 For further detail see, M. Dean,'The Drum: A History', pp. 362–365; G. D. Smith. *I Drum Therefore I Am: Being and Becoming a Drummer* (Farham: Ashgate, 2013).
8 For a wider discussion of drum kit curriculum design see, B. Stillie. 'When Is a Drummer Not a Drummer? Developing Coordination, Musicianship, and Creativity through Electronic Drum Performance', in Z. Moir, B. Powell, and G. D. Smith (eds.), *The Bloomsbury Handbook of Popular Music Education: Perspectives and Practices* (London: Bloomsbury, 2019): p. 189.
9 LCM provide a series of graded instrumental exams. Entry to the Edinburgh Napier University BA Popular Music programme is set at Grade VII, which is two levels below the Diploma. Students will have studied foundation courses in Logic Pro X and Pro Tools. Music analysis skills in this context relate to using notation and aural skills to define and describe melodic, harmonic, textural, and rhythmic elements of music.

10 G. D. Smith. 'Popular Music in Higher Education' in I. Papageorgi and G. Welch (eds.), *Advanced Musical Performance: Investigations in Higher Education Learning* (Farnham: Ashgate, 2014), pp. 33–48; D. Bennett and R. Bridgstock. 'The Urgent Need for Career Preview: Student Expectations and Graduate Realities in Music and Dance', *International Journal of Music Education* 33:3 (2015), pp. 263–277.
11 For a detailed description of this course see, B. Stillie, 'When Is a Drummer Not a Drummer?, pp. 187–201; B. Stillie. 'Electronic Solo Performance Using Drum Kit Technologies' in A. P. Bell (ed.), *The Music Production Cookbook: Ready-Made Recipes for the Classroom* (Oxford: Oxford University Press, 2020).
12 J. Bergmann and A. Sams. *Flip Your Classroom: Reach Every Student in Every Class Every Day* (Eugene, OR: International Society for Technology in Education, 2012).
13 The Roland SPD-20 forms part of the Roland OCTAPAD range. The SPD-20 is a single unit that has an eight-pad playing surface, hundreds of inbuilt sounds that can be layered (two per pad), the option to connect external triggers via TRS cables, and MIDI connectivity.
14 Sampler instruments enable playback of audio files via MIDI.
15 Hybrid drum kits combine the traditional acoustic drum kit setup with electronic drum kit technologies.
16 E. S. Tobias. 'From Musical Detectives to DJs: Expanding Aural Skills and Analysis through Engaging Popular Music and Culture', *General Music Today* 28:3 (2015), pp. 23–27 and 25; E. I. Dolan. *The Orchestral Revolution: Haydn and the Technologies of Timbre* (Cambridge: Cambridge University Press, 2013), p. 54.
17 Tobias, 'From Musical Detectives to DJs: Expanding Aural Skills and Analysis through Engaging Popular Music and Culture'.
18 D. R. Garrison and H. Kanuka. 'Blended Learning: Uncovering Its Transformative Potential in Higher Education', *The Internet and Higher Education* 7:2 (2004), pp. 95–105.
19 R. Cremata, J. Pignato, B. Powell, and G. D. Smith. 'Flash Study Analysis and The Music Learning Profiles Project', *Action, Criticism, and Theory for Music Education* 15:5 (2016), pp. 51–80; G. D. Smith, '*I Drum Therefore I Am: Being and Becoming a Drummer*'; N. R. Garner. '*The YouTube® Effect: A Paradigm Shift in How Musicians Learn, Teach and Share?*' University College London, available at: http://discovery.ucl.ac.uk/10026223/1/EprintCopyFinalThesis26092017NRG.pdf (accessed 1 September 2019); K. Zhukov. 'Exploring the Role of Technology in Instrumental Skill Development of Australian Higher Education Music Students', *Australian Journal of Music Education* 2 (2015), pp. 66–77; L. Green. *How Popular Musicians Learn: A Way Ahead for Music Education.*
20 M. J. Hannafin. 'Inter-Action Strategies and Emerging Instructional Technologies: Psychological Perspectives', *Canadian Journal of Educational Communication* 18:3 (1989), pp. 167–179; D. R. Garrison and T. Anderson. *E-Learning In the 21st Century: A Framework for Research and Practice* (London: Routledge, 2003); Garrison and Kanuka, 'Blended Learning: Uncovering its Transformative Potential in Higher Education'.
21 This is a key difference between acoustic and electric instruments in that, on the acoustic drum kit the volume is directly linked to how hard it is struck by the player. On electronic instruments the striking force (known as velocity) is independent of volume enabling these instruments to be played with force but turned down, and vice versa.
22 J. Lave and E. Wenger. *Situated Learning: Legitimate Peripheral Participation* (Cambridge: Cambridge University Press, 1991).
23 L. S. Vygotsky. *Mind in society: The development of higher psychological processes* (Cambridge: Harvard University Press 1978), p. 86.
24 Garrison and Anderson, *E-Learning In the 21st Century: A Framework for Research and Practice.*
25 See, for example, A. Jimbo. *Fujiyama: Combining Acoustic and Electronic Drums* (New York: Carl Fischer, 2003); B. Terry. *The Beginners Guide to Electronic Drums* (Milwaukee: Hal Leonard Corporation, 2011).
26 G. Chaffee. *Linear Time Playing: Funk and Fusion Grooves for the Modern Styles* (Van Nuys: Alfred Publishing, 1993); G. Chester. *The New Breed* (Cedar Grove: Modern Drummer Publications Inc., 1985); G. Chester. *The New Breed II* (Endcote: Drummers Intensive Company, 1990).
27 C. P. Cameron. *Exploring Applications of Multi-Dexterity in Drum Kit Performance* (Melbourne: Monash University, 2016).
28 T. Parkinson and G. D. Smith. 'Towards an Epistemology of Authenticity in Higher Popular Music Education', *Action, Criticism, and Theory for Music Education* 14:1 (2015), pp. 93–127.

29 C. Meskill. *Online Teaching and Learning: sociocultural perspectives* (London: Bloomsbury Publishing, 2013).

30 Cameron, *Exploring Applications of Multi-Dexterity in Drum Kit Performance*, p. 2.

31 J. M. Pignato. 'Situating Technology within and without Music Education', in A. Ruthmann, R. Mantie (eds.), *The Oxford Handbook of Technology and Music Education* (Oxford: Oxford University Press, 2017), pp. 203–215.

11 The Aesthetics of Timekeeping

Creative and Technical Aspects of Learning Drum Kit

CARLOS XAVIER RODRIGUEZ AND PATRICK HERNLY

Introduction

In this chapter we examine how drummers are taught and learn to conceptualize and execute expressive variations of familiar drumming patterns, i.e. 'feel'-based aspects, and the enabling conditions that underlie them. We draw from multiple sources including analysis of sound recordings, theoretical models proposed by philosophers, psychologists, and educators, interviews with experienced drummers, and our own teaching and performing experiences and reflections. We explain the conditions under which these technical nuances develop in the early-stage drummers we have worked with, and despite the resistance of these nuances to straightforward or specifiable instruction, their indispensability to ensemble leadership and drumming success. We first begin by exploring some of the creative and interpersonal characteristics that are beneficial to drumming success, then analyse the teaching and learning of some of the techniques themselves. We then conclude with recommendations for teaching drum kit in music classrooms and private tuition studios.

Creative Framework

Curiosity, Creativity, and Musical Expression

While straightforward to isolate drumming skills and understandings facilitating discrimination between drummers of different ability levels, it is comparatively more challenging to account for how and why some drummers learn more quickly and achieve more than others. We have observed that some learners progress by demonstrating a natural affinity for the drum kit – historically conceptualized as *talent* in music education and psychology – while others rely more significantly on tenacious *effort*. An alternative perspective might consider what helps someone maximize one's talents or efforts, suggesting that *motivation* for high achievement is the critical attribute, in which case *curiosity* might well be the best explanation for effective learning. According to Jordan Litman, curiosity is a desire to understand something that motivates exploratory behavior to acquire new information, which is pleasurable whether done for its own sake or to reduce uncertainty.[1] Curious individuals learn better and faster than those who are less curious. Curiosity is also a prerequisite condition of creativity, which in turn drives musical expression as well as many conceptions of intelligence. We will now take a closer view of intelligence, creativity, and musical expression as they pertain to drumming performance.

Robert Sternberg's multifaceted theory of *successful intelligence* is well-suited to explain the complex actions of drum kit playing.[2] According to Sternberg's theory, an intelligent person optimizes four types of skills: creative, analytical, practical, and wisdom-based. Drummers must be creative in order to extend their personality through their instrument – what allows one to recognize a drummer by listening to his or her playing. They must be analytical to understand what works best, and why, from the entire range of potentially useful ideas. They must be practical in order to convincingly unify ideation with muscular motion. They must be wise to marshal these skills in such a way that they favourably serve the interests and ensure the success of the ensemble.

The creative skill of drummers is mediated within the social matrix of an ensemble, with motivation commingling among intrinsic and extrinsic sources. At least since Teresa Amabile's study focusing on creative *situations* there is widespread acceptance that creativity is best achieved through intrinsic motivation, suggesting that drummers must negotiate their contributions in a resilient manner even while making themselves vulnerable to praise and criticism, neither of which are necessarily supportive of creative behaviour.[3] Illustrating this point, the 1997 CD reissue of The Byrds' LP *The Notorious Byrd Brothers*, the final bonus track, entitled 'Universal Mind Decoder', contains an extended dialogue in the recording studio between guitarist and singer David Crosby and drummer Mike Clarke, in which Crosby attempts to inspire Clarke to improve his performance using various approaches, all unsuccessful.[4] Sternberg and Lubart's *investment* theory of creativity is another applicable explanation of how drummers function creatively within ensembles – they often 'buy low, sell high', i.e. introduce ideas that are initially unfamiliar and unusual, persist and adjust until they are consensually accepted as part of the ensemble's 'sound', then begin the process anew.[5] Thus, drummers must be prepared to fail whilst prospecting for successful pathways.

Creativity additionally provides the foundation for musical expression, defined by Roger Scruton as 'those elements of a musical performance that depend on personal response and which vary between different interpretations'.[6] Introduced in Carl Seashore's pioneering work in the psychology of music, musical expression comprises deviations from mechanical performances of time, pitch, loudness, and timbre.[7] The feel-based constructs we review later fall neatly into these categories: using them promotes musical expression, which is essential for communicating one's personal understanding of the music. In the philosophical literature, John Dewey's *Art as Experience* provided a convincing explanation of how expression is at the core of creative reasoning, delineating expressive acts and objects as the processes and products of artistic self-definition.[8] And in the psychological literature, Alf Gabrielsson's development of systematic variation of duration (SYVAR-D) revealed that deviations from mechanical regularity are rarely either random or the same: rather, they are undertaken to emphasize the perceived importance of structural features.[9] Therefore, while drummers might enjoy the freedom to experiment with various rhythmic possibilities, they ultimately are bound by musical genres styles, and forms, and the skills and attitudes of other ensemble members.

Leveraging the Roles of Drummers in Ensembles

If drummers do enjoy some creative autonomy in their ensemble as musicians, they also inherit some responsibility as a focal point of ensemble collaboration: drummers actively negotiate and enact adjustments that benefit group cohesion. In our extensive teaching novice rock band members, we note their perceptions that drummers are considered somewhat less suitable for singing duties. Their reasons include that drummers must listen to everyone more closely than other band members, that they carry the burden of executing structural cues, and that they are more physically involved, i.e. playing with both hands and feet, making singing too difficult. While these reasons may not be limiting of singing ability, they suggest how novice band members tend to view the roles of drummers and the demands of the drum kit.

In a performance by the group Three Friends of the song 'Prologue', drummer Malcom Mortimer counts off the tune, 'leading' the group in at a pace he immediately realizes is too fast, given the complex melodic figures played by the other five performers, thus he adjusts the tempo down, momentarily 'following' the group.[10] One characteristic of a more advanced drummer is to make such adjustments without compromising personal, expressive technique. Honing and Bas de Haas studied the performances of experienced jazz drummers, finding the long-short subdivision of the beat commonly known as 'swing' is not related linearly to tempo, i.e. expressive timing is adapted to tempo variations.[11] Alternatively, John Churchville, a professional drummer, teacher, and recording artist, believes that while drummers might represent the 'swing' by first providing the beat on the ride cymbal, and round out appropriate beat divisions with the other hand, the success of the effect is group-determined, i.e. 'swing' is not initiated, controlled, or achieved solely by the drummer: rather, all ensemble members mutually participate in the process, which is mediated primarily by the level of their listening skills.[12] The extent to which creativity is encouraged, required, or exercised by drummers is contingent upon the specific performance environments. Bill Bruford characterized different 'contexts' in which experts perform, which differ in the relationship of the drummer to a group leader, whether there is a leader in the first place, and the level of creative freedom available, either 'functional' or 'compositional'.[13] It should be noted that even when drummers are performing for a leader who commands complete stylistic control over the music, there is still some room for creative thinking. Brazilian jazz drummer Airto Moreira, describing the process of finding a percussion part whilst everyone else in the group is scrambling to occupy every available space in the musical texture, said 'you just have to find a place that no one else is using, even if it is an unusual space, and fill it up and keep playing there so no one can take it away from you'.[14] Moreira further explained that performance situations which offer formative roles are attractive to drummers, since most ensembles 'need someone to help everyone else make sense of time'.[15]

The demands on drummers are varied and complex, and it requires manipulative skill, tenacity, and strong interpersonal skills to confront them. There is additionally the need for drummers to simultaneously conform to tradition while incorporating their trademark sound through selected techniques. Peter Abbs described a hypothetical aesthetic balance between tradition and innovation, which is achieved through instruction and reflection.[16] It is therefore perhaps optimal that drummers be purposefully mindful of such aesthetic balance in their playing, and search for evidence of such balance in the playing of successful drummers. For example, the late drumming legend Jeff Porcaro was perhaps best known for his much imitated 'half-time shuffle' groove, a modified rendition of Bernard Purdie's earlier 'Purdie Shuffle', and already familiar to music listeners, thus likely related to the success of Porcaro's signature sound. He further combined this element with a kick-drum rhythm – the legendary 'Bo Diddley Beat', perhaps the best-known syncopated pattern in popular music. Porcaro's effort was a perfect example of combinational thinking – fusing established sounds to produce a captivating beat pattern. Despite the literature and recordings that highlight the independently creative roles of drummers, some performance tendencies have emerged in drummers' efforts to create unique musical grooves. Danielsen *et al.* asked ten expert drummers to play a rock pattern at three different tempi using three timing styles – 'laid-back', 'on-the-beat', and 'pushed' – and noted systematic variances in intensity and timbre of snare drum strokes between tempi and styles.[17] These findings suggest the gradual formation of normative sound cues which accompany a drummer's efforts to create groove.

We now turn our attention to the practice routines and techniques associated with drum kit instruction, intending to link them to the aforementioned personal habits and challenges of successful drumming. Specifically, we identify skills associated with effective drum kit playing, map the cognitive understandings required for their execution, consider the dynamics of ensemble playing and their influence on drumming technique, and invoke the advice of expert teachers as to the optimal ways to educate young drummers. We also reintroduce the idea of aesthetics and how it may relate to the concept of timekeeping.

Technical Framework

Background

Before discussing drum kit method book literature, we first look briefly to some psychology research,[18] as well as computer modeling of neurological processes to establish some aspects of conceptual modeling for rhythm in the human mind.[19] Human beings undergo a process of informal musical learning as they grow up in a cultural setting; this includes implicit understanding of how tonal and rhythmic aspects of music 'work'. Rhythmic aspects of this framework include beat induction, meter induction, and architectonic relationships between multilayered timescales. Conceptual modeling of rhythm is significant for the teaching and learning of drum kit from multiple angles. On the one hand, recorded and live performance of drum kit playing is rooted in performers' conceptual modeling of rhythm; conversely, the ensemble members with whom they perform, as well as listeners, map the experienced music onto their own conceptual models and frameworks.

Procedural Aspects from Method Books

Method books have addressed the role of the drummer in musical settings. These books have focused on challenges facing drummers as well as recommendations for how developing drummers can work towards meeting those challenges. Jazz drumming expert John Riley addressed the need for a drummer's playing to appeal to a bandleader, stating that, 'The bottom line is, people hire drummers who make them sound good – period'.[20] Ron Spagnardi described how big band drummers cannot depend on written notation in a drum chart to tell them all details about what or how to play. 'With just a basic sketch to go by, you need to depend on your musical instinct and creativity to decide what to play, how to phrase, where to fill, and how to accompany the soloists'.[21] Daniel 'Zoro' Donnelly and Daniel Glass described common challenges facing developing drummers in the rhythm and blues idiom, citing, 'poor understanding of swung eighth notes ... improper sound balance ... misdirected motion ... lack of understanding'.[22] These challenges address the necessity of creativity, identity, and effectively fulfilling a timekeeping role with a rhythm section.

Additionally, method books have used language as an analogy to describe drummers' abilities to function authentically in diverse stylistic contexts. Towards the development of properly grooving within R&B, soul, funk, and hip-hop styles, Mike Adamo stated, 'breakbeat drumming has its own vocabulary, just as any language does'.[23] In discussing grooves particular to Afro-Cuban drumming, Ed Uribe wrote, 'your final goal in the study of a musical style should be ... strive to play this music as if you had learned it in its purest, handed-down, oral tradition ... There is a big difference between playing a beat and playing a style ... You are, in essence, learning a language'.[24] Riley emphasized the importance of listening to examples from musical styles in order to develop idiomatic understanding. 'To be fluent in any style of music, you must know the "dialect" ... All the great players we know have studied hundreds of recordings and have listened to and probably own a thousand or more jazz recordings'.[25]

Method books have also offered suggestions for how developing drummers ought to meet these challenges. Donnelly and Glass insisted on the importance of understanding historical context. 'In order to reign and rule over the groove (of rhythm and blues) and play it convincingly, you must first understand how it got there in the first place and how it evolved into what it is today'.[26] One stylistic example that they cited towards effectively grooving in early R&B idioms was the shuffle: 'When it comes to early R&B, there are three important tools that a drummer can't live without: a good shuffle, a good shuffle, and a good shuffle! ... If you start simple, focusing on sound and balance (as opposed to technique), you can develop a basic shuffle that will get you through just about any musical challenge that comes your way'.[27] Towards drummers' development of groove, individual creativity and musicianship, and effective ensemble performance, Riley's suggestions included, 'open your ears to the other players. Play together ... think like a musician. Make the other players sound good ... play your own time, not your idol's ... think consistent spacing and volume. Hypnotize with your groove ... when there are problems (with ensemble cohesion), play strong but become more supple, not more rigid'.[28] Adamo's suggestion for drummers' development of groove and pocket was 'playing along with recorded songs . . . playing along with a metronome/click track . . . feeling an underlying half-note or whole-note pulse as you practice/play various grooves'.[29]

Towards an Aesthetic of Timekeeping

If we propose there is an 'aesthetics of timekeeping' in the first place, it must be predicated on, yet transcend, requisite skills and techniques. What renders the timekeeping 'aesthetic' is a transformation from purely functional actions and executions to apprehend the expressive qualities of the activity, to engage the communicative potential of music. Drum teachers spend a lot of time, informed by method book authors, teaching students how to strike the drum, count, play four-way coordination, read charts, listen to music for dialectic fluency, balance the various instruments of the drum set, and function appropriately in music ensemble settings. Drum teachers teach these techniques and skills, hoping that creativity emerges from students' practice as they work to attain them. Our position is that these techniques and skills emerge in confluence with students' developing creativity. The most effective teaching and learning of drumming maintains focus on the aforementioned techniques and skills, executed using strategies that additionally help students develop the dispositions that are associated with creative reasoning and action. These include embracing the centrality of listening as the key to learning and ensemble performance, awareness of rhythm framework, improving negotiation of the social dynamics of being a drummer, and a personal creative style that balances tradition and innovation while continually testing new ideas amidst various enabling and inhibiting conditions.

We therefore recommend a practice repertoire of actual musical examples to supplement method book use, in which teachers saliently indicate the history and innovations of drummers from prior eras.[30] Two examples of such practice repertoire include listening and playing along to jazz standards and break beats. These two bodies of repertoire represent much of the relevant drumming idiom in the twenty-first century. Jazz drummers from the early to mid-twentieth century influenced drummers across many styles of popular music from the latter half of the twentieth century to the early twenty-first century.[31] Sampling and recreation (through performance or programming) of R&B and soul break beats has been prevalent in popular music of the past forty years. In addition to assimilating a repertoire of relevant beats and songs, study of this repertoire might well refine developing drummers' conceptual modelling for rhythm towards an increasingly detailed template for groove and pocket that includes swing, centeredness on the beat, and elasticity of time.

Given the aural tradition of the drum kit, and that ideas about swing and pocket differ among various musical styles, we recommend use of listening and play-along to help drummers develop intuitions towards idiomatic performance of musical styles. In this regard, developing a sense of pocket is akin to achieving a colloquial and conversational fluency in various musical genres and styles. Developing drummers should assimilate repertoire aurally, only using notation when necessary to achieve optimal comprehension. Learning break beats and songs by ear will engage the developing drummer in a process of disequilibrium and reconciliation, interacting as directly as possible with the music.[32] While notational skills are important in professionalizing drummers, superb aural skills are foundational in virtually every aspect of drumming, thus need not be tied to note-reading. The practice of reading musical notation should focus on norms of reading charts as musical 'road maps' with important clues about how to engage with and lead the ensemble: the details of musical interpretation should be left largely to drummers' intuitions, developed through listening and play-along repertoire. As John Churchville reports, early-stage drummers tend to be consumed with striking drums and making as much sound as possible through intense exertion, and only once they realize how this practice interferes with increasing demands on their listening, their technique can become more efficient and varied. The late drumming educator John Bergamo, one of Churchville's teachers, encouraged improved technique through examining the natural mechanics of the body (the basic 'throwing' motion), making better use of gravity, and incorporating various parts of the striking surfaces for expanded timbral range.

Indeed, developing drummers are typically preoccupied with the physical act of playing drums. Consequently, one of the challenges for a drum kit teacher is to help channel this preoccupation towards a more developed musicality and musicianship. Two groups developing drummers must learn how to please are other musicians with whom they perform, and audience members. Groove and pocket are particularly important in both instances: fellow rhythm section members judge drummers' ability to groove in a group setting (based on cognitive conceptual models of groove), and listeners' experiences of popular music include groove and pocket as well, though perhaps based on more generalized conceptual models.

Developing drummers are also listeners, however. When they commence systematic study of the drum kit, they do not do so in a musico-technical vacuum. Therefore, much of what we emphasize in teaching developing drummers about groove and pocket may be a process of making salient, thereby more consciously present, the conceptual models they bring to the studio setting as advanced listeners. This supports a student-centred model of teaching and learning, whereby we encourage students to bring their whole selves into the classroom setting. We meet them where they are as learners, developing their understanding that listening is key, guiding them towards a professional level of fluency within popular music dialects.

Feel-Based Drumming Constructs

For drummers to develop awareness of rhythmic framework, they should develop fluency within the overlapping, abstract, feel-based constructs of swing, groove, and pocket. These constructs break down into several aspects, such as beat subdivision, centredness on the beat, elasticity in interpretation of time, and dynamic balance among voices on the drum kit. Beat subdivision is also sometimes referred to as 'depth of swing'. Usually, a drummer is described as playing 'in the pocket' in relation to one or more other players, often other rhythm section players. A groove that is pocketed in one context may be completely out of the pocket in another. In this regard, pocket is an agreement among several players, often the rhythm section, as to how hard the music will swing. While there is widespread acceptance for these constructs in the Western music world and in some parts of Asia,[33] the practices themselves are familiar even when the constructs are not, as in the case of 'groove' in England.[34]

Centredness on the beat refers to how 'on top' of the beat the drummer plays, versus how far ahead or behind, meanwhile not rushing or dragging to the point of tearing from the pocket. A drummer simultaneously must match the beat-centredness of the rest of the rhythm section, but also inherits a greater responsibility than other rhythm section players in determining the beat-centredness of the entire rhythm section. Such considerations concerning micro timing signal the influence of popular music genres in modern rhythmic discourse and analysis.[35]

Elasticity refers to the dynamic pushing and pulling of time: sometimes when entering or exiting phrases, playing fills, set-ups, or ensemble hits, the time seems to organically stretch to aesthetic effect.[36] Skilled drummers strike a balance between strict adherence to metronomic time and related time scales or subdivisions versus allowing the time to 'breathe' to enhance the feel of the shared pocket. Sometimes these adjustments are significant enough to be considered displacements or grouping 'dissonances' in the meter.[37]

The dynamic balance among voices on the drum kit contributes to the pocket of the groove. Sometimes, for example, a groove may go from un-pocketed to pocketed by adjusting the balance of timekeeping in the hi-hat in relation to the kick and snare drum. By properly 'mixing', the entire drum kit part can 'sit better' in the groove. The ability to create and adjust such balance is acquired through a combination of experimentation and performance experience.[38]

These aspects occur in the social context of ensemble music making. However, in addition to the drummer's ability to creatively utilize them towards aesthetic effect, the drummer's social role in the band also impacts how freely the role of time steward is fulfilled. If the time is off, the rest of the band first blames the drummer, as the drummer is perceived as a de facto conductor who controls tempo and other time-related parameters. A drummer who is a new addition to a rhythm section may subordinate his or her timekeeping intuitions to another, more senior member of the rhythm section, usually the bass player. Indeed, drummers are commonly advised to follow the bass player during a group audition, a practice that demonstrates the physiological tendency to allow lower-sounding ensemble instruments to establish the temporal foundation of music.[39] These and other considerations are abundantly clear in drummers' verbal reports of their ensemble experiences.

Looking Forward in Teaching and Learning Drum Kit

Throughout this chapter, we have attempted to synthesize ideas from philosophy, psychology, pedagogy, and applied literature, as well as our own professional experience as musicians and educators. We have interrogated established norms for teaching and learning of the drums, and suggest a comprehensive and productive model of teaching and learning based on these norms while informed by the conceptual lens of creativity. In summary, we have substantiated the following points:

1. Curiosity, creativity, and musical expression are necessary attributes for pursuing a personal drum kit style, and they function interdependently and actively in a drummer's interactions with other ensemble members.
2. Theories of curiosity, creativity, and musical expression are relevant to the ongoing work of drum kit learning, experimentation, and ensemble performance and recording.
3. Philosophical and psychological writings support the complex work of articulating a personal style of drum kit playing while conforming to well-known styles and genres, i.e. of striking an imperceptible balance between tradition and innovation, which comprises an important aesthetic dimension of musical experience.
4. Negotiating one's individuality as a drummer is mediated by the belief systems of other group members regarding the traditional roles of drummers in groups.

Given these findings, the most effective drum kit instruction, while continuing to emphasize performance techniques and skills, should also incorporate expanded focus on creativity. We believe this can occur in the following ways:

1. Feel-based aspects of drumming technique should remain central to the instructional process.
2. Mentoring relationships between early and later-career drummers, which naturally includes transmission of generational knowledge in aural traditions, is essential.
3. Strategies helping students explore and develop the personality traits relevant to creative reasoning and execution are central to a comprehensive didactic approach to the drum kit.

The challenge of achieving a balance between tradition and innovation by drummers in ensemble practice and performance provides an opportunity for them to assimilate a repertoire that spans multiple decades of popular music history, and which recurs in contemporary popular music.[40] We believe music philosophy, having evolved through the postmodern era, can still be quite useful to developing musicians, as they seek a meaningful core for guiding their aesthetic judgements in drum kit playing.

Notes

1 J. A. Litman. 'Curiosity and the Pleasures of Learning: Wanting and Liking New Information', *Cognition and Emotion* 19:6 (2005), pp. 793–814.
2 R. J. Sternberg. 'The Theory of Successful Intelligence' in R. J. Sternberg and S. B. Kaufman (eds.), *Cambridge Handbook of Intelligence* (New York: Cambridge University Press, 2011), pp. 504–527.
3 T. M. Amabile *The Social Psychology of Creativity* (New York: Springer-Verlag, 1983).
4 'Universal Mind Decoder', The Notorious Byrd Brothers, CD Re-Issue, track 17, (1997). https://www.youtube.com/watch?v=vRQcVGr7ar8
5 R. J. Sternberg and T. I. Lubart. 'An Investment Theory of Creativity and Its Development', *Human Development* 34:1 (1991), pp. 1–31.
6 R. Scruton. The Nature of Musical Expressionin S. Sadie (ed.), *The New Grove Dictionary of Music and Musicians* (London: MacMillan, 1980), p. 327.
7 C. Seashore. *Psychology of Music* (New York: McGraw-Hill, 1938).
8 J. Dewey. *Art as Experience* (New York: Perigree, 1934).
9 A. Gabrielsson. 'Interplay between Analysis and Synthesis in Studies of Music Performance and Music Experience', *Music Perception* 3:1 (1985), pp. 59–86.
10 'Three Friends – Prologue', video and sound recording (2009) available at: www.youtube.com/watch?v=_JWk0VyFmxc.
11 H. Honing and W. Bas de Haas. 'Swing Once More: Relating Timing and Tempo in Expert Jazz Drumming', *Music Perception* 25:5 (2008), pp. 471–476.
12 John Churchville, personal communication (Ann Arbor, MI, 5 September 2019).
13 B. Bruford. *Uncharted: Creativity and the Expert Drummer* (Ann Arbor: University of Michigan Press, 2018).
14 Airto Moreira, personal communication (Tampa, FL, 24 March 2010)
15 Ibid.
16 P. Abbs. *A Is for Aesthetic: Essays on Creative and Aesthetic Education* (New York: Falmer Press, 1989).
17 A. Danielsen, C. H. Waadeland, H. G. Sundt, and M. A. Witek. 'Effects of Instructed Timing and Tempo on Snare Drum Sound in Drumkit Performance', *Journal of the Acoustical Society of America* 138:4 (2015), pp. 2301–2316.

18 S. Hawkins. 'Situational Influences on Rhythmicity in Speech, Music, and Their Interaction', *Philosophical Transactions: Biological Sciences.* 369:1658 (2014), pp. 1–11; H. Merchant, J. Grahn, L. Trainor, M. Rohrmeier, and W. T. Fitch. 'Finding the Beat: A Neural Perspective across Humans and Non-Human Primates', *Philosophical Transactions: Biological Sciences* 370:1664 (2015), pp. 1–16.

19 D. Rosenthal. 'Emulation of Human Rhythm Perception', *Computer Music Journal* 16910 (1992), pp. 64–76; F. Gouyon and S. Dixon. 'A Review of Automatic Rhythm Description Systems', *Computer Music Journal* 29:1 (2005), pp. 34–54; A. Shenoy, and Y. Wang. 'Key, Chord, and Rhythm Tracking of Popular Music Recordings', *Computer Music Journal* 29:3 (2005), pp. 75–86; G. Weinberg and S. Driscoll. 'Toward Robotic Musicianship', *Computer Music Journal* 30:4 (2006), pp. 28–45; J. J. Rehmeyer. 'The Machine's Got Rhythm: Computers Are Learning to Understand Music and Join the Band', *Science News* 171:16 (2007), pp. 248–250; A. Robertson and M. D. Plumbley 'Synchronizing Sequencing Software to a Live Drummer', *Computer Music Journal* 37:2 (2013), pp. 46–60.

20 J. Riley. *The Jazz Drummer's Workshop: Advanced Concepts for Musical Development* (Milwaukee: Hal Leonard Corporation, 2004), p. 7.

21 R. Spagnardi. *The Big Band Drummer: A Complete Workbook for Improving Big Band Drumming Performance* (Cedar Grove: Modern Drummer Publications, 2000).

22 D. Donnelly and D. Glass. *The Commandments of Early Rhythm and Blues Drumming* (Van Nuys: Alfred Publishing Co., Inc., 2008), p. 37.

23 M. Adamo. *The Breakbeat Bible: The Fundamentals of Breakbeat Drumming* (Milwaukee: Hal Leonard Corporation, 2010), p. 1.

24 E. Uribe. *The Essence of Afro-Cuban Percussion and Drum Set* (Miami: Warner Bros. Publications, 1996), p. 9

25 J. Riley. *The Art of Bop Drumming* (Van Nuys: Alfred Publishing Co., Inc., 1994), p. 71.

26 Donnelly and Glass, *The Commandments of Early Rhythm and Blues Drumming*, p. 16.

27 Ibid., p. 36.

28 Riley, *The Jazz Drummer's Workshop*, p. 7.

29 Adamo, *The Breakbeat Bible.*

30 M. Berry and J. Gianni. *The Drummer's Bible: How to Play Every Style from Afro-Cuban to Zydeco* (Tucson: See Sharp Press, 2012); Riley, *The Art of Bop Drumming*; Riley, *The Jazz Drummer's Workshop*; E. Uribe. *The Essence of Brazilian Percussion and Drum Set* (Van Nuys: Alfred Publishing Co., Inc., 1993); Uribe, *The Essence of Afro-Cuban Percussion and Drum Set.*

31 D. Gottlieb. *The Evolution of Jazz Drumming* (Milwaukee: Hal Leonard Corporation, 2010).

32 T. Solis. *Performing Ethnomusicology: Teaching and Representation in World Music Ensembles* (Berkeley: University of California Press, 2004).

33 S. Kawase and K. Eguchi. 'The Concepts and Acoustical Characteristics of 'Groove' in Japan', *PopScriptum* 11 (2010).

34 B. Bruford, personal communication (Ann Arbor, MI, 17 April 2018)

35 T. de Clercq. 'Swing, Shuffle, Half-Time, Double: Beyond Traditional Time Signatures in the Classification of Meter in Pop/Rock Music' in C. X. Rodriguez (ed.), *Coming of Age: Teaching and Learning Popular Music in Academia* (Ann Arbor: Maize Books, 2017), pp. 139–167.

36 Bruford, lecture, 'Uncharted: Creativity and the Expert Drummer', Center for World Performance Studies and School of Music, Theatre & Dance, University of Michigan (Ann Arbor, MI, 17 April 2018).

37 N. Biamonte. 'Formal Functions of Metric Dissonance in Rock Music', *Music Theory Online* 20:2 (2014).

38 J. Peckman. *Picture Yourself Drumming* (Boston: Thomson Course Technology, 2007).

39 M. Hove, C. Marie, I. Bruce, and L. Trainor. 'Superior Time Perception for Lower Musical Pitch Explains Why Bass-Ranged Instruments Lay Down Musical Rhythms', *Proceedings of the National Academy of Sciences* 111:28 (2014), pp. 10383–10388.

40 Abbs, *A Is for Aesthetic.*

12 Mentorship

Jazz Drumming across Generations

JOSEPH MICHAEL PIGNATO

Introduction

Jazz music has long been understood as a generational practice, one where older musicians mentor, encourage, and teach younger, aspiring players.[1] That tradition of tutelage is often evident in the long lineages of musicians who have graduated from the ensembles of noted bandleaders. Historical examples of such ensembles include those of Duke Ellington, Count Basie, and most germane to this volume, Art Blakey's Jazz Messengers, an ensemble celebrated for its famous alumni as much as for its spirited drummer and leader.[2]

In this chapter, I consider this tradition as it relates to two specific drum kit players: Jack DeJohnette, a major figure in the history of jazz drumming and a bandleader recognized for his history of nurturing younger musicians, and Terri Lyne Carrington, a premiere figure in contemporary jazz drumming and a celebrated leader of ensembles that feature young, developing musicians.

Specific themes include: (a) *the importance of mentors* in the lives of the participants, (b) *challenges of learning to play the drum kit*, particular to the instrument itself, (c) *the unique place and space of drummers*, behind kits, on band stands, and in the roles of leader or leader/mentor, and (d) '*something bigger than just the music*', the larger contexts of learning to play, of connecting to a community and lineage of jazz drummers.

The Participants

Although both participants are quite renowned, and full details of their extensive recording, performing, and education careers are readily available to readers elsewhere, in order to provide context for this chapter contribution, short profiles of each participant are in order. I will start with Jack DeJohnette, whom I have known for some 30 years, and who led me to Terri Lyne Carrington, and eventually to the ideas that informed this writing.

Jack DeJohnette, a name likely familiar to drum kit players reading this volume, has played with some of the most storied figures in jazz and improvised music. DeJohnette's credits include recordings, performances, and long-time associations with Miles Davis, Sonny Rollins, Thelonious Monk, John Coltrane, Bill Evans, Stan Getz, Keith Jarrett, Herbie Hancock, Dave Holland, Joe Henderson, Freddy Hubbard, Betty Carter, and Pat Metheny among many others.

Jack's creative drumming in jazz, avant-garde, fusion, and new age styles has been recognized by critics, associations, institutions, and peers so often as to preclude listing every honour in this chapter text. A quick summary of recognitions includes a Grammy Award, perennial inclusion in readers and critics polls published by each of the major US jazz magazines, *Down Beat* and *Jazz Times*, Hall of Fame status in the *Modern Drummer Magazine* readers poll, recognition with the French Grand Prix du Disc award, and induction into the Percussive Arts Society's Hall of Fame.

The honour most relevant to this chapter is a National Endowment for the Arts Jazz Master Fellowship. This award is the highest honour awarded by the US Federal Government in recognition of the life's work and contributions of notable jazz musicians. The Jazz Master designation noted Jack DeJohnette's remarkable career achievements, life-long contributions to jazz music as a cultural and artistic form, and his commitment to mentoring younger generations of aspiring jazz musicians.

Terri Lyne Carrington, one of the most highly regarded musicians of her generation, has been playing the drum kit since childhood, manifesting prodigious talent as early as ten years old. In a career that spans some 40 years, Terri Lyne Carrington has played drums, sang, and produced music for record, for television, and for marquis live events affording her opportunities to collaborate with the likes of Wayne Shorter, Herbie Hancock, George Duke, Carlos Santana, John Scofield, David Sanborn, Stan Getz, Geri Allen, Esperanza Spalding, Christian McBride, and vocalists Cassandra Wilson, Dee Dee Bridgewater, and Dianne Reeves, among countless others. A three-time Grammy Award winner, Terri Lyne Carrington is the first female recipient of the Grammy Award for Best Instrumental Jazz Album. In 2019, Carrington was awarded the Doris Duke Award in recognition of and in support of her outstanding record of achievements in jazz performance.

One hallmark of Terri Lyne Carrington's work has been the ways in which she features young musicians in her ensembles, providing opportunities early in the careers of Ambrose Akinmusire, Tineka Postma, and Morgan Guerin, among many others. Accordingly, Carrington is an esteemed educator, lauded for her work at Boston's Berklee College of Music, where she founded and, at the time of this writing, serves as Artistic Director for the Berklee Institute of Jazz and Gender Justice,[3] an organization that has mentoring young musicians as part of its stated mission.[4]

Finally, it is important for me to contextualize my own background so that readers might better understand the experiences and perspectives that have informed my analysis of the participants' expressions. I am a drummer, composer, and music education researcher. In my research, I have considered improvisation education,[5] popular music education,[6] technology in music education,[7] and music teaching and learning as it occurs outside of schools.[8] I am also an educator, holding the position of full professor at the State University of New York Oneonta, where I teach music industry courses, beat production, and direct ensembles that perform experimental music and improvised rock.

Lastly, I have extensive experience working in the jazz recording industry, including tenures at notable labels such as CMP Records, ECM Records, and RCA Victor. More recently, I am a band leader and recording artist, leading the jazz fusion group Bright Dog Red, which records for the influential Philadelphia label, Ropeadope Records. The views of and interpretations of the participant expressions presented in this chapter reflect and have been informed by these various identities, experiences, and professional activities.

Method

Given the nature of what I sought to understand, the dynamic personal and professional relationships between two expert practitioners, the phenomenon of generational mentoring, and the role of mentoring in jazz music, I selected qualitative research methods. Qualitative inquiry afforded me the opportunity to interpret the themes explored in this chapter, as they emerged and as I engaged the participants in discussion about mentoring in jazz drumming, the drum kit itself, and our collective experiences learning and teaching the instrument.[9]

I conducted two stages of data collection, both based on a protocol developed for the Music Learning Profiles Project.[10] For the first stage, I shared the twelve-question protocol with the participants and asked them to freely respond, either in writing or in spoken and recorded voice, individually and without discussing their answers. For the second stage, I interviewed both participants simultaneously, using the protocol to structure the interview. Although the protocol helped start the discussion, the participants' responses drove the discussion,[11] illuminating key themes, ideas, and expressions reflective of the participants' understandings of their relationship, of mentoring in jazz and in drumming, and of the project itself.

After conducting both stages of data collection, I reviewed the transcripts of participant responses, expressions, and thoughts. That review process allowed me to code themes, concepts, and recurrent notions, in an emergent and evolving manner.[12] As I came to understand the data, I simultaneously rethought the themes and points of focus. That iterative approach led me to the understandings, analyses, and conclusion offered in this chapter contribution.

Finally, after transcribing the data, I shared transcriptions, emerging themes, and the final draft of this chapter with Jack DeJohnette and Terri Lyne Carrington to ensure that the final work represented their perspectives, their participation, and the points they wished to communicate. The analyses, discussion, and conclusions reflect my understandings, responses to, and interpretations of Jack DeJohnette's and Terri Lyne Carrington's statements.[13]

Discussion

I have known Jack DeJohnette for some 30 years, first meeting him when I worked for the drum manufacturer Latin Percussion. A few years after working for Latin Percussion, I got to know Jack well during my time working for ECM Records, home to much of Mr. DeJohnette's recorded output. To describe Jack as a friend would not suffice. He's been a mentor, a figure of wise council, and a role model in drumming and in life. I am grateful to have gotten to know him in these ways, to have grown close to his family, and to learn so much from him over the years.

Some years ago, Jack introduced me to Terri Lyne Carrington with the aim of planning an educational endeavour, a summer camp, a school program, something that would bring the three of us together to, as Jack put it at the time, 'to work with kids and the power of music'.[14] That project did not come to fruition; however, I learned more about Jack's relationship with Terri. Already very much aware of Terri Lyne Carrington's professional accomplishments, I also learned more about her exemplary teaching and long history of mentoring younger musicians, something she shared in common with Jack DeJohnette.

Mentoring has a long history in the jazz tradition, one that has been explored at length in music education research[15] and jazz history research.[16] In the early to mid-twentieth century, jazz music was developed and learned by and among jazz musicians. Andrew Goodrich, who has written much about mentoring in the context of contemporary jazz education, explains:

> Jazz musicians originally learned to play jazz in a variety of ways: listening to and transcribing recordings, listening to live performances, and asking questions of each other. From this aural and verbal communication with

> each other came the development of mentoring, or the social language of jazz. As jazz musicians hung out with each other, they shared ideas for learning that increased their knowledge of jazz music and elevated their level of musicianship. This type of conversation, both verbal and aural, occurred before, during, and after gigs. These conversations centered around *how* to learn. (emphasis added)[17]

In the United States, during the latter part of the twentieth century, jazz education programs became a staple among collegiate and university music departments, professional associations such as the *International Association for Jazz Education* formed, and music publishers began publishing jazz charts and method and instrumental technique books expressly for school jazz contexts.[18]

Although speaking in the early twenty-first century, some seventy years since jazz music first entered the academy, the participants in this study described learning in many of the same terms as those described by Andrew Goodrich and the others I have referenced. In describing their experiences with learning the drum kit, the participants kept returning to the following themes: (a) *the importance of mentors* in their lives and in the jazz tradition, (b) *challenges of learning to play the drum kit*, particular to the instrument itself, (c) *the unique place and space of drummers*, behind kits, on band stands, and in the role of leader or leader / mentor, and (d) '*something bigger than just the music*', the larger contexts of learning to play, of connecting to a community and lineage of jazz drummers. The following sections explore those themes as they emerged in the responses of the participants.

The Importance of Mentors

Throughout our conversations, Jack DeJohnette repeatedly expressed gratitude that he was 'fortunate enough to be around other musicians, players, and you know, a mentor that' could teach and inspire him.[19] DeJohnette explained his early musical life in his hometown: 'I got guidance, what you're calling mentoring, from Chicago musicians, let's see, Von Freeman, who else, yeah, Muhal Richard Abrams was really good, a lot of others too'. As Jack recalled other Chicago area musicians, he noted some of the players he had only heard on recordings, viewing them as de facto mentors. Similarly, DeJohnette counted many of the musicians whom he had observed playing live or had worked with on bandstands as mentors:

> You know, a lot of that guidance came from listening to musicians, recordings, going to hear people play, and then playing with Roscoe Mitchell, almost every day, free improvisation, drums and piano. Playing with Muhal

> [Richard Abrams], Joseph Jarman, a variety of music professionals that were just very helpful in my development, and inspired me to do my very best, and playing with musicians of, you know, the best quality, top quality, and playing also with some of the greatest jazz artists and musicians on the planet. That helped a lot. Jackie McLean was a great help for me, of course Coltrane, and, who else, Miles Davis, of course, Bill Evans, just to name a few.

Much of Jack's drum kit learning, however, was self-directed. He started as a piano player, taking lessons, and playing that instrument with a combo of his own. The drummer in that combo left a drum kit at the DeJohnette household and between rehearsals, Jack would sit behind the kit:

> So, I got started playing the drum kit when I had a combo and I had a drummer who was a part time drummer, so we used to rehearse in my house in Chicago, and he left his drum kit there. My uncle was a DJ so I had access to the latest jazz LPs and so, it took me about a month, I would go down in my basement, in a studio, and play with the LPs, jazz LPs and It took me about two weeks to get my coordination together and the other two weeks, I would actually play pretty decent. Drums came to me very naturally.

Mentoring also figured prominently in Terri Lyne's biographical narrative. She explained, 'drumming ran in the family. My grandfather was a drummer and my dad played sax and drums. So, the drums were there and the music was always playing in the house'.

Carrington's father, Matt Carrington, introduced Terri to a slew of iconic jazz musicians, including Dizzy Gillespie and Clark Terry, among many others, affording her the opportunity to sit in and 'learn while doing it'. Many of Matt Carrington's associates became mentors for young Terri Lyne. She recalled the importance of those mentors during a particularly musical childhood, 'learning from mentors is the *most* important way to get the needed inside information. You learn by default just by being around the *right* people'.

In addition to those de facto mentors, Carrington mentioned some of her teachers, each of whom transcended their role, going above and beyond teaching how to play the drum kit to becoming important life mentors, 'my Dad was my first teacher, but I also studied with Keith Copeland and Alan Dawson, as well as Tony Tedesco and John Wooley'. Owing to her precocious talents, Terri Lyne began studying at the Berklee College of Music as early as ten years of age. As noted earlier in this chapter, Ms. Carrington is a well-regarded and innovative educator at her alma mater. During the interviews for this chapter, Mr. DeJohnette regularly remarked on Terri Lyne's 'amazing' expertise in teaching drum kit at Berklee. Despite her commitment to and expertise in jazz education,

Carrington described an extra 'element', unique to the mentor / mentee relationship, that often eludes institutionalized jazz education contexts:

> And now we have institutionalized jazz education, so people are getting a lot of the things more quickly. But there's still that element of apprenticeship in the art form, that element of *needing* to be apprenticed, and needing to be mentored to really get into the nuances of the music that you won't necessarily get in jazz education.

Terri Lyne described the importance of Jack to her development as a drummer, musician, and 'most importantly, as a human being'. Carrington has a nearly forty-year relationship with Jack DeJohnette, whom she identified as, 'my biggest mentor … critical to my development'. She explained:

> For me, Jack was definitely, and still is, that person who came to be so important on so many levels when I was 17 or 18. I remember being pretty close-minded about music, life, things in general, and I remember Jack saying, 'we have to open you up,' because I was really a jazz head, in a way, which was great to start, but there were all these other things about music and about *life* that I really needed to embrace. I moved to NY when I was 18 and I had some friends, people that were a little older than me, but nobody who took *that* much interest who could pass the important things on to me, other than my parents, or that I could go to if I needed advice or help. And, I think that for me this was crucial to my development and it also made me see how important it is for me to do the same thing. I know that in my own way, I'm trying to do the same for some other young people. And because I'm teaching, seeing so many young people, I can't do that for *everybody,* but I do pick a few. And another thing I really learned from Jack is *how* to pick the ones you help. You know, it's not something that you just give away. You can't give a gift to somebody that doesn't know what to do with it.

At this point, as Carrington and I began discussing the vast numbers of students we see each academic year, the conversation switched focus to the specific challenges posed by teaching and learning to play drum kits in jazz education.

Challenges of Learning to Play the Drum Kit

In discussing the 'learn while doing it' approach, the nature of the drum kit and the particular role of drummers became points of focus. The drum kit is essential to much of contemporary jazz and improvised music. Drummers are relied upon for time, support, and direction. While all instrumentalists must learn a fair amount before hitting the bandstand, the participants agreed that drummers had to contend with being more of a critical focus while learning on the bandstand. Terri Lyne summed up this challenge:

> I don't think you can go on stage and play without a certain amount of experience, but then you're right, you have to *get* the experience. If the drummer's horrible, then the band's not great. You could have a mediocre bass player or soloist, but a good drummer, and the band still sounds and feels good, for the most part. So, there's a lot of weight on the drummer for making a band sound good.

The participants then recalled the ways in which they dealt with this conundrum in their own lives. Some of their approaches are likely familiar to readers of this volume and echo those that have been documented in the literature: listening to recordings, watching more established drummers, asking questions, and transcribing parts. One approach, however, stood out.

Both participants recalled learning to think about time from listening to instrumentalists charged with phrasing, such as horn players, other front-line instrumentalists, or singers. Jack DeJohnette explained, 'I listened to the melodies. Learning the melody can actually improve your time because you have to follow the phrasing, understand where things end up'. Terri Lyne Carrington concurred, 'to this day, I listen to the horn soloists, the singers, sometimes more than I do the bass player. In fact, I don't even really want to listen to the bass player so much, at least not as the start'.

Honing in on melodic instruments or singers, as a gauge to mark time, figured into the learning processes for both participants. Terri Lyne Carrington recalled taking this approach in her earliest days, while playing with records:

> When I would play with records, and even today, I would listen to the phrasing and the rhythm of the horn, so if I'm playing with somebody who's phrasing and time is impeccable, I'm playing with *that* and it makes me play different. So, it's all kinds of elements coming together. When you're playing with great records, you're playing with great people that had great *time*, and that helps you to learn what to listen for. And if you're playing along with great pianists, that comp in the right places, you know what it sounds like when somebody's comping good.

These discussions led the participants to think about other approaches to learning that helped them develop on the drum kit prior to 'learning by doing it' on bandstands.

Jack DeJohnette noted that the drum kit does not have explicit melodic or harmonic capability, which could make developing players think of the instrument as 'just about rhythm or time'. Terri Lyne Carrington repeatedly turned to the concept that practicing along with records, had to have 'playing musically, like a great singer or a great accompanist' as its ultimate goal. DeJohnette interjected, 'if it's possible, I would encourage young drummers to also get experience on a melodic instrument, like a guitar, or vibes, or piano'.

As noted earlier, Jack DeJohnette started playing piano before taking up the drum kit. Throughout our discussions, DeJohnette repeatedly emphasized the influence playing melodies and understanding harmony had on his own development on the drum kit. Terri Lyne Carrington, concurred, recalling the importance of singing melodies in her own education. She recounted how Alan Dawson, one of her teachers and primary influences, encouraged singing while practicing:

> If you don't have access to an instrument, maybe you don't have a piano, there's singing. When I studied with Alan Dawson, he made us sing while we played, sing the melodies of the standards while we played them, and that really helped because I actually learned *how* to learn them. I learned the intervals and I had to have that kind of razor-sharp understanding of pitch and intervals because I didn't want to be [chuckling] embarrassed.

At this point, I shared my own experiences studying composition along with the drum kit, inspired by my own interest but strongly encouraged by each of my primary drum kit teachers, noted drum pedagogue Sal LaRocca and iconic jazz drummer Max Roach. Mr. Roach used to say, 'don't be just a drummer. Other musicians will hold it against you for the rest of your life'. His point, as I understood it, was that development as a drummer required development as a musician in the fullest sense.

Jack DeJohnette returned to a topic from earlier in the conversation, one referenced at the start of this chapter section, the challenges posed by learning to play the drum kit on the bandstand with minimal experience:

> Still, at some point, you have to *do* it and you can't play just what you practiced, you have to do it with other musicians, on the bandstand, in real-time and get that feedback, keeping time, supporting, but also encouraging or directing a bit. That's a very different experience and it's just as important to learning, but it's hard because you're in the back surrounded by drums but you're also kind of the center of everything.

Our discussions then pivoted to the drum kit's status as a backline instrument and the unique place and space of drummers within jazz performance practice.

The Unique Place and Space of Drummers

The drum kit which, in a sense, isolates its player, enclosing the drummer in a formation of metal, wood, and reinforced hardware, is generally considered a backline instrument. Consequently, the instrument is often placed in the back, centre or off-centre, on bandstands and stages positioning the drummer further from the rest of the ensemble. With frontline instrumentalists facing the audience, eye-contact can be limited. Both participants noted these tendencies and described the ways in which they countered them.

Jack DeJohnette noted that a competent drummer can lead from wherever, and although eye-contact is essential, good drummers 'can still communicate and direct, whether leading the band or as part of the band. Where you set up is second to good communication, you know, between all the instruments, based on cues that you give on the drum kit'. Both DeJohnette and Carrington described taking pains to position themselves for optimal communication, facilitating eye contact with their ensembles, and respecting the desire of audiences to feel, as Jack put it, 'part of the group'. DeJohnette explained:

> We kind of deal with that position of the drums in relation to the other musicians by setting up to have the best possible eye contact. I set up my drums almost facing the instruments, bass in the middle, if there's piano so I can see it. You know, when I play with Ravi [Coltrane] and Matt [Garrison], we kind of face each other so we could have the eye contact, and not necessarily have the drums facing the audience. I want to be comfortable, where I can have eye contact and hear, and it's also, you know, people will see, they like the players to be intimate with each other, you know, so they can see the eye contact and the *sound* contact as well. And it's not dissing the audience because I can turn to the left and look at the audience, sort of on an angle.

Jack's description of how he sets up, and the reasons for why he sets up in the described manner sparked an exchange with Terri Lyne, in which they shared how they position their drums to balance their needs as leaders, the needs of the musicians they work with, and the needs of audiences. Terri Lyne Carrington positions her drum kit in a particular manner, whether serving as leader or as a member of another leader's ensemble:

> I make sure that I can see everybody I'm playing with, whether I'm the leader or not. I also make sure I'm not in the back, no matter who the leader is. When I get to a venue, whatever the stage plot is, I normally move the drums up some. So, the best position for me is when the drum throne is parallel with the bass amp and, therefore, I'm getting some sound from the bass amp, and it's not so far away. I don't want it way behind me either. And then the piano to the right of the bass, generally, and kind of at an angle where he or she would be looking at me, and making sure the bass player is not standing right in that view, and often I have guitar on the left, on the hi-hat side, and horns, kind of in front but to the left so nobody's standing directly in front of me

> because we wouldn't be able to have any eye contact like if a horn player's standing right in front of the drum set. So, those things are all super important, and the closer, the better, ultimately, in a jazz setting.

Jack brought the conversation back to the ultimate goal of positioning and placement, eye contact with other musicians:

> I mean, I think eye contact is crucial. It's very important, as well as the listening, you know, to be supporting and leading at the same time, simultaneously, and having an interchange or interaction with the ensemble and someone who's soloing too. In other words, you have that sort of democratic kind of, reciprocal interaction with everybody, even though somebody's soloing, the drummer can still, not dictate, but sort of direct. Ultimately, you want everyone, the musicians, the audience, to feel like they're part of something, something bigger than just the music.

Terri Lyne concurred, returning to the role of mentoring, explaining how Jack had taught her about life as much as about music or how to play drum kit. Jack agreed, recalling, 'it was funny because we didn't talk about drums all that much, right? We didn't talk about the technical aspects of the instrument. We just hung. We talked about music, about life, right'? The notion of something bigger returned. Something mentors impart beyond the particulars of the drum kit, beyond jazz drumming or technique or how to play well.

Something Bigger than Just the Music

Terri Lyne picked up on the notion of 'something bigger', recounting discussions about musicality with Herbie Hancock, 'the one thing that the musicians that I like the most have, well it comes down to things that *aren't* related to music, things that make you a good musician, like compassion, sensitivity, empathy'. One something bigger was the notion of belonging, of connecting to and becoming an enduring part of a community of musicians, the lineage of jazz drummers. Carrington identified belonging as a motivation for mentoring:

> I think that anybody that cares about the music has to take it upon themselves to mentor, at some point, or I don't know how you really care about the music. I think we spend a lot of our earlier years trying to get it together, trying to learn enough and don't really think of ourselves as teachers or mentors but, at some point, you want to see the music move *forward*. You want, also to, and even thinking selfishly, about your own legacy, you want to leave one that connects, like we talked about lineage earlier, the only way you have lineage is if you embrace others that are still learning how to play. Teach them as much as you can about what you know.

> They'll never be you, of course, but that influence ends up being part of the lineage. That extra step of encouragement, and insight and wisdom that you pass down, can be the tipping point that makes somebody go from good to great.

Jack DeJohnette summed it up beautifully, 'we're talking about humanity, you know, teaching *that* aspect, which is ultimately what's important, as we all agree, in the music'. Jack continued, observing that he has found teaching part of his own lifelong learning. He explained, 'you know, students can mentor us too. It's a two-way street. That exchange is priceless'.

Conclusions

Mentoring has played a central role in the development of jazz musicians for some 100 plus years. The drum kit players presented in this chapter represent two leading figures firmly established in that tradition. Not surprisingly, their statements and expressions chronicled here underscore the importance of mentoring, in general, and, more specifically, in the participants' personal histories, experiences as bandleaders, and teaching practices.

Further, both acknowledged a particular set of challenges associated with mentoring drummers and with learning to play the drum kit, rooted in the instrument's size, location on bandstands, and essential role in jazz ensembles.

Finally, both participants saw mentoring other drummers and other musicians as a part of a something bigger. Mentoring served a larger mission, to help their mentees develop as human beings, and as an essential part of their life's work and contributions to a jazz lineage.

Notes

1 P. F. Berliner. *Thinking in Jazz* (Chicago: University of Chicago Press, 1994); I. Monson *Saying Something: Jazz Improvisation and Interaction* (Chicago: University of Chicago Press, 1996); K. E. Prouty. 'The History of Jazz Education: A Critical Reassessment', *Journal of Historical Research in Music Education* 2 (2005), pp. 79–100.

2 A. Goldsher. *Hard Bop Academy: The Sidemen of Art Blakey and the Jazz Messengers* (Milwaukee: Hal Leonard, 2002).

3 Berklee Institute of Jazz and Gender Justice, available at www.berklee.edu/jazz-gender-justice (accessed 4 October 2019).

4 Ibid.

5 J. Pignato. 'Angelica Gets the Spirit out: Improvisation, Epiphany and Transformation', *Research Studies in Music Education* 35:1 (2013), pp. 21–38. DOI: http://10.1177/1321103X13486569.

6 B. Powell, A. Krikun, and J. M. Pignato. '"Something's Happening Here!": Popular Music Education in the United States', *IASPM Journal* 5:1 (2015), pp. 4–22.

7 J. M. Pignato and G. M. Begany. 'Deterritorialized, Multilocated and Distributed: Musical Space, Poietic Domains and Cognition in Distance Collaboration', *Journal of Music, Technology & Education* 8:2 (2015), pp. 111–128; J. Pignato. 'Situating Technology within and without Music

Education' in S. A. Ruthmann and R. Mantie (eds.), *The Oxford Handbook of Technology and Music Education* (Oxford: Oxford University Press, 2017), pp. 203–215.

8 J. M. Pignato. 'Red Light Jams: A Place Outside of All Others' in R. Mantie and G. D. Smith (eds.), *The Oxford Handbook of Music Making and Leisure* (Oxford: Oxford University Press, 2017), pp. 405-423; R. Cremata, J. M. Pignato, B. Powell and G. D. Smith. *The Music Learning Profiles Project* (New York, Routledge Focus, 2018).

9 C. Glesne. *Becoming Qualitative Researchers: An Introduction* (New York: Pearson, 2016).

10 Cremata, Pignato, Powell, and Smith, *The Music Learning Profiles Project*, Appendix A.

11 I. E. Seidman. *Interviewing as Qualitative Research* (New York: Teachers College Press, 2006).

12 Glesne, *Becoming Qualitative Researchers*, p. 200.

13 J. A. Smith, P. Flowers, and M. Larkin. *Interpretive Phenomenological Analysis: Theory, Method, and Research* (London: Sage, 2009).

14 Personal correspondence with the author.

15 A. Goodrich. 'Social Language of Jazz' in C. West and M. Titlebaum (eds.), *Teaching School Jazz: Perspectives, Principles, and Strategies* (Oxford: Oxford University Press, 2019), p. 30.

16 Berliner, *Thinking in Jazz*; Monson, *Saying Something*; Prouty, 'The History of Jazz Education'.

17 Goodrich, 'Social Language of Jazz'.

18 Prouty, 'The History of Jazz Education'.

19 Unless otherwise noted, quotations from the participants that appear in this chapter come from two sets of interviews, one conducted with each individual participant and another conducted with both, in simultaneous conversations. Their words appeared as they said them with some editing for clarity. Italics in quoted statements reflect natural emphasis in the participants' voices.

13 Leadership

The View from behind the Kit

BILL BRUFORD

Introduction

Leadership means different things to different people around the world, and different things in different situations. Community, religious, military, and political leadership, for example, all have their several dimensions. A traditional organisation requires the leader to manage by breaking down the task and coordinating members so the (usually) intended outcome is achieved with maximum efficiency in a timely fashion. However, leadership in the creative collaboration of a music group could scarcely be more different. Despite the recent emergence online of those such as the YouTube drummers whose music generation is mostly self-governed, large swathes of popular music performance continue to demand a real time association with others in a wide variety of collectives governed generally by some form of leadership. This chapter investigates the many overt and covert forms this leadership takes, the several conditions from which it emerges, and its relationship, if any, to the drummer-leader's interpretation of a successful music outcome.

Here I adopt a broad definition of leadership in music performance as guiding, influencing, directing, or otherwise controlling the music actions of a group of performers. Irrespective of the type or quality of the music outcomes, leadership seems to be irrevocably present and impossible to purge whenever one musician collaborates with another. There may have been prior manifestations of a hierarchical power in the selection of the music to be performed; the musicians to perform it; the time, place and other conditions of its performance; or the counting off of a tempo to commence the performance. Irrespective of any explicit desire for leaderless performance, some lead and some follow. In its most microscopic manifestation, someone will arrive at the second note first. From then on the generative process likely will fall under some sort of organisational, administrative, or inspirational leadership.

Leaders include the unchosen, the unappointed, the self-appointed, and those imposed from within and from outside the ensemble, and their actions or inactions may help or hinder the achievement of shared goals in varying degrees. 'Leader', 'leadership', 'supporting musician', and their various definitions are not cast in stone – clearly there are degrees of adoption of these identities and their functions – but forthwith the dyads 'leader/follower' and 'leader/subordinate', originating from business and commerce will be eschewed in favour of the nearest equivalent understanding in popular music: leader/supporting musician. The term 'group' is used throughout this discussion to indicate a music ensemble of any size.

Music leadership may be irrevocably present, but interest in it as a research topic appears everywhere in retreat. Recent studies of collaborative music making in closely related domains such as composition, Broadway musicals, or collective online music making make no mention of leadership at all.[1] Nevertheless, even as older, overt forms of leadership in music groups appear to dissipate, issues of leading, following and the distribution of power remain very much alive, if perhaps more covert. The 'band leader', 'lead' guitarist, orchestral 'section leader', virtuoso, or 'lead' singer are less easily identified in today's interactive and democratised ecology of popular music making. Practitioners may collaborate increasingly across the less-bordered roles of 'producer' or 'music inventor', but the forces of power and control remain ever-present whether or not they are mediated by one or more of the many forms that leadership may assume. Correctly interpreting the several conceptions of leadership that may be present in a group becomes a useful skill for the instrumentalist, often required to perform at short notice and with minimal contextualizing information.

Unfortunately, leadership models appropriated from the worlds of business management and administration, organizational and emotional psychology, sports management, or the military have poor transference to the performing arts, in which successful outcomes tend to be less quantifiable.[2] While certain kinds of decentralised leadership structures have been associated with better performance within sales teams than others, the evaluation and quantification of collaborative 'success' in the performing arts remains problematic.[3] The music leader needs to transform the values, preferences, and aspirations of sidemen from self-interest to collective interest to best secure the music outcomes required.[4]

Leadership in Theory

Music ensembles are specialised organisations often perceived to be endowed with paradigmatic levels of interactional skills that are nurtured and coordinated through leadership. Several nuanced models have emerged to explain the profound effects of leadership upon the performers.

I collate thinking into three strands that, woven together with and through participant data, may prove helpful in illuminating the various degrees of leadership 'fit' in music performance.

The One-Way Street: A Dominant-Linear-Hierarchical Model

For much of their known existence, kit drummers have operated as a breed apart, a breed below, and a breed under the authoritarian control of a band leader or conductor.[5] Classical orchestras, big bands (such as those of Buddy Rich or Duke Ellington) and soul revues (James Brown's Famous Flames, the Ike and Tina Turner Revue) of previous generations were perceived as functioning better with a leader, if only to coordinate large numbers of performers. Typically adopted was the dominant-authoritarian model of leadership, complete with reinforcement behaviours and sanctions for sidemen who transgressed. Leaders embody the rules held as being most valuable by the group: they 'attract the group members and assume the right to control or influence them'.[6] A directive perspective such as this tends now to be seen as not only inherently limited but also out of step with contemporary ideas of inclusive interaction.

The Two-Way Street: A Visionary-Transformational Model

Mid-twentieth-century hierarchical conceptions of leadership are only now just beginning to be supplanted by a suite of more nuanced models better suited to explain the many ways in which leadership exists in music. The principle aspects of the charismatic', 'inspirational', 'transformational', or 'visionary' styles have been gathered under the rubric of a 'new genre' of leadership theories that establish trust, appeal to ideological values, proffer intellectual stimulation and high expectations for performance beyond the call of duty.[7]

Followers have complete faith in charismatic leaders, feel proud to be associated with them, and trust their capacity to overcome any obstacle. Inspirational leadership involves the arousal and heightening of motivation among followers. The transformational model foregrounds the bringing about of change, rather than the maintenance and steady improvement of current performance, while a visionary style of leadership highlights clear depiction of the shared goals, stirs the imagination and generates thoughts and insights. Individualised consideration involves giving personal attention to followers who seem neglected, treating each follower individually, and helping each follower get what she wants.[8] Trumpeter Miles Davis exemplifies the two-way street when he asserted that: 'I don't lead musicians, man. They lead me. I listen to them to learn what they can do best'.[9]

Collectively, the new genre of leadership has profound effects on followers through strong engagement with followers' self-concepts in the interest of the mission articulated by the leader.[10] Effective leaders tend to set strategy, motivate followers, create a sense of mission, and build a culture.[11] Leadership is increasingly interpreted as a process rather than a possession held by someone; less about influencing others to do what the leader wants, more about helping a community to make meaning in its specific context.

The Shared Street: A Plural-Distributed Model

This line of thinking suggests a processual view of leadership that acknowledges its fluidity and plurality. In this shared space the segregation between potentially multiple leaders and sidemen is minimised. Leadership is seen as distributed and emergent; a plural process where some or all group members are actively involved in the realization of aims and objectives.[12] Notwithstanding the valid theoretical ideal of distributed leadership in which every person is equally a leader and a follower, leadership tends to be relatively centralised in human groups: only a very small percentage of group members actually emerge as leaders within a group at any point in time.

Central to effective leadership here is whether the formal and emergent leaders are able to coordinate effectively. In work groups with a formally appointed leader, informal leaders may emerge for a variety of reasons.[13] When formal and emergent leaders do not recognize one another's leadership, the group can literally be torn apart. When they do, they should be better able to synchronize their leadership efforts so that decision making and action are more effectively channelled within the group. This kind of distributed and coordinated leadership echoes Gronn's notion of 'conjoint agency', in which a few individuals emerge as leaders within a group and are able to synchronize their actions through reciprocal influence.[14]

Leader–Member Exchange

Helpful here is Leader-Member Exchange theory of leadership (LMX), drawn from management and business organisation. This frames the quality of the relationship between music leader and supporting musician in terms of an exchange of resources.[15] LMX has been shown to be positively related to support, and creates obligations in individuals who then reciprocate through higher levels of performance. The extent to which the leader and subordinate exchange resources and support beyond what is expected based on the formal employment contract evidences a high LMX [23]. High LMX relationships may be forged under the charismatic or transformational leadership of some drummers and their band leaders,[16] and are characterised by mutual trust, loyalty, and behaviors that extend outside the employment contract. The drummer supplies the unfailingly high-quality groove essential to the leader's satisfactory performance. In exchange, the charismatic leader of global star-quality confers status, respect, and cultural capital upon the drummer. To the extent that the needs of both are met to mutual satisfaction, the ensemble is built on sound foundations. A low LMX relationship is one in which the employee performs within the bounds of the employment contract but contributes nothing extra.[17]

Method

The research project that informs this chapter combines autoethnographic self-reflection of my own experience of music leadership, as both leader and supporting musician, with narrative expressions of a small group of high-level peak-performance instrumental colleagues. I take autoethnography as a form of qualitative social science research that combines an author's narrative self-reflection with analytical interpretation of the broader contexts in which that individual operates.[18] As a scholar-practitioner, I use the robust intellectual framework of autoethnography to link concepts from the literature to the narrated personal experience while seeking to avoid the production of so-called mesearch – work that merely draws upon the author's autobiographical description in an academic context.[19]

Nine participants, selected for their many years of experience in giving, receiving, and sharing leadership functions, provided interview data. They were divided into two groups. The reflections of a primary group of five drummer-leaders comprising Chad Wackerman, Asaf Sirkis, Cindy Blackman Santana, Mark Guiliana, and the author were culled from preexisting research and personal correspondence.[20] A secondary group of four non-drummers with similar levels of leadership experience consisted of Tony Levin (bassist), Django Bates (pianist, tenor horn player), Tim Garland (saxophonist), and Iain Ballamy (saxophonist): all have shared performance experience with the author. This group completed a written questionnaire focused specifically on giving, receiving, and sharing leadership with drummers, with, in some cases, follow-up correspondence for clarification. These data were drawn upon to identify emergent themes and their fit with the theoretical models discussed above.

The analysis generated a number of different elements that were identified as having a reported impact on music decision making. Central and emergent themes were identified and their commonality, if any, assessed across participant responses. These clustered around three main umbrella categories: a) Identification and Location; b) Function and Purpose, and c)

Giving and Receiving. As in any kind of personal and qualitative writing, I make choices and create narratives and subtext while both maintaining my own voice as a participant-observer and looking for common threads to buttress or negate perspectives from the literature.

Leadership in Practice

Identification and location

While expert drummers see themselves as performing on a powerful instrument able to effect radical change in performance outcomes, neither they nor the culture in which they exist typically see theirs as a lead instrument. Most drummers will never lead an ensemble from behind a drum kit: almost all will experience leadership from in front of it. The requirements and constraints they suffer as drummer-leaders differ remarkably little from those suffered by a leader on any other instrument. Chad articulates one view of core function in terms of dynamics: 'Usually as drummers – as leaders – we're always shaping the dynamics of the band and the transition points to the second verse, the chorus, the bridge. We are the ones who are building it or making it go dynamically'. The work of building, making comfortable and making go, to name but three dimensions of drummer action, remain central to effective performance, irrespective of any real or imagined leadership function.

Drummers tend to see the assumption of the leadership role first, as a catalyst for action; second, as a way of designing and controlling a vehicle for creative expression, thereby decreasing the chances of expressive dilution. Mark's perception of leadership is typical of many in its requirement for 'much more of the "producer" mentality in the moment; thinking about the big picture and the ensemble sound and just trying to accommodate that'. He feels obliged to seek the imaginative exploitation of all the possibilities of his ensemble. Different leadership models might be adopted for different, sometimes simultaneous, projects, ranging from the loose assembly of musically compatible individuals to the complete control of all aspects of the collective performance.

Common to all is the creation of a musical space. Leaders provide both the space in which creative action is developed and the conditions under which it is nurtured and sustained, but that space may be elusive to locate. Working with James Taylor, Chad is surprised at the source of actual rather than nominal leadership:

> We're playing with an orchestra; the drum set is right in front of the conductor, you know, the first violins are to my right, seconds and violas are behind me, I'm playing really quiet, a lot of brushes. But Clifford Carter, the

> keyboard player, was saying 'You know, basically you have to realise . . . we're all following you, you've got to be the leader. Even though there's a conductor' . . . he said 'Look, actually James [Taylor] hired the conductor to follow the rhythm section'.

Part of Chad's expertise (and a necessary skill for drummers in general) resides in the accurate, speedy assessment of the locus of actual rather than nominal leadership in the music situation. His anecdote suggests that structures of power within a given performance space tend to be fluid, contested, less straightforward than might be imagined and arising in unexpected ways that may require negotiation. In his view 'we're hired by the leader, they have the final say on things but it's our band. It's the drummer's band, always'. Observations such as this not only reflect the multiple evocations of the adage about a band being only as good as its drummer, but also evoke a conspiratorial view of the covert nature of the power structure. From the practitioner's point of view the ball always remains in the drummer's court, even though the client or leader may not know it.

Participant notions of ideal leadership gather around a handful of recurring core ideas. Tim and Django invoke the 'two-way' model when they insist a leader must be a visionary. 'In a group where the aim is to maximise unique creative input from all other members' asserts Tim, 'a leader must develop the capacity to strongly envisage the end result and how an audience will respond to this'. According to Django, a leader should possess self-confidence – 'the strong belief that their ideas deserve to be performed. Performing for a leader, I get to be part of someone else's musical vision. When their vision is clear . . . I am led to play in very different ways in service of [that] vision, *which I trust*'. The ineffective leader, in Tim's opinion, 'lacks vision, focus, or personality, and depends rather on 'derivatives, platitudes and sometimes on the sidemen to somehow make up for that emotive, explosive kernel that [the leaders] themselves should possess'. Unclear expression is a marker of ineffective leadership for Iain and Tim, as is a lack of openness to what others have to say about the way the performance is being directed. As Iain puts it: 'A sense of belonging is important. By not inviting input from musicians a leader can leave them feeling like a note on a keyboard rather than an active and valuable member of the band'.

An early function of the leader is to select appropriate co-performers to collaborate in the realisation of this vision, and they may be people from whom the leader can learn. Tim points to the 'terrific tradition of mentorship in our [jazz] music where both parties end up learning from each other, co-creating . . . I know I am learning from playing with musicians now who are half my age'. In his view a good leader will not be content just to let the sidemen shine; they'll be wanting to actually develop themselves, as an eternal student'. In my own group Earthworks, an older, more experienced but less technically capable leader was able to offer an international platform to younger, less experienced but more technically capable sidemen who hitherto did not have access to one. The exchange was balanced and to mutual advantage, supporting the development of all parties and auguring well for a successful outcome. Moreover, this exchange went *beyond the expected.*

Purpose

To the extent that the leader's over-arching function is interpreted by the performers as the provision of, and direction to, a shared goal, as for example a group identity or a hit record, then the first purpose of leadership might be to create the conditions under which that may be enabled. Iain's perception of working with me in the late 1980s was that I was the leader of Earthworks and 'clearly the most established among us . . . we managed to collaborate, share, write and work together to create the music we made. I believe that process was the only way we could have arrived at the eventual musical result we achieved'. From this we might infer that the freedom of input on offer in that situation was both necessary and sufficient to arrive at the shared goal.

In Venkat Krishnan's view, transformational leaders 'broaden and change the interests of their followers, and generate awareness and acceptance of the purposes and mission of the group. They stir their followers to look beyond their self-interest for the good of the group'. He suggests that four factors are at play: 'charismatic leadership or idealized influence, inspirational leadership or motivation, intellectual stimulation, and individualized consideration'.[21] These styles tend to emphasize 'vague and distal goals and utopian outcomes. It is here that Bass refers to charismatic leaders' use of "symbolism, mysticism, imaging and fantasy"'.[22] This chimes with my own experience in the rock group King Crimson: 'I wasn't given a set list when I joined the band, more a reading list. Ouspensky, J. G. Bennett, Gurdjieff, and Castaneda were all hot. Wicca, personality changes, low-magic techniques, pyromancy: all this from the magus in the court of the Crimson King'.[23]

A second important purpose of leadership is to foster mutual trust, identified earlier as an essential component of a high LMX. Characterised as the 'willingness to be vulnerable',[24] trust becomes a critical component in any untroubled relationship between leader and follower. Expert drummers emphasize its reciprocal nature, emerging as: 1) the leader's perception of the trustworthiness of the support musician; 2) the support musician's perception of how much the leader trusts him or her; 3) the leader's perception of how much the support musician trusts him or her; 4) the support musician's perception of the trustworthiness of the leader.[25] A two-way street requires both trust and respect: with insufficient of either, matters default to the authoritarianism of the one-way street. On the topic of performing in my group a decade after Iain, Tim states that 'there was trust and a good deal of mutual respect' engendered between us at an early age, as he grew up with my music as a teenager. Iain echoes Tony when he says that he 'trust(s) the people I book and they are chosen carefully for their skills and qualities – therefore I feel it is intelligent of me to give them the freedom to bring ideas that could add greatly to the music'. Touching upon the idea of rotational leadership at the level of the bar or phrase, he positions leadership as 'a trust and shared understanding that any member (may) lead and initiate (through making sound or leaving space) and that they can support and follow the direction the music is taking if someone else is taking the lead at a that moment'. The authoritarian model of leadership, by contrast, is predicated upon a lack of trust that engenders what Cindy identifies as a 'lack of letting and allowing'. The one-way street allegedly beloved of Rich, Brown, and Turner has been rejected as much in the classical string quartet as in high level popular music performance.[26]

A third purpose of leadership identified by participants is to avoid or resolve conflict. Ideally leaders on the shared street understand the creative nature of dialogue and the always emerging nature of leadership. Success rests on the ability of group members to resist indulging their ego and to embrace an '*ethics of reciprocity* – of living well with others'.[27] Not all conflicts are resolved smoothly, however, and feelings may fester. Leadership may be challenged or be in semi-permanent negotiation with others such as the record company or its agent in situ. Sidemen may be shackled to a dysfunctional or disputed form of producer/artist co-leadership. 'That is often the case in the recording studio, where there can be said to be two leaders, the record producer and the artist' says Tony, a position exacerbated should the drummer-leader also be the producer.

The shared space of plural leadership acknowledges the possibility of leadership as a distributed phenomenon in which there may be several formally appointed and/or emergent leaders within a group.[28] In the 1990s I performed with a group called Bruford Levin Upper Extremities (BLUE). The case of BLUE is instructive in that the group incorporated two formally appointed leaders. Tony frames leadership here in reference to our respective differing compositional methodologies:

> My approach was not just to have the players that would get something musically exciting going, but to let them do the composing, albeit in a low

> key way . . . [I] didn't need to even say the words, just let the music go that way. I wouldn't call [that approach] 'leadership', just being smart about the concept, a fairly wide open concept, I had. The Bruford compositions were complete compositions, and your leadership method involved telling the players what you wanted, and then judging, as the pieces came together, whether to rein them in or let them vary things for the better.

This exemplifies the close relationship that many jazz musicians have with the leader-as-composer paradigm. Perhaps because the compositional elements he brought to the music consisted of no more than his own bass parts, Levin appears to disavow this approach as leadership in any meaningful sense: he was 'just being smart about the concept'. Being smart also involved minimal explication: 'Didn't need to even say the words'. In apparently doing little, this leader did a lot.

In ensembles such as BLUE, to the extent that leadership could be said to be present in any shape or form, it was covert, unannounced, and to be found in the lightest of light touches, the smallest of small suggestions, planted or ignored. A visitor to the recording studio would have likely been unable to discern any overt leadership whatsoever. All group members contributed in any way that seemed appropriate in the context of the nascent composition, improvised in private in the studio or in public on stage. Certainly no one instructed anyone else on what to do: any friction between formally-appointed and emergent leaders was indiscernible. The many years of experience and the recorded options already made in so many music situations, it was assumed, would lead to a satisfactory outcome. All parties reserved the right to change any aspect of their contribution at any time prior to or during performance. Within the best co-operatives, leadership is translucent, unnoticed, and practically inert. It becomes overt only when necessary, and then anyone may lead.

Giving and Receiving

Three of the four performance contexts mentioned earlier demonstrate perceptions of the compounding severity of extra-musical concerns when giving and receiving leadership. *Performing with* David Torn and Tony in David's group Cloud About Mercury, I was without organisational concerns and thus removed from the extra-musical complexities of recording contracts, agents, diaries, and visas. *Performing as* a co-leader of BLUE, my name was 'on the marquee', and many of the above considerations returned. Finally, as the sole leader of Bill Bruford's Earthworks, concerns both musical and extra-musical became, in combination, all but insuperable. Ultimately, *performing without* a leader in a duo format proved to be by far the most amenable scenario.

In contrast, Tony is 'pretty oblivious to my role in the band, be it leader or backup player or some other variation. In the bands where I've clearly been the leader . . . I'll have chosen or written the material and the style we're playing in, and have chosen players to implement that well, and left the rest to them. So nothing during the performances impacts on that'. For Django, 'a lot of my leadership has happened before the performance . . . my leadership during performance becomes more about subtle choices that shape the structure of that music, such as cueing the next section or sending signals through the music that lead everyone to a change in dynamic, tempo, or anything else'.

In Earthworks I sought a leadership style that 'eschewed hierarchy in preference to the more difficult and perhaps more time-consuming work of maintaining "relational integrity", avoiding both the passive compliance of groupthink and the potential for offence by overly confrontational and combative argument'.[29] Music leadership in that group tended to be assumed by, or devolved to, the individual composer of the work at hand; a reasonably democratic model of what Tony calls a 'revolving' leadership and common enough practice in the jazz community. Iain and Django were contemporaries in Earthworks. They now generally perform as leaders and prefer that condition, but Iain is 'happy to be led, provided I'm given the freedom to input that I would offer my own musicians', They describe their position in the group as being 'the kids figuring out how things worked'. Indeed, investigators in the realm of musicians' motivations confirm that intrinsic motivation for music is reinforced in an environment that is perceived as allowing personal autonomy.[30] The provision of a portable performance workshop in which 'the kids' could figure out how things worked is an example of both informal learning and one side of the exchange of resources beyond what is expected based on the formal employment contract that is a requirement of the LMX framework.

Conclusion

Visionary-transformational models that foreground visionary thinking and the bringing about of change, rather than 'transactional leadership' designed to maintain and steadily improve current performance were predominant in drummers' perceptions of leadership. The application of LMX theory to the data has been useful in illuminating the reasoning behind an individual continuing to perform with any given ensemble. The one-way, two-way, and shared streets metaphor provided a robust framework in which to depict interpretations of leadership. Unsurprisingly, the two-way street of the visionary/inspirational model of leadership attracted far more support than the one-way street of the dominant/ hierarchical model, generally seen as ineffective at best or a hindrance at worst. A distributed, plural type of leadership surfaced predominantly in discussions of collective improvisation.

Evidence from within high-level music performance suggests that:

- leadership is more than a top-down process between a formal leader and group members
- multiple leaders within a group may exercise simultaneous or sequential leadership
- practitioners oscillate between the supporting musician and leader roles as the situation demands
- practitioners privilege group-based leadership processes rather than those generated through individual agency

Broad consensus is evident on four further issues. An ideal leader will:

- know what she wants and be able to express it clearly
- provide a vision of, and direction towards, a group identity
- foster mutual trust and respect
- promote 'living well with others' through conflict resolution

In sum, identifying, locating, giving, and receiving leadership have become skills to be continually refined as part of the drummer's habitus. The leadership styles in evidence in this collective today will differ in subtle but important ways in that collective tomorrow: being well-adapted to swimming in these ever-changing waters may remove one potential level of stress for the practitioner. The chapter should contribute to a growing body of knowledge of use to the drummer in her development of a suite of 'off-instrument' skills now seen as every bit important as her suite of 'on-instrument' ones.

Notes

1 S. Hayden and L. Windsor. 'Collaboration and the Composer: Case Studies from the End of the 20th Century', *Tempo* 61:240 (2007), pp. 28–39; B. Uzzi and J. Spiro. 'Collaboration and Creativity: The Small World Problem', *American Journal of Sociology* 111:2 (2005), pp. 447–504; M. K. Koszolko. 'Crowdsourcing, Jamming and Remixing: A Qualitative Study of Contemporary Music Production Practices in the Cloud', *Journal on the Art of Record Production* 10 (2015).

2 H. H. Brower, F. D. Schoorman, and H. H. Tan. 'A Model of Relational Leadership: The Integration of Trust and Leader–Member Exchange', *The Leadership Quarterly* 11:2 (2000), pp. 227–250; V. R. Krishnan. 'Leader-Member Exchange, Transformational Leadership, and Value System', *EJBO-Electronic Journal of Business Ethics and Organization Studies* (2005); P. Chelladurai. 'Leadership in Sports, A Review', *International Journal of Sport Psychology* 21:4 (1990), pp. 328–354; L. Wong, P. Bliese, and D. McGurk. 'Military Leadership: A Context Specific Review', *The Leadership Quarterly* 14:6 (2003), pp. 657–692.

3 A. Mehra, B. R. Smith, A. L. Dixon, and B. Robertson. 'Distributed Leadership in Teams: The Network of Leadership Perceptions and Team Performance', *The Leadership Quarterly* 17:3 (2006), pp. 232–245.

4 B. Shamir, R. J. House, and M. B. Arthur. 'The Motivational Effects of Charismatic Leadership: A Self-Concept Based Theory', *Organization Science* 4:4 (1993), pp. 577–594.
5 B. Bruford. 'A Breed Apart and a Breed Below: Creative Music Performance and the Expert Drummer', *Popular Music* 39:2 (2020).
6 S. R. Covey cited in J. P. Carnicer, J. Gustems, D. C. Garrido and S. O. Requena. 'Music and Leadership, the Role of the Conductor', *International Journal* 3:1 (2015), p. 85.
7 Shamir, House, and Arthur, 'The Motivational Effects of Motivational Leadership', pp. 577–578
8 B. M. Bass. 'Two Decades of Research and Development in Transformational Leadership', *European Journal of Work and Organizational Psychology* 8:1 (1999), pp. 9–32.
9 N. B. Wakan and R. Artmonsky. *Music Works* (Artmonsky Arts Publishing, 2002), p. 105.
10 Shamir, House, and Arthur, 'The Motivational Effects of Motivational Leadership', p. 577
11 D. Goleman. *Leadership: The Power of Emotional Intelligence* (Northampton: More than Sound, 2011).
12 R. Bathurst and D. Ladkin. 'Performing Leadership: Observations from the World of Music', *Administrative Sciences* 2:1 (2012), p. 115.
13 T.A. Judge, J. E. Bono, R. Ilies, and M. W. Gerhardt. 'Personality and Leadership: A Qualitative and Quantitative review', *Journal of Applied Psychology* 87:4 (2002), p. 765.
14 P. Gronn. 'Distributed Leadership as a Unit of Analysis', *The Leadership Quarterly* 13:4 (2002), pp. 431–432.
15 C. R. Gerstner and D. V. Day. 'Meta-Analytic Review of Leader-Member Exchange Theory: Correlates and Construct issues', *Journal of Applied Psychology* 82:6 (1997), p. 827; R. C. Liden, B. Erdogan, S. J. Wayne, and R. T. Sparrowe. 'Leader-Member Exchange, Differentiation, and Task Interdependence: Implications for Individual and Group Performance', *Journal of Organizational Behavior: The International Journal of Industrial, Occupational and Organizational Psychology and Behavior* 27:6 (2006), p. 723.
16 See for example, those between Cindy Blackman Santana and her leader-employer rock star Lenny Kravitz; drummer Ralph Salmins and leader-employer singer Van Morrison, Chad Wackerman, and leader-employer Frank Zappa in B. Bruford (ed.), *Uncharted: Creativity and the Expert Drummer* (Ann Arbor: University of Michigan Press, 2018).
17 Brower, Shoorman, and Tan, 'A Model of Relational Leadership', p. 229.
18 For more on this see H. Chang. *Autoethnography as Method*, Vol. 1 (Routledge, 2016).
19 The term is used in 'Beyond 'Mesearch': Autoethnography, Self-Reflexivity, and Personal Experience as Academic Research in Music Studies', Conference at the Institute of Musical Research, Senate House, London, 16–17 April 2018.
20 B. Bruford. *Uncharted: Creativity and the Expert Drummer* (Ann Arbor: University of Michigan Press, 2018).
21 Krishnan, 'Leader-Member Exchange, Transformational Leadership, and Value System', p. 14.
22 B. M. Bass. *Leadership and Performance beyond Expectations* (New York: The Free Press, 1985) p. 6.
23 B. Bruford. *Bill Bruford: The Autobiography: Yes, King Crimson, Earthworks, and More* (London: Jawbone Press, 2009) pp. 145–146.
24 Mayer, Davis, and Schoorman (1995) in D. M. Rousseau, S. B. Sitkin, R. S. Burt, and C. Camerer'Not So Different After All: A Cross-Discipline View of Trust', *Academy of Management Review* 23:3 (1998), p. 394.
25 Brower, Shoorman, and Tan, 'A Model of Relational Leadership', p. 233.
26 D. Waterman. 'Playing Quartets: A View from the Inside' in R. Stowell and J. Cross (eds.), *The Cambridge Companion to the String Quartet* (Cambridge: Cambridge University Press, 2003), pp. 100–101.
27 A. L. Cunliffe and M. Eriksen. 'Relational Leadership', *Human Relations* 64:11 (2011), p. 1439.
28 Mehra, Smith, Dixon, and Robertson, 'Distributed Leadership in Teams', p. 2.
29 Bathurst and Ladkin, 'Performing Leadership', pp. 102–103.
30 A. C. Lehmann, J. A. Sloboda, and R. H. Woody. *Psychology for musicians: Understanding and Acquiring the Skills* (New York: Oxford University Press, 2007), p. 49.

PART IV

Drumming Bodies, Meaning, and Identity

14 The Meaning of the Drumming Body

MANDY J. SMITH

For me, playing drums is . . . as involving to an athletic degree as a marathon is, but at the same time your mind is busy as an engineer's is, with all the calculations a drummer has to make. NEIL PEART[1]

In the book *The Meaning of the Body* – after which this essay is titled – cognitive scientist Mark Johnson puts forth a philosophy of meaning based on the visceral human experience. He situates the arts among the best places to find examples of how meaning works. In his chapter on music, he claims it can 'present the flow of human experience, feeling, and thinking in concrete, embodied forms – and this is meaning in its deepest sense'.[2] I can think of no musical experience more obviously visceral than the act of drumming.

Drumming is often pigeonholed as *solely* a visceral experience. But it undoubtedly has cognitive components as well, as Rush's Neil Peart aptly points out in the epigraph. This fact supports Johnson's central argument 'that what we call "mind" and what we call "body" are not two things, but rather aspects of one organic process, so that all our meaning, thought, and language emerge from the aesthetic dimensions of this embodied activity'.[3] Johnson goes on to identify 'at least' five levels of embodiment of mind and meaning: the body as a biological organism, the ecological body, the phenomenological body, the social body, and the cultural body.[4]

In this essay, I analyse John Bonham's performance on Led Zeppelin's 'When the Levee Breaks' (1971) to demonstrate how these five dimensions of the human body can reveal meaning in drumming, and how drumming – a type of music-making where it is almost impossible to hide its bodily nature – supports the idea of music as an embodied activity. I apply all five of Mark Johnson's levels to the song one at a time in order to peel back layers of meaning. In Johnson's final level, the cultural body, I propose what I term a Tonic Beat Pattern Theory based on tension and release that serves as a method of drum analysis across rock music to explain how drummers contribute to affect and meaning.

'When the Levee Breaks'

In 1968, John Bonham, John Paul Jones, Jimmy Page, and Robert Plant formed The New Yardbirds in London – and later changed the name of

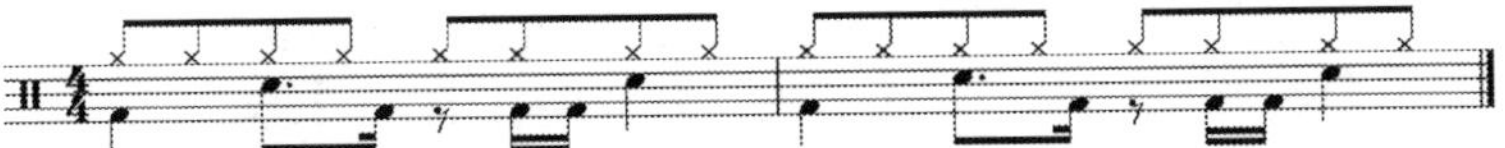

Example 14.1 Beat played by Bonham in 'When the Levee Breaks' (0:00)
Note: In standard drum kit notation, the bass drum appears on what in treble clef would be the F space, snare drum on C space, and hi-hat on the G above the staff.

this band to Led Zeppelin. Their sound ranged from hard rock, heavy metal, and psychedelic rock to blues and folk. Zeppelin drew up a blueprint for generations of rockers with their mix of drums-bass-guitar-vocals, endless touring, contributions to both arena rock and album-oriented rock, theatric self-presentations onstage, and high level of musicianship. The group released their untitled fourth album – often called *Zoso* or *IV* – in November 1971. They first tried recording the album at Island Records' Basing Street Studios, eventually returning to a combination they found successful for *III*. They used the Rolling Stones mobile recording studio – also used to record the Stones' album *Sticky Fingers* – and Headley Grange, a structure originally built in 1795 as a House of Industry for the sick, elderly, orphans, and illegitimate children.[5] *IV* contains classic Zeppelin tracks such as the raucous 'Rock and Roll' and the epic 'Stairway to Heaven'.

The album's final track, 'When the Levee Breaks', is Zeppelin's take on a song that blues artists Kansas Joe and Memphis Minnie wrote about the Great Mississippi Flood of 1927. Plant's sparse but powerful vocals soar over the drone created by Jones and Page. The groove of the song is deep and sluggish, and the main beat Bonham plays throughout the song appears in Example 14.1.

Bonham plays this beat for nearly every section of the song. Andy Johns engineered the session, and he and Bonham recorded the drums at the bottom of a three-story tall staircase in an open hallway at Headley Grange, resulting in a classic drum sound that has been sampled by everyone from the Beastie Boys ('Rhymin & Stealin') and Eminem ('Kim') to Björk ('Army of Me') and Beyoncé ('Don't Hurt Yourself').

The Biological Body

Johnson's first and most narrow dimension of the human body is the body as conceptualised completely separately from the mind: 'the body as biological organism'. He describes the biological body as follows: '[t]he principal physical locus of my being-in-the-world is the living, flesh-and-blood creature that I call "my body"'.[6] Given this definition, John Bonham's performance on 'When the Levee Breaks' contains a biological dimension: what his body actually did to make the drums generate sound.

This level reveals Bonham's physicality as he enacted the beat patterns, fills, and groove. He struck the bass and snare in a call-and-response manner, with his right foot and left hand, in which the second bass drum part of the conversation has three syncopated hits. Meanwhile, Bonham kept time on the hi-hat with his right hand. All this activity would have made his heart beat faster than at resting, causing his blood to pump harder through his veins. His muscles, ligaments, and tendons tensed and released to allow bodily motion throughout his arms and legs. This extreme physical exertion may have caused him to sweat as well. While this reveals what Bonham is physically doing, the analysis of the drum pattern is fairly basic and perhaps the least insightful of Johnson's five levels. It describes how the sounds the listener hears are generated, but it does not reveal why listeners find pleasure in this grooviest of grooves.

The Phenomenological Body

Johnson defines the phenomenological body succinctly as 'our body as we live it and experience it'.[7] Unfortunately for me, I did not play on Led Zeppelin's fourth album. But I can begin to understand John Bonham's experience of drumming during the recording by turning to how it feels for me as a drummer to play this pattern, drawing on Elizabeth Le Guin's work, which she calls 'carnal musicology', a connection between people who play and write about music and the composers of that music. She writes of this connection:

> at its best and sweetest we might call it intimate, implying that it is somehow reciprocal. I will contend two things here: first, that the sense of reciprocity in this process of identification is not entirely wistful or metaphorical, but functions as real relationship; and second, that this relationship is not fantastic, incidental, or inessential to musicology. It can and should be a primary source of knowledge about the performed work of art.[8]

Le Guin's insights prompt questions. How does my body carnally connect with John Bonham when I drum this pattern? What can my analysis gain from my experience of drumming? The answer is simple; my body feels as if it is in the ultimate state of groove.

But what does it mean to be 'in a groove'? In *Presence and Pleasure: The Funk Grooves of James Brown and Parliament*, Anne Danielsen wants to understand funk 'as lived experience'.[9] She writes, '[b]eing in a groove, feeling the right feeling, letting presence happen, from the inside, from a position within time, within the experiential now, this is probably what funk is all about'.[10] Here, Danielsen attempts to capture in words the essence of being in a groove, and her claim could apply to many groove-based musics, including 'When the Levee Breaks', in which a single beat pattern takes up the vast majority of the song. When one impulse happens for such a long time in a song, it brings you into the present moment of that song in a way that songs with more defined sections do not. *Rhythm* magazine readers certainly agree, naming 'When the Levee Breaks' the '[g]reatest groove of all time'.[11] The song often ranks on lists of the most sampled breaks in hip-hop alongside legendary funk grooves such as The Winstons' 'Amen, Brother' and James Brown's 'Funky Drummer'.[12]

Bonham's infectious groove – in Example 14.1 – oozes with laid-back ease. This pattern is as unbelievably satisfying to play as it is to hear. As I play it, I connect carnally with Bonham. The basic drum pattern consists of three components. First, as in any standard backbeat pattern, the snare strikes on two and four. The tempo enables my hand to fall into place for a slow crack on the snare – where I have plenty of time to lift my left hand high and smack it down firmly in the pocket. The ever-so-slightly-open hi-hat keeps time with straight eighths, a very common way to keep time over a backbeat. At that tempo, my right hand can remain loose in a way that it cannot at some fast or even mid tempos, allowing for a slack push-and-pull in the groove. The bass drum simply pounds on beat one for the first half of the pattern, leaving loads of aural space until the first snare crack on beat two.

The true magic happens with the bass drum in the latter part of the one-measure pattern. The bass drum feels early, entering a sixteenth note before beat three and making my body sway a bit as I play it – yearning not so much with anticipation, but with pleasure. The 'early' hit feels natural, almost necessary, because of the groove's depth and almost sluggish tempo. Difficult to get just in the sweet spot, this early bass drum hit's payoff is simply euphoric. Beat three aches because of the absence of the bass drum, which flirts with the beat but never touches it. Then, I anticipate the snare backbeat on four with a couple gallops of the bass drum, filling in significantly more of the space in the second part of the measure than the first.

But one musical element both enriches and complicates the phenomenological dimension of this analysis: tempo. I cannot connect fully to Bonham's bodily experience of playing because I do not know at what tempo he recorded this beat. The wash of the cymbal indicates that the drums were recorded faster and slowed down for the track – but I can only confirm this because of my experience as a drummer, who has heard and played so many cymbals throughout my life.[13] When my body plays along with the recording, my physicality does not actually enact the pattern in the way that Bonham does on the record. The link between his phenomenological experience and mine is not broken, but it is fractured. Still, the result of this phenomenological layer of analysis is a deep, pleasurable groove for the listening experience.

The Ecological Body

The final three dimensions all relate to environment – ecological, social, and cultural. Johnson takes into account the environment because '[h]uman mind and meaning require at least a partially functioning human brain within at least a partially functioning human body that is in ongoing interaction with complex environments that are at once physical, social, and cultural. These environments both *shape* and *are shaped by* the humans who inhabit them'.[14] Under the third dimension – the ecological body – he explains, '[t]here is no body without an environment, no body without the ongoing flow of organism-environment interaction that defines our realities'.[15] Our interactions with the world define and shape our bodies. In the case of 'Levee', I turn to two factors of ecological environment: the physical, architectural space around the drums at the famous recording spot Headley Grange, and the sonic space created by the Binson echo unit used in production.

The physical reverberation of the stone walls of Headley Grange 'had a significant impact on the sound. Because stone is, acoustically speaking, a highly non-absorbent material, the sound waves were reflected within the stairwell with a greater intensity than if the walls were composed of a more absorbent material'.[16] But the engineers still needed to capture the natural echo on record. Andy Johns remembers hanging 'two ambient Beyer M160 stereo microphones over the kit, one 10 feet up, the other about 20''.[17] This mic placement in combination with the open, echo-producing stone structure gave the drums a fabricated live sound.

Do not confuse this physical echo with the sixteenth-note delay on the track. For that, Johns went beyond the literal space of Headley Grange to layer a sonic space onto the already-complex body/environment Bonham enacted with his drumming. Outside, in the Rolling Stones mobile studio, Johns put the drums into two channels, compressed them, and ran the signal through a Binson echo unit: a machine owned by Jimmy Page that used an analogue magnetic drum recorder to produce a signal delay.[18] This machine – not the natural echo of Headley Grange – translates to the delay that falls a sixteenth note after each drum hit. Example 14.2 shows the result, which is closer to what the listener actually hears.

Because the delay lands exactly a sixteenth note after the physical hits, it ends up sounding like John Bonham is playing ghost notes after every snare and bass hit – the key component that makes the beat so unique. This delay

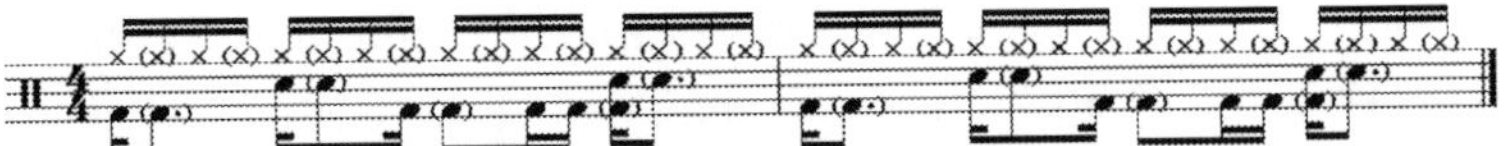

Example 14.2 Heard Beat Pattern for 'When the Levee Breaks' (0:00)

adds texture to the sounds, creating a spatial effect of being in an even bigger, more echo-filled space than Headley Grange – a canyon, perhaps. The large space between the hits allowing for the sixteenth-note delay also creates a disconnect between what Bonham's biological body enacts and what the listener ends up hearing and connecting to, which is Bonham's bodily engagement with both physical and technological environments.

In the early 1970s – an era when most drummers dampened their drums and engineers recorded them with close microphones – the full, life-like sound that Bonham and Johns produced stands out. It forges a bond between listener, Bonham, and the multiple spaces of the song. The physical spaces of John Bonham's drum kit and Headley Grange affect the listening experience, but so does the virtual space of the Binson Echo unit. Together, they create a new space that only exists in 'When the Levee Breaks'.

The Social Body

All of the previous levels ended with a consideration of the listener, leading us to Johnson's fourth level: the social body. He writes, '[t]he human environment of which the body partakes is not just physical or biological. It is also composed of intersubjective relations and coordinations of experience'.[19] For 'When the Levee Breaks', the biological body is the force that generates the sounds that the listener hears. The phenomenological body allows listeners and performers to carnally connect to the groove of the song. The multifaceted spaces surrounding the recording of the drums affect the ecological body.

Significantly, Bonham's body, manipulated technologically by Johns (another agent), interacts with the listener – though not in real time. When listeners can't help but move to 'When the Levee Breaks', their bodies connect to more than Bonham's physical, biological body, even more than the phenomenological experience of simply being in the groove; they connect to the reverberant, stone-walled space of Headley Grange and to the technological space that allowed for a perfect delay that fit smack dab in the middle of those wide open spaces between drum hits. Perhaps this explains why Led Zeppelin only played 'Levee' in concert a few times: the technological environment required for the groove and feel of the track – which went beyond Bonham's drums to include tempo manipulation, panning, and a backward echo effect on the harmonica – could not be adequately recreated in a live setting in the 1970s. The magic just didn't translate.

The Cultural Body

The listener cannot find meaning in 'When the Levee Breaks' if it exists in a vacuum. Johnson's fifth and final dimension, the cultural body, provides the greater context that makes the first four dimensions matter. Johnson explains:

> Our environments are not only physical and social. They are constituted also by cultural artifacts, practices, institutions, rituals, and modes of interaction that transcend and shape any particular body and any particular bodily action . . . Cultural institutions, practices, and values provide shared ('external') structures that influence the development of our bodily way of engaging our world.[20]

The main culture that affects 'When the Levee Breaks' and its relation to Bonham's body is Western rock music. And the backbeat occupies a central cultural locus of meaning in Western rock drumming. In another essay in this volume, Steven Baur calls the backbeat 'one of the single most prevalent features of Western popular music'.[21] Audiences learned to expect and desire the backbeat well before the rock era, and it gained cultural power when both its adherents and detractors emphasised its centrality to the new sound during the 1950s Big Bang of rock and roll.[22] People figured out how to move to it and the seemingly endless patterns in which it can occur not only through its affective dimensions, but also, through cultural institutions of rock such as variety shows (e.g. Ed Sullivan, Milton Berle), dance music party shows (e.g. American Bandstand, Soul Train), and live concerts. In many ways, the backbeat *is* rock culture; it is how our bodies culturally interact with rock music.

I want to distinguish between the backbeat and what I call the backbeat pattern. The backbeat is the accent on the weak beats of the measure – in standard 4/4, beats two and four – most often played in rock by the snare drum. The backbeat *pattern* includes the backbeat itself, but also two other components. The bass drum falls on or around beats one and three and creates a call and response pattern with the snare backbeat. For the final component, drummers designate an instrument – often a cymbal – to perform a steady time-keeping function.

In his essay on soul music, Robert Fink demonstrates that rhythmic goal direction occurs in popular music, that a single song can exhibit both groove and teleology, and that certain beat patterns can serve as a rhythmic 'tonic' that allows for patterns of tension and release. For his example of this phenomenon, he looks at another core beat pattern: the Motown four-on-the-floor pattern.[23] Drummers apply this tactic in all genres and styles, and rock drummers most often manipulate audience expectations of the backbeat pattern. I term the core groove of a given song – that beat that the drummer plays that feels like 'home' – the tonic beat pattern. A song's tonic beat pattern is often some variation of the backbeat pattern, or of another core stylistic beat pattern – i.e. disco four-on-the-floor, train beat, or reggae. While multiple variations of the backbeat might appear in a particular song, each song only has one true tonic beat pattern.

Drummers go away from, and return to, the tonic beat pattern to design these tension and release patterns in several ways, and this is the crux of the Tonic Beat Pattern Theory. It can take place on a small scale when, say, drummers build tension through drum fills. These embellishments instill unease in the listener because they momentarily obscure the integrity of the tonic beat pattern, temporarily compromising the song's underlying stability. For this reason, fills regularly lead into new sections of the songs, as they make the return of a beat that much more satisfying. In Nirvana's 'Smells Like Teen Spirit', for example, Dave Grohl uses largely sixteenth-note-based snare drum fills to transition between sections. He plays a steady backbeat pattern through the verse, modifies it slightly for the pre-chorus, and plays loud sixteenth notes to build tension before the explosion of the chorus, where he plays a louder, more complex backbeat pattern. In effect, Grohl establishes a steady beat, uses a fill to create tension, and then releases that tension through going into another steady beat.[24]

The Tonic Beat Pattern Theory also works on a larger scale. Some drummers withhold a steady backbeat for a section of a song, often saving it for the chorus. Benny Benjamin's thumping tom-tom pattern emphasises beats one and three in verse one of Barrett Strong's 'Money', eliminating the backbeat and the snare altogether. When the chorus pattern comes in with snare backbeat on two and tom backbeat on four, it feels utterly resolved. Other drummers take this practice to its logical conclusion by holding back that which becomes a tonic beat pattern for minutes of a song. In Hole's 'Violet', Patty Schemel alternates two patterns: one obscures the backbeat by offsetting the first snare hit a half a beat, while in the other, she simply plays a quiet four-on-the-floor bass with uneven rim clicks on the snare. These patterns feel partially resolved at times – particularly after interruptive drum fills – but there is clearly something missing. In the very last chorus, she unleashes that ever-gratifying, full-blown backbeat almost three minutes into the song – finally supplying the listener with the song's tonic beat pattern. Try as I may, I cannot find a single tune in rock music that has drumming that does not adhere to the Tonic Beat Pattern Theory. These tension and release patterns work always and only culturally. They are the primary way that drummers shape musical meaning and steer the narrative in rock music.[25]

'When the Levee Breaks' is no exception, and applying the Tonic Beat Pattern Theory to it reveals deeper meanings than Johnson's first four levels. The tonic beat pattern as played by Bonham appears in Example 14.1, whereas the tonic beat pattern as heard appears in Example 14.2. The form diagram of the song appears in Table 14.1.

The song contains two large-scale iterations of essentially the same thing – instrumental verse, interlude, verse, interlude, bridge – bookended by an intro and outro. The song lacks any true chorus, significantly, which contributes to the drone-like feeling of the piece, as does the literal drone in the guitar and bass in the intro, verses, and outro. The tonic beat pattern

Table 14.1 *Form diagram of 'When the Levee Breaks'*

LARGE FORM	FORM	TIME	PHRASING (in mm.)	BEAT PATTERN	FILL
INTRO	Intro	0:00	2	tonic	
ITERATION I	Instrumental verse	0:07	16+2	tonic	tonic+
	Interlude	1:08	4+1	tonic backbeat+ alternating w/ punches	(silence)
	Verse	1:25	7+7	tonic	tonic+
	Interlude	2:12	4	tonic backbeat+ alternating w/ punches	
	Bridge	2:25	4+4+4	silence/crash; backbeat w/ active BD; backbeat w/ fills	one busy SD/ tom; others simple
ITERATION II	Instrumental Verse	3:04	14	tonic	tonic+
	Interlude	3:51	4+1	tonic backbeat+ alternating w/ punches	(silence)
	Verse	4:08	8+6 (vox) [7+7 (gtrs)]	tonic	tonic+
	Interlude	4:55	4	tonic backbeat+ alternating w/ punches	
	Bridge	5:09	4+4+4	backbeat w/ active BD	more virtuosic throughout
OUTRO	Outro	5:47	10+8+3½	tonic	few; SD/rolls

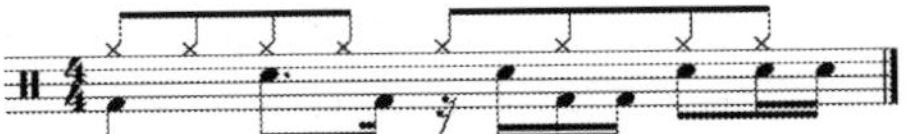

Example 14.3 Fill at the end of the verses in 'When the Levee Breaks' as played by Bonham (1:03)

occurs even more frequently than the drone part – in every section except the two bridges and every other measure in the interludes. Aaron Liu-Rosenbaum performs an analysis of the song's recording techniques and production to make a fairly convincing argument that drums, bass, and rhythm guitar signify the rising rain water, the villain that threatens to break the levee.[26] However, my reading takes into account these tension and release patterns, as well as the cultural signification of the backbeat, to argue that the drums signify the steadfast levee itself.

Bonham always plays the same fill at the ends of the verses, transcribed in Example 14.3.

Notice that this simple fill contains the tonic beat pattern within it, with three extra snare hits added. Incorporating the tonic beat pattern within the fill makes it less disorienting than, say, some kind of highly syncopated fill. The listener still knows where the backbeat and groove fall. Through the extra snare hits, you can start to hear points in the levee crack and erode. These fills also signal a formal change into the interludes.

In the interludes, a slight variation on the tonic beat pattern alternates with a 'Ba-DOO' punching figure where snare falls on every beat. This 'Ba-DOO' punching figure proves particularly jarring for three reasons: the main groove is so infectious, the tonic beat pattern saturates the track, and many of Bonham's deviations still contain the tonic beat pattern within them. The levee here endures major hits as the tide charges forth every other measure, and more jolting, intense cracking of the levee ensues. The first three of these punching deviations lead into silence. Here, in the silence, the tide has temporarily gone out, and the levee gets a much-needed break from its hard work of holding back the villainous rain.

But the final 'Ba-DOO' punching figure in the last interlude occurs before the second bridge, in which the drums deviate significantly from the first bridge. Instead of a measure of silence and a measure of crashes with bass drum hits, the second bridge kicks right into a backbeat pattern with an active bass drum. Add to that the fact that the second bridge features significantly more virtuosic drum fills than the first – including a thirty-second note fill and Bonham's signature bouncing-bass-drum-snare-sextuplet combo – and this section comes to represent the point where the levee starts to surrender to leakage and overtopping. The water is making headway. This struggle continues into the outro, with another sextuplet fill and a few rolls on the snare. Then in the middle of a measure, the tonic beat pattern abruptly stops. The levee has reached catastrophic failure through massive collapse. Water flows freely, and the vocalist's fears have come true. The listener can only hope he actually started his journey to Chicago before it was too late.

Just as Liu-Rosenbaum showed how close attention to recording practices can help understand 'Levee', my analysis shows how close consideration of drums can contradict those meanings. In his reading, the backbeat is the water – the dangerous antagonist. The drums in this song do not feel dangerous at all, however; the backbeat rarely does to fans. The backbeat in general, and the tonic beat pattern in 'Levee' specifically, feel pleasurable, comforting, and reliable – like an old friend. They constitute what audiences have come to expect through decades of reinforcement. In Mark Johnson's chapter about music in *The Meaning of the Body*, he states, 'music is meaningful because it can present the flow of human experience, feeling, and thinking in concrete, embodied forms – and this is meaning in its deepest sense'.[27] Throughout 'When the Levee Breaks', John Bonham does just that – by harnessing the cultural, bodily signifying abilities of the backbeat, he crafts the song's narrative and contributes to its affective meanings.

The Power of the Drums

In '"The Pride of Noise": Drums and Their Repercussions in Early Modern England', Christopher Marsh writes about the myriad signifying possibilities of the drum at that time, demonstrating how drums were used as powerful communication tools. He writes:

> the meanings of drumming were absorbed at a personal level by a kind of cultural osmosis. Just as the soldier learned to heed the signals beaten out by the military drummer, so the civilian developed the ability to interpret the rhythms that cut through the air in town and village. The beating of a drum was an irresistible sound, capable of stimulating not only hope, happiness, excitement and bravery but also anxiety, fear, anger and misery. It all depended on where one stood and how one listened.[28]

For Marsh, the drum held immense power to communicate in Early Modern England. In rock, the same thing holds true; listeners absorb the narratives that drummers weave by a kind of cultural osmosis. Through their lifetime's worth of knowledge of, and experience with, the tension and release patterns drummers craft, rock fans are expert listeners and interpreters of the moves drummers make. When session drummer Hal Blaine omits half the backbeats on his iconic 'Boom ... boom boom CRACK' beat pattern at the beginning of the Ronettes' 'Be My Baby' and then resolves that tension by playing all backbeats in the chorus, and when Meg White withholds the powerful crash cymbal timekeeper until the choruses of the White Stripes' 'Seven Nation Army', they show how drummers create musical trajectories in songs that not only make fans wiggle our hips, move our feet, and bang our heads, but also, create just about any affect the song calls for.

My hope for this essay is that it provides popular music scholars the necessary theory and methods to weave drummers' musical contributions more fully into the conversation. The Tonic Beat Pattern Theory provides insights into just about any song in the twentieth or twenty-first centuries that has anything meant to fill the role of a drummer: from acoustic and electronic drum kits to drum machines and computer patches. We can no longer ignore or diminish the instrument that most urges people to move and groove and connects to their bodies. In the words of James Brown, 'give the drummer some'.

Notes

1 W. F. Miller. 'Neil Peart', *Modern Drummer* (February 1994), p. 64.
2 M. Johnson. *The Meaning of the Body* (Chicago and London: University of Chicago Press, 2007), p. 236.
3 Johnson, *The Meaning of the* Body, p. 1.
4 Johnson, *The Meaning of the* Body, pp. 275–78.
5 B. Hoskyns. *Led Zeppelin: Zoso* (New York: Rodale, 2006), p. 59.
6 Johnson, *The Meaning of the* Body, p. 275.
7 Johnson, *The Meaning of the* Body, p. 276.
8 E. Le Guin. *Boccherini's Body: An Essay in Carnal Musicology* (Berkeley: University of California Press, 2005), p. 14.
9 A. Danielsen. *Presence and Pleasure: The Funk Grooves of James Brown and Parliament* (Middletown: Wesleyan University Press, 2006), p. 11.
10 Danielsen, *Presence and Pleasure*, p. 204.
11 C. Welch and G. Nicholls. *John Bonham: A Thunder of Drums* (London: Backbeat Books, 2001), p. 157.
12 See, for example, G. Akkerman. *Experiencing Led Zeppelin: A Listener's Companion* (Lanham: Rowman & Littlefield, 2014), p. 61; D. S. 'These Are the 5 Most Sampled Drum Beats in Hip Hop', *Produce Like a Pro* (14 September 2007), available at: https://producelikeapro.com/blog/5-most-sampled-drum-beats-in-hip-hop/; and C. Reiff. 'These Are the Breaks: 10 of the Most Sampled Drum Beats in History', *AV Club* (26 August 2015), available at: https://music.avclub.com/these-are-the-breaks-10-of-the-most-sampled-drum-beats-1798283974.
13 C. Eddy. 'The Making of Led Zeppelin's Zoso', *Rolling Stone* (15 May 1997), p. 74.
14 Johnson, *The Meaning of the* Body, p. 279. Italics his.
15 Johnson, *The Meaning of the* Body, p. 276.
16 A. Liu-Rosenbaum, '"A Kind of Construction in Light and Shade": An Analytical Dialogue with Recording Studio Aesthetics in Two Songs by Led Zeppelin', unpublished dissertation, City University of New York (2009), p.31.
17 Hoskyns, *Led Zeppelin*, p. 107.
18 'The Truth behind Led Zeppelin's When the Levee Breaks' video explains this process well. Rick Beato, 'The TRUTH Behind Led Zeppelin: When the Levee Breaks', *YouTube*, available at: www.youtube.com/watch?v=XZYDDX1DHDU (accessed 15 October 2019).
19 Johnson, *The Meaning of the* Body, p. 277.
20 Ibid.

21 S. Baur. 'Toward a Cultural History of the Backbeat', in M. Brennan, J. Michael Pignato, and D. Akira Stadnicki (eds.), *The Cambridge Companion to the Drum Kit* (Cambridge: Cambridge University Press, 2021).

22 Ibid.

23 R. Fink. 'Goal-Directed Soul? Analyzing Rhythmic Teleology in African American Popular Music', *Journal of the American Musicological Society* 64:1 (Spring 2011), pp. 197–237.

24 Notice how Grohl enters the song with a drum fill, demonstrating that drummers do not need to start with the tonic beat pattern.

25 At first, I thought 'Heroin' by the Velvet Underground broke the rule, but Maureen Tucker clearly plays with the faster galloping pattern as the tonic beat pattern, using silence, fewer drum hits, and slower tempos as the tension to the gallop's release.

26 Liu-Rosenbaum, 'A Kind of Construction in Light and Shade', pp. 33–41.

27 Johnson, *The Meaning of the* Body, p. 236.

28 C. Marsh. '"The Pride of Noise": Drums and Their Repercussions in Early Modern England', *Early Music* 39:2 (May 2011), p. 216.

15 Disability, Drumming, and the Drum Kit

ADAM PATRICK BELL AND CORNEL HRISCA-MUNN

Introduction

See the trick is only pick on those that can't do you no harm,
like the drummer from Def Leppard's only got one arm. FROM THE BLOODHOUND GANG'S 'WHY'S EVERYBODY ALWAYS PICKIN' ON ME' (1996)

What is especially significant about this ableist mid-1990s popular culture reference is that Def Leppard's Rick Allen has long been the public face of the disabled drummer. As the Bloodhound Gang's lyrics make clear, Allen has more often than not been identified primarily by his disability (e.g. 'the one-armed drummer' and so on), as opposed to by his name, or solely by his role (e.g. 'the drummer'). Like some disabled musicians that came before him such as Chick Webb, Django Reinhardt, and Ray Charles, Allen's disability is visible, and as a result, for many in the music-consuming public, his disability defines him more so than his musicianship. Such perceptions are typically tied to the tired trope of overcoming disability, which is rooted in an implicitly or explicitly held belief in a normal body,[1] and that it ought to conform to the built environment such as musical instruments, and more specifically in our case, the drum kit. In the case of music, this 'normal performance body' is above-average with regard to the musculature and dexterity needed to play an instrument.[2] Applying this theory to the drum kit, drummers are presumed to play their instrument with two hands and two feet.

In this chapter we examine the intersection of drumming and disability. Whilst Rick Allen is undoubtedly the most famous drummer with a disability, he is certainly not the only drummer with a disability. The World Health Organization estimates that fifteen percent of the global population have disabilities, and therefore by extension we can safely presume that many drummers do or will experience disability at some point in their lifetimes.[3] By seeking to learn about the experiencers of other drummers with disabilities, the drumming community can broaden and deepen its understanding of how disabilities affect drumming, if at all. To this end, what began as a conversation initiated by adam wanting to learn from Cornel about his experiences drumming as a person with disabilities soon morphed into this co-authored chapter on drumming and disability. Our research process took the form of the following stages: First, we engaged in multiple semi-structured conversations to generate possible themes and topics to examine at the confluence of drumming and disability.[4] These conversations were then transcribed to text and analysed for their most salient ideas. We mutually agreed upon how we would address or illustrate the key ideas we wish to communicate in this medium, and settled on the overarching concept of how disability, drumming, and the drum kit intersect with each other. Using narrative sections written by Cornel about his experiences as a drummer with a disability, we apply concepts from the field of disability studies to drum kit studies and consider the significance of our discussion for the drumming community at large.

We commence our chapter with a discussion of relevant concepts from the field of disability studies. We presume readers may not have engaged with disability studies literature, and therefore we provide a brief primer on core concepts from the field such as the medical and social models of disability, relevant critiques of these paradigms as they relate to drumming, and how they influence societal perspectives on drumming.

Drumming and Disability Studies

In the interest of brevity, our summary of disability studies as it relates to drumming is admittedly condensed. Our aim is to provide sufficient foundational information such that readers with little to no familiarity with the field of disability studies can grasp some of the basic concepts and terms employed throughout the chapter. As a starting point, both the terminology itself and the understandings of terms within the field of disability studies are contentious;[5] it is like the jazz of academic fields: there is no resolve. Entering into the field of disability studies is less like wading into warm waters and more like a polar bear plunge: it is invigorating, awakening, and for some, a shock to the system. In Western societies, we tend to accept the idea that there are 'average' things such as bodies, but, 'there is no such thing as average body size . . . Our modern conception of the average person is not a mathematical truth but a human invention'.[6] Disability studies scholars point out that our conceptions of 'average' or 'normal' are unfounded yet continue to deeply influence our understanding of the construct of disability. During the nineteenth century, 'Medical knowledge determined the boundaries between "normal" and "abnormal" individuals' and by the end of that century, 'the individual approach to disability located in medical knowledge was widely accepted . . . It focused on bodily "abnormality", disorder or deficiency and how this "causes" functional limitation or "disability"'.[7] This line of thinking that centres on the individual as disabled is what is commonly referred to as the *medical model of disability.*

In contrast, the *social model of disability*, takes aim at the failings of society to support people with *impairments* – bodily differences – which as a result leads to experiences of disability:

> This approach does not deny the significance of impairment in disabled people's lives, but concentrates instead on the various barriers, economic, political and social, constructed on top of impairment. Thus "disability" is not a product of individual failings but is socially created.[8]

Pitted as binary opposites, applying medical- and social-model thinking to drumming and disability lead to rather limiting understandings. In practice, if a drummer and drum kit are seemingly ergonomically incompatible, we do not attempt to adjust one or the other, we do both. Drumming is but one activity in a long list that exposes the inadequacy of either/or medical- and social-model thinking. More nuanced understandings based on peoples' lived experiences help to make sense of disability theory, and we use examples from Cornel's life as a drummer to highlight the importance of complexity and context. In particular, Tobin Siebers' conception of 'complex embodiment' as a way of understanding disability as the result of both the effects of the environment *and* the effects of the body meshes well with Cornel's perspectives on drumming and disability.[9]

Drumming, Disability, and Social Media

We proceed with a narrative by Cornel on how he has experienced others' perceptions of him through his online presence on various internet and social media platforms. Notably, 'while social media is becoming an increasingly important part of our lives, its impact on people with disabilities has gone largely unscrutinized'.[10] By having Cornel present his perspective in the first person we gain valuable insights into his experience as a drummer with an online presence and how others' perceptions of his disability are expressed to him and affect him.

> **Cornel:** As a disabled person who was determined to escape the stereotypes of disability, for years I avoided what many people believed would be an obvious path for me; that is, to engage with and study disability, particularly when considering musicianship and drumming. As I became more serious about music, and as my musical presence (particularly online) became more known, I came to realise that further study into disability did not only increasingly pique my interest, but in fact became simply unavoidable. I was

on something of a musical 'quest' to be praised and scrutinised for my music alone, disability notwithstanding.

Particularly noticeable are the online comments stemming from two standpoints. The first of these is what I like to term 'inspiration at all costs'. This standpoint includes comments that are positive to the point of being disingenuous, completely ignoring the music itself, ignoring any aspect of playing ability, and simply addressing me as 'inspirational' due to my disability. Although not abusive in their nature, these comments carry undertones of me being inferior because of my disability. It seems that the fact that I do more than sit around being cared for by other people is enough to amaze people – the proficiency of my playing does not matter. These comments are indicative of the attitudes of a large online community towards disability: disability is primary, and music is secondary. This attitude highlights the concept of 'inspiration porn'[11] – the portrayal of people with disabilities as inspirational solely due to their disability. My musical ability is of a proficient standard (I have had professionals confirm this for me), yet I have been called inspirational for my ordinary daily activities (in extreme cases, being able to hold an apple whilst I ate it) as well as for my music. Placing these two activities under the same banner of 'inspiration' belittles the value of the one, and unduly elevates the value of the other. These types of 'inspiration at all costs' comments create a culture of disabled people existing for the sole purpose of being saint-like inspirations for non-disabled people. This attitude fuels an 'us and them'-type culture between disabled and non-disabled people and holds disabled people as 'serving' non-disabled people through simply living their lives. I do not play music to inspire people. I play music because I enjoy it, because I am motivated to improve my playing, and because I want to be taken seriously as a musician in the possible hope of a musical career in some capacity.

The second standpoint regarding online comments are the overtly negative perspectives, primarily perpetuated by internet trolls whom spread abusive comments relating to my disability. These consist of derogatory terms, ableist assumptions about my capabilities, and threats (although these have been incredibly rare). These negative comments do not move me in any particular way, positively or negatively. I do not spend much time dwelling on these because they have a negligible impact on my music and my overall views on disability. The other type of negativity stems from non-disabled musicians suggesting ergonomic improvements to my drum kit, reinforcing the belief that disabled people could not possibly know best about their own needs, requirements, and preferences. I have been painstakingly honing and experimenting with for over 16 years! This attitude is also exemplified in online comments from non-disabled people such as 'now I have no excuse not to play', implying that simply not having a disability is enough for a person to play an instrument, and play it better than the person with a disability.

Cornel's experiences of being the object of others' inspiration porn or trolling on social media highlight how difficult it is for him to be regarded solely as a drummer; instead, he is compartmentalized as a 'disabled drummer':

> **Cornel:** My large online following knows me primarily as the disabled drummer (a combination of two aspects of my character). Musicians become known and identified by their art form. I am subject to a step further in external identification, by my art form, and by my disability. My disability does not constitute 100 percent of my identity; it occupies a very small percentage of my identity, but also, (surprisingly for some) neither does drumming. Drumming and playing music are huge passions of mine. There is nothing I would rather do professionally than play music every day. This is, however, something that I do, not who I am.

Cornel Plays 'Everlong'

Given that Cornel wishes his drumming to be perceived as something that he does as opposed to something that he is, we proceed with a description of how he plays his drum kit, which requires some contextualization. We begin with Cornel describing his disability and how it affects his drumming. Following, Cornel describes his approach to playing 'Everlong' (1997) by Foo Fighters, a rite of passage for many drummers as it requires considerable experience and practice to rival the performance of the original recording by Dave Grohl or the live performances of Taylor Hawkins. To the reader we pose this question: in the act of playing 'Everlong' on his drum kit, is Cornel disabled? From an auditory-only perspective, if the same notes are being played, there would be no way of knowing about Cornel's disability. But, in our visual-centric society, watching Cornel play his drums in addition to hearing him play them is integral to the listening experience. How we see Cornel play drums changes how we hear him play drums. As Cornel explains, understanding how he plays 'Everlong' necessitates not only a description of his performance, but also his disability and his drum kit:

> To fully understand how I played this song, I believe it is important to understand two things at the outset: the nature of my physical disability, and my drum kit, which is tailored for my disability in a very individualized way.
>
> *My disability:* The best way to describe my disability is multi-limb deficient. The most obvious manifestation of this is that my arms do not go below the elbow on either side. I have neither a left nor right elbow joint. I do however have a digit on my left side, which allows me to grip items (with a high degree of strength, as well as allowing for variation in that strength). In relation to drumming, this is where I hold one of my two drumsticks. On my

right arm, I have no digit, and in terms of drumming, my stick on this side is held on using a leather and Velcro strap, which allows for tightening and loosening; however, most of my dynamic stick control on my right side comes from a muscle in my right arm, which I relax and contract accordingly to vary dynamic control depending on the requirement of the piece that I am playing. A less obvious aspect of my disability is that I have had my right leg amputated above the knee, due to being born with a fully formed leg and foot being twisted around completely. I therefore wear a prosthesis, which has a functioning mechanical knee joint, socket, shin, and foot.

*My Drum kit***:** My drum kit has not required any equipment modifications; rather, it has been a case of years of ergonomic adjustment and movement of various drums, cymbals, and other percussion variants. If one assumes a 'standard' right-handed drum kit consists of a drummer sitting with a snare drum between their legs, their left foot on the hi-hat pedal, their right foot on the bass drum pedal, with toms above the bass drum and floor tom to the right of the drummer, then my drum kit does not appear vastly different. The first, and arguably most important adjustment to my drum kit is the heights of my drums and cymbals. I am 180cm tall, yet I require my drum kit to be much higher for me. This is primarily because of the angle of attack on my drums, which is most obvious when considering my snare drum. Because my arms are shorter, I have less reach low down for a good angle of attack when my drums are too low, and often end up impacting the snare head almost with the top of the tip of my stick. Raising my drums means I have to reach a shorter distance lower, meaning I can angle my stick more effectively. The most obvious adjustment to my drum kit, however, is the positioning of my feet. Due to my prosthetic foot being less able to move quickly than my 'real' foot, I play with my left (real) foot on the bass drum, and right (prosthetic) foot on the high-hat pedal for faster bass drum strokes. This means that I play angled facing to the right of my kit, with the hi-hat moved to the right hand side over the floor tom (instead of the 'typical' position over the snare), my left foot on the bass drum pedal, with the floor tom between my legs. This is a very comfortable drumming position for me. I am able to play a right-handed drum kit (I lead sticking with my right), yet utilise my faster moving, 'real' foot for bass drum strokes. Within this setup here lies an issue: the distance between the hi-hat cymbal and the snare drum is great, meaning that, for example, playing a fast 4/4 beat with 16th notes on the hi-hat interplaying with the snare is exceedingly difficult. To circumvent this issue, I have added another, closed set of hi-hats in the 'traditional' position left of my snare drum, to use for extra accents, as well as fast hi-hat/snare interplay. This is particularly conducive to playing songs such as 'Everlong'.

Drumming 'Everlong': I have chosen 'Everlong' by Foo Fighters to demonstrate the similarities (and indeed, differences) of how I play. The intro and verses of this song are played in 4/4, with fast 16th note hi-hats carrying the right-hand rhythm, with the snare played on 2 and 4 in the verses. The intro to this song, 16th notes on the hi-hats with a gradually opening crescendo into the verses I play on my primary pair of hi-hats, controlled by my right foot on the pedal, to the right of my floor tom. It was learning to play this song on drums that encouraged me to devise a solution to the issue of reach between my hi-hat cymbals on the right, and my snare on the left. The solution was a secondary pair of hi-hats, closed with a clutch, on the left-hand side of the snare in the 'traditional' place. This allowed me to play the fast 16th note rhythm on the hats, whilst also managing not only the main snare beat on 2 and 4, but also to play fills, which interplayed these two parts of the drum kit. This is how I am able to play this beat effectively in the verses. As the song progresses, I experience fatigue in my left arm whilst playing the 16th notes, which usually sets in towards the end of the second verse. This is due to the unnatural position of my body whilst playing the secondary hi-hats, as I am twisting my whole body to reach and play this effectively. This fatigue is also especially prevalent in my upper arms and shoulders. Whereas most drummers would play fast single and roll strokes using wrist control, I am using the entirety of my arms and shoulders. I overcome this through regular practice and lifting weights. I notice that if I practice these motions even for a couple of hours one day, the next day I feel noticeably less fatigued when playing, especially concerning the fast 16th notes.

In the verses, my bass drum pattern is different from the original recording. Played with my left foot, I elaborate a little on the almost '4 on the floor' type bass drum rhythm that Dave Grohl plays on the original track. This is a stylistic variation to the song and does not concern my disability. My ability to play 4 on the floor or more complex bass drum patterns is not impacted simply because I play the bass drum with my left, 'real' foot, rather than my right, 'prosthetic foot'.

In the build-up crescendo from the verse to the pre-chorus, Grohl opens up his hi-hat foot pedal to create a louder, trashier-sounding build up to the verse. The hi-hats that I am using to play the main 16th notes rhythm are closed shut with a clutch; therefore, I compensate for this by striking the side of the closed cymbals (causing them to create some openness) with the thicker sides of my sticks, whilst increasing how hard I hit the cymbals, thus increasing volume.

The pre chorus I play very close to how Grohl played in the original recording, with the snare and crash-led fill leading into a 4/4 beat at the end of each subsection, played with bass drum, snare, and on my primary hi-hats situated to the right of the floor tom, playing 8th notes instead of 16ths. The same is true in the build to the chorus and the chorus itself. In the chorus, I switch to leading with 8th notes on the ride cymbal, interplaying with fills using the snare, bass, and crash. In these fills and in the main beat in the chorus, I noticeably use ghost notes and accents. I am able to do so using the digit on my left arm, controlling how strongly I hold the stick, allowing for a hard hit, light hit, single stroke, or multiple-stroke role. I achieve this with the stick strapped to my right arm using the muscle in my arm which is in direct contact with the stick, contracting the muscle for harder, single stroke hits, and relaxing the muscle for ghost notes and multiple-stoke roles. This abruptly changes for the last couple of bars of the chorus, where I play an 8th note floor tom-led beat, before going straight back across my drum kit to the hi-hats to play the fast 16th notes into the second verse.

The entire song allows me to demonstrate a variety of drumming techniques, such as switching from 8th to 16th back to 8th notes, as well as fast single strokes, ghost notes, dynamic variation, and tightness of playing. Through minor ergonomic adjustments to my drum kit (higher drums and cymbals, as well as moving my primary hi-hat to the right hand side and adding a closed, secondary hi-hat on the left), I am able to play this, and other songs, perfectly capably, whilst adding improvised embellishments to various sections of the song.

Enacting Evolution on the Drum Kit

Considering Cornel's explication of his approach to drumming 'Everlong', it is clear that he engaged in a thoughtful and complex process to determine the optimal approach for himself to play this particular song. While Cornel's drum kit setup for 'Everlong' deviates from the supposed 'standard' drum kit configuration, the changes he makes to the standard configuration are less than those required by a left-handed drummer because the standard configuration presumes right-handedness. Despite this fact, in Cornel's experience, observers of his drumming tend to pay more attention to his body than his drum kit. Such a perspective exemplifies medical model thinking as the focus is on the individual as opposed to the environment (the drum kit in this case). Following, Cornel details how he is often compared to Rick Allen of Def Leppard, and explains why this comparison is problematic when we compare their respective approaches to playing the drum kit:

I am frequently compared to the drummer from Def Leppard, Rick Allen. On the surface, these comparisons appear obvious – we are both drummers with limbs missing. One does not have to dig too much deeper, however, to understand the flaws in this comparison, particularly when considering the ergonomics of a drum kit, as well as the vastly differing methods that Allen and myself have for playing drums. First and foremost, our circumstances are entirely different. I was born with no lower arms, and my right leg was amputated in my infancy (nearly a decade before I started playing drums). This means that all I have known is my disability. I have been aware of my capabilities and limitations for as long as I can remember and have adapted this to my drumming. I have never known what it was like to be a drummer playing the 'standard' way, with all four limbs fully formed and fully working.

> The case of Rick Allen is vastly different. He was a drummer in an established rock band for many years before he acquired his disability and had to adapt his drumming after his arm was amputated. The second thing to consider is the vastly different natures of our disabilities. I have arms to my elbows, but no joints and no fully formed hands. I also only have one fully working leg, with my right leg being an above-knee amputation, on which I wear a prosthesis. Allen has one fully working arm and hand, but on the other side, has an amputation up to his shoulder joint, with no part of a working arm whatsoever. What Allen does have, however, is two fully-formed, fully working legs and feet, which appears to be the key to his drumming. With two working feet, Allen has adapted his drumming using an adjusted drum kit, which involves pedals not only for the bass drum and hi-hat cymbals, but for multiple drums too. This shows a distinct variation from the majority of other drum kits, which only have the two pedals (or maybe three if a double bass player or with multiple hi-hats and effects), therein lies an entirely unique ergonomic drum kit setup for Allen, but also, a completely individual way of playing. Allen's feet will be doing a lot of the work that a non-disabled drummer's hands would be doing, and so, a complete rethink of rhythm and playing would have been required as a complementary exercise to the ergonomic adjustments to Allen's drum kit. My drum kit setup is vastly different to Allen's in that its setup is remarkably similar to a 'typical' non-disabled drummer's setup. I use no uniquely crafted equipment to play. What is individual to my kit setup is the placement of the drums and cymbals. Last, but certainly not least, one should not assume that all ergonomic changes to drum kit setups made by disabled people are due to disability, as many I am sure will be stylistic.

Cornel has to adjust his drum kit to his body, but also adjust his body to his drum kit in order to play. Is this statement not true for any drummer? We forward that drumming inherently requires 'complex embodiment', a blend of medical and social model thinking about being in our environment (i.e. playing the drum kit). In comparison, many other musical instruments are much less modifiable and therefore either exclude a potential player due to bodily difference or demand the player adapt to it. And, while other musical instruments may be adapted or modified, they are often singled out for being just that, such as the one-handed bass guitar.[12] The drum kit requires no qualifying terms – there is no one-handed drum kit even though there are one-handed drummers.

The construct of a drum kit is in flux – it can take on many different configurations and be made of many different materials and yet be recognized and referred to simply as a drum kit. Why this might be is beyond the scope of this chapter, but we suspect that the drum kit's relative newness compared to other musical instruments that have arrived at fairly fixed designs over time helps to explain this phenomenon. At the beginning of the twentieth century, all of the elements that comprise a drum kit as we now know it existed, but they were not played together by one person.[13] The drum kit has a history of being amorphous and modular – components can be added or subtracted yet it will still be acknowledged by both drummers and non-drummers as a drum kit. Some of the technological advances of the drum kit have afforded evolved and new techniques,[14] but for drummers with disabilities, it is often the necessity to deviate from the norm – not artistic aims nor the recognition of the possibilities afforded by new technologies – that drive innovation. While the modularity of the drum kit is an important factor in making it accessible to people with disabilities, how disabled drummers are able to adapt techniques, often in personalized ways, is also an important factor to consider.[15] Not only does adapting tried-and-trusted techniques make playing the drum kit more accessible, it also challenges established ideas about technique and opens up previously undiscovered possibilities of the instrument. In this way, all drummers are engaged in a critical role of evolving the very conceptualization of the instrument itself because our instruments are extensions of ourselves.[16]

Final Fill: Conclusions

Am I a drummer? Am I a musician? Am I a disabled musician? Am I a combination of all of these things? Part of the problem that exists here is the disparity between other people's perceptions of my identity, and my own. CORNEL

Perhaps it is not possible to completely bridge the disparity of which Cornel speaks, but drummers can and will play a pivotal role in how the intersection of disability and drumming is perceived; it is imperative and inevitable. Given that 1 billion of the people on this planet will experience disability at some point in their lifetime, Cornel's case is not an anomaly. The specifics of Cornel's disability and how it affects his drumming may be unique, but the broader idea that drummers will experience disability playing the drum kit is not. Cornel's case exemplifies that, 'Having a disability is something that makes you different, but not something that by itself makes you worse off because of that difference. Being disabled is simply something that makes you a minority – it is a way of having a *minority body*'.[17]

Cornel's approach to playing 'Everlong' is different than that of Foo Fighters' Dave Grohl and Taylor Hawkins, but does this difference constitute 'disabled drumming'? Who decides? Whom does it affect? Why does it matter? These are questions that drummers need to contemplate both for themselves and for those they mentor. Kat Holmes observes, 'As we age, we all gain and lose abilities. Our abilities change through illness and injury. Eventually, we all are excluded by designs that don't fit our ever-changing bodies'.[18] As we have detailed, the infrastructure of the drum kit can potentially be changed to accommodate our ever-changing bodies. How far from the standard configuration of a drum kit can we deviate before we cross the undefined threshold of dis/ability? If we cannot adapt our drum kits to our changing bodies, can we adapt our drumming techniques? Aspiring to be a lifelong drummer demands an acceptance of the reality that our bodies change over time.

Beyond the physical, disability not only dictates how a drummer plays, but how a drummer is perceived. The drummer's identity hangs in the balance of public perception, be it on social media or elsewhere. A disability identity may be chosen by an individual, assigned by a government agency, or presumed by others – in all cases, disability identity, whether a drummer chooses it or not, affects how they are perceived as a drummer. Considering how disability affects drummers physically and socially, if we are not already, we drummers ought to be ever-conscious of our own complex embodiment, and continually contemplate how to navigate the intersection of disability, drumming, and the drum kit.

Notes

1 R. Garland Thomson. *Extraordinary Bodies: Figuring Physical Disability in American Culture and Literature* (New York: Columbia University Press, 1997).

2 B. Howe 'Disabling Music Performance' in B. Howe, S. Jensen-Moulton, N. Lerner, and J. Straus (eds.), *The Oxford Handbook of Music and Disability Studies* (New York: Oxford University Press, 2016), pp. 191–209.

3 D. Goodley. *Dis/ability Studies: Theorising Disablism and Ableism* (London: Routledge, 2014).

4 S. Kvale. *InterViews: Learning the Craft of Qualitative Research Interviewing* (Los Angeles: Sage, 2009).

5 G. Pullin. *Disability Meets Design* (Cambridge: The MIT Press, 2009).

6 T. Rose. *The End of Average* (New York: HarperOne, 2016), p. 11.

7 C. Barnes and G. Mercer. *Exploring Disability: A Sociological Introduction* 2nd ed. (Cambridge: Polity Press, 2010), p. 18.

8 C. Barnes, M. Oliver, and L. Barton. 'Introduction' in C. Barnes, M. Oliver, and L. Barton (eds.), *Disability Studies Today* (Cambridge: Polity Press, 2002), p. 5

9 T. Siebers. *Disability Theory* (Ann Arbor: The University of Michigan Press, 2008).

10 K. Ellis and M. Kent. 'Introduction: Social Disability' in K. Ellis and M. Kent (eds.), *Disability and Social Media: Global Perspectives* (Abingdon: Routledge, 2017), p. 1.

11 B. Haller and J. Preston. 'Confirming Normalcy: "Inspiration Porn" and the Construction of the Disabled Subject?' in K. Ellis and M. Kent (eds.), *Disability and Social Media: Global Perspectives* (Abingdon: Routledge, 2017), pp. 41–56.

12 J. Harrison and A. P. McPherson. 'Adapting the Bass for One-Handed Playing', *Journal of New Music Research* 46:3 (2017), pp. 270–285.

13 P. Avanti. 'Black Musics, Technology, and Modernity: Exhibit A, the Drum Kit', *Popular Music and Society* 36:4 (2013), pp. 476–504.

14 J. Packman. 'Way beyond Wood and Skin: Drum Sets, Drumming, and Technology', in R. Hartenberger (ed.), *The Cambridge Companion to Percussion* (Cambridge: Cambridge University Press, 2016), pp. 211–226.

15 For another example of a drummer with a disability adapting techniques see Mover. 'Ray LeVier: Living the Dream', *Drumhead* (March 2018), available at: www.drummersresource.com/wp-content/uploads/2018/03/DH_Ray_LeVier.pdf (accessed 31 August 2019).
16 A. Evens. *Sound Ideas: Music, Machines, and Experience* (Minneapolis: University of Minnesota Press, 2005), p. 84.
17 E. Barnes. *The Minority Body: A Theory of Disability* (New York: Oxford University Press, 2016), p. 78.
18 K. Holmes. *Mismatch: How Inclusion Shapes Design* (Cambridge: The MIT Press, 2018), p. 29.

16 Seen but Not Heard

Performing Gender and Popular Feminism on Drumming Instagram

MARGARET MACAULAY AND VINCENT ANDRISANI

Introduction

According to musicologist Rita Steblin, the masculinization of the drums has roots extending as far back as the Renaissance.[1] In the fifteenth century, European sensibilities discouraged women from playing physically demanding percussion instruments in favour of *quieter*, more *subdued* (and thus *feminine*) instruments such as psalteries and lutes. This very same sentiment is alive and well still today, making the drum kit one of the most explicitly gendered instruments in Western popular music. The result is that, at both the professional and amateur levels, women and gender minority drummers remain severely underrepresented. For instance, in 2011 *Rolling Stone* magazine created a list of the top 100 drummers of all time and featured zero women. The magazine subsequently published another list in 2016, this time increasing the number of women drummers to five. And *Modern Drummer*, the industry's most widely-read magazine published monthly since January 1977, has featured only eight women on its cover – with three of those covers sharing space with men. To be sure, there are more than a few examples of accomplished women drummers: Karen Carpenter, Sheila E, Terri-Lyne Carrington, and Cindy Blackman-Santana, among many others. Yet these women are the exception and not the rule, which suggests the ongoing need for women to mobilize as a distinct drumming community.

Like other communities of interest, social media offers a space to do so. Nowhere is this more apparent than on Instagram: a social media platform that affords participation through both photos and video. 'Drumming Instagram' is a vibrant online community where drummers share photos of their gear and performance venues, videos of their practice routines, live performances, and jam sessions, and other moments in their professional and personal lives. Here, users can learn about new performers; acquire new skills and techniques; find inspiration; and offer support to others on their musical journeys. For women, Drumming Instagram does all these things while also enabling a form of public visibility and real-time interaction with other drummers that has not been otherwise possible. As a result, drummers like Anika Nilles (@anika.nilles), Taylor Gordon

(@thepocketqueen), and Sarah Thawer (@sarahtdrumguru) (among many others!) have gained recognition within the professional drumming scene, in large part because of their vibrant social media presence. These artists are among the most followed drummers on Instagram regardless of gender, and their contributions have gone a long way for inspiring other up-and-coming women drummers globally. The momentum surrounding the participation of professional and amateur women drummers offers a form of networked visibility that makes Instagram a productive space to challenge the historically gendered norms of drum kit performance.

This networked visibility, however, is highly ambivalent. Just as Drumming Instagram supports women's participation in a traditionally male-dominated musical domain, it also sets them up for public scrutiny and unwanted attention. From gendered critiques of their performances to sexual objectification, the participatory nature of social media presents a series of challenges that are specific to the experiences of women drummers. In light of these challenges, we ask, what is the range of public responses to women's visibility on Drumming Instagram? What are the social norms and codes that guide participation in this networked public? And is Instagram a space where an emancipatory feminist politics can emerge? To answer these questions, we examined three notable Instagram accounts dedicated to the promotion of women drummers: @femaledrummers, @tomtommag, and @hitlikeagirlcontest. While they differ in terms of their publishing aims and approaches, each account functions as a community hub while highlighting how Drumming Instagram is a contested site of meaning and power. Borrowing from feminist literature on the politics of online visibility, we argue that visibility is a currency that both legitimizes women on Drumming Instagram while simultaneously rendering them more vulnerable to public scrutiny and unwanted attention. The digital drum kit performance space may make it easy for *women to be seen*, but it remains challenging for *feminists to be heard.*

Emergent Online Communities and Popular Feminism

This study of women's participation on Drumming Instagram builds upon a series of distinct, yet interrelated bodies of literature. Among them are studies of gender, sexuality, and musical performance developed in the sociology of music.[2] Over the past several decades, questions of gender and sexuality have offered an important conceptual framework for the study of musical subcultures,[3] particular celebrities,[4] and audiences alike.[5] Alongside this body of research, scholars have also raised questions about music education and participation, and how gender mediates the "acceptability" of instruments for particular groups of people.[6] This discussion extends into women's instrumental performance in contemporary music, although work in this area tends to highlight the role of guitarists, bassists, and vocalists at the expense of drummers.[7] Layne Redmond's *When the Drummers Were Women* (1997), Meghan Georgina Aube's dissertation *Women in Percussion* (2011), Angela Smith's *Women Drummers* (2014), and most recently, Matt Brennan's *Kick It: The Social History of the Drum Kit* (2020) are notable exceptions, offering revisionist histories that question the gendered norms of contemporary drumming culture. Our research contributes to this body of literature by examining an emergent drumming community where gender plays a central role. However, we do so by considering musical performance through the lens of digital media, which is a (and perhaps *the*) primary channel for the circulation of popular music.[8]

For this reason, we also borrow from existing research in the area of feminist media studies. As feminism has enjoyed a 'new luminosity in popular culture' scholars have considered the political implications of this growing visibility.[9] Although the proliferation of images of strong and powerful women in media and advertising is indeed a welcome departure from the past, it has the potential to give rise to a postfeminist sentiment that sexism no longer exists and collective struggle is no longer necessary.[10] Feminist scholarship remains largely ambivalent to this notion, which is made tangible by 'hashtag feminism': a media practice that has fundamentally altered how we discuss gender and sexism, who participates in that conversation, and what types of political actions are possible.[11] Generating visibility and attention through the deployment of buzzwords and catchy political slogans while encouraging others to signal boost its message in the hopes of 'going viral', hashtag feminism is a type of performative politics that aims to disrupt the status quo by presenting an alternative version of the world (i.e. #YesAllWomen, #MeToo). However, like other identity-based movements, scholars have questioned whether this emphasis on visibility and attention overshadows structural inequities.[12] In other words, a demand for visibility and recognition within a system may come at the expense of dismantling or even challenging that system.

Feminist media scholarship also reminds us that visibility may at times even run counter to feminist goals. Under late capitalism, feminism can become vulnerable to co-optation and commodification when marketers regularly use images of 'empowered' women to sell everything from soap to clothing and cosmetics in the name of feminism.[13] Visibility can also engender certain kinds of vulnerability, with Larisa Kingston Mann listing the male gaze[14] and the hypervisibility of black female bodies[15] as examples where visibility itself is not necessarily liberatory.[16] This becomes particularly clear when we consider the paradoxically symbiotic relationship between 'popular feminism' – a feminism widely accessible across the mediascape – and 'popular misogyny'.[17] As part of the contemporary backlash against feminism, popular misogyny aims to silence women who 'make too much noise'.[18] In this sense, popular feminism in digital culture refers to media content *meant to be seen* rather than political demands that are *meant to be heard.*

Although the scholarly discussion about the politics of online feminism is robust, its applicability to women's online drumming communities is not quite so straightforward. Most of the existing scholarly discussion concerns women as media consumers and not as content producers.[19] And when it does consider women as producers of digital content, it mainly applies to young women engaged in explicitly feminist activities online.[20] In the case of women's online drumming communities, and Drumming Instagram in particular, women are both the producers *and* consumers of media content. Commodities may be a part of the discussion (through mention of specific brands of sticks, drums, cymbals, or other performance accessories), but do not figure as prominently as in other online communities such as influencer marketing spaces. And although the visibility of women performers in the highly male-dominated world of drumming is not politically insignificant, the motivations of women posting their videos may not be as explicitly political as those of young feminists aiming to confront sexism and misogyny in 140 characters or less. Taking this into consideration, we ask the following questions: What is the range of public responses to women's visibility on Drumming Instagram? What are the social norms and codes guiding participation in this networked public? And is Instagram a space where an emancipatory feminist politics can emerge?

Method: A Content Analysis of Drumming Instagram

Our analysis is based on an examination of three popular Instagram accounts dedicated to the promotion of women drummers: @femaledrummers (~75k followers), @tomtommag (~15k followers), and @hitlikeagirlcontest (~5,300 followers). @femaledrummers is the largest community-based account for women drummers on Instagram. Rather than developing original content, @femaledrummers amplifies individual performers' content by reposting one-minute videos of amateurs and professionals alike. Launched in 2016, the @femaledrummers Instagram account (and corresponding website) has since accrued a steadily growing audience that – at the time of our study – totalled over 75,000 followers. @tomtommag is the official Instagram account for *Tom Tom Magazine*, an online and paperback publication dedicated to showcasing and promoting women, queer, and non-binary drummers. The only trade publication made by and for women, the New York-based *Tom Tom Magazine* is distributed in the United States, Europe, Australia, South America and Japan. Lastly, @hitlikeagirlcontest is the official Instagram account for the annual women's drumming competition Hit Like a Girl, featuring women artists and promotional content. The Hit Like a Girl competition began in 2011 through the work of drum industry marketing exec David Levine and is presented in in association with *Tom Tom Magazine*. Together, these Instagram accounts function as foundational digital infrastructure that networks the women's online drumming community.

Because there is much to learn from the visual, auditory, and textual content of every Instagram post, our initial thoughts were to develop a critical analysis of discrete posts. We quickly realized however, that in order to learn about audience reception and popular discourse it would be necessary to focus not on content, but instead, on discussion. For this reason, our study examines user comments and the dynamics of the online conversation by, and about, women on Drumming Instagram. Our data set is comprised of comments (n=3,370) from the 100 most recent posts for each of the three accounts (i.e. @femaledrummers = 100, @tomtommag = 100, @hitlikeagirlcontest = 100). To generate the data set, we made use of ExportComments.com: a freemium online tool that converts comments from Instagram accounts into spreadsheets. Once downloaded, we imported the spreadsheets into NVivo (qualitative research software) for further investigation using content analysis: a research method involving the systematic reading, interpretation, and coding of texts to quantify patterns in communication materials.[21] A staple in media analyses, content analysis is an ideal method for the study of women on Drumming Instagram as its context-sensitivity makes it suitable for analysing large and varied social media datasets. The flexibility of NVivo software allowed us to refine categories as the analysis progressed, eliminating redundancies while aggregating similar coding items to produce more sensitive results.

Our coding protocol was developed through a pilot study conducted in early 2019 using only the @femaledrummers account. During this phase, we developed a series of broad categories according to the function and overall meaning of comment types. These include the following: 'Compliment/Enthusiasm/Support' (all of which fall under the broad category of positive feedback); 'Conversational' (which could be an expression of gratitude, a question, a reply, a user challenging a comment, or tagging a friend); 'Unsolicited Comments' (typically criticism or sexualization); 'Self-Promotion' (typically the assertion of one's own artistic merit or promoting an outside interest); and 'Other'. Although these categories adequately captured the range of sentiments expressed, there are nevertheless limitations to the approach: Since we limited each comment to a single code, it was at times challenging to decide which category took precedence when comments straddled different categories (i.e. tagging a friend while also complimenting the drummer). Additionally, it was also challenging to decipher the meaning of particular comments. For instance, when do flame and heart emojis signal admiration and when do they signify sexualization? This required careful decision-making, and it illustrates the highly interpretive dimension of content analysis and internet research.

The following chart illustrates each category, its corresponding definition, and examples of the comments that are typical to each.

TYPE OF COMMENT	DEFINITION	EXAMPLE
Compliment/ Enthusiasm/Support	User expresses a positive sentiment regarding the drummer's skill or expresses agreement with the post's overall message	'Wow!!! ' 'Amazing ' 'GET IT ' 'TOP ' 'YASSSSS '
Conversational	User comment engages other users	
e.g. Gratitude	User thanks another user	'OMG! TY for the feature! ' 'I love this! Thank you so much!'
e.g. Question	User posts a query in response to the post	'Wow! What's the name of this drummer?' 'What kind of sticks are you using?' 'Whoa! How did you do that?'
e.g. Reply	User responds to another user	'@username you're welcome ' '@username right?! The best!'
e.g. Challenging commenter	User counters another user's comment	'Cheers to the users who actually appreciate her talent instead of commenting on how she looks' 'I can't believe you all are giving her a hard time. She is way better than most of us. Her playing might not be pro, but she played it well. Nicely done!'
e.g. Tag a friend	User tags another user	'@username check her out'
Unsolicited Comments	User comment is deemed negative or inappropriate	
e.g. Criticism	User expresses negative judgement towards another user or post	'It's all about attention these days. She thinks she's the best even though her drumming sucks' 'Finally, a drummer who has REAL talent, not just another hot girl'
e.g. Sexualization	User reduces drummer to their physical appearance	'Wow, so talented AND beautiful!' 'Super sexy'
Self-Promotion	User comment serves to promote own interests	'Awesome! Check out my bio @username if you want to jam sometime' 'Hey everyone, check out my new track on YouTube! http://link.com'
Other	Function not listed here (i.e. user expresses a neutral fact or observation) or translation of non-English was unclear	'The name of this song is Highway to Hell. She was last year's winner.'

Interpreting the Data

Our analysis is based on a sample of 3,370 comments from the 300 posts we examined. In terms of distribution between the three accounts, the majority of these comments (69%, n=2,309) came from @femaledrummers, 25% came from @tomtommag (n=826), and 7% (n=236) came from @hitlikeagirlcontest. While there was user activity on all three accounts, it was clear that @femaledrummers attracted the greatest amount of participation, largely due to the size of its following.

	@femaledrummers		@hitlikeagirlcontest		@tomtommag		sum	percentage
Compliment	1396	60%	152	65%	456	55%	2004	59%
Conversational or Interactive	687	30%	68	29%	330	40%	1,085	32%
Gratitude	95	4%	27	11%	38	5%	160	5%
Question	49	2%	7	3%	18	2%	74	2%
Reply	165	7%	10	4%	159	19%	334	10%
Challenging commenter	7	0%	0	0%	0	0%	7	0%
Tag a friend	377	16%	24	10%	115	14%	516	15%
Unwanted	143	6%	3	1%	3	0%	149	4%
Criticism	95	4%	1	0%	2	0%	98	3%
Sexualization or Objectification	34	1%	2	1%	1	0%	37	1%
Self-Promotion	41	2%	5	2%	16	2%	62	2%
Other	41	2%	7	3%	21	3%	69	2%
Sum	2,309		235		826		3,370	
Percentage	69%		7%		25%			

Overwhelmingly, the discussion that takes place within all three accounts expresses a sentiment that is positive, supportive, and encouraging. In fact, nearly 60% (n= 2,004, 59%) of all comments fell into the category 'Compliment/Enthusiasm/Support'. Participants regularly complimented the abilities of featured performers and expressed support for women drummers and the musical initiatives with which they are associated (including bands, events, competitions, etc.). In terms of the individual accounts, this sentiment appeared most frequently on @hitlikeagirlcontest (n=152, 65%), which we paradoxically attribute to the competitive dimension of the initiative. Although it is ultimately a competition that might otherwise produce antagonistic sentiments, @hitlikeagirlcontest is foremost an organization designed to encourage participation among women, girl, and gender minority drummers. Its posts consist not only of competition winners who almost always earn public congratulations, but also of general competitors, finalists, and advertising and promotion for the event, all of which also generates public interest and support. The prevalence of such enthusiastic and supportive forms of dialogue, not only on @hitlikeagirlcontest but across all three accounts, are typical markers of feminist online communities, where maintaining a positive and encouraging atmosphere is a part of the social infrastructure and genre.

It is also worth mentioning some of the secondary but no less important types of communication operating in the online community of women drummers. Nearly a third of comments (32%, n=1,085) were conversational or interactive in tone. For instance, tagging a friend comprised 15% of all posts (n=516), which was done to share content with others who may have particular interest in a given post while also initiating further commentary and discussion. 10% of all comments were replies to other users in the context of dialogue (n=334), 5% expressed gratitude (n=160), and 2% posed a question (n=74). All of this activity is an important part of community dialogue, where users aim to interact with artists, acquire new techniques, or thank others for their posts. These types of comments most commonly appeared on @tomtommag (40%, n=330), where user dialogue was more prominent than the expression of enthusiasm and support for female participation we saw on other pages. We read the nature of @tomtommag's dialogue as an expression of a community with aims extending beyond visibility, instead gravitating around questions of artistry and curiosity amongst distinct musical cultures.

In the context of community dialogue and conversation, gratitude was particularly apparent and operated as a type of community currency. For instance, drummers whose original content was reposted on any one of the three accounts regularly thanked account administrators for their support and recognition. Similarly, amateur drummers often took the time to personally acknowledge the compliments of other users through their own expression of gratitude. Gratitude appeared in 5% of comments (n=160), typically in the form of drummers thanking account moderators for posting or reposting their content. This was most common on @hitlikeagirlcontest (11%, n=27), where users regularly thanked page moderators for sharing their content or organizing the competition itself. This type of activity indicates the highly supportive and reciprocal nature of this online community.

Our data shows, however, that no matter how supportive, the public and visible nature of these online communities does not insulate them from criticism. Although only a minority of comments (4%, n=149) were negative and fell into the 'unsolicited' category, they nevertheless warrant discussion. Such comments tended to be either rude, critical, or sexualizing, and were often misogynistic in tone. Unsurprisingly, the vast majority of these comments appeared on @femaledrummers posts (6%, n=143), which is perhaps expected in light of the visibility and popularity of this particular account. Some of these negative comments came off as slightly patronizing when they contained terms like 'dear' or 'sweetie', but they more commonly appeared in criticisms of a performers' technique or appearance (4%, n=95), or even in sexually-objectifying language (1%, n=34). Criticism sometimes occurred as a form of disruption, usually interrupting a stream of praise (i.e. 'she sucks!'). But it also occurred in comments where users criticized women drummers *generally* as a way to compliment a woman drummer *specifically* (i.e. 'You should post talented drummers like this more often instead of ones that just look good on camera'). We also found that some of the most vitriolic comments appeared not when drummers posted videos of themselves playing, but when they made political statements about gender and drumming. In user responses to one such video, some users replied that the video was shitty', that the drummer needed to 'shut the f*** up', and repudiated identity politics altogether, asserting that gender had little to do with music. Although the comments in our sample were for the most part positive, we wondered how that might change if drummers in this space had made more politically charged – and therefore controversial – statements.

What it may have also done, however, was increase the frequency by which users challenged those who left critical comments on performers' videos. In our sample, we found seven instances where users defended performers against unfair critiques, suggesting that community members will enforce informal norms around keeping Drumming Instagram a positive and supportive space for women. On one post we examined where various commenters made inappropriate comments about the drummer's appearance and performance style, we saw a number of users come to the performer's defence. One user in particular accused those leaving harsh comments of being envious of her talent and feeling unfulfilled in their personal lives. They reiterated their support for women drummers and encouraged critics to have a more positive outlook. Remarks such as these demonstrated both the strength and the resilience of the community, and the fact that its members feel strongly committed to defending fellow performers from the unfair critique and occasional vitriol that accompanies women daring to be seen *and heard* on Drumming Instagram.

The Ambivalence of Networked Performance

That user responses on @femaledrummers, @tomtommag, and @hitlikeagirlcontest were overwhelmingly positive was somewhat unexpected in light of the negative discourses that surround discussion of online culture and commenting – particularly when it comes to gender and equity-related issues in historically male-dominated spaces. We attribute this to the fact that the relatively niche and emergent nature of this online community means that many members and visitors are already personally invested in and supportive of women and gender minority drummers. This suggests that, as questions of identity-based online participation goes, context certainly matters. For example, the supportive tone of comments may have differed on more general Drumming Instagram accounts (i.e. @drumeo, @modern_drummer, or @drumlads), just as they would likely differ on accounts supporting more mainstream feminist efforts (i.e. those that promote visibility of women in STEM or campaigns to promote a wider representation of women's bodies in media).

We also found that women's Drumming Instagram provided more opportunities for users to interact with one another. Far from serving as a site where users passively consumed content, users regularly commented and replied to each other. Although the majority of this interactive process involved users tagging one another as a means of sharing content, it was also common to ask questions and respond to one another's comments. This again demonstrated the communitarian nature of this space as well as its users' commitments. The majority of the users in this space shared a common goal of supporting the increased visibility of women and gender minority drummers, with networked information technologies serving as integral communal infrastructure.

Given the overwhelming positivity of this space, it was unsurprising that hostile and misogynist commentary was uncommon. Whether due to careful moderation by the page owners or the relatively quiet feminism of the content, the popular misogyny evident in so much of online discourse about gender was relatively absent. We wondered how this might have differed had the content been more political or the pages more mainstream. Indeed, content and audience size play an important role in shaping reception. For example, we observed that @tomtommag tended to post more explicitly political content than @femaledrummers (for instance, by posting a photo in support of Dr Christine Blasey Ford during the Kavanaugh hearing), with its smaller audience perhaps insulating it from the backlash one might typically expect. @femaledrummers, on the other hand, had a much wider userbase and online presence that inadvertently courted backlash the few times it posted explicitly political content. Thus, the feminism of women's Drumming Instagram is a complex and uneven phenomenon that is still evolving.

The nature of this uneven, emergent form of feminism on Drumming Instagram makes it difficult to say whether or not it is a space where an emancipatory feminist politics can emerge. Insofar as women's Drumming Instagram promotes positive images of women and gender minority drummers that are often side-lined in popular and niche music scenes, it succeeds at making them visible. This is a feminist politics of visibility that is not about individual empowerment nor about unfettered consumption but is about recuperating and celebrating marginalized people's contribution to music. This visibility is not restricted to white and normatively gendered bodies (though user comments indicate which bodies are seen as worthy of attention and engagement) but is inclusive of a range of different identities. In other words, women's Drumming Instagram does not exactly resemble the feminist online efforts that tend to be analysed in the scholarly literature.

However, the extent to which women's Drumming Instagram is *emancipatory* is complicated because the underlying political struggle that gives life to this community remains relatively muted. Images of women and gender minority performers exist in this space, and they are rewarded with compliments and occasional feminist solidarity. Yet the few times where performers explicitly address the politics of gender and drumming renders them vulnerable to the online vitriol one would come to expect in other online spaces. We would answer our own question with another: although women and gender minority performers may be *visible* on Instagram, are their demands as feminists in fact being *heard*?

Conclusion

This study explored the relationship between online visibility, social norms, and political change in the emergent online community of women on Drumming Instagram. What we found, among other things, was that context matters: in online spaces dedicated to promoting women drummers, users are generally supportive because they are explicitly seeking out images that are otherwise side-lined in the mainstream world of drumming. We also found that women's Drumming Instagram is not so different than other online communities insofar as it invites both detractors and defenders. The openness of online communities, regardless of type, means that users with little personal investment will occasionally leave disruptive or hostile comments that will not go unchecked.[22] And although a minority of comments were overly critical or even sexualizing, committed users regularly challenged them while enforcing the shared values of the space (i.e. encouraging and supporting women drummers of all abilities).

Ultimately however, what emerged from this exploration was that women's Drumming Instagram affords women drummers a specific type of networked visibility that both supports *and* limits the possibilities for change. Although the increased visibility of women drummers in historically male-dominated spaces is a welcome departure from the past, we wonder about the emancipatory potential of a politics that begins and ends with visibility alone. The drummers on this page received acclaim when their content was about *drumming*, but courted backlash when the content was explicitly about *gender*. This may discourage drummers from speaking up on political issues, thus muting the political possibilities of their visibility. In short, Instagram is a space where women drummers are *seen*, but it remains unclear whether or not we, the broader drumming community, are willing to truly *listen*.

Notes

1 R. Steblin. 'The Gender Stereotyping of Musical Instruments in the Western Tradition', *Canadian University Music Review* 16:1 (1995), pp. 128–44.

2 R. Walser. *Running with the Devil: Power, Gender, and Madness in Heavy Metal Music*, Music/Culture (Hanover: University Press of New England, 1993); S. Whiteley (ed.), *Sexing the Groove: Popular Music and Gender* (New York: Routledge, 1997).

3 M. Leonard. *Gender in the Music Industry: Rock, Discourse, and Girl Power* (Aldershot, Hampshire, England; Burlington: Ashgate, 2007).

4 C. D. Abreu. 'Celebrity, "Crossover," and Cubanidad: Celia Cruz as "La Reina de Salsa," 1971–2003', *Latin American Music Review / Revista de Música Latinoamericana* 28:1 (2007), pp. 94–124; A. N. Edgar. 'Blackvoice and Adele's Racialized Musical Performance: Blackness, Whiteness, and Discursive Authenticity', *Critical Studies in Media Communication* 31:3 (2014), pp. 167–81; J. A. Mena and P. K. Saucier. '"Don't Let Me Be Misunderstood": Nina Simone's Africana Womanism', *Journal of Black Studies* 45:3 (1 April 2014), pp. 247–65.

5 J. D. Brown and L. Schulze. 'The Effects of Race, Gender, and Fandom on Audience Interpretations of Madonna's Music Videos', *Journal of Communication* 40:2 (1 June 1990), pp. 88–102.

6 H. Abeles. 'Are Musical Instrument Gender Associations Changing?' *Journal of Research in Music Education* 57:2 (July 2009), pp. 127–39; E. Koskoff. 'When Women Play: The Relationship between Musical Instruments and Gender Style', in *A Feminist Ethnomusicology: Writings on Music and Gender* (Champaign: University of Illinois Press, 2014), pp. 122–32; L. Green. *Music, Gender, Education* (Cambridge: Cambridge University Press, 2009).

7 M. A. Clawson. 'When Women Play the Bass: Instrument Specialization and Gender Interpretation in Alternative Rock Music', *Gender & Society* 13:2 (1999), pp. 193–210.

8 N. K. Baym. *Playing to the Crowd: Musicians, Audiences, and the Intimate Work of Connection*, Postmillennial Pop (New York: New York University Press, 2018).

9 Rosalind Gill. 'Post-Postfeminism?: New Feminist Visibilities in Postfeminist Times', *Feminist Media Studies* 16:4 (July 2016), pp. 610–630.

10 R. E. Dubrofsky and M. M. Wood. 'Posting Racism and Sexism: Authenticity, Agency and Self-Reflexivity in Social Media', *Communication and Critical/Cultural Studies* 11:3 (July 2014), pp. 282–287; A. McRobbie. *The Aftermath of Feminism: Gender, Culture and Social Change* (Los Angeles, London: SAGE, 2009).

11 H. Baer. 'Redoing Feminism: Digital Activism, Body Politics, and Neoliberalism', *Feminist Media Studies* 16:1 (January 2016), pp. 17–34; R. Clark-Parsons. '"I SEE YOU, I BELIEVE YOU, I STAND WITH YOU": #MeToo and the Performance of Networked Feminist Visibility', *Feminist Media Studies* (June 2019), pp. 1–19.

12 See also N. Fraser. 'Heterosexism, Misrecognition and Capitalism: A Response to Judith Butler', *New Left Review*, no. 228 (1998), pp. 140–149.

13 S. Banet-Weiser. *Empowered: Popular Feminism and Popular Misogyny* (Durham: Duke University Press, 2018).

14 L. Mulvey. 'Visual Pleasure and Narrative Cinema', *Screen* 16:3 (September 1975), pp. 6–18.

15 b. hooks. *Black Looks: Race and Representation* (Toronto: Between The Lines, 1992).

16 L. K. Mann. 'What Can Feminism Learn from New Media?', *Communication and Critical/Cultural Studies* 11:3 (July 2014), pp. 293–297.

17 Banet-Weiser, *Empowered*.

18 Gill. 'Post-Postfeminism?: New Feminist Visibilities in Postfeminist Times'; S. Faludi. *Backlash: The Undeclared War against American Women*, 15th anniversary ed., 1st Three Rivers Press ed. (New York: Three Rivers Press, 2006).
19 Banet-Weiser, *Empowered*; McRobbie, *The Aftermath of Feminism*; Gill, 'Post-Postfeminism?: New Feminist Visibilities in Postfeminist Times'.
20 J. Keller. *Girls' Feminist Blogging in a Postfeminist Age* (London; New York: Routledge, 2017); Clark-Parsons, '"I SEE YOU, I BELIEVE YOU, I STAND WITH YOU"'.
21 K. Krippendorff. *Content Analysis: An Introduction to Its Methodology*, 3rd ed. (Los Angeles; London: SAGE, 2013).
22 W. Phillips. *This Is Why We Can't Have Nice Things: Mapping the Relationship between Online Trolling and Mainstream Culture*, The Information Society Series (Cambridge: The MIT Press, 2015).

17 Building Inclusive Drum Communities

The Case of Hey Drums

NAT GRANT

Introduction

Hey Drums (2016-present) is a blog documenting the work and experiences of Australian female and gender diverse drummers.[1] The site also features percussionists but is largely focused on promoting a diverse intersection of players of an instrument widely and predominantly accepted as the territory of cis gendered men: the drum kit.[2] Just as 'drummers have largely been neglected in scholarly literature on music and education',[3] non-male drummers are routinely underrepresented in drum kit culture, to the point where these artists are required to write their own histories and document their own contributions. Much literature and media surrounding the instrument is not representative of the diversity of drummers out there, which *Hey Drums* (amongst other publications and movements) seeks to address.

At the time of writing, interviews with more than 145 drummers from across the Australian continent have been published on the site and promoted on *Hey Drums* social media platforms and there is a dedicated Spotify playlist featuring bands with female and gender non-conforming (GNC) drummers. The project has grown into an online and real-life community of drummers, regular articles in a nationwide drumming magazine, live performance, and teaching events, as well as academic outcomes. This chapter will document the genesis, goals, and evolution of *Hey Drums* and affiliated projects, highlighting some of the individual artists and the broad range of areas in which they work.

A Woman's Work

A woman's work is never done. Or it's erased from history books. DYSON, STRINGER, CLOHER 'FALLING CLOUDS'

As early as 2001, I wanted to do something to counter the incessant feedback I had received throughout my teens which continued into my twenties, that 'girls don't play drums', with some kind of project listing and profiling all the Australian non male drummers I could find.

I began the *Hey Drums* blog in 2016 as an acknowledgement of the people I already knew, and to learn about others. It started with some personal emails and a public call on Facebook, which resulted in more than twenty candidates within an hour. There has been a steady stream of willing and eager interviewees ever since, demonstrating the great need and enthusiasm for this project. I find interview participants mostly by word of mouth. Some are self-nominated. Some are suggested by band-mates or friends. Some are found at gigs and on social media. The need for the project is affirmed almost every time I contact a new drummer and explain what the project is (often now they have heard of the project), and receive many replies affirming I haven't been alone in feeling isolated as a non-male drummer. Melbourne based session drummer Julia Watt, for example, says that:

> Since beginning my professional drumming career, I have truly felt like the odd one out and felt I was the only one of my kind out there in the big bad world of the music industry. This was especially true before the days of social media when finding other non-male drummers was quite a challenge. Through their love of drumming and the *Hey Drums* program, Nat has managed to bring together and create this lovely community of drummers and like-minded creatives. It is so nice to be a part of something so wonderful and to feel connected and inspired by my non-male peers.[4]

The birth of the blog and beginning to pen feature articles for *Drumscene* magazine happened almost simultaneously in mid-2016.[5] I was starting to collect all this information and saw the possibility of doing something more than simply presenting it on the *Hey Drums* blog. A chance discovery of the female-focused drumming magazine *Tom Tom* in a music store in New Orleans in 2015 had me reflecting on Australia's own drumming magazine, *Drumscene* and its lack of representation of female and gender diverse drummers.[6] It was evident that a wider audience could be reached, at the same time as challenging the typical male drummer stereotype very much reinforced by previous issues of *Drumscene.*

A few email exchanges later with editor and founder of the quarterly magazine, Frank Corniola, and I was to become a regular writer for the print publication, contributing articles about all aspects of life as a drummer that just happened to feature non-male artists. Frank was aware of the lack of representation in the magazine and was open to doing something about it together.

The articles do not mention gender unless it is something that the interviewees specifically bring up. They instead focus (just as in all the other articles in the magazine) on different elements of drumming and drumming related experiences. I have been careful to avoid sensationalising the people in the articles.

You Can't Be What You Can't See

The desired outcome of this work is the normalisation of seeing and hearing women and gender diverse folks behind the drum kit: to simultaneously increase representation and raise awareness that these drummers exist. It is just as important for these drummers to see themselves represented as it is for younger aspiring drummers to see themselves represented in print.[7]

Since 2016, I have penned more than fifteen articles for *Drumscene*, including profiles of dozens of Australian drummers both here and overseas – articles on touring, session playing, yoga for drummers, inclusive music education programs for young people, practice hacks, promoting yourself as a drummer on social media, and interviews with international superstars Terri Lyne Carrington, Cindy Blackman Santana, and Vera Figueiredo.

Each artist featured on the *Hey Drums* blog answers the same set of questions.[8] There is no common theme amongst the answers given, except perhaps in the final question: 'What advice would you give your younger drumming self?' There is a strong sense of solidarity amongst the interviewees and their less experienced selves; a combination of many variations on 'don't be so hard on yourself' and 'don't let annoying old man drummers try and intimidate you with useless facts about what kind of cymbals you should be using' [9].

There are three main goals of *Hey Drums*:

1. The documentation of Australian drummers;
2. The inclusion across all iterations of the project of trans and GNC people;
3. The promotion of all the interviewed drummers the same way regardless of level of experience, 'fame', 'chops', or genre.

Documentation

The number one goal of *Hey Drums* has always been to satisfy the need for documentation of female and non-binary artists in a traditionally male dominated field: to present unequivocally the existence of and creative work being done by female and non-binary drummers around Australia, despite a still common perception that these people don't belong or are a rarity behind the kit.

My experience as a young drummer in the early 2000s is not an uncommon one: being confronted, even accosted, in drum shops and at gigs, by men who felt the need to either point out or challenge the fact that I was a drummer and also not a man. Having had (only a few but very influential) incredible female mentors – very established artists in their own right – ten to twenty years my senior, I wondered what it must have been like for them at my age (and now). Each generation seems to be continually surprised that women and GNC people are drumming, perpetuating what feminist author Dale Spender describes as a submergence of information,[10] the erasure of the achievements and experiences of non males at every age. As Australian author and journalist Jane Caro writes, 'the revolution that has occurred in the lives of women remains relatively unacknowledged. It's as if each step forward is regarded in isolation'.[11] And, as Catherine Strong writes in her essay *Grunge, riot Grrrl and the forgetting of women in popular culture*, 'women are generally written out of historical accounts of music in order to reinscribe the creative dominance of men in this field'.[12]

Though only three years old, the *Hey Drums* blog represents an important historical document that will, hopefully, continue to be added to for years to come. By providing a snapshot of women and gender diverse people working in the music industry it serves and will continue to serve as a resource for musicians, music fans, students, and researchers alike.

The Importance of Inclusion: Trans and GNC Artists

For the first twelve months the blog was called *She Drums*. I knew this was not inclusive of trans and GNC artists, but I was not yet sure how to make it so. At the same time, I wanted to make it clear that I wasn't going to be interviewing or featuring cis-male drummers With the encouragement and advice of some patient non binary drummers who were enthusiastic but reluctant to participate in a project titled 'she' (with good reason), *Hey Drums* (a reference to the gender neutral pronoun 'they') was created in its place.

The second goal of *Hey Drums*, the importance of the inclusion of trans, non-binary, and gender non-conforming drummers, cannot be understated. In a time where these people are being actively excluded, bullied, and vilified in the arts, in sport, this is a movement, like any feminist movement, that must be trans and GNC inclusive.[13]

It is important to note, however, that this is not a project seeking to 'out' anyone. There are no check boxes around gender identification that accompany the drumming questionnaire. There are drummers who feature on the blog who are non-binary but not public about this, or trans but not public about it. There are others who are very much out and outspoken. The blog and affiliated events are safe spaces that are inclusive but respectful of the drummers' privacy; places they need not feel like 'a specimen with all the lights bearing down'. It is important that all of these artists are seen as people, as drummers, first.[14]

Snapshot of Drummers: Diversity

The third important element of this project is that it does not discriminate in terms of level of experience, technical ability, or genre of music played by the drummers in question. In fact, the very opposite is true: the diversity of the featured artists in terms of playing level and style is part of what makes this community and this project both interesting and unique. The range of stories and experiences is important: to hold a mirror up to as many different types of musical practices as possible; to show that there are many different ways one can be a drummer and that they are all valid. There is not one type of female or GNC drummer, just as there is no one type of male drummer.

This sentiment has been echoed by Dr Louise Devenish, Chair of Percussion at UWA Conservatorium of Music. Louise explains:

> Being interviewed in *Hey Drums* made me feel part of a bigger drums and percussion community, a much bigger community than I knew was out there. I learned about so many other musicians from different cities and genres that I otherwise would never have come across. One of the great things about it is that it is inclusive in lots of ways, so there are many ways to connect with and through *Hey Drums* for musicians of all genders, all genres and all modes of making . . . *Hey Drums* is incredibly important for the drum community and overall music community within Australia and internationally!![15]

At the time of writing this chapter, more than 145 drummers and percussionists (overwhelmingly drum kit players) have been interviewed. These drummers include some of Australia's most seasoned players such as Sonja Horbelt (co-founder of the Melbourne Women's International Jazz Festival), Julia Day (Do-Re-Mi), Jen Sholakis (Jen Cloher, Laura Jean, The Orbweavers) and Clare Moore (Dave Graney). There are interviews with well-known artists such as Lozz Benson, who drums for folk pop star John Butler and was awarded first prize in 'Australia's Best Female Drummer' competition in 2016, Leanne Cowie of 'The Scientists' fame, and pop sensation G Flip, who belts out powerful original songs from behind the kit. Alongside Lozz, Leanne, and G are dozens of little known and non-professional but regularly gigging drummers, all with their own experiences and all given equal weight within the project.

The drummers I interviewed are regulars with bands, freelance drummers, touring artists, teachers, session musicians, as well as professionals in other fields who maintain steady side careers as musicians. They are students, activists, booking agents, multi instrumentalists, electronic musicians, composers, and collaborators. Some have formal musical training. Some are self taught. Some strive to make a living from music. Some have no desire to, or even a strong urge not to combine their love of music making with the stress of trying to make a living.

There is Tanja Bahro who started playing at age forty-seven and now gigs regularly in Melbourne with her traditional jazz band, and sixty-year-old student of African drumming Anne Harkin who also began drumming in her forties. There are a number of Australian born drummers currently living and playing overseas such as Latin percussionist Nasrine Rahmani (Madrid) and jazz drummer Jodie Michael (New York), and those born in other countries who now call Australia home such as Bonnie Stewart (born in Ireland, now Sydney based) and drummer/composer, Cissi Tsang (born in Hong Kong, now based in Perth). There are performers across rock, pop, metal, improvisation, jazz, noise, experimental music, circus, and cabaret.

There is blind from birth drummer, Renee Kelly, who was made famous through a series of short films by the Australian Broadcasting Commission focusing on disabled artists.[16] There is yoga teacher and arts manager, Holly Norman, who has turned her focus to the mental and physical wellbeing of those working in the performing arts. There is ex Circus Oz drummer and Edinburgh Festival regular, Bec Matthews, performance artist, Tina Havelock Stevens, who plays drums underwater and in abandoned aeroplane hangers, and electro pop percussion duo, Feels, who are crusaders for gender parity in their own right through their creation of WOMPP: Women of Music Production Perth,[17] a community-focused label and series of education groups for female and GNC music makers in Western Australia.

Approximately two thirds of the drummers interviewed for *Hey Drums* hail from Melbourne. This is inevitable as it as it is where I am based, but it is also the city with the highest number of music venues per capita in the world.[18] Almost ten percent are based in New South Wales (mostly Sydney) and there are representatives from all the other states and territories in Australia, as well as a number of Australian born drummers living, working, or studying overseas.

Outcomes

Outcomes of the *Hey Drums* project so far include the online interviews, the articles in *Drumscene* magazine, several live performance events, a conference presentation, and drum lessons that are open to the public. There is an online community of the drummers who have been involved on Facebook; a place to ask for advice, offer support, and share opportunities. Most of the 100+ members have done an interview or a gig for *Hey Drums* at some point, and many use the private group to advertise that they are looking for work or gigs, that someone they know is after a drummer for project, to offer education opportunities for young women and GNC artists, to borrow gear when travelling, or to ask advice when buying new equipment. The larger and more diverse the community becomes the greater the opportunities for collaboration.

Holly Norman, drummer and Program Manager for the Melbourne International Jazz Festival describes *Hey Drums* in the following manner:

> An incredible resource for drummers and percussionists on the Australian music scene. Not only does the blog promote a strong sense of community between female and [GNC] musicians . . . but it provides a platform to profile players to the broader musical and arts community. I've met many new musical peers and colleagues through *Hey Drums* and always love seeing the articles come out to get to know new players. [19]

In May 2018, *Hey Drums* curated an event at the *Make It Up Club*,[20] which is a weekly experimental and avant-garde sound art and performance event that has been running in Melbourne for the past twenty-two years. Fifteen drummers set up five drum kits and performed three sets of completely improvised music to a full house. The reactions from performers and audience alike were electric – and the performances were incredibly diverse and engaging – with veteran noise and experimental drummers playing alongside jazz, and punk artists – all finding a way to listen and work with each other. This *Hey Drums* takeover of the *Make It Up Club* has now become an annual event.

In 2019, a summer night market in the Melbourne CBD featured a pop up speed drum lesson event, with two experienced teachers and *Hey Drums* representatives offering rolling ten-minute drum lessons to members of the public, who could then have a go at jamming along with a favourite pop tune. Preference was given to female and GNC 'students' and this event was picked up by Melbourne Music Week for a similar event in Bourke St Mall, in the heart of the CBD.[21] This event provided a way to engage the public in something fun whilst also raising awareness of *Hey Drums*.

An event at the Melbourne Recital Centre, also in 2019, saw original electro pop outfit *Cool Explosions* collaborate with *Hey Drums* in an hour-long concert and soundscape performance for drums, percussion, vocals, synths, and electronics.[22] The band specifically sought out *Hey Drums* in order to collaborate with non-male drummers and percussionists.

In the same year, I presented a paper at the 'Gender Diversity in Music and Art' conference at the University of Western Australia.[23] That presentation began with a talk about *Hey Drums* and ended in a collaborative improvised performance with five other drummer/percussionists who were in attendance at the conference. Some of the performers were WA locals

(Genevieve Wilkins, Cissi Tsang, Flick Dear) and some were visiting from interstate and overseas (Vanessa Tomlinson: Brisbane, Robyn Schulkowsky: Berlin). All the participants, with the exception of Schulkowsky, had been previous interviewees for *Hey Drums* and were keen to be involved to promote the work being done by the blog.

2020 will feature a collaboration with the Melbourne Museum and Melbourne Fashion Festival, Australian drum maker Entity,[24] as well as monthly drum lessons at an iconic Melbourne venue the Esplanade Hotel.

Context

The musical landscape in Australia is changing and the representation of minority groups including people of colour, people with disabilities, LGBTQIA+, women and GNC artists is very much a big issue. The 2019 fourth annual 'By the Numbers' study of the gender gap in Australian music found that 'the diversity of acts represented on major Australian festival line-ups improved significantly; for the first time in the report's history, a festival analysed achieved gender parity, with fifty percent of acts on Falls Festival's 2018/2019 line-up featuring at least one woman'.[25] Further, fifty-two percent of year 12 (final year high school) students undertaking a music subject in 2018 were female. However, a discrepancy exists between these figures and those female musicians being recognised as practising professionally. While women represent forty-five percent of those with a tertiary music qualification and fifty percent of those that study music, they make up just twenty percent of those registered to receive royalties.[26] In a report on the 'gender gap in Australian music', Ange McCormak noted that:

> If you turned on the radio in 2018, you were more likely to hear songs performed by men than women. Only 21 per cent of the top 100 most-played tracks on Australian radio stations in 2018 were by solo female acts or all-female groups; however, 27 per cent of songs were by acts with men and women, or featuring a female vocalist.[27]

On 8 March every year both national and community broadcasters turn the airwaves over to female and gender diverse presenters and recording artists for International Women's Day programming.[28] This initiative sees a significant spike in representation, but the above statistics show there is still much room for improvement.

Hey Drums is part of a wider series of grassroots movements in Australia, part of a broader landscape of organisations striving for greater access and inclusion. Music Victoria is an advocacy group with a motto of 'Advocate, Support, Celebrate'. The independent body has created a variety of initiatives focusing on gender equity, safety, and inclusivity in the live music scene, among which is their 'Best Practice Guidelines for Live Music Venues', which includes a chapter for venues on how to deal with sexual harassment.[29] Music Victoria also hosts regular panel events, training, and mentoring for female and GNC musicians and music producers.

LISTEN (established in 2014) 'is a new music initiative focusing on fostering change, using a feminist perspective to promote the visibility and experiences of women, gender non-conforming and LGBTQIA+ people, people of colour, Aboriginal and Torres Strait Islander people, people with disabilities and other marginalised folk in Australian music'.[30] LISTEN began as an online community, has hosted conferences, gigs, talks and events, now incorporates a record label, and is host to the Listen Lists: databases of female and GNC sound engineers, performing acts, session musicians, DJs, and producers (beat makers).[31]

All In, based in Melbourne 'exists to create a more inclusive environment for musicians and audience members in the Melbourne jazz scene'.[32] Through a variety of strategies, they are trying to address the aforementioned discrepancy between number of female music students and professionals, with activities including:

- Advocating for policy change in venues and institutions;
- Listening directly to marginalised people's experiences of the scene and taking action;
- Sharing valuable knowledge, stories and perspectives;
- Helping to foster sustainable careers;
- Boosting the profiles of diverse artists;
- Promoting a broader range of gigs and events.[33]

Girls Rock! Australia is a national network of music camps focused on rock and pop music. Held during the school holidays, the program is 'independently run by a team of musicians and educators passionate about empowering girls, trans and gender-diverse young people through music education and mentorship'.[34] They have held camps and concerts in all the major Australian cities since 2016 and are aligned with the Global Girls Rock Camp Alliance.[35]

The combined effects of these movements, organisations, and activities puts pressure on bookers, broadcasters, and festival organisers to be proactive in regards to gender representation. Worldwide, there is also a groundswell around inclusivity of female and gender diverse instrumentalists.

The formerly mentioned quarterly New York based publication *Tom Tom Magazine* was founded by drummer Mindy Abovitz in 2009 and is 'the only magazine and media company in the world dedicated to female and GNC drummers, beat makers and producers'.[36] Like *Hey Drums*, *Tom Tom* has expanded from the page and screen to include live performance and installation events, a drum academy, and a podcast. Also, like *Hey Drums, Tom Tom* recently changed their focus from 'female' drummers to be inclusive of GNC artists.

Hollywood drummer and teacher, Liz Aponte, offers online lessons for women and girls, to 'help female drummers who are feeling frustrated with their progress reach the next level and absolutely CRUSH it in a male dominated music world'.[37] She also makes drums through her own business, The Respira Collective,[38] and makes jewellery and other accessories from broken cymbals through her company Full Circle Co.[39]

The annual 'Hit Like a Girl' contest is an amateur contest for women and girls where female percussionists and drummers of all ages and levels are encouraged to participate. Its purpose is 'to spotlight female drummers/percussionists and encourage drumming and lifelong musicianship for girls and women, regardless of age or playing level. The event is produced by the Hit Like A Girl Contest and our activities are made possible by the generous support of artists, individuals and companies in the music and music products industries'.[40]

The contest was conceived by a team of drum industry and media veterans (along with *Tom Tom*'s Mindy Abovitz) as a way to promote and raise the profile of female drummers. Since 2011, it has attracted more than 5000 contestants from over fifty countries.

Australia's *Drumscene* magazine ran a similar competition from 2016 to 2018. Their Best Female Drummer award was a new category created in a long-standing yearly competition. The category has now been subsumed back into the existing competition.

Conclusion

Strangers now contact me when they are looking for a drummer, percussionist, or teacher. Artists and audience are invested in diversity and there is a growing movement in Australia of acknowledging privilege when employing musicians and looking around for who is not currently being represented. People are realising the importance and relevance of supporting, acknowledging the work being done by female and GNC people in a traditionally male dominated area. Alex Roper, a Melbourne-based freelancer and one of the first interviewees for *Hey Drums*, explains the importance of the blog:

> It gives a platform for people who might not have had one in the same way previously. I know I have been found through the website and my interview and have done gigs because of it and connected with people I wouldn't have

> otherwise. I was able to see myself as a professional and people to see me that way too. I even got a job at a prominent Melbourne drum shop & school because of *Hey Drums*![41]

The project offers value to the music community and music audiences in Australia via the blog, private and public social media groups and platforms. It has great value as a resource and a work of advocacy. What is unique about *Hey Drums* is that it assumes first and foremost that everyone who is interviewed, who has a lived experience of being a gigging drummer, deserves to be there. GNC, non-binary, and non-male analyses are critical for truly representative future studies of the drum kit, and there is a great opportunity to include a diverse range of voices from a relatively early stage in the burgeoning field of drum kit related academia.

Historically, women drummers have been separated out in literature – female artists separated out into articles such as 'the best female ... of the 90s' or '5 female drummers you should know' and GNC artists are all but written out of history. *Tom Tom* Magazine, Angela Smith's *History of Women Drummers* and Layne Redmond's *When the Drummers Where Women* fill a substantial gap in the literature. *Hey Drums* is attempting to do the same and, though unfortunate that this is still at all necessary, will continue to do so until sensationalised articles about female drummers claim 'girls can do it all', 'breaking the mold', 'marching to their own beat', are no longer tolerated or relevant – until 'alternate histories' of drumming no longer need to be written.

Notes

1 'Hey Drums', available at: http://heydrums.com (accessed 12 November 2020).
2 From hereon in when the author mentions 'men' or 'male' drummers they are referring to cisgendered men.
3 G. D. Smith. *I Drum, Therefore I Am: Being and Becoming a Drummer* (Farnham: Ashgate, 2013), p 2.
4 Email correspondence with author, January 2020
5 'Drumscene Magazine', available at: www.drumscene.com.au/ (accessed 12 November 2020).
6 'Tom Tom Magazine', available at: http://tomtommag.com (accessed 12 November 2020).
7 M. W. Edelman. 'It's Hard to Be What You Can't See', Children's Defense Fund (21 August 2015), available at: www.childrensdefense.org/child-watch-columns/health/2015/its-hard-to-be-what-you-cant-see/ (accessed 12 November 2020).
8 Questions
    Name
    Where are you based?
    How long have you been playing drums? And what initially drew you to the instrument?
    Do you play any other instruments?
    What bands/projects/collaborations are you involved in right now?
    What else have you previously been involved in (bands/shows/projects etc)?
    Do you write music or develop your own shows? What are they about/how have they come about?
    What are your thoughts on collaboration in music and in the projects you're involved in or the projects you run?
    Who are you listening to/whose music are you enjoying right now?

Do you have any favourite drummers? Or other musicians who inspire you? why?
How would you describe the kind of music or projects you're mostly involved in? And what kind of unique perspective/sound do you bring to these gigs?
Do you have a particular warm up or practice routine? Or favourite exercises?
Does social media play a big part in how you promote yourself as an artist and your various projects?
Do you promote your work in other ways?
Do you make a living from music? What different types of work does this comprise?
Where's the coolest place that music has taken you?
If you could give your younger drumming self some advice what would it be?
Other thoughts/info

9 'Bianca Raffin', interview from Hey Drums, available at: www.heydrums.com/home/bianca-raffin (accessed 12 November 2020).
10 D. Spender. 'Women of Ideas: And What Men Have Done to Them' (1982), p. 15.
11 J. Caro. 'Accidental Feminist' (2019), p. 2.
12 C. Strong. 'Grunge, riot Grrrl and the Forgetting of Women in Popular Culture', *The Journal of Popular Culture* (2011).
13 R. Dembroff 'Trans Women Are Victims of Misogyny Too', *The Guardian* (19 May 2019), available at: www.theguardian.com/commentisfree/2019/may/19/valerie-jackson-trans-women-misogyny-feminism (accessed 12 November 2020).
14 A. Sicardi 'My Gender Is: Mind Your Business' (28 November 2018), available at: www.them.us/story/my-gender-is-mind-your-business (accessed 12 November 2020).
15 Email correspondence with author, December 2019
16 'Drummer Girl', Seed Series 1, Episode 1, ABC iview, available at: https://iview.abc.net.au/video/RA1808H001S00 (accessed 12 November 2020).
17 'Women of Music Production Perth', available at: http://wompp.com.au (accessed 12 November 2020).
18 P. Donoughue 'Melbourne Is the Live Music Capital of the World, Study Says', *Double J* (12 April 2018), available at: www.abc.net.au/news/2018-04-12/melbourne-is-the-live-music-capital-of-the-world-census-shows/9643684 (accessed 12 November 2020).
19 Email correspondence with author, December 2019
20 'Make it up Club', *Bar Open*, available at: http://baropen.com.au/make-it-up-club/ (accessed 12 November 2020).
21 'Melbourne Music Week', *City of Melbourne*, available at: https://mmw.melbourne.vic.gov.au (accessed 12 November 2020).
22 'Arrhythmia', Melbourne Recital Centre (15 June 2019), available at: www.melbournerecital.com.au/events/2019/arrhythmia/ (accessed 12 November 2020).
23 'Gender Diversity in Music and Art', *University of Western Australia* (16–19 July 2019), available at: www.uwa.edu.au/able/schools/conservatorium-of-music/conservatorium-of-music-events/gender-diversity-conference (accessed 12 November 2020).
24 'Entity Drums', available at: https://entitydrums.com/ (accessed 12 November 2020).
25 A. McCormack 'By the Numbers 2019: The Gender Gap in Australian Music Revealed', triple j HACK (8 March 2019), available at: www.abc.net.au/triplej/programs/hack/by-the-numbers-2019-the-gender-gap-in-australian-music-revealed/10879066 (accessed 12 November 2020).
26 Ibid.
27 Ibid.
28 'International Women's Day 2020', *3CR Community Radio*, available at: www.3cr.org.au/iwd (accessed 12 November 2020).
29 'Best Practice Guidelines for Live Music Venues', *Music Victoria*, available at: www.musicvictoria.com.au/reports/best-practice-guidelines (accessed 12 November 2020).
30 'LISTEN', available at: www.listenlistenlisten.org/ (accessed 12 November 2020).
31 'Listen Lists', LISTEN, available at: www.listenlistenlisten.org/lists/ (accessed 12 November 2020).
32 'All in Melbourne', available at: www.allinmelbourne.com (accessed 12 November 2020).
33 Ibid.
34 'Girls Rock! Australia', available at: www.girlsrockaustralia.com.au/ (accessed 12 November 2020).
35 'Girls Rock Camp Alliance', available at: www.girlsrockcampalliance.org/ (accessed 12 November 2020).
36 'Tom Tom Magazine', available at: http://tomtommag.com (accessed 12 November 2020).

37 'Liz Aponte: Drum Lessons for Female Drummers', available at: http://lizapontedrums.com (accessed 12 November 2020).
38 'Respira Collective', available at: www.lizapontedrums.com/respira-collective (accessed 12 November 2020).
39 'Full Circle Co.', available at: https://fullcirclecompany.co/ (accessed 12 November 2020).
40 'Hit Like A Girl Contest', available at: http://hitlikeagirlcontest.com (accessed 12 November 2020).
41 Email correspondence with author, December 2019.

18 A Window into My Soul

Eudaimonia and Autotelic Drumming

GARETH DYLAN SMITH

I Like Playing Drums

I really like playing the drum kit. In important ways, drumming and being a drummer define who I am. For about as long as I have been a drummer, and all the more since I have taken this habit with me into adult life, through numerous moves from one apartment or house to another, between cities, and recently between countries, I have wondered why I keep doing it. Let me be clear: I have never considered *not* being a drummer, but it has occurred to me from time to time that I have not really articulated the reasons why I find drumming, in the various forms in which I do it, so very compelling. As I have noted before, 'I have found fulfillment through every aspect of being a drummer'.[1] Not playing drums or not having the opportunity to play drums is unimaginable to me. While such a claim might seem outrageous to some, me this is very real indeed. As drummer-scholar, Bill Bruford acknowledges, drumming 'is what I do, and what I do is who I am'.[2] There are numerous possible reasons why I find drumming so necessary, and in this chapter I focus on two possible rationales – autotelicity and eudaimonia (both explained below). I have written before about drumming in relation to these ideas,[3] and in this essay I look at possible connections and contradictions between the two concepts.

While being a drummer necessarily involves numerous activities (such as maintaining the instrument, learning songs, and driving to shows and rehearsals) I limit my writing here to experiences of (or that mostly comprise) playing the drums. I should emphasize here that my focus is not on *performing*, but on *playing*. I do not play drums exclusively in, or in preparation for, performance. When I perform, however, I do so largely because doing so means that I get to play drums. I have previously suggested that drumming for me is an autotelic (inherently worthwhile) activity. I wrote the following about rock drumming in particular, and the sentiment is also true of the other drumming that I do:

> [Rock] drumming for me is a particularly autotelic experience. I do it because I need to feel that autotelic experience as part of a meaningful life being me. I do it because it is intrinsically valuable in and of itself.[4]

In what follows, I interrogate this notion that drumming is 'intrinsically valuable in and of itself', because playing drums is core to what Laing terms my 'ontological security'.[5] Playing drums provides me with 'a feeling and a condition ... [which] signals that the present activity ... is in harmony with the daimon that is [my] true self'.[6] I do not value drumming 'for itself', but rather because of what doing it does for me. With research into drums, drummers, and drumming being a relatively new field, there is no literature, to my knowledge, that connects philosophy and drumming (by which I mean, in this context, playing the drum kit). There is helpful, resonant writing on the philosophy of play,[7] including Rathunde and Isabella's conception of 'leisure play' as 'an intrinsically motivated and deeply enjoyable activity'.[8] It is this notion of the intrinsic about which I am less than convinced. Schmid, writing about sports, and whose findings and assertions that I find analogous here to drumming, notes that 'the philosophical literature defines autotelic play as an activity pursued for factors intrinsic to the activity'.[9] Schmid, however, 'find[s] this conception of autotelic play and its justification unsatisfactory'.[10] I am inclined to concur, since I do not play the drums just to play the drums – that would not make any sense. I play the drums because of the rewards I reap from doing so. Per what Schmid terms a 'hedonistic' account, 'it is not the activity itself that is intrinsically valuable but [my] enjoyment or pleasure derived from the activity'.[11] Richard Shusterman also captures some aspects of this derived pleasure, in his writing about aesthetic experience, which is:

- Essentially valuable and enjoyable;
- Something vividly felt and subjectively savoured, affectively absorbing us and focusing our attention on its immediate presence;
- Meaningful experience, not mere sensation.[12]

As I explore below, the meaningful experience of playing drums is more than mere pleasure; drumming is often as challenging as it is thrilling. In this vein, Ryan, Huta, and Deci construe eudaimonia as comprising more than mere pleasure and residing in 'living a complete life, or the realization of valued human potentials', such as (for me) drumming.[13] I prefer, then, to consider that I find eudaimonia in drumming.[14]

Bauman describes individuals who live this way as possessing an autotelic personality,[15] seeking optimal, flow experiences that exist at the crossroads of challenge and reward.[16] Csikszentmihalyi writes that people with an autotelic personality do things for the sake of doing them, rather than in order to attain later, external goals.[17] Wrigley and Emerson tell us that during such intense flow experiences, 'the experience becomes autotelic, that is, [those taking part] experience a high level of intrinsic enjoyment as a result'.[18] I am unsure that the kinds of experience these commentators describe are truly as autotelic as they claim. I offer instead this claim: that the rewards I feel and seek *derive from* drumming, but are not, or at least not mostly, *intrinsic to* drumming.

As I have noted elsewhere, extant scholarship on drumming tends, with very few exceptions, to ignore experiential accounts, but for me as a drummer, the value, interest and meaning in drumming lie primarily in the experience of playing the drums [3]. In the tradition of autoethnographic research, I therefore present this deeply personal account of the meaningfulness and value of drumming, realizing that my experiences and expressions are not generalizable to the broader population of drummers.[19] However, as Tomlin notes, 'reality, in fact, is indeterminable and empty of inherent existence . . . the notion of . . . independent categories for the things we experience and perceive in the world, unwisely ignores or blocks out the fact that objects, perceptions and thoughts are non-essential, irreducible, interdependent and impermanent'.[20] Experiences of drumming, then, while undoubtedly related, are as varied as the drummers who experience them. It is an honour to share with readers some of mine.

I am writing this essay almost two years since moving to the United States, having spent the first forty years of my life living in the United Kingdom. I recently became a legal permanent resident in the United States, which means I am on the fourth visa I have used to travel and live in this country in two years. This feels like an especially salient time to be thinking about drumming and eudaimonia, since until I recently acquired permanent resident status, I have been unable to play drums professionally, and therefore unable to seek to do so – an altogether disorientating experience, having spent the prior twenty years earning a good portion of my income from playing drums, and always with the option to do so. With all the social, emotional logistical, financial, and professional turmoil of the past two years, playing drums has occupied an unprecedented type of niche in my life; I have craved every chance to play, yet felt a huge part of me being suppressed by the infrequency of playing opportunities. I was recently able to make the down-payment on a home, and in the garage there I have set up a small drum kit – the first time in my professional or adult life that I have had an acoustic drum kit I can play in my home.

In this essay I present personal accounts of drumming in a rock band and practising alone at the drum kit. I have chosen to write about these particular contexts that capture the places, purposes and modes of drumming in my life now, because my interactions with drummers and other musicians suggest that similar experiences can be at the core of what it means to know oneself as a musician. While the experiences I describe are unique to me and are therefore not generalizable, I hope that my observations about playing the drums may resonate (no pun intended!) with some readers. I discuss drumming as amateuring, which Regelski notes is '*time well spent*, even when it requires strenuous effort'[21] (emphasis in original). Amateur musicians are often not highly regarded; 'amateur' and the more derogatory 'amateurishness', are often presented in contrast with 'professional' or 'professionalism', and tend to denote poor quality of craftsmanship and artistry. However, Kratus reminds us that 'amateur' derives etymologically from 'love' and 'lover', and that 'an amateur musician is one who engages in music purely for the love of doing so'.[22] Following this definition, I feel no shame in being a profoundly amateur musician. Moreover, it is in musical amateuring at the drums that I find community, meaning and peace.

Black Belt Jesus

For most of the last two years I have been living in temporary accommodation, unsure of where my family would settle, and mostly on visas not permitting me to work outside of my day job. These factors all conspired to mean that I have not been in a tight, belting rock band that rehearses regularly and has unrealistic dreams beyond its potential (hallmarks of each of the dozens of bands I have been in from the age of fourteen), since before I moved to the United States from London. That has been a gaping hole at the core of my being. After one abortive audition for a band with a megalomaniacal singer who insisted on recording all the instruments for the band's demo EP despite a demonstrable weakness playing most of them, I again visited the local Craigslist pages and searched for 'Stoner Rock Band'. I found one band – Black Belt Jesus – in need of a drummer, had a quick phone call with the guitarist and main writer, learned a song on my commute to and from work, and auditioned for them the following week. When I turned up at the address for the audition, I found three guys with an album's worth of material and a yearning to fill the gap left when their excellent singer departed the drum chair a year ago to take on the vocals. We start playing the epic, repeated riff that announces the mid-tempo rock song 'Bo Huesley'. The playing is loud, immersive, and feral. It does not sound all that loud in my ears because I am wearing earplugs as I have done when drumming since I was twelve years of age. High volumes have never really been what attracted me to making rock music. I feel the most alive, though – the best alive – when making the movements required to make loud rock music authentically on the drums in a band,[23] and especially in a rehearsal space.[24]

Férdia Stone-Davis describes the physical character of musical experience 'disclos[ing] a first-order mode of being, one that involves a suspension of the distinction between subject and object (promoting instead their mutuality), or, rather, a retrieval of the pre-reflective moment before this distinction asserts itself'.[25] I have previously described how:

> When I am drumming, this feeling in my body, and the conscious, embodied knowledge that I am core to the band creating and perpetuating the sound that I hear and feel around me, compel me to continue making the music, making and luxuriating in the perpetual now.[26]

The sound envelopes me while I play, while the band all plays together. Everyone is into it – laying down fat, fat beats and riffs that are all we are in that moment. I recall Theodore Gracyk's description of 'rock creat[ing] a cocoon of sound', which, 'physical and sensual, felt and heard . . . invites us to crank the volume and overwhelm consciousness'.[27] Gracyk was writing about the experience of hearing rock music, which is magnified when also creating that sound.[28] This all resonates with the 'authenticity of expression, or what I also term "first person authenticity"' identified by Alan F. Moore, which 'arises when an originator (composer, performer) succeeds in conveying the impression that his/her utterance is one of integrity, that it represents an attempt to communicate in an unmediated form'.[29] For Moore, that communication happens between performer(s) and audience, but I recognize this phenomenon as occurring between band members who are playing for themselves, not necessarily performing.

When we finished rehearsing in Tony the bass player's converted garage rehearsal space (and man cave), I said aloud to no one in particular 'It feels really good!' Tony agreed, adding that 'it takes you off the planet for a while – it's peaceful'. Tony was right – everything else melted away while we played and we shared an immersive, collective experience that none of us could create without the others. As I have noted previously:

> When I am drumming, this feeling in my body, and the conscious, embodied knowledge that I am core to the band creating and perpetuating the sound that I hear and feel around me, compel me to continue making the music, making and luxuriating in the perpetual now.[30]

On this evening, I got the distinct impression from the others that all experienced the same feeling. This unmediated, non-verbal communication of rocking out collaboratively was a tonic for my soul, reminding me how and why playing drums in a rock band is so vital to me being a human – so core to my eudaimonia.

One aspect I love about playing original music is that I get to create or individualize my drum parts and I get to decide when they are right. Subbing in for a band's regular drummer leaves me anxious that I will not play the things that I should at the tempo that I should, and that the band will be unhappy, or at best unfamiliar and therefore uncomfortable, with my playing. Similarly, playing cover songs is fun, but it is never fully satisfying as I know I do not sound like the commercial release of the original that audiences and band members want to hear. When I make up the drum parts and play them like only I can, it is all so much easier to get right. It is also affirming and reassuring when bandmates tell me, as they did after this audition/rehearsal, things like 'you got the groove, bro!' and 'we're so happy you're in the band'. As far I'm concerned, the groove is created collectively, and I am elated to be in the band – drumming alone is not the same (although it can be fulfilling in a whole set of other ways, as I explore below).[31]

Playing in a rock band such as Black Belt Jesus fills a need that is core to my sense of who I am, and recalls 'Erikson's definition of identity as "the style of one's individuality . . . that . . . coincides with the sameness and continuity of one's meaning for significant others in the immediate community"'.[32] While it is early to consider men I have now rehearsed with twice 'significant others' in the traditional sense, they are truly significant in terms of the role they now play, and moreover, the role they enable me to play, in my life. June Boyce-Tillman captures the singularity of this drumming experience:

> I am calling the moment when all the other domains fuse in a single experience – a time when body, mind, spirit, and emotions come together – Spirituality . . . Spirituality represents the reintegration of the body (Materials), the emotions (Expression), the reason/intellect (Construction), and the culture (Values).[33]

Playing in a rock band such as Black Belt Jesus is for me, then, a spiritual experience.

Personal Practice

I am immensely fortunate to have somewhere at home to practise my drums. I cannot play very loudly as they are set up in my garage, which is not isolated or insulated for sound. This has proven rather wonderful, though, as it presents me with the opportunity to play with brushes and light sticks and to coax more nuanced and delicate combinations of sounds from the kit than are typical of the 'tub-thumping' approach I take to the rock drumming that would ordinarily be my go-to. I have a rubber pads drum kit set up in the garage too, on which I have done the majority of my personal practice for over twenty years. This is where I practise rock music; the pads are aesthetically disappointing to play, but perfect for working through big, fast motions and learning song structures without inviting noise complaints from neighbors or the property owners association.

A wonderfully gratifying aspect of playing and practising drums is that I get to control the experience. I decide when to start, when to stop, what to play, how to play it, what my goals are, how long I have to reach them, and all the while my physical, emotional, and mental faculties are having the time of their lives. I quickly become bored and irritable if not stimulated, and become impatient and angry if I feel demands being made on me are unreasonable, so being in control of what I do helps to keep me in or approaching a state of flow. Better yet, the time that I spend playing drums is nearly always uncluttered by the constant conscious mental activity that troubles the rest of my life every day. I also cannot hear the phone ringing, nor SMS, email, or social media notifications above the sound of the drums. As I note elsewhere, 'practising provides a beautiful cocoon that shields me from the cacophony of the world'.[34] I am always happier after practising drums. I am usually calmer, kinder and more focused. I feel more fulfilled. I am a better version of myself for the rest of the day, having connected with something so deeply meaningful to who I am. With the drums ready and waiting in my garage now, I am sometimes able to pop in there three or four times a day for a short session, even just for a few minutes while the kettle boils for a cup of tea.

I enjoy gradually warming up when I first play the drums on a given day and welcome the time I must allow for that process. I have been playing mostly without ear plugs in the garage because the volume is low and the practice sessions brief enough as not to pose a threat to my health. It was been wonderfully rewarding to hear the full variety of overtones produced by the drums and the beautiful, complex shimmer of the sounds from cymbals. I have luxuriated in the numerous blended sounds of my drum kit, and in teasing more from one place or another – less ride, more of the handmade crash-turned-sizzle cymbal that I made with my Dad. Appreciation of the sound of the instrument is usually lost to protective ear plugs and a rock aesthetic that privileges loudness, accuracy, and punctuation over nuance, richness, and sipping the sumptuous sibilance from the cymbals along with the width of the sound of a stick contacting a drum and leaving the air alive with bountiful, colourful tones. It is like savouring the tastes of a perfectly prepared meal, where each morsel is gorgeous and the flavours from foods combine with one another while the sommelier's perfectly paired selection of wine creates sensations utterly sublime.

It has been a joy to feel the stick in my hand playing jazz time on the ride cymbal, the bounce-and-rebound of the double-stroke, and the finger control of playing three rapid notes in a row – techniques that are largely lost to me when I play less technically sophisticated rock music. It has also been wonderful to reconnect with the delicate swish of a brush, tracking circles in constant motion around the head for that unending background swoosh, or waving rhythmically back and forth across the head to make eighth notes that are as relentless and vague as the points in time on the arc of a conductor's baton, yet all the while the ensemble of my arms and feet and legs and hand and fingers all dance to weave coherently through time. I have been practising a one-handed roll technique I first worked on a few years ago when I had access to acoustic drum kits to practise at the college where I taught. I have not kept this up for the last seven years, so have enjoyed developing interdependence with my other limbs as they coordinate with this unfamiliar motion from my left hand operating a stick or brush on the edge of the snare drum. It is exciting and rewarding to hear the development of my playing.

Playing the drums like this is deeply sensuous – it feels selfishly indulgent because I am both making and consuming the sound. As I noted before about rock drumming, but which rings true for practising quietly alone in my garage:

> Sound and touch are . . . not so distinct, but are bound up through perception as indistinguishable, or aspects of the same phenomenal experience. When I strike my drums, the hearing and feeling are experienced as two parts of the same sense – each is necessary to me for the other to feel real.[35]

Percussionist Evelyn Glennie has called hearing 'a form of touch' and said that we 'hear through the body'.[36] Nancy extends hearing to understanding, suggesting that somatic understanding exists 'between a sense (that one listens to) and a truth (that one understands), although one cannot . . . do without the other'.[37] Communing with this touch, this truth, and this understanding is a crucial component of why I play drums. I often sit at the drum kit with no particular goal in mind other than to be with the drums, and I am nearly always inspired when I do so; I cannot resist the urge to play. Even when the practice session is more mundane, I derive great satisfaction from the physical sensation of stick or brush striking drums and cymbals. I still just revel in the glorious sound and the fact that I get to produce it and hear it. Norton describes eudaimonia as the feeling of 'being where one wants to be, doing what one wants to do', where that something feels meaningful and worthwhile.[38] Playing my drums alone is for me a site of self-knowledge, self-understanding, and self-acceptance: eudaimonia.

From Autotelicity To Eudaimonia

I have attempted to show that I play the drums because I love to do so, and that the activity fulfils in me needs other than drumming. Drumming for me *seems* autotelic, but scratching to just beneath the surface reveals some of the complexity of which this supposed autotelicity is comprised.

Drumming fulfils in me some 'basic psychological needs, which differ conceptually and functionally from the conception of autotelicity'.[39] These needs are twofold:

1. Doing something I know I can do, a place and time where I feel competent, confident, empowered and able to succeed;
2. Transcendence and transformation of my *self*, the ability of drumming seemingly to transport me to another plane of existence.

The examples above of Black Belt Jesus and practising alone illustrate how these two motivators for me playing drums correlate to 'autonomy', 'competence' and 'relatedness', the 'three innate human needs central to motivation' that Schmid identifies in self-determination theory.[40] I play drums because of *intrinsic motivation* to do so, but 'what reasons count as "intrinsic" [is] an empirical matter determined by the effects of those reasons on [my] behaviors and participatory satisfaction'.[41] For me, drumming is vital to eudaimonia, rather than something that I do, or arguably even could do, explicitly and purely for its own sake. Waterman notes that 'eudaimonia includes a constellation of subjective experiences, including feelings of rightness and centeredness in one's actions, identity, strength of purpose, and competence'.[42] Drumming holds this key to my self-actualization), individuation and identity realization.[43] Per Frankel's observation, the 'search for meaning is the primary motivation in [one's] life … This meaning is unique and specific in that it must and can be fulfilled by him alone; only then does it achieve a significance which will satisfy his own will to meaning.[44] I play the drums in order to be me and to get the most out of being me. Playing drums is thus not an autotelic pursuit, but a eudaimonic one.

Drumming allows me to feel success. My life is full, as much adult life seems to be, of incomplete tasks and struggling to meet requirements, deadlines and expectations – emails to respond to, tax forms to file, papers to review, essays to grade, meals to make, a car to keep on the road. I meet enough expectations in an adequate enough way to get by, and in some things I possibly excel, but none of them sounds as sweet or feels as satisfying as drumming. Drumming is the one place to which I know I can return and where I know everything will be all right (and it if it isn't, then it very soon will be, and even fixing drumming things is part of the joy, the fulfilment of it all). Rarely are such experiences construed as success; in music and music learning circles, we tend to think of commercial recognition, accrual of financial resources, celebrity, or an acknowledged display of a particular kind of artistic virtuosity as indicative of success. However, as Heidi Partti suggests, there is success in experiencing agency. I revel and take solace in the fact that in playing drums I am able to experience a modicum of such success.[45] As noted above, I am a proud and true musical amateur.[46]

I gave a conference paper in 2019, during which I played drums in a range of styles, beginning with a rock juggernaut, moving through a hectic jazz fusion composition and finishing with a soft, slow singer-songwriter ballad.[47] After the talk, a colleague approached me and said, 'I just saw into your soul, man'. I suspected the gentleman of well-intentioned hyperbole and perhaps mild weekend intoxication, but he may actually have hit the mark – I certainly hide nothing when playing at my fullest, and on that occasion there were no barriers, no filters to the real me. Maybe I really did bare my soul. I hope so. Boyce-Tillman proposes that 'part of self-actualization within a musical experience can be seen as the last remaining place for the soul in Western society'.[48] Drumming, then, is where my soul resides.

Notes

1 G. D. Smith. '(Un)popular Music Making and Eudaimonia', in R. Mantie and G. D. Smith (eds.), *The Oxford Handbook of Music Making and Leisure* (New York: Oxford University Press, 2016), pp. 151–170.

2 B. Bruford. *The autobiography: Yes, king Crimson, Earthworks, and More* (London: Jawbone Press, 2009).

3 G. D. Smith. 'Embodied Experience of Rock Drumming', *Music + Practice* 3 (2017), available at: www.musicandpractice.org/ (accessed 19 January 2020); G. D. Smith. 'Let There Be Rock: Loudness and Authenticity at the Drum Kit', *Journal of Popular Music Education* 3:2 (2019), pp. 277–292; Smith, '(Un)popular Music Making and Eudaimonia'.

4 Smith, 'Let There Be Rock: Loudness and Authenticity at the Drum Kit'.

5 R. D. Laing. *The Divided Self* (Harmondsworth: Penguin Books Ltd, 1960).

6 D. L. Norton. *Personal Destinies: A Philosophy of Ethical Individualism* (Princeton: Princeton University Press, 1976).

7 H. G. Gadamer *Truth and Method* (London: Bloomsbury, 2004); J. Huizinga. 'Nature and Significance of Play as a Cultural Phenomenon' in R. Schechner and M. Schuman (eds.), *Ritual, Play, and Performance: Readings in the Social Sciences/Theatre* (New York: Seabury, 1976), pp. 46–66.

8 K. Rathunde and R. Isabella. 'Playing Music and Identity Development in Middle Adulthood: A Theoretical and Autoethnographic Account' in R. Mantie and G. D. Smith (eds.), *The Oxford Handbook of Music Making and Leisure* (New York: Oxford University Press, 2016) pp. 131–150.

9 S. E. Schmid. 'Beyond Autotelic Play', *Journal of the Philosophy of Sport* 38:2 (2011), pp. 149–166.

10 Ibid.

11 Ibid.

12 R. Shusterman. *Performing Live: Aesthetic Alternatives for the Ends of Art* (Ithaca: Cornell University Press, 2000).

13 R. M. Ryan, H. Veronika, and E. L. Deci. 'Living Well: A Self-Determination Theory Perspective on Eudaimonia', *Journal of Happiness Studies* 9 (2008), pp. 139–170.

14 D. V. Dierendonck and K. Mohan. 'Some Thoughts on Spirituality and Eudaimonic Well-Being', *Mental Health, Religion and Culture* 9:3 (2006), pp. 227–238; Smith, '(Un)popular Music Making and Eudaimonia'.

15 N. Baumann. 'Autotelic Personality' in S. Engeser (ed.), *Advances in Flow Research* (New York: Springer, 2012), pp. 165–186.

16 M. Csikszentmihalyi. *Flow: The Psychology of Optimal Experience* (New York: Harper Perennial 1991).

17 M. Csikszentmihalyi. *Finding Flow: The Psychology of Engagement with Everyday Life* (New York: Basic Books, 1997).
18 W. J. Wrigley and S. B. Emmerson. 'The Experience of the Flow State in Live Music Performance', *Psychology of Music* 41:3 (2011), pp. 1–14, DOI: http://10.1177/0305735611425903.
19 H. Chang. *Autoethnography as Method* (Walnut Creek: Left Coast Press, 2008); T. Muncey. *Creating Autoethnographies* (London: SAGE, 2010); N. Denzin. *Interpretive Autoethnography*, 3rd ed (Thousand Oaks: SAGE, 2014).
20 A. Tomlin. 'Introduction: Contemplating the Undefinable' in R. Shusterman and A. Tomlin (eds.), *Aesthetic Experience* (New York: Routledge, 2008), pp. 1–13.
21 T. A. Regelski. 'Amateuring in Music and its Rivals', *Action, Criticism, and Theory for Music Education*, 6:3 (2007), pp. 22–50.
22 J. Kratus. 'A Return to Amateurism in Music Education', *Music Educators Journal* 106:1 (2019), pp. 31–37.
23 A. F. Moore. 'Authenticity as Authentication', *Popular Music* 21:2 (2002), pp. 209–223.
24 Smith, 'Let There Be Rock: Loudness and Authenticity at the Drum Kit'.
25 F. J. Stone-Davis. *Musical Beauty: Negotiating the Boundary Between Subject and Object* (Eugene: Cascade Books, 2011).
26 Smith, 'Embodied Experience of Rock Drumming'.
27 T. Gracyk. *Rhythm and Noise: An Aesthetics of Rock* (London: I. B. Taruis & Co., 1996).
28 J. L. Nancy. Listening, C. Mandell, translator (New York: Fordham University Press, 2007); Smith, 'Embodied Experience of Rock Drumming'.
29 A. F. Moore. 'Authenticity as Authentication', *Popular Music* 21:2 (2002), pp. 209–223.
30 Smith, 'Embodied Experience of Rock Drumming'.
31 G. D. Smith. *I Drum, Therefore I Am: Being and Becoming a Drummer* (Abingdon: Routledge, 2013); Smith, 'Embodied Experience of Rock Drumming'.
32 E. H. Erikson. *Childhood and Society* (New York: W. W. Norton & Co., 1950).
33 J. Boyce-Tillman. 'An Ecology of Eudaimonia and its Implications for Music Education' in G. D. Smith and M. Silverman (eds.), *Eudaimonia: Perspectives for Music Learning* (New York: Routledge, 2020).
34 G.D. Smith. 'A Drummer in All That I Do', available at: https://drdrumsblog.com/a-drummer-in-all-that-i-do/ (accessed 19 January 2020).
35 G. D. Smith, 'Embodied Experience of Rock Drumming'.
36 *Touch the Sound: A Sound Journey with Evelyn Glennie* (DVD Perivale: Signum Records, 2009).
37 Nancy, *Listening*.
38 Norton, *Personal Destinies: A Philosophy of Ethical Individualism*.
39 Schmid, 'Beyond Autotelic Play'.
40 S. Waterman. 'The Humanistic Psychology–Positive Psychology Divide: Contrasts in Philosophical Foundations', *American Psychologist* 68:3 (2013), pp. 124–133; Schmid, 'Beyond Autotelic Play'.
41 Schmid, 'Beyond Autotelic Play'.
42 Waterman, 'The Humanistic Psychology–Positive Psychology Divide: Contrasts in Philosophical Foundations'.
43 Smith, *I Drum, Therefore I Am*; A. H. Maslow. *Toward a Psychology of Being* (Bensenville: Lushena, 2014); C. G. Jung. *Modern Man in Search of a Soul* (Oxford: Routledge, 1933).
44 V. E. Frankel *Man's Search for Meaning* (New York: Washington Square Press, 1959).
45 H. Partti. *Learning from Cosmopolitan Digital Musicians: Identity, Musicianship, and Changing Values in (In)formal Music Communities* (Helsinki: Sibelius Academy, 2012);G. D. Smith 'Seeking "Success" in Popular Music', *Music Education Research International* 6 (2013), pp. 26–37
46 Regelski, 'Amateuring in Music and Its Rivals'; Kratus, 'A Return to Amateurism in Music Education'.
47 G. D. Smith. *Drumming, Daimon, and Music Education: Cardiff Rock, London Blues, Texas Ink, and New York Noise*. Visions of Research in Music Education conference, Westminster Choir College, Princeton, NJ (24 May 2019), available at: www.youtube.com/watch?v=9qRxhCRzKB4 (accessed 19 January 2020).
48 Boyce-Tillman, 'An Ecology of Eudaimonia'.

Index

Printed in the United States
by Baker & Taylor Publisher Services